Immigration

Law, Politics, and Crime

FIRST EDITION

Immigration

Law, Politics, and Crime

Edited by Jeffrey Bumgarner

North Dakota State University

Bassim Hamadeh, CEO and Publisher
Mieka Portier, Senior Acquisitions Editor
Tony Paese, Project Editor
Sean Adams, Production Editor
Emely Villavicencio, Senior Graphic Designer
Alexa Lucido, Licensing Associate
Natalie Piccotti, Director of Marketing
Kassie Graves, Vice President of Editorial
Jamie Giganti, Director of Academic Publishing

Copyright © 2020 by Cognella, Inc. All rights reserved. No part of this publication may be reprinted, reproduced, transmitted, or utilized in any form or by any electronic, mechanical, or other means, now known or hereafter invented, including photocopying, microfilming, and recording, or in any information retrieval system without the written permission of Cognella, Inc. For inquiries regarding permissions, translations, foreign rights, audio rights, and any other forms of reproduction, please contact the Cognella Licensing Department at rights@cognella.com.

Trademark Notice: Product or corporate names may be trademarks or registered trademarks and are used only for identification and explanation without intent to infringe.

Cover image copyright© 2014 iStockphoto LP/Rpsycho; © 2015 iStockphoto LP/Bill Oxford.

Printed in the United States of America.

CONTENTS

Preface ix

CHAPTER ONE
History of American Immigration 1

READING 1
Immigration and Growing Diversity 5
By John Iceland

CHAPTER TWO
Controlling Immigration and Visitation: A Plenary Power of the President or a Due Process Issue? 37

READING 2
Plenary Power: Should Judges Control U.S. Immigration Policy? 39
By Jon Feere

CHAPTER THREE
Legal Immigration: Visas, Green Cards, and Refugees 75

READING 3
Permanent Legal Immigration to the United States: Policy Overview 77
By William A. Kandel

CHAPTER FOUR
Immigration and Federal Law Enforcement   95

READING 4

The Department of Homeland Security and the Immigration
Enforcement Regime of the Twenty-First Century   99
By Tanya Maria Golash-Boza

CHAPTER FIVE
Immigration and State/Local Law Enforcement   137

READING 5

Insecure Communities: How an Immigration Enforcement Program
Encourages Battered Women to Stay Silent   141
By Radha Vishnuvajjala

CHAPTER SIX
Sanctuary Cities/Counties   171

READING 6

Tackling Sanctuaries   173
By Dan Cadman and Jessica Vaughan

CHAPTER SEVEN
Immigration and Crime   199

READING 7

Divergent Perspectives: Social Disorganization and
Segmented Assimilation   201
By Vincent A. Ferraro

CHAPTER EIGHT
Immigration and Terrorism   **237**

READING 8
Terror of Immigration and War on Immigrants   239
By Samantha Hauptman

READING 9
Homeland Security and Support for Multiculturalism, Assimilation, and Omniculturalism Policies among Americans   253
By Fathali Moghaddam and James Breckenridge

CHAPTER NINE
Immigration and Elections   **269**

READING 10
Do Non-citizens Vote in U.S. Elections?   271
By Jesse T. Richman, Gulshan A. Chattha, and David C. Earnest

READING 11
The Contextual Presidency: The Negative Shift in Presidential Immigration Rhetoric   289
By Damien Arthur and Joshua Woods

PREFACE

For the 2016 American presidential race, immigration was one of the issues front and center during the campaign and about which there was much debate. Curbing illegal immigration at our borders and restricting legal immigration from countries thought to be especially prone to generating terrorists were major campaign themes of Donald Trump. Given the millions of legal and illegal immigrants in the United States, candidate Trump's views on immigration were roundly criticized by Democrats, many fellow Republicans, and pro-immigration activists. But the issue did not go away and Donald Trump didn't retreat from his positions.

For example, when Trump formally announced his bid for the presidency on June 16, 2015, he spoke of the problems on America's southern border in a way that outraged the opposition. In his first speech as a candidate he said that "when Mexico sends its people, they're not sending their best. ... They're sending people that have lots of problems, and they're bringing those problems with them. They're bringing drugs. They're bringing crime. They're rapists. And some, I assume, are good people." Even his Republican primary opponents pounced on this generalization as hateful rhetoric. People assumed that such a rhetorical mistake by Trump at the very outset of his campaign portended that his political life would be short indeed and everyone else would be able to move on to the consideration of serious candidates.

But Donald Trump stuck around, and so did his views on immigration. He did not shy away from his position that unchecked immigration was destroying communities and denying Americans jobs. He moderated his language about immigration only a little. Importantly, his messaging about securing the border, keeping terrorists out, confronting crime committed by immigrants, and protecting jobs of the American worker resonated with a significant number of American people. According to the Pew Research Center, 70% of voters in the 2016 election listed immigration as a "very important" issue to them. Among Trump supporters, the figure was 79%. Other key issues for Americans included the economy and terrorism, with 84% and 80% of the voters, respectively, identifying those issues as "very important." Of course, woven into the issues of the economy and terrorism is that of immigration. This was a real, rather than imagined, matter of concern to voters in the United States.

This book attempts to explore immigration along the fault lines that have galvanized people around this issue. It does so through an assemblage of selected readings regarding immigration that have been previously published in other venues. The topics to be explored in this collection of readings include the history of immigration in the United States, the current laws regarding immigration, the authority of different branches of the federal government to implement immigration policy, the different law enforcement players effecting immigration enforcement, immigration's purported links to crime and terrorism, and immigration's impact on elections. Each of the chapters also include discussion questions to help readers pull out the most salient points and to think through one's own positions regarding immigration in an informed way.

My hope is that the book contributes to a civil, educated, and productive dialogue regarding immigration and the many public policies that attach to it.

Jeffrey B. Bumgarner, Ph.D.
North Dakota State University

CHAPTER ONE

History of American Immigration

Introduction

There are many platitudes, from all sides, that are voiced in the debate about immigration policy in the United States. Perhaps the one most frequently used is the phrase "we are a nation of immigrants." America certainly is a nation of immigrants. America was colonized by the British, gained its independence, and then saw its population grow over a span of 200 years due in large part to migration from various European, Latin American, and Asian countries. The nation's population was also bolstered by the importation of slaves from Africa, although African Americans were denied the benefits of citizenship and civil rights throughout America's first century as a nation. Even the indigenous population of various tribes of American Indians has its origins somewhere else—most likely Asia or Oceana.

That America is a nation of immigrants is self-evident from its heterogeneity. But how exactly did immigration into the country unfold in the past and how does it do so today? This chapter's piece by John Iceland addresses this question. It takes us through the history of American immigration laws and trends. Further, he considers the primary concerns that attach to increased immigration.

Iceland identifies two key concerns that Americans and their elected officials have had and do have about immigration—particularly immigration on a large scale. The first concern regards assimilation. This concern relates to the ability and willingness of immigrants to "Americanize." In other words, do those who migrate to the United States, both legally and illegally, desire to embrace American freedoms, traditions, values, and culture? Or, do migrants prefer to settle down in ethnic and cultural enclaves that isolate them from the rest of American society and at times puts them at odds with it?

Many in the United States who are dubious of large-scale immigration point to continued use of a mother tongue as evidence of a lack of assimilation. Naturally, migrants from non-English-speaking countries will often arrive with an inability to communicate in English, so speaking in their native language is their only option. But what of those immigrants who appear uninterested in learning English? In some neighborhoods, and even in some cities and counties at large in the United States, English is a second language to Spanish. Does this reflect a lack of assimilation? It could. But it wouldn't be the first time. For example, German immigrants to the United States in the 19th century didn't assimilate easily. They held on to their language and customs. School instruction and church services were delivered in German. Whole communities in the Midwest in places such as Minnesota, Wisconsin, and North Dakota reflected German culture. These people remained proudly German.

This reluctance to abandon German culture held fast for decades in the late 19th and early 20th centuries; however, when the United States entered World War I against Germany, it became increasingly difficult to hold on to one's German identity. Arguably, the holding on to one's ethnic and cultural identity is normal, and so is its cessation at the proper time. It is fine to belong to a group. But when the group is associated with enmity toward the United States, one may well feel the need to modify one's identity in order to demonstrate fidelity to America, as German Americans did in the first half of the 20th century.

Assimilation is open to definition. Most who study immigration and immigrant communities today say that assimilation is a two-way street whenever there is a convergence of communities. Immigrants must learn the culture, laws, customs, and morays of their new home; Americans must learn to accept others who are perhaps different from themselves into the tapestry that is American society. There is much that can be learned and embraced from each other. Of course, critics of cultural appropriation muddy the waters of two-way assimilation when they cry foul at the embracing of aspects of an immigrant community's practices and culture. In 2017, a burrito shop in Portland, OR, was pressured into closing its doors after critics declared that its owners had committed the sin of cultural appropriation. The owners had taken a trip to Mexico and learned how to make their tortillas in an authentically Mexican way. After a deluge of protestations via social media, the owners finally shut down the business. In essence, they learned how tortillas were made in Mexico, found it superior to their own way, and embraced the Mexican way. If the behavior of two White women in this instance was inappropriate, then there could never be two-way assimilation, or even one-way assimilation, for no one from one community would ever be allowed to adopt the favored practices of another community.

The second key concern identified by Iceland in this chapter is the economic and social effect of immigration. It is the concern about societal effect that is most relevant to the intersection of crime and immigration, although assimilation is also relevant to crime. Iceland takes the reader through a summary of the history and the evidence regarding the impact immigration has on society.

Iceland highlights America's historical practice of setting quotas for legal immigration, which favored European countries. For example, the Immigration Act of 1924 capped the number of immigrants from any particular country to 2% of the number of people from that country already living in the United States. This scheme favored countries such as Ireland, England, and Germany and worked against countries in Asia or Africa. The effect was to severely limit immigration from underdeveloped countries and to lower the immigration numbers overall. The Hart-Celler Act of 1965 amended America's immigration laws to make them less discriminatory. But the legislation only passed after assurances were made there would not be large increases in immigration nor would there be a threat to the ethnic balance that existed in the United States. Even so, immigration dramatically increased after this law came into effect.

People began to resettle from countries in Asia, Africa, and Latin America that theretofore had not been sources of immigrants. Additionally, the birthrates of these immigrant groups have outpaced that of White Americans, further contributing to Hispanics and Asians holding growing shares of the U.S. population since 1970.

Iceland also notes that with regard to the concern of crime and immigration, the evidence suggests there is at worst a neutral, and possibly an inverse, relationship between crime and immigration. In particular, first-generation immigrants tend to exhibit a lower propensity toward criminal conduct than do later generations or Americans in general. In this discussion, Iceland cites Robert Sampson, a Harvard sociologist known for his seminal research on immigration and crime, particularly among Mexican migrants in the United States. Iceland concludes there are certainly good reasons for being rational in our approach to immigration and perhaps even favoring some groups over others (e.g., skilled and educated over unskilled). At the same time, however, he suggests one must concede that the intuitive arguments against immigration, including broad concerns about crime, tend not to hold up in light of America's experiences to date.

READING 1

Immigration and Growing Diversity

By John Iceland

....

The United States is often said to be a land of immigrants—and with good reason. Immigration from a wide variety of other countries has continuously changed the character of this country. The initial wave of colonial settlement from England and around it—along with the large number of involuntary immigrants from Africa sold into slavery—eventually gave way to immigration from the rest of northern and western Europe in the early to mid-1800s. The stream of immigration then shifted to eastern and southern Europe by the end of the nineteenth century. Immigration slowed to a trickle after the passage of restrictive laws in the 1920s, aided and abetted by two world wars and a deep depression, before once again accelerating in the last decades of the twentieth century. During this last wave, immigrants came from an even broader array of countries spanning the globe—millions from Asia, Latin America, and Africa.

For a land of immigrants, however, the subject of immigration has long been a source of considerable political contention in the United States. Debates have generally centered around two issues: (1) the extent to which immigrants are assimilating and (2) the overall social and economic impact of immigration on the nation. New groups of immigrants from differing origins have long been viewed with suspicion by a substantial portion of the native-born population. Many have worried that immigrants weaken the character of the country or that they are too different from the native born to assimilate or, worse yet, indifferent to assimilating altogether. Others have fretted that immigrants are a drain on the economy, or that they bring crime and social disorganization to our nation's cities and communities, or that they take jobs away from native-born Americans. These debates on immigration have echoed across generations.

For example, many nativists reacted with alarm to the increasing immigration of Catholics from Germany and Ireland in the early eighteenth century. Catholics, who were associated with the pope

John Iceland, "Immigration and Growing Diversity," *A Portrait of America: A Demographic Perspective*, pp. 107-137, 221-223. Copyright © 2014 by University of California Press. Reprinted with permission.

and other monarchies of Europe, were viewed by some as an internal threat who might undermine the republic. As historian Roger Daniels recounts:

> When relatively large numbers of Irish and German Catholic immigrants, many of them desperately poor, began to arrive in the late 1820s and early 1830s, what had been a largely rhetorical anti-Catholicism became a major social and political force in American life. Not surprisingly, it was in eastern cities, particularly Boston, where anti-Catholicism turned violent, and much of the violence was directed against convents and churches. Beginning with the burning down of the Ursuline Convent just outside Boston by a mob on August 11, 1834, well into the 1850s violence against Catholic institutions was so prevalent that insurance companies all but refused to insure them.[1]

By the end of the century, when immigrants from southern and eastern Europe were pouring in, the targets of the nativists changed, though many of the underlying concerns were the same. As Daniels again relates:

> But lurking behind and sometimes overshadowing these [religious and economic] objections to continued immigration was a growing and pervasive racism, a racism directed not against non-white races, but against presumed inferior peoples of European origin.... According to one of its founders [of an immigration restriction league], the question for Americans to decide was whether they wanted their country "to be peopled by British, German and Scandinavian stock, historically free, energetic, progressive, or by Slav, Latin and Asiatic races (this latter referred to Jews rather than Chinese or Japanese), historically down-trodden, atavistic and stagnant."[2]

As immigration from non-European countries picked up steam after changes in immigration policy enacted in 1965, many commentators again raised the alarm of immigration's effect on the character of the nation. Writing in 1995, immigration policy critic Peter Brimelow argued that the 1965 law resulted in immigration that is "dramatically larger, less skilled, and more divergent from the American majority than anything that was anticipated or desired ... is probably not beneficial to the economy ... is attended by a wide and increasing range of negative consequences, from the physical environment to the political ... [and] is bringing about an ethnic and racial transformation in America without precedent in the history of the world—an astonishing social experiment launched with no particular reason to expect success." Indeed, he asks, "Is America still that interlacing of ethnicity and culture we call a nation—and can the American nation-state, the political expression of that nation, survive?"

Given that his book is titled *Alien Nation: Common Sense about America's Immigration Disaster,* one may not be surprised to find out that Brimelow offers a pessimistic answer to this question.[3]

The rest of this chapter addresses issues raised in these immigration debates by tackling the following basic questions: To what extent is immigration changing the racial and ethnic composition of the country? Are immigrants being successfully integrated into society? What is the economic and social impact of immigration? How does America's experience with immigration compare with those of other countries? A review of the research on these issues can give us a better sense of the types of policies the United States should consider pursuing, keeping in mind that policy is usually driven by a diverse set of constituents with sometimes competing goals.

Immigration Policy and Current Immigration Patterns

From the founding of the country until about 1875 the United States had an open-door immigration policy. The Naturalization Act of 1790 allowed immigrants to acquire citizenship after several years of residence in the United States, and there were no legal restrictions on the number of immigrants or on places of origin. From time to time throughout the nineteenth century there was serious opposition to immigration—or at least to immigrants from certain origins—but these efforts did not have a significant impact on national policy. As noted above, the feeling was sometimes quite vehement, resulting in periodic violence against certain groups, such as Roman Catholics from Ireland.[4]

By the end of the nineteenth century there was considerable debate about the number of immigrants from southern and eastern Europe. In addition, on the West Coast many opposed immigration from China and Japan, as these immigrants were seen as undercutting the economic prospects of the native born.[5] In all cases, racism undoubtedly played a role, for these groups were often considered inferior to the native stock, and the extent to which they could assimilate into American society was also questioned. After the passage of mainly minor laws that barred the entry of convicts and prostitutes in 1875, Congress passed the Immigration Act of 1882, which prohibited immigration from China.[6] Japanese immigration was later limited in 1907 with the "Gentleman's Agreement," in which Japan was pressured to agree not to issue passports to Japanese citizens interested in immigrating to the United States, and the United States agreed to accept the presence of Japanese immigrants already in the country.

The Immigration Act of 1921 was the first law to put a ceiling on the overall number of immigrants allowed entry into the United States, followed by the even tougher Immigration Act of 1924. The 1924 law limited the number of immigrants from any country to 2 percent of the number of people from that country who were already living in the United States in 1890. By using 1890 as the base year for the quotas, the law had the effect of reducing the number of immigrants from southern and eastern Europe, who came in large numbers to the United States especially after that time. Levels of immigration plummeted after these legislative acts and remained low also in part because of the Great Depression in the 1930s and World War II in the early 1940s.[7]

Immigration policy generally became less restrictive in a number of small ways during and after World War II. Perhaps in part a reaction to the racist excesses of Nazism, overt racism in the United States increasingly fell out of favor. In general, many Americans felt that more effort should be made to harmonize policies with basic American ideals of liberty and equality of opportunity.[8] President Franklin Delano Roosevelt, for example, passed an executive order in 1941 that forbade racial discrimination by defense contractors. The Chinese exclusion laws were repealed in 1943, and the Luce-Celler Act of 1946 prohibited discrimination against Indian Americans and Filipinos, who were accorded the right to naturalization. The Immigration and Nationality Act of 1952 revised the quotas, basing them on the 1920 census (rather than the 1890 census).

In the meantime, immigration from Mexico began increasing in the 1940s and 1950s, largely as a result of the Bracero Program, which aimed to bring contract laborers temporarily to the United States to fill labor shortages, especially in agriculture. Workers were paid low wages, often endured difficult working conditions, and were expected to return to Mexico after their contract expired. The Bracero Program was extended several times before formally ending in the mid-1960s.[9]

At about this time another momentous piece of immigration legislation was passed—the 1965 amendments to the Immigration and Nationality Act (also known as the Hart-Celler Act). This act did away with the discriminatory national quota system and instead set more uniform annual quotas across countries. While supporters of the bill sought to make immigration policy less discriminatory, they did not think it would drastically affect immigration patterns. Senator Edward Kennedy, chair of the Senate Immigration Subcommittee that was managing the bill, asserted, "First, our cities will not be flooded with a million immigrants annually. Under the proposed bill, the present level of immigration remains substantially the same. … Secondly, the ethnic mix of this country will not be upset."[10] The bill set an overall cap of 170,000 visas per year, later raised to 290,000. A number of people were, and continue to be, exempt from quotas, including spouses, children, and parents of U.S. citizens, as well as refugees and other smaller categories of immigrants. In 2009, for example, about 47 percent of the 1.1 million people who gained legal permanent residential status in the United States were immediate relatives of U.S. citizens who were exempt from the numerical quotas.[11]

Senator Kennedy's assurances notwithstanding, the most significant effect of the Hart-Celler Act was that it spurred immigration from countries that had little recent history of sending immigrants to the United States, especially Asia and later Africa. (Immigration from Latin America had been in increasing in the years before the passage of the law, so it is not clear whether the law was responsible for spurring any further migration from that region.)[12] Figure 1.1 shows the number and changing origins of the immigrant population from 1900 to 2009. While the number of immigrants arriving annually was higher between 1900 and 1909 than in the middle decades of the twentieth century, by the 1990s the number of immigrants arriving surpassed all previous levels. The United States received a historical high of over 1 million legal immigrants annually in the 2000s, with many more undocumented immigrants as well. (About 11 million undocumented immigrants lived in the United States

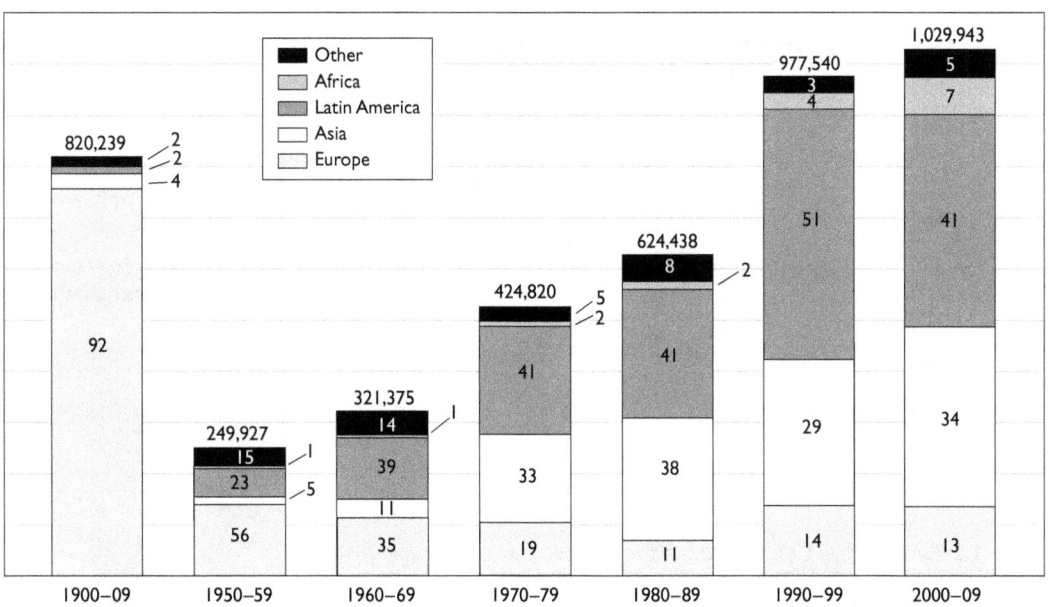

Figure 1.1 Annual Number of Legal U.S. Immigrants, by Decade, and their Percentage Distributions, by Region of Origin, 1900–2009.

Note: The Y axis demarcates numbers of immigrants in increments of a hundred thousand. The shadings and numbers *within* the graph's bars indicate percentages of immigrants from the different regions of origin. The Latin America category includes Mexico, Central America, the Caribbean, and South America. The Other category consists mainly of immigrants from Canada in the 1950–59 and 1960–69 periods, though it also includes immigrants from Oceania and a small proportion of immigrants whose origin was not known in the 1980–89 and 2000–2009 periods.

Source: U.S. Department of Homeland Security 2012.

in 2011.)[13] However, because of the smaller population base at that time, the proportion of the population that was foreign born in 1910 (15 percent) was still higher than the proportion foreign born a hundred years later in 2010 (13 percent).[14]

Whereas 92 percent of all legal immigrants were from Europe in the 1900–1909 period, this dropped to just 19 percent in the 1970s and 13 percent in the first decade of the 2000s. Meanwhile, the proportion of immigrants from Latin America grew from only 2 percent in 1900–1909 to 23 percent in the 1950s to a peak of 51 percent in the 1990s, before dropping back to 41 percent in the 2000s. The proportion of immigrants from Asia grew rapidly in the 1960s through the 1990s; by the 2000s Asians constituted about a third of legal immigrants. Since 2009, the number of immigrants from Asia has surpassed the number from Latin America.[15] Immigration from Africa was negligible over most of the period, though it has increased in the last couple of decades, such that African immigrants made up 7 percent of all immigrants in the 2000s.[16]

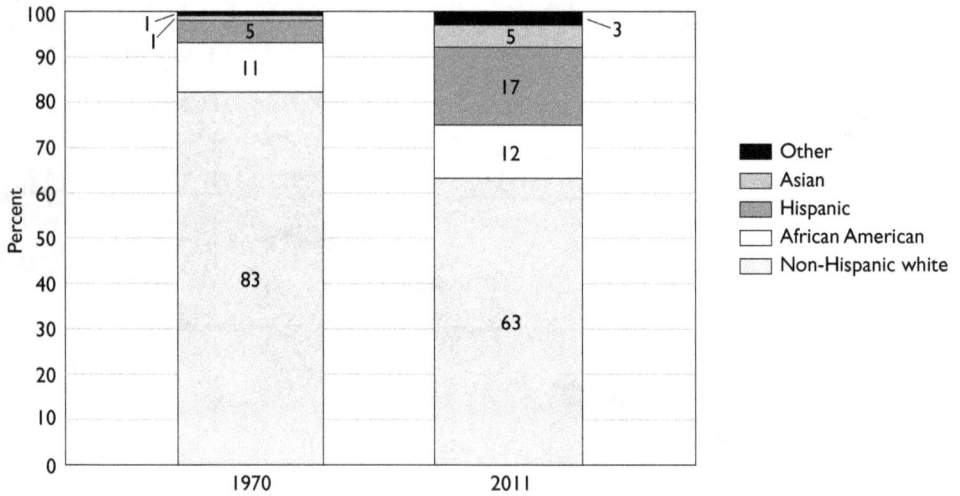

Figure 1.2 Racial/Ethnic Composition of the United States, 1970 and 2011.

Sources: 1970 data from Martin and Midgely 2010, 3; 2011 data from Motel and Patten 2013, table 1.

Changing immigration patterns and differential fertility rates (higher fertility rates among minority groups than among whites) have had a major effect on the racial and ethnic composition of the U.S. population. Figure 1.2 shows that 63 percent of the population was non-Hispanic white in 2011, down from 83 percent in 1970. The percentage of the population that is African American held steady, constituting 12 percent of the total population in 2011. Meanwhile, the percentage of the population that is Hispanic has increased rapidly, from 5 percent in 1970 to 17 percent in 2011. The Asian population has likewise increased significantly, from 1 to 5 percent over the period. The U.S. Census Bureau projects that by 2060, just 43 percent of the population will be non-Hispanic white, 13 percent will be African American, 8 percent will be Asian, and 31 percent will be Hispanic.[17] These projections, however, should be viewed with caution, as they incorporate assumptions about immigration trends, fertility rates, and future patterns of racial and ethnic identification. For example, recent research has shown that Latino fertility rates may not be as high as commonly thought, and that how people view their identity over time and across generations often changes.[18] Nevertheless, it is safe to say that racial and ethnic diversity in the United States will continue to increase in the coming decades.

Immigrant Assimilation

What does assimilation mean in the United States today? Researchers and commentators have struggled with the concept, as have immigrants themselves. A newspaper article from the 1990s relates the following story:

> Night is falling on South Omaha, and Maria Jacinto is patting tortillas for the evening meal in the kitchen of the small house she shares with her husband and five children. Like many others in her neighborhood, where most of the residents are Mexican immigrants, the Jacinto household mixes the old country with the new.
>
> As Jacinto, who speaks only Spanish, stresses a need to maintain the family's Mexican heritage, her eldest son, a bilingual 11-year-old who wears a San Francisco 49ers jacket and has a paper route, comes in and joins his brothers and sisters in the living room to watch "The Simpsons."
>
> Jacinto became a U.S. citizen last April, but she does not feel like an American. In fact, she seems resistant to the idea of assimilating into U.S. society. "I think I'm still a Mexican," she says. "When my skin turns white and my hair turns blonde, then I'll be an American."[19]

The article goes on to argue that the changing demographics of the country challenge the notion that immigrants will be able to assimilate, because many newcomers are visible minorities, and, unlike in the past, many immigrants themselves resist assimilation, not wanting their children to assimilate into a culture that they view as being different from and in many ways inferior to their own.

While debates on these issues are far from settled, the evidence tends to indicate—contrary to the implications of the article above—that immigrants in the newest wave are successfully integrating into American society, though the pace and extent of integration vary significantly across groups. In the next section I delve into these issues by defining assimilation, reviewing the empirical evidence on the issue, and describing why the pessimism expressed in the article above is for the most part unwarranted.

What Is Assimilation?

Assimilation refers to the reduction of ethnic group distinctions over time. In the past the term has sometimes been used to mean Anglo conformity; that is, assimilation occurs when an immigrant group adopts the mores and practices of old-stock native-born white Americans. More recent assimilation theorists emphasize that assimilation need not be a one-way street on which minority members become more like the majority group members. Rather, assimilation involves a general convergence of social, economic, and cultural patterns that typically also involve the upward mobility of immigrants and their children.[20]

Assimilation is often not a conscious decision in which an immigrant decides to shed his or her cultural practices and heritage in the pursuit of another culture's. Rather, as Richard Alba and Victor Nee note, assimilation is a lengthy process that typically spans generations: "To the extent that assimilation occurs, it proceeds incrementally as an intergenerational process, stemming both from individuals' purposive action and from the unintended consequences of their workaday decisions.

In the case of immigrants and their descendants who may not intentionally seek to assimilate, the cumulative effect of pragmatic decisions aimed at successful adaptation can give rise to changes in behavior that nevertheless lead to eventual assimilation."[21]

Commentators who believe that immigrants of old were eager to assimilate—unlike contemporary immigrants—are not well acquainted with the historical record. Historian Roger Daniels describes how German immigrants in the nineteenth century came mostly for economic reasons, remained very proud of their homeland, and sought to retain their cultural practices:

> Indispensable for most cultural institutions that were intended to endure beyond the immigrant generation was some way of ensuring that the second and subsequent generations learn and use the ancestral language—what scholars now call language maintenance. ... Beginning with parochial schools, largely but not exclusively Lutheran and Catholic, Germans eventually turned to the public schools and political action in [an] attempt to make German instruction in all subjects available when enough parents wanted it. In such public schools, English might be taught as a special subject as if it were a foreign language, which, of course, it was and is to many young children of immigrants raised in essentially monolingual homes. And in many parochial schools, English was not taught at all.[22]

Daniels notes that German culture remained very strong and proudly expressed until World War I, when the conflict pitting Germany against England, France, and eventually the United States led to strong anti-German feeling in many quarters. Still, even today many communities in the Midwest have strong German roots and cultural heritage.

Ties to the United States were also, at least initially, weak among many immigrants from a number of other sending countries. For example, of the 4.1 million Italians recorded as entering the United States between 1880 and 1920, anywhere from about 30 percent to nearly half returned to Italy.[23] Over the years, many immigrants have been attracted primarily by economic opportunities rather than by the notion of becoming American. Italians, like many other immigrant groups, were also concentrated in particular neighborhoods of particular cities (such as Little Italy in New York City), and they were concentrated in specific occupations as well, such as in low- and semiskilled trades like construction and pushcart vending. Many native-born Americans stereotyped Italians as criminals, pointing to tight-knit criminal organizations such as the Mafia.[24] Here we see that contemporary concerns with crime in immigrant communities (e.g., Hispanic gangs today) and the stereotyping of immigrant groups are nothing new.

Still, just because immigrants of previous waves of immigration from Europe assimilated does not mean that more recent immigrants from Latin America, Asia, and Africa will have the same experience. Commentators have pointed to a number of differences in the conditions under which these different waves have arrived in the United States.[25] Perhaps the most prominent of the arguments is that immigrants today are racially more distinct than those in the past. The counterview is that despite our perception of previous waves of immigrants from Europe as essentially "white," historical accounts indicate that many among those immigrant groups, including the Irish, Jews, and Italians, were perceived to be racially distinct from the majority of native-born Americans. As Daniels writes: "However curious it may seem today, by the late nineteenth century many of the 'best and brightest' minds in America had become convinced that of all the many 'races' (we would say 'ethnic groups') of Europe one alone—variously called Anglo-Saxon, Aryan, Teutonic, or Nordic—had superior innate characteristics. Often using a crude misapplication of Darwinian evolution, which substituted these various 'races' for Darwinian species, historians, political scientists, economists, and, later, eugenicists discovered that democratic political institutions had developed and could thrive only among Anglo-Saxon peoples."[26] The idea that immigrants from different European countries constituted different races diminished only over time as various groups achieved socioeconomic mobility.[27]

Nevertheless, a number of people remain skeptical about the successful integration of many of today's immigrant groups into American society. A competing theoretical perspective—*ethnic disadvantage*—holds that even if new immigrants learn the language and customs of their new country, they may still not be able to achieve significant socioeconomic mobility or acceptance by the white mainstream. Discrimination, for example, may put many educational opportunities or jobs out of reach for newcomers.

One viewpoint somewhere between the two (assimilation and ethnic disadvantage) is *segmented assimilation.* This perspective focuses on divergent patterns of incorporation among contemporary immigrants.[28] It asserts that the host society offers uneven possibilities to different immigrant groups, some of whom might achieve upward mobility and be successfully assimilated into the mainstream, others who will be marginalized and will adopt harmful cultural practices of disadvantaged native-born groups and experience downward mobility, and yet others who will retain strong ethnic ties and still achieve high levels of socioeconomic success. According to this perspective, racial discrimination and the range of economic opportunities available in a particular place at a particular time may shape assimilation trajectories of immigrants and their children. A number of studies have tested these perspectives.

Evidence on Assimilation

While one could study many different dimensions of assimilation (social, political, economic, etc.), I will focus on three dimensions of broad interest that are indicative of immigrants' general position in U.S. society: education, earnings, and residential segregation patterns. Taking generational change into account is critical in these comparisons, as assimilation is thought to occur mainly over time and across generations. Beginning with education, figure 1.3 shows years of education for different ethnic groups by generation and age averaged over the 1995 to 2007 period. (Multiple years of Current Population Survey data were needed to have large enough samples of relatively small groups, such as second-generation Puerto Ricans, to calculate reliable averages.) It should be noted that individuals

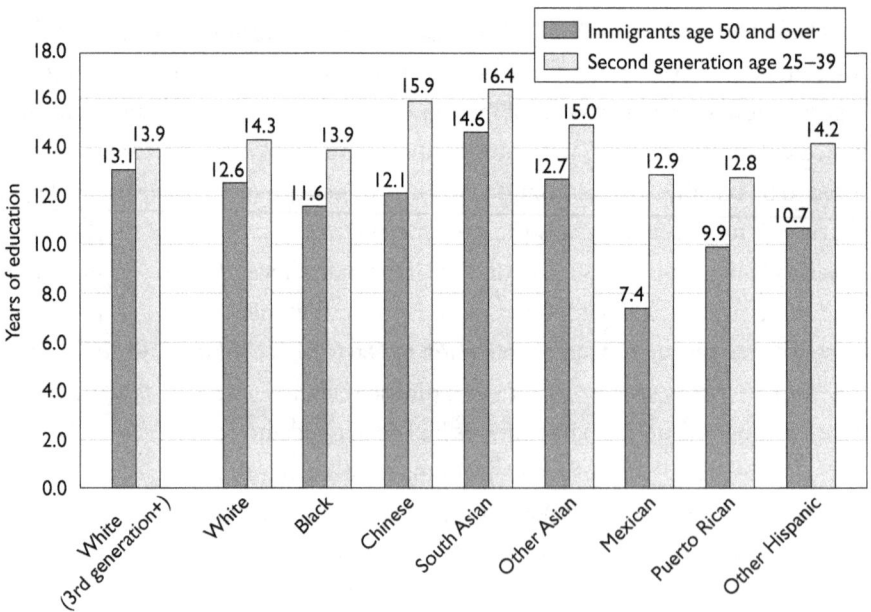

Figure 1.3 Years of Education, by Generation, Age, and Ethnic Origin, Among U.S. Native Born and Immigrants, 1995–2007.

Note: The first set of bars refers to native-born populace; all others refer to immigrants or their offspring. Following the same key that pertains to the other categories, the first bar in the set for 3rd generation+ whites refers to whites 50 and over, and the second bar refers to 3rd-generation whites ages 25–39.

Source: Reitz, Zhang, and Hawkins 2011, table 1, using Current Population Survey data.

born in Puerto Rico, although U.S. citizens at birth, are considered to be "foreign-born" in the analysis on the basis of their shared experiences as newcomers to the mainland United States, whereas their children and subsequent generations are "native-born." On the left-hand side of the figure, we see that third- and higher-generation whites age 50 and over have, on average, 13.1 years of education. This number is higher than the figure among similarly aged immigrants of all origins except South Asians, indicating a general educational advantage among the native-white population.

However, we see that the second generation has experienced considerable increases in mean education levels compared with the first generation, and that most groups have closed the gap or surpassed the educational attainment of third- and higher-generation whites of the same age. For example, while the third-generation or more whites of ages 25 to 39 averaged 13.9 years of education, this figure was 14.3 among children of white immigrants, 13.9 among second-generation blacks, 15.9 among second-generation Chinese, and a high of 16.4 among second-generation South Asians. The two second-generation groups that had lower levels of educational attainment than third-generation or more whites were Mexicans (12.9 years) and Puerto Ricans (12.8 years). However, even though these groups did not reach parity with whites, they far surpassed their respective first generations

(7.4 years among Mexican immigrants age 50 and over and 9.9 years among similar Puerto Ricans). The second generation of many groups often does better than third-generation whites, because their parents—especially those with high education themselves—are often a "select" group: many immigrated to the United States because they sought economic mobility, and they push their children to excel in school.[29] These general findings about the upward mobility across immigrant generations are in line with the conclusions of other studies that have analyzed this issue with other approaches and nationally representative data. In other words, while many immigrant groups are initially quite disadvantaged compared with the native mainstream, their upward trajectory suggests that some measure of integration is occurring.[30]

These findings do not mean that there is no cause for any concern. First, the immigrants themselves and their children vary considerably in their educational attainment. The United States attracts both very highly educated professionals (e.g., computer programmers and engineers in Silicon Valley) and low-skill laborers who toil away on farms or construction sites across the country. Even among Hispanics we see considerable variation, with Mexicans having the lowest initial levels of education, while education among "Other Hispanics" is considerably higher.

Second, while generational progress among the Mexican-origin population is impressive, Mexican American educational attainment at this time still lags behind other groups. The lack of documentation among many Mexican-origin immigrants tends to impede integration, because such individuals and their children do not have the same means to access the full range of jobs and educational opportunities that others can in the United States.[31] Researchers Michael White and Jennifer Glick find that adolescents from lower socioeconomic backgrounds tend to lag behind their more advantaged peers regardless of racial and ethnic background, and this can serve to slow continued educational progress across generations. White and Glick further note that while the effect of race may be declining in American society, the effect of race and ethnic origin on educational attainment has not disappeared altogether, even after accounting for many other family background factors.[32]

Turning to the second dimension of assimilation, income, figure 1.4 shows differences in household income by age and generation for the same ethnic groups shown in figure 1.3. The household income measure is adjusted for household size to produce an "individual-equivalent" measure. Some groups have larger households on average, so this measure provides more of a per capita household income estimate that also takes into account economies of scale enjoyed by larger households.[33] Figure 1.4 shows that second-generation households have higher incomes, on average, than first-generation ones among all ethnic groups. In addition, whereas all first-generation immigrant groups except South Asians had lower incomes than third-generation+ whites, the second generation of many groups (whites, Chinese, South Asians, other Asians, and other Hispanics) had higher average incomes than third-generation+ whites in the same age range. Second-generation blacks, Mexicans, and Puerto Ricans all continued to have lower incomes than whites, even if the gap (as compared with the first-generation white gap) was narrower. More sophisticated analyses that take into account differences in education, marital status,

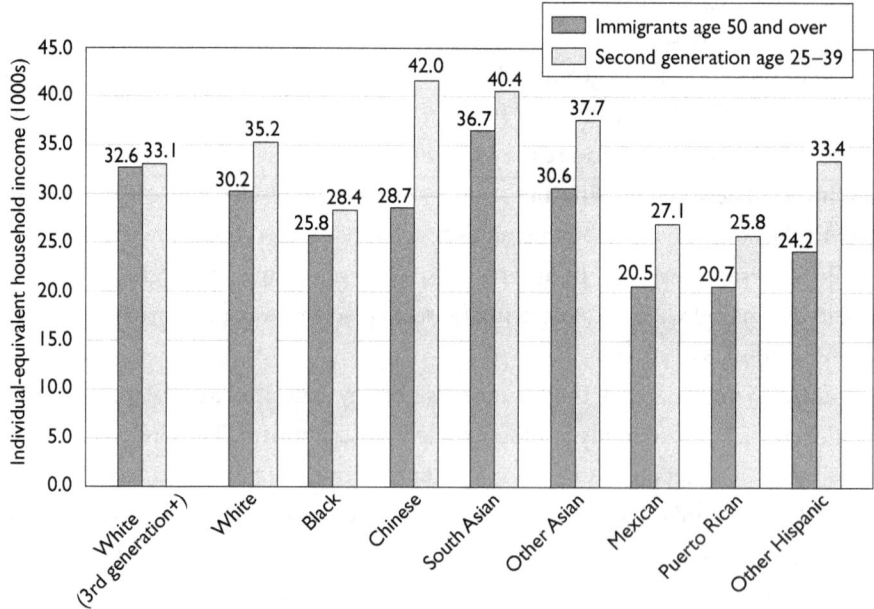

Figure 1.4 Household Income (Adjusted for Household Size), by Generation, Age, and Ethnic Origin, 1995–2007 (in 1,000s of Dollars).

Note: The first bar in the set for 3rd-generation+ whites refers to whites age 50 and over, and the second bar refers to 3rd-generation of whites ages 25–39. Income is in constant 2001 dollars. Household income is divided by the square root of the number of persons in the household.

Source: Reitz, Zhang, and Hawkins 2011, table 3, using Current Population Survey data.

and geographic location across groups tend to find small to negligible differences between whites and Asians but lower incomes among African Americans and Hispanics.[34] Other research confirms lower earnings for African Americans, though more mixed findings for Hispanics once many background factors are taken into account.[35] It is not clear why the gap between whites and African Americans, and perhaps Hispanics, exists, though labor market discrimination might play a role. Some studies have found higher levels of disadvantage particularly among blacks and darker-skinned Hispanics, suggesting the existence of a black-nonblack divide in American society abetted by discrimination.[36] American color lines are discussed in more detailed in the following chapter.

With respect to the final dimension of assimilation to be discussed, immigrant residential patterns, I previously conducted research on this issue by examining how levels of residential segregation vary by racial/ethnic group and nativity. The conventional wisdom has long been that new immigrants prefer to settle in ethnic enclaves so that they can live near people who share their common history and culture. Living among friends and family can bring comfort to those in a very unfamiliar environment. Immigrants' social networks also draw them to live in particular neighborhoods. According to the assimilation perspective, however, immigrants would be more likely to move out of these enclaves the longer they are in the host country, and certainly we would expect to see later generations living in a broader array of neighborhoods with groups other than immigrants themselves.

I used the most common indicator of residential segregation, the dissimilarity index, to measure the distribution of different groups across neighborhoods in metropolitan areas across the United States. The index ranges from 0 to 100, where 0 indicates complete integration (ethnic groups are evenly distributed across all neighborhoods) and 100 indicates extreme segregation (ethnic groups live wholly homogeneous neighborhoods with co-ethnics). The general rule of thumb is that scores above 60 are considered high in absolute terms, a score between 30 and 60 indicates moderate segregation, and scores under 30 are quite low.

Figure 1.5 shows average levels of segregation of Hispanics, Asians, and blacks from native-born non-Hispanic whites (hereafter termed "whites") across metropolitan areas in the United States, as calculated with 2000 census data. We see that in general, blacks are highly segregated from whites (an overall dissimilarity score of 67), followed by Hispanics (52) and Asians (43). Of particular relevance to testing the assimilation perspective, native-born Hispanics, Asians, and blacks are less segregated from whites than their immigrant counterparts.[37] In additional analyses, I found that, consistent with the assimilation perspective, some of these differences by nativity are explained by the average characteristics of the foreign born that are generally associated with higher levels of segregation, such as their lower levels of income and English-language fluency, meaning that gains in those attributes generally translate into greater residential integration. I also found that immigrants who have been in the United States for longer periods of time were generally less segregated from whites than new arrivals.[38]

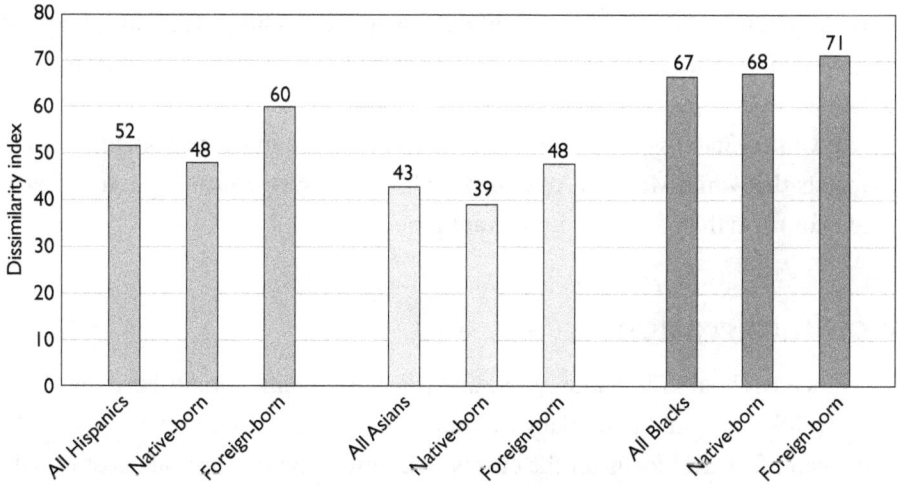

Figure 1.5 Segregation of Racial/Ethnic Groups from Native-Born Non-Hispanic Whites, by Nativity, According to the Dissimilarity Index, 2000.

Source: Iceland and Scopilliti 2008, table 1.

Nevertheless, we do see that patterns vary across racial and ethnic groups, with very high levels of segregation between blacks and whites regardless of nativity. On the one hand, this could provide some support for the segmented assimilation perspective. Clearly, blacks tend to live in very different neighborhoods from those of whites, especially in metropolitan areas in the Northeast and Midwest such as Detroit, Milwaukee, Chicago, and New York.[39] On the other hand, as will be shown in chapter 7, black-white segregation has been declining significantly over the years (this also shows up in 2010 census data), such that the residential (and social) distance between blacks and whites will likely continue to narrow in the coming years.

Despite these findings on the generational improvement in education and income and the decline in residential segregation, some commentators remain skeptical about whether all immigrant groups are assimilating. They rightly point out, for example, that Hispanic immigrants have been met with considerable hostility in many communities and question whether Hispanics will eventually be accepted into American society.[40] Many people also view strict anti-illegal immigration laws passed in states such as Arizona (2010) and Alabama (2011) as condoning racial profiling against Hispanics. Others base their skepticism about assimilation on research; one large study of a sample of Mexican-origin individuals in San Antonio and Los Angeles found that while there was considerable linguistic assimilation among Mexican Americans (i.e., most native-born Mexican Americans were fluent in English), educational and earnings mobility was only modest between the first and second generation, with little additional progress thereafter.[41]

Studies using nationally representative data, however, tend to show slow but steady generational progress among Mexicans. In a careful comparison of assimilation patterns of Mexicans in recent years with Italians and other southern and eastern European groups a century ago, Joel Perlmann concludes that Mexican socioeconomic mobility is slowly progressing such that it may take them "four or five generations rather than three or four to reach parity with the native-white mainstream."[42] That is, the low socioeconomic starting point of Mexican immigrants, combined with the fact that many are in the United States without valid visas (and thus have limited opportunity for upward mobility), suggests that while Mexican Americans will make socioeconomic progress over time, it may take longer for them than for other immigrant groups.[43]

Impact of Immigration

In addition to concerns about assimilation, some question whether immigrants have a positive impact on U.S. society. While one could potentially examine the impact of immigration on just about any aspect of American life, here I focus on the effects of immigration on three areas of broad interest and concern: the economy, social solidarity and social capital, and crime.

Economic Impacts

One economic issue frequently raised is whether immigrants drive down the wages of native-born workers. The answer comes down to whether immigrants are *complements* to American workers or *substitutes* for them. If they are complements, they are not directly competing for existing jobs. Instead, they work in jobs that employers have trouble filling with existing native-born workers (such as in agriculture in some parts of the country), they work in jobs that only marginally compete with native-born businesses (e.g., bodegas that serve ethnic communities), or they even generate job growth because they are entrepreneurs or consumers of goods and services produced by native-born workers. In these cases, immigrants are complementing the existing native workforce and not taking away their jobs. However, if immigrants are substitutes, they are essentially replacing native-born workers or competing enough with them to drive down their wages.

Economists have debated this issue at length over the years, as different methodological approaches have at times yielded different findings. A number of years ago a National Academy of Sciences panel of accomplished social scientists investigated this issue and concluded that the effect of immigration on the earnings of the native-born workforce is on the whole quite small. Immigration does not reduce the earnings of most native-born workers. Those most susceptible to the negative effects of immigration are low-skill workers, including less-educated African Americans, but even here the effects are small. The evidence suggested that immigrants tend to compete most with immigrants from earlier waves of immigration, for whom the recent immigrants are at times substitutes in the labor market.[44] The findings of the panel have been supported by a more recent review of the research on this topic as well.[45]

The fiscal impact of immigration depends on whether immigrants pay more in taxes than they consume in public services. Calculating the overall impact is quite complicated, as taxes are paid at the federal, state, and local levels via a variety of mechanisms (e.g., income taxes, payroll taxes, sales taxes, etc.), and public services are likewise offered by different levels of government. Moreover, the effects of immigration are both short term and long term, with the latter depending on not only the tax and consumption patterns of current immigrants but also those of the children of immigrants. Both the National Academy of Science panel mentioned above and more recent work have concluded that once all of these elements are balanced, the fiscal effects of immigration are generally small, and they depend on the characteristics of immigrants. Less-educated immigrants tend to consume more public services and contribute less in taxes, as do immigrants over the age of fifty. The federal government tends to benefit from immigration in the form of payroll taxes paid, because even many illegal immigrants with counterfeit Social Security cards have such taxes withheld from their paychecks. Meanwhile, local governments are more likely to bear the brunt of the costs of immigration (at least in the short run), such as in the form of staffing public schools with sufficient support services for immigrant children and health care for a growing local population.[46]

Immigration has a number of other economic benefits to the United States. Immigrants tend to lower the cost of many goods and services as a result of low wages. Higher-income consumers may benefit the most from this because they consume more "immigrant-intensive" products and services, including child care, restaurant food, and landscaping.[47] Among other economic benefits, immigrant entrepreneurs contribute to economic growth, immigration can boost struggling industries and cities, immigrants strengthen America's commercial ties with the rest of the world, immigrants contribute to the United States' engineering and scientific prowess, and immigration counteracts the aging of the native-born population.[48]

Regarding the first of these additional benefits—the contribution of immigrant entrepreneurs—immigrants to the United States have long been economic innovators. Among them, readily recognizable today are Andrew Carnegie (in the steel industry), Alexander Graham Bell (communications), and John Nordstrom (retailing).[49] Even today immigrants are more likely than native-born Americans to start companies. Immigrants, for example, make up 18 percent of all small business owners in the United States, though they are 13 percent of the U.S. population and 16 percent of the labor force.[50] Their impact on the rise of technology businesses and corporations in Silicon Valley in recent years has been immense. One study estimated that immigrants were on the founding teams of just over half of all technology companies in Silicon Valley, including companies such as Google, Sun Microsystems, and SpaceX.[51] In debates about immigration policy, one point many observers agree upon is that high-skill immigrants should be able to get visas to come to the United States more easily than current policy rules allow. As Alex Salkever and Vivek Wadhwa argued in a column on immigrant entrepreneurs:

> Allowing skilled immigrant entrepreneurs to more easily enter America, where they can create good jobs and pay taxes, is the closest thing to an economic free lunch that we are likely to get. In the words of New York Mayor Michael Bloomberg, we are committing "economic suicide" by making it hard for skilled immigrants to stay in the U.S. and contribute to our economy. ... [Foreign-born inventors are most prevalent] in cutting-edge fields such as semiconductor device manufacturing, where 87 percent of patents named an immigrant inventor; information technology, where 84 percent of patents named an immigrant inventor. ... Unfortunately, difficulties in obtaining visas are forcing many founders and innovators to either delay their start-up dreams or to relocate to more hospitable countries.[52]

Illustrating this very point, an article in the *Washington Post* recounted the following visa woes of two aspiring entrepreneurs who were postdoctoral mechanical engineers at MIT and, by extension, the impact this problem might have on our economy if it persists:

Anurag Bajpayee and Prakash Narayan Govindan, both from India, have started a company to sell the[ir water decontamination] system to oil businesses that are desperate for a cheaper, cleaner way to dispose of the billions of gallons of contaminated water produced by fracking.

Oil companies have flown them to Texas and North Dakota. They say they are about to close on millions of dollars in financing, and they expect to hire 100 employees in the next couple of years. *Scientific American* magazine called water-decontamination technology developed by Bajpayee one of the top 10 "world-changing ideas" of 2012.

But their student visas expire soon, both before summer, and because of the restrictive U.S. visa system, they may have to move their company to India or another country. "We love it here," said Bajpayee, a cheerful 27-year-old in an argyle sweater and jeans. "But there are so many hoops you have to jump through. And you risk getting deported while you are creating jobs."[53]

Immigration has also boosted struggling industries, such as the fruit and vegetable industry in California and the garment industry in New York, and has revitalized many inner cities, such as Miami, Los Angeles, New York, and Philadelphia.[54] In Philadelphia, for example, the immigrant population grew by 113,000 just between 2000 and 2006, by which time immigrants constituted 9 percent of the total population. Audrey Singer and her coauthors conclude that immigrants are revitalizing the city by bringing "fresh energy, entrepreneurship, and vibrancy to many parts of the region. They are breathing life into declining commercial areas, reopening storefronts, creating local jobs, and diversifying products and services available to residents. Immigrants are repopulating neighborhoods on the wane and reviving and sustaining housing markets. Across the region, they are helping to make greater Philadelphia a more global, cosmopolitan center, with stronger connections to economies and cultures abroad."[55] On the other hand, Singer also notes that immigration produces challenges for local institutions, such as in the overcrowding of public schools and the need for more services targeted at non-English-speaking individuals. On the whole, however, immigration has been an economic boon for the city. Recognizing the economic potential of immigration, many other places, such as Dayton, Ohio, Michigan, and Iowa, have tried to lure more immigrants.[56] For all of these reasons, the National Academy of Sciences panel concluded that immigration delivers a significant net economic gain for U.S. residents.[57]

Social Cohesion and Social Capital

The arrival of a large number of immigrants naturally changes the dynamics of communities. Many long-standing community members may view the newcomers with distrust and perhaps fear that immigrants are going to change the character of a familiar place. Sometimes animosity can arise in a struggle for power, as established residents may wish to keep their control over resources while new groups fight for recognition and for what they view as their fair share. For example, discussing racial and ethnic tensions in Los Angeles in the 1990s, researcher James Johnson and his colleagues argued, "Tensions, conflicts, and community instability associated with heightened immigration—especially of nonwhite immigrant groups—threaten to balkanize America. ... We believe that the undercurrent of racial and ethnic intolerance that undergirds the nation's changing demographic realities strongly challenges, and may very well threaten, our ability to establish viable, stable, racially and ethnically diverse communities and institutions."[58]

Johnson and his colleagues provide the example of neighborhood change in the city of Compton, a suburb of Los Angeles. It was initially an all-white community that experienced racial tension and white-to-black population succession in the 1960s. In the following decades, Hispanic migration to the area caused new schisms. On the one hand, black residents resented having to share social services and social institutions with the newcomers. On the other hand, newly arriving Hispanics complained about the lack of access to municipal jobs and leadership positions in the local government and about staffing positions in the school system and the content of the school curriculum.[59]

In 2006, in what was viewed by many as a law targeting Hispanics as a whole, Hazleton, Pennsylvania, passed a law that penalized employers for hiring illegal immigrants and landlords for renting to them. The law was declared unconstitutional in 2010 by a federal appeals courts, but the next year the U.S. Supreme Court upheld a similar law in Arizona and ordered a court of appeals to review Pennsylvania's law. Hazleton is a largely white, conservative community that had experienced a slow demographic decline since the 1940s in large part because of the decline of local industries (coal mining and the garment industry). In the 2000s it became a new destination for immigrants, who have in many ways revitalized the city. Hispanics made up 37 percent of the population in 2010, up from only 5 percent just ten years earlier. But this immigration has also been a source of tension, as it has changed the character of the city.

As a news story looking at relations in Hazleton reported, "Hispanic residents said they felt their entire population was stigmatized by the crackdown on illegal immigrants. Felix Perez, a Walmart employee with two daughters, 2 and 9, recalled a time he hesitated at the wheel of his car, unsure which way to turn, and the non-Hispanic driver behind him got out with a gun in his hand. 'He saw my face, he knew I was Spanish,' Mr. Perez said. 'They believe we are all the same because we look the same.' "[60]

According to the same story, some longtime residents are not entirely happy with the changes in their community. "The people in this town, we're becoming a minority," said Chris DeRienzo, 30, a wedding photographer who opposes a pathway to citizenship for illegal immigrants. "It hurts. I grew up here. It's not what it used to be."

One recent study by the well-known political scientist Robert Putnam examined the effect of diversity on social solidarity and social capital. He found that social cohesion was indeed lower in more diverse communities, at least in the short run. As he puts it, "In ethnically diverse neighborhoods residents of all races tend to 'hunker down.' Trust (even of one's own race) is lower, altruism and community cooperation rarer, friends fewer."[61] For example, survey respondents in relatively homogeneous areas, such as Bismarck, North Dakota, and Lewiston, Maine, were more likely to report that they trust their neighbors "a lot" than those in diverse places like San Francisco, Los Angeles, and Houston. Putnam also cites Richard Alba and Victor Nee, who note, "When social distance is small, there is a feeling of common identity, closeness, and shared experiences. But when social distance is great, people perceive and treat the other as belonging to a different category."[62]

While Putnam's main analysis focuses on this point, he does provide a word of optimism at the end of his published lecture, saying that these low levels of trust might be fleeting. "In the long run, however, successful immigrant societies have overcome such fragmentation by creating new, cross-cutting forms of social solidarity and more encompassing identities. Illustrations of becoming comfortable with diversity are drawn from the US military, religious institutions, and earlier waves of immigration."[63] It should be said that Putnam's analysis should not be taken as the last word on these issues. The results of his study have been criticized on both conceptual and methodological grounds, though empirical studies have tended to support (though not uniformly) his general conclusion about the negative association between diversity and social solidarity.[64] Thus, immigration can lead to a decline in social cohesion, at least in the short run, though a negative long-term impact is far from inevitable.

Regarding a related issue, the effect of immigration on the incidence of crime, conventional wisdom has long held that immigration is associated with social disorganization, ethnic gangs, and many types of criminal activity. However, an emerging consensus among scholars is that immigration to the United States in recent decades has generally not increased crime and in fact has often served to reduce it.[65] For example, sociologist Robert Sampson, one of the leading scholars in this area, found that, controlling for individual and family background characteristics, first-generation Mexican immigrants in Chicago were considerably less likely to commit crimes than later generations. He also found that living in a neighborhood of concentrated immigration was directly associated with lower violence, once a number of other neighborhood attributes were accounted for. More generally, he notes that immigration was increasing in the 1990s just when national homicide rates were plunging. He concludes that the beneficial (or at least unharmful) association between immigration and crime may be due to immigration's role in helping to revitalize many declining inner-city neighborhoods and to the positive influence that many immigrants may have on local cultures, given that immigrants themselves are not prone to crime or violence and for the most part do not come from particularly violent cultures.[66]

International Comparisons

International migration has been increasing around the globe in recent decades. Most of the discussion below focuses on comparisons between the United States and other peer (mainly wealthy) countries of Europe and the OECD, but it should be noted that many countries in a wide variety of regions have very high net migration rates, ranging from the United Arab Emirates on the Arabian Peninsula to Singapore in Southeast Asia to Botswana in sub-Saharan Africa.[67]

Many European countries that had been senders of migrants (and colonizers) in the nineteenth century became destinations for immigrants in the post–World War II period. Germany, for example, experienced labor shortages in the 1950s as it continued to rebuild and grow after World War II. It first looked to southern Europe, then Turkey, and then North Africa for temporary laborers. Other European countries with guest-worker policies included, among others, Austria, Switzerland, and Sweden. Some countries, particularly Great Britain, France, the Netherlands, and Belgium, also received immigrants from their former colonies. When a sharp recession hit Europe in the early 1970s, countries with guest-worker programs terminated them. However, a significant proportion of supposedly temporary immigrants did not wish to be repatriated to their countries of origin and stayed in their adopted countries. Many European countries have struggled with their growing diversity, and public opinion remains divided on appropriate levels of immigration. Nevertheless, immigration to many European countries both from their neighbors and from non-European countries continues.[68]

The United States continues to attract more immigrants than any other OECD country. For example, the United States had nearly 40 million foreign-born persons in 2010, followed next by Germany, with nearly 11 million.[69] However, because the United States has a much larger total population than any of these other countries, the percentage of its population that is foreign born is lower than in many others, as shown in figure 1.6. Countries with the highest percentage of foreign-born

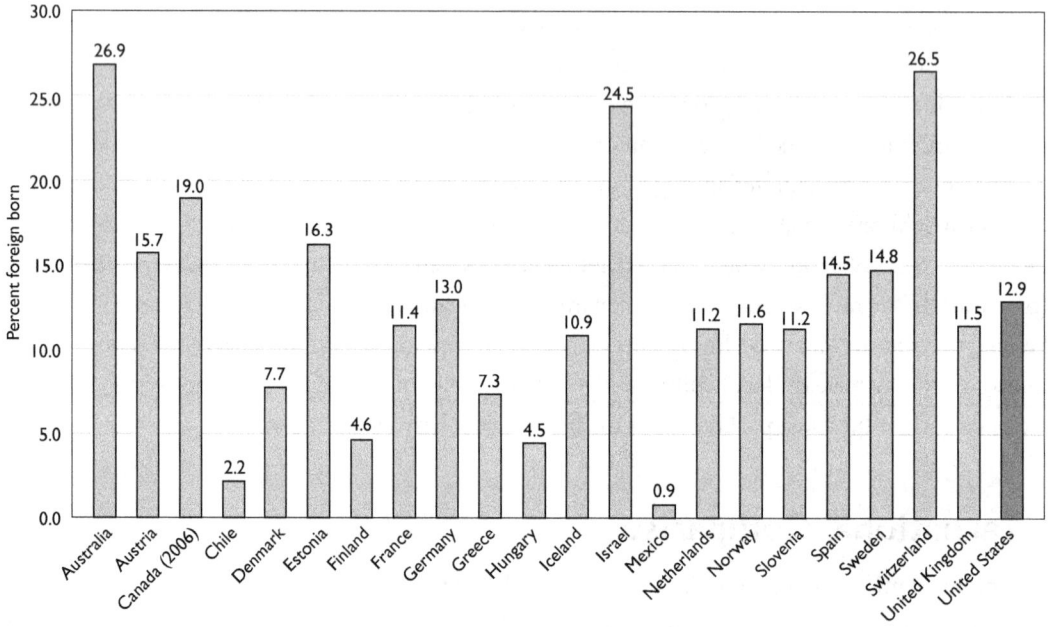

Figure 1.6 Percentage of the Population Foreign Born in Selected OECD Countries, 2010.

Source: OECD 2013d.

residents in 2010 were Australia (26.9 percent), Israel (24.5 percent), and Switzerland (26.5 percent). Canada (19.0 percent) also had a higher proportion of foreign-born residents than the United States (12.9 percent). A number of OECD countries had a relatively low percentage of foreign-born residents, such as Mexico (0.9 percent), Chile (2.2 percent), and Hungary (4.5 percent). Overall, however, immigration is both bolstering the populations of many countries that would otherwise be facing the prospect of future demographic decline because of low fertility and also transforming the character of these countries.

A few of the OECD countries, such as Canada and Australia, have long histories of immigration, whereas for others it is a much more recent phenomenon. The extent to which immigrants are assimilating and otherwise affecting OECD countries varies, for the countries themselves vary considerably in terms of the timing of immigration, the composition of the immigrants, their policies toward immigrants, and the economic and social conditions at the time of reception.

In terms of differences in immigration policy, Germany, for example, initially denied citizenship to all immigrants who could not trace their familial roots back to Germany. Over time this became untenable, as many guest workers originally from Turkey and North Africa, and then their children, were clearly in Germany to stay. Thus, laws regarding citizenship were eventually reformed in 1999 to make it easier for immigrants to gain German citizenship.[70] The United Kingdom had more multicultural policies from the 1970s onward, recognizing the rights of different groups and their claims on public resources. In recent years there has been some backlash against multiculturalism—many feeling that it is divisive—and a greater emphasis on promoting integration and community cohesion.[71] France, in contrast, has long had an assimilationist approach to immigration, expecting that immigrants should adopt French customs and culture. This approach informed the 2004 passage of what is sometimes referred to as "the veil law," which forbade any visible sign of religious affiliation in schools, and a 2010 law that banned the wearing of veils that cover the face in public places. Despite policies strongly promoting assimilation, many immigrants and their children in France, especially if they are "visible" minorities (those perceived as different because of skin color, language, accent, self-presentation, or surname), report that others perceive them as not being French, though they do experience at least some measure of integration over time and across generations.[72]

Concerns about immigrant integration in many European countries, such as the United Kingdom, France, the Netherlands, and Sweden, frequently focus on the assimilability of Muslim immigrants in particular. There is a broad fear of Islamic radicalism and a skepticism about whether the values of religious immigrants are compatible with the culture of secular humanism that predominates in many European countries.[73] Muslim immigrants in turn often feel that they are viewed with suspicion and discriminated against by the native-born mainstream.[74]

Studies that have systematically investigated immigrant incorporation into Europe and other OECD countries for the most part find that the second generation often does better than the first, as in the United States, though significant variation occurs across immigrant groups. One study of education, unemployment, and occupational attainment outcomes among the second generation in ten countries in Europe (Austria, Belgium, Great Britain, Denmark, France, Germany, the Netherlands, Norway, Sweden, and Switzerland) finds that upward mobility occurs among the second generation but that second-generation minorities from non-European countries still tend to experience some disadvantage, such as those of Turkish ancestry in Belgium, Germany, and the Netherlands; those of Moroccan or other North African ancestry in Belgium, France, and the Netherlands; individuals of Caribbean or Pakistani ancestry in Britain; and those of Surinam ancestry in the Netherlands.[75]

Another cross-national comparison of immigrant integration into the United States, Canada, and Australia finds common patterns of high achievement among the Chinese and South Asian second generation in these countries. Children of black immigrants tend to fare less well in all contexts, though the second generation still does better than the first. Across these host countries, some specific differences appear in relation to the starting points of the immigrants and the extent of generational change, but on the whole the similarities among these countries seem to outweigh the differences.[76] In short, in many different contexts, children from low-status immigrant families lag behind the children from native families, but immigrant incorporation is the dominant trend.[77]

A Final Note on Immigration Policy

Immigration reform has been discussed from time to time in recent years in the United States, mostly focusing on reducing the number of illegal immigrants currently in the country and attracting immigrants that would boost our economy. In some quarters, support for an expanded guest-worker program in the United States is considerable, especially among large businesses that would like to recruit low-wage workers for agricultural work or other labor-intensive work. While there may be good short-term economic reasons to have a guest-worker program, the entry of a large number of temporary, low-skill workers with relatively few rights or prospects for legal incorporation through citizenship may result in the growth of a socially, economically, and politically marginalized constituency. As indicated above, the record of guest-worker programs in western European countries suggests that such immigrants are not usually content to simply go home after they are no longer needed. In fact, approximately 25 to 40 percent of undocumented immigrants in the United States are visa overstayers rather than people who crossed the border illegally.[78] For similar reasons, providing the means for current undocumented immigrants to eventually attain citizenship will likely help them and their children more easily integrate into American society.

On the other hand, policies that favor admitting more immigrants on the basis of education and skills could serve to boost our economy, as such immigrants often engage in highly productive work. They are also more likely to have a positive fiscal impact on national, state, and local budgets through the higher taxes that they pay as compared with lower-skill immigrants. As noted above, the children of high-skill immigrants are also more likely to do well in school and in the labor market and are thus less likely to be marginalized and isolated. Of course, it should be said that immigration policy should not be shaped only on the basis of economic cost-benefit analyses. Immigration policy has long had an important humanitarian component that should help inform policy decisions as well. For example, many countries, including the United States and those of Europe, have policies that allow refugees from dangerous, war-torn countries to immigrate, believing that it would be inhumane to allow them to face extreme hardship or death if they remained. Over the years, such groups have included Jewish refugees during World War II, Vietnamese refugees from the Vietnam War, and Somali refugees in the 2000s seeking to escape the anarchy and clan warfare occurring in many parts of the country.

Conclusions

Immigration has contributed to increasing racial and ethnic diversity in communities across the United States. While the United States is a land of immigrants, fears about the impact of immigration and whether new immigrants are capable of assimilating have been frequently expressed over the years and continually crop up in policy debates on the issue. Research on the recent, post-1965 wave of immigration tends to show that immigrants are by and large being integrated into American society. The second generation tends to have higher levels of education and earnings than their immigrant parents, and that generation also achieves greater parity with whites. The native-born second generation also tends to be less residentially segregated than the first generation. Nevertheless, there is significant variation across immigrant groups, with Asians having the highest levels of attainment. Asian immigrants tend to have relatively high levels of education, and this confers advantages to their children in school and in the labor market. Hispanic immigrants come with relatively low levels of education, and while their children tend to do better than their parents, on average they do not achieve parity with whites. The children of black immigrants likewise achieve some measure of mobility but remain disadvantaged relative to the mainstream; racial discrimination may impact their life chances.

Many studies have also examined the economic and fiscal impacts of immigration. They have generally found that immigrants do not have much of an impact on the employment or wages of most of the native born, though there might be a small negative effect on the wages of low-skilled native-born workers. This effect is generally small because immigrants are often complements of rather than substitutes for American workers; also immigrants often create jobs and are consumers too, which can spur economic growth. Indeed, immigrants are more likely to be entrepreneurs than native-born workers, and high-skill immigrants have been crucial in spurring innovative economic activity in science and technology, such as in Silicon Valley.

The fiscal impact of immigration is small in the aggregate. Immigrants consume government services (such as public education), but they also pay taxes. Highly educated immigrants tend to pay more than they consume in public services. The federal government budget may benefit from immigration, because a large majority of immigrants (including many illegal immigrants with fake

Social Security cards) pay federal payroll taxes, though some local governments are harder hit because of small tax collections from immigrants and the cost of locally financed services (such as schools).

More diverse areas sometimes experience intergroup conflict and have less social cohesion and social capital than more ethnically homogeneous areas, at least in the short run, but communities that can successfully incorporate immigrants often forge larger, more inclusive identities over the long run. In the United States at least, immigration in recent decades has not been associated with more crime; immigrants themselves often contribute economically to poor communities and are not particularly prone to criminal activity or violence.

International migration is increasing worldwide. Many European countries that used to send migrants elsewhere in the nineteenth century have, in the post–World War II period, received many immigrants from abroad. These countries struggle with many of the same issues that immigration raises in the United States, such as the considerable concern about whether immigrants and their children—particularly those who are "visible minorities"—will integrate into society. While different host countries and different immigrant groups experience considerable variation, there are signs that integration is occurring in many European countries as well. These trends have not silenced debates on immigration in the United States or abroad, as many are still concerned about how immigration will continue to change the character of their country and how immigrants of the future will fare.

Notes

1. Daniels 2002, 266.
2. Daniels 2002, 275–76.
3. Brimelow 1995, 9 and 232.
4. Daniels 2002, 267–69.
5. Martin and Midgley 2006, 12. See also Daniels 2002, 271.
6. Martin and Midgley 2006, 12.
7. Daniels 2002, 287.
8. Daniels 2002, 329.
9. Daniels 2002, 310–11.
10. Brimelow 1995, 76–77.
11. Martin and Midgley 2010, 2.
12. Daniels 2002, 311.
13. Passel and Cohn 2012.
14. Daniels 2002, tables 6.4 and 16.2; Migration Policy Institute 2012b.

15. Pew Research Center 2013.
16. U.S. Department of Homeland Security 2012.
17. U.S. Census Bureau 2012i.
18. Parrado 2011; Parrado and Flippen 2012; Duncan and Trejo 2011b.
19. Branigin 1998.
20. Alba and Nee 2003, 11.
21. Alba and Nee 2003, 38.
22. Daniels 2002, 159.
23. Daniels 2002, 189.
24. Daniels 2002, 195–98.
25. See Alba and Nee 2003 for a detailed discussion of these issues.
26. Daniels 2002, 276.
27. Alba and Nee 2003, 131–32.
28. Portes and Zhou 1993; Zhou 1999, 196–211.
29. Reitz, Zhang, and Hawkins 2011, 1064.
30. Park and Myers 2010; White and Glick 2009; Bean and Stevens 2003. For a careful and fascinating study of immigrant assimilation in New York, see Kasinitz et al. 2008; and Kasinitz, Mollenkopf, and Waters 2004.
31. Bean et al. 2013; Brown 2007.
32. White and Glick 2009, 111.
33. Specifically, individual-equivalent household income is calculated by dividing household income by the square root of the number of persons in the household. For more details, see Reitz, Zhang, and Hawkins 2011, 1054.
34. Reitz, Zhang, and Hawkins 2011, table 5.
35. White and Glick 2009, 148.
36. J. Lee and Bean 2007, 2012; Golash-Boza and Darity 2008; Frank, Akresh, and Lu 2010.
37. Note that the bar for All Blacks is below that of both Native-born and Foreign-born blacks. While the average segregation for the group as a whole is typically between the segregation experienced by the two component groups, it does not have to be. Each of the component groups could live in different segregated neighborhoods, but if combined into one group, they may be spread across a broader array of neighborhoods.
38. Iceland and Scopilliti 2008.
39. Iceland, Sharp, and Timberlake 2013.

40. Lippard and Gallagher 2011, 1–23.
41. Telles and Ortiz 2008.
42. Perlmann 2005, 117.
43. See also Brown 2007.
44. Smith and Edmonston 1997, 6.
45. Holzer 2011.
46. Smith and Edmonston 1997; Holzer 2011.
47. Holzer 2011, 10.
48. Smith and Edmonston 1997.
49. Immigrant Learning Center 2013.
50. Fiscal Policy Institute 2012.
51. Salkever and Wadhwa 2012.
52. Salkever and Wadhwa 2012.
53. Sullivan 2012.
54. Smith and Edmonston 1997.
55. Singer et al. 2008, 29.
56. Jackson 2011.
57. Smith and Edmonston 1997, 4.
58. Johnson, Farrell, and Guinn 1997, 1055–56.
59. Johnson, Farrell, and Guinn 1997, 1074–75.
60. Gabriel 2013.
61. Putnam 2007, 137.
62. Alba and Nee 2003, 32.
63. Putnam 2007, 137.
64. Portes and Vickstrom 2011.
65. M. T. Lee and Martinez 2009; Sampson 2008; Martinez, Stowell, and Lee 2010; Stowell et al. 2009; Wadsworth 2010.
66. Sampson 2008, 28–33.
67. Central Intelligence Agency 2013.
68. Hansen 2003.

69. OECD 2013d.
70. Hansen 2003.
71. Modood 2003; BBC News 2011.
72. Simon 2012, 1.
73. See Caldwell 2006; Modood 2003.
74. Modood 2003; Simon 2012.
75. Heath, Rothon, and Kilpi 2008, 218.
76. Reitz, Zhang, and Hawkins 2011, 1063–64.
77. Alba, Sloan, and Sperling 2011.
78. Passel 2005.

References

Alba, Richard, and Victor Nee. 2003. *Remaking the American Mainstream: Assimilation and Contemporary Immigration.* Cambridge, MA: Harvard University Press.

Alba, Richard, Jennifer Sloan, and Jessica Sperling. 2011. "The Integration Imperative: The Children of Low-Status Immigrants in the Schools of Wealthy Societies." *Annual Review of Sociology* 37: 395–415.

BBC News. 2011. "State of Multiculturalism Has Failed, Says David Cameron." Online article, February 5. Available at www.bbc.co.uk/news/uk-politics-12371994 (accessed March 13, 2013).

Bean, Frank D., and Gillian Stevens. 2003. *America's Newcomers and the Dynamics of Diversity.* New York: Russell Sage Foundation.

Bean, Frank D., James D. Bachmeier, Susan K. Brown, Jennifer Van Hook, and Mark A. Leach. 2013. *Unauthorized Mexican Migration and the Socioeconomic Integration of Mexican Americans.* Research Report, US2010: Discover America in a New Century, Russell Sage Foundation, May.

Branigin, William. 1998. "Immigrants Shunning Idea of Assimilation." *Washington Post,* May 25, A1.

Brimelow, Peter. 1995. *Alien Nation: Common Sense about America's Immigration Disaster.* New York: Random House.

Brown, Susan K. 2007. "Delayed Spatial Assimilation: Multigenerational Incorporation of the Mexican-Origin Population in Los Angeles." *City and Community* 6 (3): 193–209.

Central Intelligence Agency. 2013. "The World Factbook: Net Migration Rate." Internet datatables. Available at www.cia.gov/library/publications/the-world-factbook/rankorder/2112rank.html (accessed March 13, 2013).

Daniels, Roger. 2002. *Coming to America.* 2nd ed. New York: Perennial.

Duncan, Brian, and Stephen J. Trejo. 2011b. "Tracking Intergenerational Progress for Immigrant Groups: The Problem of Ethnic Attrition." *American Economic Review* 101 (3): 603–8.

Fiscal Policy Institute. 2012. *Immigrant Small Business Owners: A Significant and Growing Part of the Economy.* Fiscal Policy Institute Immigration Research Initiative Report, June. Available at fiscalpolicy.org/wp-content/uploads/2012/06/immigrant-small-business-owners-FPI-20120614.pdf (accessed March 12, 2013).

Frank, Reanne, Ilana Redstone Akresh, and Bo Lu. 2010. "Latino Immigrants and the U.S. Racial Order: How and Where Do They Fit?" *American Sociological Review* 75 (3): 378–401.

Gabriel, Trip. 2013. "New Attitude on Immigration Skips an Old Coal Town." *New York Times,* March 31.

Golash-Boza, Tanya, and William Darity. 2008. "Latino Racial Choices: The Effects of Skin Colour and Discrimination on Latinos' and Latinas' Racial Self-Identifications." *Ethnic & Racial Studies* 31: 899–934.

Hansen, Randall. 2003. "Migration to Europe since 1945: Its History and Its Lessons." *Political Quarterly* 74, S1: 25–38.

Heath, Anthony F., Catherine Rothon, and Elina Kilpi. 2008. "The Second Generation in Western Europe: Education, Unemployment, and Occupational Attainment." *Annual Review of Sociology* 34: 211–35.

Holzer, Harry J. 2011. *Immigration Policy and Less-Skilled Workers in the United States: Reflection on Future Directions for Reform.* National Poverty Center Working Paper Series no. 11–01, January. Available at npc.umich.edu /publications/u/working_paper11-01.pdf (accessed January 22, 2013).

Iceland, John, and Melissa Scopilliti. 2008. "Immigrant Residential Segregation in U.S. Metropolitan Areas, 1990–2000." *Demography* 45: 79–94.

Iceland, John, Gregory Sharp, and Jeffrey M. Timberlake. 2013. "Sun Belt Rising: Regional Population Change and the Decline in Black Residential Segregation, 1970–2009." *Demography* 50 (1): 97–123.

Immigrant Learning Center. 2013. "Immigrant Entrepreneur Hall of Fame." Online list. Available at www.ilctr.org/promoting-immigrants/immigrant-entrepreneur-hof/ (accessed March 14, 2013).

Jackson, Geena. 2011. *Declining Cities Look to Immigrants to Revitalize Economies and Increase University Enrollment.* Immigration Impact report. Available at http://immigrationimpact.com/2011/10/03/declining-cities-look-to-immigrants-to-revitalize-economies-and-increase-university-enrollment/ (accessed March 12, 2013).

Johnson, James H., Walter C. Farrell, and Chandra Guinn. 1997. "Immigration Reform and the Browning of America: Tensions, Conflicts and Community Instability in Metropolitan Los Angeles." *International Migration Review* 31 (4): 1055–95.

Kasinitz, Philip, John H. Mollenkopf, and Mary C. Waters. 2004. "Worlds of the Second Generation." In *Becoming New Yorkers: Ethnographies of the New Second Generation,* edited by Philip Kasinitz, John H. Mollenkopf, and Mary C. Waters. New York: Russell Sage Foundation.

Kasinitz, Philip, John H. Mollenkopf, Mary C. Waters, and Jennifer Holdaway. 2008. *Inheriting the City: The Children of Immigrants Come of Age.* Cambridge, MA: Harvard University Press.

Lee, Jennifer, and Frank D. Bean. 2007. "Reinventing the Color Line: Immigration and America's New Racial/Ethnic Divide." *Social Forces* 86 (2): 561–86.

———. 2012. *The Diversity Paradox: Immigration and the Color Line in Twenty-First Century America.* New York: Russell Sage Foundation.

Lee, Mathew T., and Ramiro Martinez. 2009. "Immigration Reduces Crime: An Emerging Scholarly Consensus." *Sociology of Crime Law and Deviance* 13: 3–16.

Lippard, Cameron D., and Charles A. Gallagher. 2011. "Introduction: Immigration, the New South, and the Color of Backlash." In *Being Brown in Dixie: Race, Ethnicity, and Latino Immigration in the New South*, edited by Cameron D. Lippard and Charles A. Gallagher. Boulder, CO: First Forum Press.

Martin, Philip, and Elizabeth Midgley. 2006. "Immigration: Shaping and Reshaping America." Population Reference Bureau, *Population Bulletin* 61 (4) (December).

———. 2010. "Immigration in America 2010." Population Reference Bureau, *Population Bulletin Update* (June).

Martinez, Ramiro, Jacob I. Stowell, and Matthew T. Lee. 2010. "Immigration and Crime in an Era of Transformation: A Longitudinal Analysis of Homicides in San Diego Neighborhoods, 1980–2000." *Criminology* 48 (3): 797–829.

Migration Policy Institute. 2012b. "2010 American Community Survey and Census Data on the Foreign Born by State." Data Hub information. Available at www.migration-information.org/datahub/acscensus.cfm (accessed September 18, 2012).

Modood, Tariq. 2003. "Muslims and the Politics of Difference." *Political Quarterly* 74, S1: 100–115.

OECD (Organisation for Economic Co-operation and Development). 2013d. "Stock of Foreign-Born Population by Country of Origin." OECD StatExtracts, International Migration Database. Available at stats.oecd.org (accessed March 13, 2013).

Park, Julie, and Dowell Myers. 2010. "Intergenerational Mobility in the Post-1965 Immigration Era: Estimates by an Immigrant Generation Cohort Method." *Demography* 47 (2): 369–92.

Parrado, Emilio A. 2011. "How High Is Hispanic/Mexican Fertility in the United States? Immigration and Tempo Considerations." *Demography* 48: 1059–80.

Parrado, Emilio A., and Chenoa A. Flippen. 2012. "Hispanic Fertility, Immigration, and Race in the Twenty-First Century." *Race and Social Problems* 4 (1): 18–30.

Passel, Jeffrey S. 2005. *Unauthorized Migrants: Numbers and Characteristics*. Pew Hispanic Center Research Report, June 14. Available at pewhispanic. org/files/reports/46.pdf (accessed March 13, 2013).

Passel, Jeffrey, and d'Vera Cohn. 2012. *Unauthorized Immigrants: 11.1 Million in 2011*. Pew Research Hispanic Trends Project Brief. Available at www.pewhispanic.org/2012/12/06/unauthorized-immigrants-11-1-million-in-2011/ (accessed August 19, 2013).

Perlmann, Joel. 2005. *Italians Then, Mexicans Now: Immigrant Origins and Second-Generation Progress, 1980 to 2000*. New York: Russell Sage Foundation.

Pew Research Center. 2013. *The Rise of Asian Americans*. Pew Research, Social and Demographic Trends Report, June 19, 2012, updated on April 4, 2013. Available at www.pewsocialtrends.org/2012/06/19/the-rise-of-asian-americans/ (accessed August 20, 2013).

Portes, Alejandro, and Erik Vickstrom. 2011. "Diversity, Social Capital, and Cohesion." *Annual Review of Sociology* 37: 461–79.

Portes, Alejandro, and Min Zhou. 1993. "The New Second Generation: Segmented Assimilation and Its Variants among Post-1965 Immigrant Youth." *Annals of the American Academy of Political and Social Science* 530 (November): 74–96.

Putnam, Robert D. 2007. "*E Pluribus Unum:* Diversity and Community in the Twenty-First Century: The 2006 Johan Skytte Prize Lecture." *Scandinavian Political Studies* 30 (2): 137–74.

Reitz, Jeffrey G., Heather Zhang, and Naoko Hawkins. 2011. "Comparisons of the Success of Racial Minority Immigrant Offspring in the United States, Canada, and Australia." *Social Science Research* 40: 1051–66.

Salkever, Alex, and Vivek Wadhwa. 2012. "Why Entrepreneurship Needs Immigrants." *Inc.com,* October 15. Available at www.inc.com/alex-salkever/why-entrepreneurship-needs-immigrants.html (accessed March 12, 2013).

Sampson, Robert J. 2008. "Rethinking Crime and Immigration." *Contexts* 7 (1): 28–33.

Simon, Patrick. 2012. *French National Identity and Integration: Who Belongs to the National Community?* Migration Policy Institute Report, May. Available at www.migrationpolicy.org/pubs/frenchidentity.pdf (accessed March 13, 2013).

Singer, Audrey, Domenic Vitiello, Michael Katz, and David Park. 2008. *Recent Immigration to Philadelphia: Regional Change in a Re-emerging Gateway.* Brookings Institution Metropolitan Policy Program Report, November.

Smith, James P., and Barry Edmonston, eds. 1997. *The New Americans: Economic, Demographic, and Fiscal Effects of Immigration.* National Academy of Sciences, Committee on Population and Committee on National Statistics. Washington, DC: National Academy Press.

Stowell, Jacob I., Steven F. Messner, Kelly F. McGeever, and Lawrence E. Raffalovich. 2009. "Immigration and the Recent Violent Crime Drop in the United States: A Pooled, Cross-Sectional Time-Series Analysis of Metropolitan Areas." *Criminology* 47 (3): 889–928.

Sullivan, Kevin. 2012. "Other Countries Court Skilled Immigrants Frustrated by U.S. Visa Laws." *Washington Post,* February 18. Available at http://wapo.st/12ZVrZF (accessed March 14, 2013).

Telles, Edward E., and Vilma Ortiz. 2008. *Generations of Exclusion: Mexican Americans, Assimilation, and Race.* New York: Russell Sage Foundation.

U.S. Census Bureau. 2012i. "Table 4. Projections of the Population by Sex, Race, and Hispanic Origin for the United States: 2015 to 2060." Population Division release NP2012-T4. Available at www.census.gov/population/projections/data/national/2012/summarytables.html (accessed February 15, 2013).

U.S. Department of Homeland Security. 2012. "Table 2. Yearbook of Immigration Statistics: 2011." Data on Legal Permanent Residents. Available at www.dhs.gov/yearbook-immigration-statistics-2011-1 (accessed September 18, 2012).

Wadsworth, Tim. 2010. "Is Immigration Responsible for the Crime Drop? An Assessment of the Influence of Immigration on Changes in Violent Crime between 1990 and 2000." *Social Science Quarterly* 91 (2): 531–53.

White, Michael J., and Jennifer E. Glick. 2009. *Achieving Anew: How New Immigrants Do in American Schools, Jobs, and Neighborhoods.* New York: Russell Sage Foundation.

Zhou, Min. 1999. "Segmented Assimilation: Issues, Controversies, and Recent Research on the New Second Generation." In *The Handbook of International Migration: The American Experience,* edited by Charles Hirschman, Philip Kasinitz, and Josh DeWind. New York: Russell Sage Foundation.

DISCUSSION QUESTIONS

1. In what ways was the 19th century-debate about immigrants from Eastern and Southern Europe similar to the debate today about immigrants from Latin American, Africa, and the Middle East?

2. Starting with the Naturalization Act of 1790, list and explain the major laws governing immigration and naturalization that have been enacted in the United States over its history.

3. According to John Iceland, what is "assimilation?" In your view, is there a particularly American culture into which immigrants to the United States ought to assimilate? Explain.

4. What is "ethnic disadvantage?" What implications flow from this theoretical perspective with regard to the notion that assimilation is the most important thing immigrants can do to improve their lot in the United States?

5. Among immigrant communities in the United States, in what ways do the second and later generations do better than their parents and grandparents who immigrated to America? In what ways do the second and later generations do worse than the first-generation immigrants?

6. Explain "social cohesion." How is social cohesion affected by large influxes of immigration?

7. How does America's experience with immigrants and immigration compare with that of European countries?

CHAPTER TWO

Controlling Immigration and Visitation

A Plenary Power of the President or a Due Process Issue?

Introduction

On January 27, 2017, President Donald Trump signed Executive Order 13769. This order capped the number of refugees the United States would be willing to take in 2017 to 50,000. It also suspended any new refugees from entering the country for 90 days and suspended the admission of Syrian refugees for an indefinite period of time. The order also prioritized admission for refugees due to religious persecution. These aspects of the order were controversial with some. But the most controversial part of the executive order was the temporary (90-day) ban on all admissions into the country from seven specific nations: Iraq, Iran, Libya, Somalia, Sudan, Syria, and Yemen. These countries had been identified by both the Obama and Trump administrations as especially dangerous places and prone to harbor terrorists. Because we did not have diplomatic relations with Iran, and the remaining six countries were embroiled in civil wars, the administration found it difficult to fully screen visitors from those countries and therefore ordered the temporary travel ban.

Given that these countries were overwhelmingly Muslim in their populations, critics of the president saw this as a partial fulfillment of his campaign pledge to ban Muslims from entering the country until such time that "our country's representatives can figure out what the hell is going on." President Trump later moderated his position, both during the campaign and after his election. But this initial sweeping promise to shut down Muslim travel to the United States would prove to be a big mistake as it served as the backdrop for challenging his temporary travel ban with regard to the seven countries listed in the executive order. Indeed, opponents of the ban on travel from these seven Muslim countries claimed it was unconstitutional because it was motivated by a bias against Islam. The opponents merely pointed to the president's previous statements during the campaign as evidence for making their case. Additionally, the sudden announcement and implementation of the ban put a number of foreign travelers in limbo, stranding them at international airports because they were refused entry. Opponents of the ban said the way it was implemented violated the travelers' and would-be travelers' due process rights. The attorneys general for the states of Washington and Minnesota filed a lawsuit to halt the ban. A federal judge in the state of Washington agreed the travel ban was unconstitutional and issued an injunction against its continued implementation.

The U.S. Justice Department made the argument that President Trump had evolved in his position, that no politician had ever been impeded in implementing policies due to campaign rhetoric (which can get heated and exaggerated), that the ban obviously wasn't anti-Muslim as most Muslim countries were not listed in the ban, and in any case that immigration policy as it relates to refugees, visa holders, and visitors has always been viewed as a plenary power of the president under his or her responsibilities to set and execute foreign policy. A plenary power is a power given to a person or body (in this case, the president) that is absolute and not subject to limitation or review. The administration's legal team argued that the judicial branch had no authority to review or interfere with this plenary power of the president due to the separation of powers between the branches of government. What's more, they argued that foreign nationals, particularly abroad, do not have due process rights under the U.S. Constitution. Foreign nationals, despite their status as a relative or friend of someone in the United States who does possess due process rights, do not receive those rights vicariously.

The federal Ninth Circuit Court of Appeals, based in San Francisco, considered the case and upheld the injunction against the ban. In response to the appellate decision, President Trump signed a modified executive order that removed Iraq from the list of banned countries and also allowed permanent residents and current visa holders to enter the country. Federal district judges in Maryland and Hawaii, however, blocked that order, and the Fourth Circuit Court of Appeals in Richmond, VA, upheld the Maryland judge's injunction. In fact, by the summer of 2017, several federal courts around the country had weighed in on one aspect or another of Trump's evolving travel ban.

Finally, in July 2017, the Trump administration attained a legal victory. The United States Supreme Court vacated the injunctions in place and allowed the executive order to be implemented. It did, however, require that the government permit visitors from the six identified countries when there is a bona fide family relationship between those visitors and residents of the United States.

In this chapter, readers will get an opportunity to fully consider the various perspectives regarding the powers of the political branches (i.e., those belonging to the president and to Congress) to restrict who may enter the country. Immigration law expert Jon Feere explains in detail the history of the Congress's plenary powers in immigration and naturalization and presidential plenary power regarding foreign affairs, and by extension visitation, and the legal arguments for both a broad and narrow reading of the scope of these powers.

READING 2

Plenary Power

Should Judges Control U.S. Immigration Policy?

By Jon Feere

The U.S. Constitution provides no direction to any branch of government on "immigration," although it does invest the power of "naturalization" in Congress.[1] Immigration law has developed over time through numerous statutes and regulations created and adopted by the legislative and executive branches—the political branches of the United States government. Historically, the U.S. Supreme Court has taken a hands-off approach when asked to review the political branches' immigration decisions and policymaking. The ability of Congress and the executive branch to regulate immigration largely without judicial intervention is what has come to be known as the political branches' "plenary power" over immigration.[2] Ever since immigration became an issue of political significance more than 100 years ago, the political branches have been able to exclude and deport aliens or deny certain benefits according to political, social, economic, or other considerations, largely without being second-guessed by the judicial branch. The Supreme Court, in fact, did not seek to assert judicial authority and instead recognized that immigration decisions "are frequently of a character more appropriate to either the Legislature or the Executive than to the Judiciary."[3] Ultimately, for much of America's history, immigration-related decisions were made within the political branches by politically accountable actors according to legislation written by elected representatives of the American citizenry.

Courts have articulated numerous justifications for keeping immigration regulation largely within the confines of the political branches. Some of those justifications include:

- **Political Question Doctrine:** Federal courts generally refuse to hear cases that involve policy questions best resolved by elected officials. The logic is that elected officials are more accountable to the public and can best represent the public's interests. Elected officials are

John Feere, "Plenary Power: Should Judges Control U.S. Immigration Policy?," *Center for Immigration Studies Backgrounder* (Feb 2009). Copyright © 2009 by Center for Immigration Studies. Reprinted with permission.

also more likely to understand the political implications of their decisions. The connection between immigration and foreign affairs, national security, and similar policy-related fields has often resulted in courts invoking this doctrine.

- **Lack of Capacity:** Courts are designed to adjudicate legal issues and simply lack the institutional capacity to make political judgments. Immigration law is inherently political because it's created entirely within the political branches. Any judicial invalidation of immigration statutes almost always requires some amount of "legislating from the bench" and, even still, courts simply do not have the ability to remedy the potentially far-reaching political, social, and economic effects of a ruling that goes against statutory law.[4]

- **Uniformity:** The specifics of immigration (how many, who gets admitted, who gets deported, etc.) are regulated by federal-level political-branch policies. If lower courts become too involved in this process and craft unique statutory interpretations, there is a strong likelihood of an inconsistent immigration system that varies from one jurisdiction to another. This would arguably be in direct violation of the Constitution, which requires a "uniform rule of naturalization." Such a result would make it difficult for citizens to change the system if so desired. Aliens would also find it difficult to navigate the system.

- **Efficiency:** From a resource perspective, a court-run immigration system would be problematic. Judges are already grappling with the ever-escalating onslaught of immigration cases; reducing the authority of the political branches to easily remove or exclude aliens would obviously increase the caseload.

- **Immigration Enforcement Is Not Punishment:** The Supreme Court has held that due process protections apply when an individual faces punishment in the form of deprivation of life, liberty, or property, but that an alien being returned to his homeland or denied entry to the United States is not being punished and therefore cannot expect the courts to grant him these protections. Deportation and exclusion is simply an administrative procedure.

- **History:** The great weight of legal authority is in support of judicial deference to the political branches on the issue of immigration. The concept of *stare decisis*, which stands for the principle that past holdings should be respected by the courts, ensures that the plenary power doctrine cannot easily be abandoned.

While the plenary power rests on a solid history, attempts to weaken the plenary power doctrine and undermine the role of Congress and the executive branch in the realm of immigration regulation have been afoot for years. This is, in part, a result of an increased judicial focus on individual rights, a willingness of courts to dissect and/ or rewrite statutes (what some might call "legislating from the bench"), and the general tendency of those granted power by the state to aggrandize that power. At the same time, open-border immigration attorneys have been desperately searching for an argument that would erase decades of Supreme Court precedent and the authority of the political branches to regulate immigration at all, their aim being more opportunities for appeal and a more lenient immigration policy over all. Outside academia, they have been largely unsuccessful, save for a few anomalous and narrow Supreme Court holdings, critiqued below, and an increasing willingness on the part of a number of lower courts to openly evade the plenary power doctrine by applying their own inconsistent statutory interpretation methodology to even the most basic immigration cases.

This attempt at erasing the plenary power must not go unaddressed. Without the plenary power doctrine, the judicial branch—rather than elected members of the political branches—would be in control of much of the nation's immigration system as courts apply constitutional or "constitutional-like" standards to all exclusion and deportation cases. Theoretically, the ability of the political branches to determine who should be welcomed to our shores, who should stay, and who should go could be almost completely abolished in favor of a judge-regulated immigration system. Immigration policy decisions would be less likely to be shaped through the political process and would therefore lessen the power of the electorate to control the nation's future and to decide who we are as a nation and who we will be. Furthermore, detailed political considerations appropriate to expert agency officials may not be adequately considered by judges who are generally without the requisite immigration expertise. This is good for neither citizens nor aliens. Fortunately, the plenary power doctrine rests on a solid foundation and will remain strong, provided that the political branches steadfastly rebuff any attempts to weaken it.

This *Backgrounder* provides a brief history of the plenary power doctrine and attempts to discredit the case law highlighted by those seeking to weaken the doctrine. It concludes with recommendations on how to protect the political branches' power over immigration. On a basic level, Congress must make sure that immigration laws are clear and decisive as to the issue of authority and the executive branch must vigorously defend its regulation and enforcement of those laws. Without attention to this matter, the courts will continue to encroach upon immigration regulation and policy.

The Immigration Courts

To appreciate a century of plenary power history, a basic understanding of the immigration court system is necessary. An alien charged with violating immigration law initially faces an administrative process separate and distinguishable from the traditional court system. After being detained by immigration authorities and placed in removal proceedings, an alien's first contact with a judicial-like authority is an Immigration Judge (IJ) in the Immigration Court; this assumes, of course, that the alien actually gets into court and is not summarily deported via expedited removal at the border, for example.[5] The IJ determines if the alien is removable or inadmissible under federal immigration statutes, and also whether the alien is entitled to some form of relief (e.g., asylum). If the alien loses in this court and chooses to appeal, he appeals to the Board of Immigration Appeals (BIA), which generally reviews the lower court's hearing on paper rather than by a new trial. These courts make up the Executive Office for Immigration Review (EOIR) and fall under the U.S. Department of Justice, an executive branch agency. This is notable for the fact that, unlike traditional courts of law, the Immigration Court and the BIA are not part of the judicial branch. One clear difference is that the U.S. Attorney General can review a BIA decision, vacate it, and issue his own decision in its place; due to separation of powers issues, the Attorney General obviously cannot do the same for decisions rendered by judicial branch (Article III) courts. Although this is only one difference between the immigration courts and judicial branch courts, it illustrates how the regulation of immigration falls squarely within the executive branch. Nevertheless, should the alien lose administratively, Congress has authorized appeal to the judicial branch in some instances. There are numerous exceptions to how and when an alien is granted the right to appeal into an Article III court, and the process is ever-changing as Congress amends and tightens the process; those opposing the plenary power doctrine are constantly looking to expand opportunities for appeal.[6]

Plenary Power: A Brief History

When immigration to the United States became a political issue over a century ago, the original understanding of each of the three branches of government was that immigration was to be regulated administratively by the political branches with minimal court intervention. One of the earliest and most significant immigration cases in Supreme Court history is *Chae Chan Ping v. United States* (1889), also known as the "Chinese Exclusion Case." At issue in this case was whether an 1882 law barring all future immigration of Chinese laborers should work to exclude Chae Chan Ping, a Chinese immigrant residing in the United States who left in 1887 for what he thought would be a brief visit to China. Although the 1882 law contained a waiver provision designed to allow previously-admitted Chinese laborers like Chae Chan Ping to leave and return, that provision was discontinued by a new act of Congress in 1888 while Chae Chan Ping was on his return voyage to the United States. Upon arrival, he was denied entry. In upholding his exclusion, the Court recognized an inherent federal power to exclude non-citizens, even though such power is not clearly written into the Constitution. In a unanimous decision, the Court held:

> "That the government of the United States, through the action of the legislative department, can exclude aliens from its territory is a proposition which we do not think open to controversy. Jurisdiction over its own territory to that extent is an incident of every independent nation. It is a part of its independence. If it could not exclude aliens it would be to that extent subject to the control of another power."[7]

Most significantly, the Court held that decisions by the "legislative department" to exclude aliens are "conclusive upon the judiciary."[8] The Court continued:

> "Whether a proper consideration by our government of its previous laws, or a proper respect for the nation whose subjects are affected by its action, ought to have qualified its inhibition and made it applicable only to persons departing from the country after the passage of the act, are *not questions for judicial determination*. If there be nay just ground of complaint on the part of China, it must be made *to the political department of our government*, which is alone competent to act upon the subject."[9] (emphasis added).

By holding as it did, the Court affirmed the political branches' authority to exclude aliens as the branches see fit. The Court signaled an unwillingness to second-guess what it considered policy-based decisions and gave strong deference to both Congress and the executive branch in the area of immigration, thus forming the basis of the plenary power doctrine.

Three years later, the Court largely rejected due process limits—namely, the right of the alien to appeal the executive branch's immigration decision—in *Nishimura Ekiu v. United States* (1892).[10] In this case, Nishimura Ekiu, a citizen of Japan, arrived in the United States by boat, claiming that she was to meet up with her husband. Ekiu did not know the husband's address and carried with her only $22. For various reasons the immigration officer did not believe Ekiu and denied her entry under a statute that directed immigration officers to deny admission to anyone likely to become a public charge. Ekiu appealed her case up to the Supreme Court arguing that complete judicial deference to immigration decisions made by executive branch immigration officers amounted to a denial of due process. The Court disagreed. It held that the statute that empowered the immigration officials to make admission decisions also entrusted the final fact-finding to these officials. In other words, the Court again held that the judicial branch was not to second-guess the political questions inherent in any immigration decision. The Court explained:

> "An alien immigrant, prevented from landing by any such officer claiming authority to do so under an act of Congress, and thereby restrained of his liberty, is doubtless entitled to a writ of habeas corpus to ascertain whether the restraint is lawful. Congress may, if it sees fit ... authorize the courts to investigate and ascertain the facts on which the right to land depends. But ... the final determination of those facts may be entrusted by Congress to executive officers; and in such a case, as in all others, in which a statute gives a discretionary power to an officer, to be exercised by him upon his own opinion of certain facts, he is made *the sole and exclusive judge* of the existence of those facts, and *no other tribunal,*

unless expressly authorized by law to do so, is at liberty to reexamine or controvert the sufficiency of the evidence on which he acted."[11] (emphasis added).

The Court also explained its definition of "due process" in the context of immigration proceedings:

"It is not within the province of the judiciary to order that foreigners who have never been naturalized, nor acquired any domicile or residence within the United States, nor even been admitted into the country pursuant to law, shall be permitted to enter, in opposition to the constitutional and lawful measures of the legislative and executive branches of the national government. As to such persons, the decisions of executive or administrative officers, acting within powers expressly conferred by Congress, *are due process of law.*"[12] (emphasis added).

One year later, in 1893, the Court extended the principles in the two exclusion cases above to the issue of deportation in *Fong Yue Ting v. United States.*[13] After reaffirming the holdings in both *Chae Chan Ping* and *Ekiu*, the Court held that:

"The power of Congress ... to expel, like the power to exclude aliens, or any specified class of aliens, from the country, may be exercised entirely through executive officers. ..."[14]

The Court also held that because deportation is "not a punishment," the due process protections of the Constitution are not applicable:

"The order of deportation is not a punishment for crime. It is not a banishment, in the sense in which that word is often applied to the expulsion of a citizen from his country by way of punishment. It is but a method of enforcing the return to his own country of an alien who has not complied with the conditions upon the performance of which the government of the nation, acting within its constitutional authority and through the proper departments, has determined that his continuing to reside here shall depend. He has not, therefore, been deprived of life, liberty or property, without due process of law; and the provisions of the Constitution, securing the right of trial by jury, and prohibiting unreasonable searches and seizures, and cruel and unusual punishments, have no application."[15]

Taken together, *Chae Chan Ping*, *Ekiu*, and *Fong Yue Ting* represent the foundation of the political branches' plenary power over immigration. The principles in these cases have since been reiterated by the courts numerous times and they have never been overturned.[16]

Over the decades that followed, the Supreme Court advanced the plenary power doctrine even further, culminating in a series of cases in the 1950s that are considered by some legal scholars to be the high-water mark for the doctrine. These cases strengthened the Court's deference to the political branches and continued to limit non-citizens' rights to due process and, in one case, held that excluded non-citizens were not entitled to a day in court even if the result was indefinite detention. In other words, in the realm of exclusion, the political branches of the government had absolute and unreviewable authority.[17]

In 1950, the Court affirmed the exclusion of Ellen Knauff, a German-born war bride working for the U.S. War Department in Germany who sought naturalization in the United States after having married a U.S. citizen employed in the U.S. Army.[18] She was detained on Ellis Island and ordered excluded by immigration officials on national security grounds. In affirming the executive branch decision to exclude her without a hearing, the Court reasoned as follows:

> "An alien who seeks admission to this country may not do so under any claim of right. Admission of aliens to the United States is a privilege granted by the sovereign United States Government. Such privilege is granted to an alien only upon such terms as the United States shall prescribe. It must be exercised in accordance with the procedure which the United States provides."[19]

And:

> "[T]he decision to admit or to exclude an alien may be lawfully placed with the President, who may in turn delegate the carrying out of this function to a responsible executive officer.... The action of the executive officer under such authority is final and conclusive. Whatever the rule may be concerning deportation of persons who have gained entry into the United States, it is not within the province of any court, unless expressly authorized by law, to review the determination of the political branch of the Government to exclude a given alien."[20]

The Court then reaffirmed *Ekiu*, discussed above:

> "Whatever the procedure authorized by Congress is, it is due process as far as an alien denied entry is concerned."[21]

After the ruling, newspaper editorials decried her exclusion and Congress decided to intervene on Knauff's behalf. Hearings were held, private bills were introduced, and eventually—over two years after the exclusion order—the U.S. Attorney General granted Knauff a hearing before the immigration Board of Special Inquiry. After testimony from government witnesses who claimed that Knauff was involved in espionage with the Czechoslovakian government, the Board ruled against Knauff and returned her to Ellis Island. Soon after, Knauff appealed the ruling to the Board of Immigration Appeals which reversed in her favor and ordered that she be admitted into the United States. The Attorney General accepted the ruling and Knauff became a lawful permanent resident.[22]

Knauff illustrates the importance of the plenary power doctrine. The Supreme Court recognized the limited role of the judicial branch in immigration proceedings and the decision appropriately forced the political issues surrounding Ellen Knauff to be debated within political branches rather than in the court system. This ensures that agency experts rather than Article III judges make the final determination. It also allows citizens to control their nation's immigration policy through the ballot box.

In 1952, the Supreme Court reasoned similarly in affirming the deportation of three aliens who were former members of the Communist Party in *Harisiades v. Shaughnessy*.[23] Here, however, the aliens were longtime residents who were fighting against their removal. The Court seemed to note the severity of deporting aliens who had resided within the country for a lengthy period of time, but noted that such expulsion, "is a weapon of defense and reprisal confirmed by international law as a power inherent in every sovereign state."[24] In affirming the deportations, the Court held:

> "[A]ny policy toward aliens is vitally and intricately interwoven with contemporaneous policies in regard to the conduct of foreign relations, the war power, and the maintenance of a republican form of government. Such matters are so exclusively entrusted to the political branches of government as to be largely immune from judicial inquiry or interference."[25]

And:

> "[N]othing in the structure of our Government or the text of our Constitution would warrant judicial review by standards which would require us to equate our political judgment with that of Congress."[26]

In supporting deference to the political branches, the Court held that the aliens' proposition that the judicial branch should review and uphold immigration policy only after a finding of "reasonableness" is a proposition "not founded in precedents of this Court."[27] The Court explained:

"Under the conditions which produced this Act, can we declare that congressional alarm about a coalition of Communist power without and Communist conspiracy within the United States is either a fantasy or a pretense? This Act was approved by President Roosevelt June 28, 1940, when a world war was threatening to involve us, as soon it did. Communists in the United States were exerting every effort to defeat and delay our preparations. Certainly no responsible American would say that there were then or are now no possible grounds on which Congress might believe that Communists in our midst are inimical to our security.... It would be easy for those of us who do not have security responsibility to say that those who do are taking Communism too seriously and overestimating its danger. But we have an Act of one Congress which, for a decade, subsequent Congresses have never repealed but have strengthened and extended. We, in our private opinions, need not concur in Congress' policies to hold its enactments constitutional. Judicially we must tolerate what personally we may regard as a legislative mistake."[28]

The Court also noted that less deference to the political branches would unwisely turn judges into international policymakers:

"[I]t would be rash and irresponsible to reinterpret our fundamental law to deny or qualify the Government's power of deportation. However desirable world-wide amelioration of the lot of aliens, we think it is peculiarly a subject for international diplomacy. It should not be initiated by judicial decision which can only deprive our own Government of a power of defense and reprisal without obtaining for American citizens abroad any reciprocal privileges or immunities. Reform in this field must be entrusted to the branches of the Government in control of our international relations and treaty-making powers."[29]

Justice Frankfurter's concurring opinion reiterates that it is not the responsibility of the judicial branch to make or rewrite policy and ultimately puts the onus back on Congress:

"Though as a matter of political outlook and economic need this country has traditionally welcomed aliens to come to its shores, it has done so exclusively as a matter of political outlook and national self-interest. This policy has been a political policy, belonging to the political branch of the Government wholly outside the concern and the competence of the Judiciary ... In recognizing this power and this responsibility of Congress, one does not in the remotest degree align oneself with fears unworthy of the American spirit or with hostility to the bracing air of the free spirit. One merely recognizes that the place to resist unwise or cruel legislation touching aliens is the Congress, not this Court."[30]

In 1953, the Court went further in *Shaughnessy v. United States ex rel. Mezei*, holding that a non-citizen facing exclusion is not entitled to any due process whatsoever, even if the result was indefinite detention.[31] In this case, Ignatz Mezei, an eastern European immigrant who had lived in the United States for more than 25 years, left the country, apparently to visit his dying mother in Romania. He was denied entry there, and instead remained in Hungary for 19 months. Thereafter, he returned to the United States, ultimately arriving at Ellis Island where he was then permanently denied entry by the U.S. government on the basis of national security. In an effort to relocate, Mezei shipped out to both Britain and France; each country denied him admission, and Mezei returned to Ellis Island. The U.S. Department of State unsuccessfully negotiated with Hungary to send Mezei there, and Mezei himself unsuccessfully applied for entry to approximately a dozen other countries.[32] Eventually, both the U.S. government and Mezei ended their search. After 21 months of living on Ellis Island, Mezei applied for a writ of habeas corpus, arguing that his exclusion from the United States amounted to an unlawful detention.

Although a lower court granted Mezei's request, the U.S. Supreme Court reversed the decision, holding that the exclusion was a "fundamental sovereign attribute exercised by the Government's political departments largely immune from judicial control."[33] And in citing more precedent, the Court held:

> "Whatever the procedure authorized by Congress is, it is due process as far as an alien denied entry is concerned. And because the action of the executive officer under such authority is final and conclusive, the Attorney General cannot be compelled to disclose the evidence underlying his determinations in an exclusion case; it is not within the province of any court, unless expressly authorized by law, to review the determination of the political branch of the Government. In a case such as this, courts cannot retry the determination of the Attorney General."[34]

And:

> "In sum, harborage at Ellis Island is not an entry into the United States. For purposes of the immigration laws, moreover, the legal incidents of an alien's entry remain unaltered whether he has been here once before or not. He is an entering alien just the same, and may be excluded if unqualified for admission under existing immigration laws."[35]

Mezei remained on Ellis Island for nearly four years until he was released on humanitarian grounds and paroled into the United States by the U.S. Attorney General after hearings.[36] Like the decision to admit Ellen Knauff into the United States, discussed above, Mezei's parole was the result of political decisions made within the political branches and involved, for example, private bills in Congress and hearings in executive branch immigration courts. Once again, the plenary power doctrine appropriately placed political decisions in the hands of policymakers.

Many additional Supreme Court cases have affirmed the plenary power doctrine and, like each of the previous cases, the following cases have been citied approvingly many times:

- 1954: *Galvan v. Press*—The Supreme Court affirms a security statute and the deportation order under that statute of a communist Mexican alien. In reaffirming the plenary power doctrine, the Court explains, "[T]he slate is not clean. As to the extent of the power of Congress under review, there is not merely 'a page of history,' but a whole volume. Policies pertaining to the entry of aliens and their right to remain here are peculiarly concerned with the political conduct of government. In the enforcement of these policies, the Executive Branch of the Government must respect the procedural safeguards of due process. But that the formulation of these policies is entrusted exclusively to Congress has become about as firmly imbedded in the legislative and judicial tissues of our body politic as any aspect of our government." The Court affirmed the deportation even while recognizing that the alien "legally became part of the American community" and had lived in the country for 36 years with an American wife and four children.[37]

- 1972: *Kleindienst v. Mandel*—The Supreme Court upholds the exclusion of a self-described "revolutionary Marxist" Belgian author who had been invited to speak at Stanford, Princeton, Columbia, and other universities. In deferring to the executive branch's decision to exclude the author, the Court explained that its own "reaffirmations of [the plenary power doctrine] have been legion. The Court without exception has sustained Congress' plenary power to make rules for the admission of aliens and to exclude those who possess those characteristics which Congress has forbidden."[38] The Court also cited an important case from 1895, holding that the power of Congress "to exclude aliens altogether from the United States, or to prescribe the terms and conditions upon which they may come to this country, and to have its declared policy in that regard enforced exclusively through executive officers, without judicial intervention, *is settled* by our previous adjudications."[39] (emphasis added). After calling the power "firmly established" the Court explained that "when the Executive exercises this power negatively on the basis of a facially legitimate and bona fide reason, the courts will neither look behind the exercise of that discretion, nor test it ..."[40]

- 1976: *Mathews v. Diaz et al.*—The Supreme Court upholds a statute requiring a five-year period of admission as a prerequisite for aliens wishing to receive Medicare. In reaffirming the plenary power doctrine, the Court held: "For reasons long recognized as valid, the responsibility for regulating the relationship between the United States and our alien visitors has been committed to the political branches of the Federal Government. Since decisions in these matters may implicate our relations with foreign powers, and since a wide variety of classifications must be defined in the light of changing political and economic circumstances, such decisions are frequently of a character more appropriate to either the Legislature or the Executive than to the Judiciary. This very case illustrates the need for flexibility in policy choices rather than the rigidity often characteristic of constitutional adjudication. Appellees Diaz and Clara are but two of over 440,000 Cuban refugees who arrived in the United States between 1961 and 1972."[41] The Court noted the significant political, social, and economic impact a decision in favor of the aliens—and against the plenary power—would have: "An unlikely, but nevertheless possible, consequence of holding that appellees are constitutionally entitled to welfare benefits would be a further extension of similar benefits to over 440,000 Cuban parolees." In being asked to substitute its judgment for that of Congress, the Court simply responded: "We decline the invitation."[42] The Court understood that it lacked the capacity to rein in the political implications a decision in favor of the alien would have in this case.

The Courts Get Involved in Immigration Policy

Despite decades of judicial support for the political branches' plenary power over immigration, the doctrine is not without some cracks. Soon after the early *Chae Chan Ping*, *Ekiu*, and *Fong Yue Ting* cases and prior to the *Knauff* decision in 1950, the Supreme Court softened the plenary power doctrine in a number of cases and carved out some exceptions, especially for individuals facing deportation who claimed to be U.S. citizens.[43] But most of these small exceptions were short-lived as the plenary power was reinvigorated by *Knauff*, *Mezei*, and the other cases discussed above. Nevertheless, with the inevitable appointment of new justices to the Supreme Court and an increasing focus on individual rights during the 1960s and 70s came a judicial willingness to wield "a scalpel [and] dissect the administrative organization of the Federal Government," at least according to a dissenting Justice Rehnquist in his defense of the plenary power doctrine.[44] As the judicial branch expanded the number and types of immigration claims it would hear, the result was a chipping away of the plenary power doctrine. But trying to make sense of the high court's inconsistent immigration decisions has justifiably been a challenge for the brightest of legal scholars. Quite simply, the agenda of judges opposed to the plenary power doctrine has been to slowly begin applying semi-constitutional norms—what some academics call "phantom norms"—to basic immigration cases that would not otherwise escape the reach of the plenary power doctrine.[45] The thinking is that if the Supreme Court could squeak out a few cases that superficially apply constitutional norms in the immigration context (e.g., the use of a First Amendment analysis as a bar against deportation, race-based civil rights claims as an argument against exclusion, protections against cruel and unusual punishment), then slowly, over time, the entire notion of dragging nearly every deportation or exclusion hearing into the judicial branch and granting constitutional protections to all aliens—both those within and outside the country—would become the status quo. The resulting decisions, logically, are much more sympathetic to the alien as the increasingly powerful judiciary finds more and more justifications for denying exclusions and deportations. The overall outcome is that political decision-making in immigration law becomes usurped by unelected, and largely unaccountable, Article III judges with little or no understanding of the political implications of their decisions.

A few notable cases seem to have abandoned decades of precedent while simultaneously enlarging the role of judges to that of immigration policymakers. Although some of the cases are heralded as "groundbreaking" by anti-plenary power attorneys, it is likely that these cases represent an anomalous, narrow, and temporary deviation that will not hold up, particularly after the deaths of nearly 3,000 people at the hands of 19 immigrants on September 11, 2001. Post-9/11 developments and possible strategies for reinvigorating the plenary power are discussed later in this report.

The attempted movement away from the plenary power doctrine can be observed in a series of holdings beginning in the mid-1940s in which the Supreme Court over time began applying constitutional norms to immigration cases that could otherwise be decided with a basic application of the plenary power doctrine. This waning and waxing anti-plenary movement included—and continues to include—detailed judicial examinations of immigration statutes and their legislative histories, routine questioning of the executive's handling of immigration cases, and a focus on the impact of deportation on the alien. The end goal for anti-plenary power judges and attorneys, of course, is the complete envelopment of immigration cases by standard constitutional law analysis, an analysis that is much more beneficial to the alien than it is to the government. Cases representing this judicial intervention are examined below.[46]

In the 1948 case *Fong Haw Tan v. Phelan*, a statute regarding the deportation of criminal alien repeat offenders was at issue after Fong Haw Tan was convicted of two different murders and received a life sentence for each during a single trial. The statute required that "any alien...who is sentenced more than once [to imprisonment for a term of one year or more] because of conviction...of any crime involving moral turpitude, committed at any time after entry shall, upon the warrant of the Attorney General, be taken into custody and deported."[47] Both the immigration court and the Ninth Circuit Court of Appeals were not swayed by Fong Haw Tan's argument that the statute did not apply to him because he could not actually serve two life sentences, nor were the courts swayed by the alien's humanitarian appeal. In showing strong deference to the executive branch's interpretation of the statute, the appeals court held simply: "In our opinion there is no harsh injustice involved that justifies a judicial search for a limitation of the plainly expressed scope of the statute."[48] Upon appeal, the Supreme Court reversed in favor of Fong Haw Tan. Instead of deferring to the executive branch interpretation of the statute, the Court dug into the statute's legislative history to find quotes from the statute's authors which emphasized a concern about repetition of offenses by an alien. The

Court held that the two murders committed by Fong Haw Tan did not represent the type of repeat offender at whom the statute was aimed and that it authorized deportation "only where an alien having committed a crime involving moral turpitude and having been convicted and sentenced, once again commits a crime of that nature and is convicted and sentenced for it."[49] Additionally, on humanitarian grounds the Court sided with the alien rather than the executive branch, a clear abandonment of basic plenary power deference:

> "We resolve the doubts in favor of that construction because deportation is a drastic measure and at times the equivalent of banishment or exile. It is the forfeiture for misconduct of a residence in this country. Such a forfeiture is a penalty. To construe this statutory provision less generously to the alien might find support in logic. But since the stakes are considerable for the individual, we will not assume that Congress meant to trench on his freedom beyond that which is required by the narrowest of several possible meanings of the words used."[50]

This holding clearly conflicts with *Fong Yue Ting*, discussed earlier, where the Court held that deportation is "not a banishment" and "not a punishment."[51] Clearly, respect for *stare decisis* must be abandoned by those wishing to eliminate the plenary power doctrine. Interestingly, Congress amended the language of this statute not long after this holding so as to render an alien deportable if he is twice convicted of crimes involving moral turpitude, *regardless* of whether the two convictions are in one trial or separate trials, and *regardless* of whether the alien is actually sentenced to a term of imprisonment as a result of such convictions. The exact motive for rewriting the statute is unclear, but it might be evidence of Congress's attempt to override judicial intervention in immigration regulation of the kind noted in *Fong Haw Tan*.[52] While the new statute renders the case *holding* somewhat irrelevant from a legal standpoint, this case nevertheless represents one of the early movements away from absolute judicial deference to the political branches on immigration enforcement and remains highlighted by anti-plenary advocates.

At issue in the 1953 case *Kwong Hai Chew v. Colding* was the exclusion of a returning lawful resident alien who was deemed to be a threat to national security by immigration authorities. After temporarily leaving the United States working as a seaman, Kwong Hai Chew was detained upon reentry, ordered excluded, and not provided a hearing or made aware of the charges against him because executive branch officials believed that to do so would harm national security. In holding in favor of the government, and noting that the statutes in the case did not provide for judicial review, the district court reiterated much of the strong plenary power reasoning in *Knauff*, discussed above, holding that "whatever the rule may be concerning deportation of persons who have gained entry into the United States, it is not within the province of any court, unless expressly authorized by law, to review the determination of the political branch of the Government to exclude a given alien."[53] The district court also reaffirmed *Ekiu*, another strong plenary power case discussed above, noting that "the admission of aliens is a privilege granted upon such terms as the United States may prescribe."[54] The Second Circuit Court of Appeals upheld the decision largely along the same lines.[55] The Supreme Court, however, reversed in favor of Kwong Hai Chew in what one influential legal scholar has called one of the Court's "feats of creative interpretation."[56]

The statute keeping Kwong Hai Chew from reentering clearly provides that "the alien may be denied a hearing ... if the Attorney General determines that he is excludable under one of the [statutorily defined] categories ... on the basis of information of a confidential nature, the disclosure of which would be prejudicial to the public interest."[57] The Court admitted that an alien arriving to the shores of the United States can be excluded and denied any due process under this statute. But because Kwong Hai Chew was a lawful permanent alien, the Court decided that in evaluating Kwong Hai Chew's due process rights it would "assimilate [his] status to that of an alien continuously residing and physically present in the United States" even though he clearly left the country and was physically outside the border during his detention (i.e. he was detained on a boat).[58] This legal fiction was enough to put Kwong Hai Chew outside the reach of the statute because the statute dealt with "exclusion" rather than "deportation." The Court majority seemed to feel that aliens in Kwong Hai Chew's situation should be entitled to due process protections, but it did not want to go so far as to deem the statute unconstitutional and declare outright that all aliens facing exclusion could invoke the Due Process Clause. In later decisions, however, the Court would admit that this decision set the precedent for doing just that.[59] This was an example of a "phantom" constitutional holding that would later be turned into a real constitutional holding.[60]

The fact that this was not yet a "true" constitutional holding was made clear a month later in *Shaughnessy v. United States ex rel. Mezei*, discussed earlier, where the Court—citing the same statute in *Kwong Hai Chew*—denied the alien bound to Ellis Island any procedural due process, holding:

> "Whatever the procedure authorized by Congress is, it is due process as far as an alien denied entry is concerned. And because the action of the executive officer under such authority is final and conclusive, the Attorney General cannot be compelled to disclose the evidence underlying his determinations in an exclusion case."[61]

The *Mezei* Court explained the seemingly contradictory holdings by noting that while Kwong Hai Chew had previously undergone a security clearance as a requirement for his seaman position, Mezei left the country "apparently without authorization or reentry papers."[62] Still, anti-plenary advocates cite *Kwong Hai Chew* as another example of the Court's willingness to move away from absolute deference to the political branches on immigration enforcement—a move they believe represents the beginning of the end of the plenary power doctrine. The decision did clear the way for the Court to—in a future case discussed below—grant an alien like Kwong Hai Chew constitutional protections under the Due Process Clause without first "assimilating" the arriving resident alien's status to that of an alien residing within the country.

No More "Phantom" Constitutional Norms

Most of the early constitutional "phantom" norm cases involved the Supreme Court simply interpreting the statutes at issue in a way that would provide some sort of constitutional-like protections to the alien. None of these early cases actually *overturned* a statute by holding it "unconstitutional."[63] Until *Landon v. Plasencia* in 1982, the Court tried to avoid creating new, significantly *constitutional* holdings in the realm of immigration partially due to the principle of *stare decisis,* which directs courts to generally adhere to previous holdings when rendering new decisions, and partially as a result of the doctrine of "constitutional avoidance," where courts try to resolve the issue at hand without creating a new constitutional holding that might upset other cases or raise additional questions that result in an onslaught of new litigation. But by the 1980s, the foundation had been set, and analyzing an immigration case through a fully constitutional lens was the next obvious step for those in the anti-plenary movement. The argument is that the constitutional-like holding in *Kwong Hai Chew* was transformed into "real constitutional immigration law" in *Plasencia*.[64]

In *Plasencia*, permanent resident alien Maria Plasencia traveled from the United States to Tijuana, Mexico, for the purpose of smuggling several illegal aliens into the United States. Plasencia provided the aliens registration cards belonging to her children. Immigration officers detained Plasencia at the border as she tried to reenter with six illegal aliens in her vehicle and charged her under a section of the Immigration and Nationality Act (INA) that provides for the exclusion of any alien seeking admission "who at any time shall have, knowingly and for gain, encouraged, induced, assisted, abetted, or aided any other alien to enter or to try to enter the United States in violation of law."[65] The immigration judge at the exclusion hearing found that Plasencia's trip to Mexico was a "meaningful departure" from the United States and that her return here was an "entry" under the law and, on the basis of these findings, ordered her "excluded and deported."[66] The Board of Immigration Appeals denied Plasencia's appeal, but via a writ of habeas corpus, the District Court vacated the decision finding no meaningful departure. The District Court declared that Plasencia was entitled to a *deportation* hearing rather than an exclusion hearing and that the government could re-litigate the question of "entry" at that proceeding. The District Court noted that an alien who loses at a deportation hearing is provided more statutory rights than the alien who loses at an exclusion hearing.[67] The Ninth Circuit Court of Appeals affirmed the District Court.[68]

The Supreme Court reversed, holding that an exclusion hearing is an appropriate place for immigration authorities to determine whether an alien was attempting to enter the United States and whether the alien is excludable. Plasencia was *not* entitled to a deportation proceeding where she would be afforded more rights. *However*, the Court then turned to the question of whether an alien facing exclusion who is a "continuously present permanent resident"—just like Plasencia claimed to be—should be afforded a right to due process as articulated by the Due Process Clause of the 5th Amendment of the U.S. Constitution. The Court held that such an alien is protected by the Due Process Clause. However, the Court was clearly attempting to reframe the debate and inject a greater amount of judicial involvement. In citing a variety of due process-related cases, the Court noted that:

> "The constitutional sufficiency of procedures provided in any situation…varies with the circumstances. In evaluating the procedures in any case, the courts must consider the interest at stake for the individual, the risk of an erroneous deprivation of the interest through the procedures used as well as the probable value of additional or different procedural safeguards, and the interest of the government in using the current procedures rather than additional or different procedures."[69]

Here, the Court granted Plasencia constitutional protections by analyzing her case through a modern constitutional due process test. The Court did not feel the need to "assimilate" her status or avoid the statute at issue. The plenary power was not mentioned once. Unlike in *Kwong Hai Chew*, the Court had reached the constitutional issue and turned phantom constitutional norms into real immigration law.[70]

Although the anti-plenary crowd heralded this decision as the death of the plenary power doctrine, the holding is not as far-reaching as some claim it to be. The Constitutional protections were only granted to a small, specific type of defendant: returning legal permanent resident aliens, generally continuously present in the United States, with social ties that create a "stake" in living here, and who had been absent from the country for "only a few days."[71] Furthermore, although the Court held that Plasencia was protected by the Due Process Clause, the Court never articulated precisely *what* process is due and instead remanded the case to the lower court for that determination. In other words, the Court did not want to completely abolish the plenary power doctrine and did not speak on the appropriate level of due process afforded an alien.

Developments After the 9/11 Attacks

About two months before the terrorist attacks of September 11, 2001, the Supreme Court took a more active role in immigration regulation than it ever had before in *Zadvydas v. INS*, a case that some argue also signals the abandonment of the plenary power.[72] To be sure, the Court's dissection of specific immigration statutes in this case—as well as the dissection of the executive branch's enforcement of those statutes—was an assault on the plenary power doctrine. But the holding was limited in scope and legislation that came about in the following months as a result of the 9/11 attacks assures a partial reinvigoration of the plenary power doctrine. Nevertheless, *Zadvydas* remains a vivid example of how invasive a court not recognizing the plenary power can be in the realm of immigration regulation. The case is also noteworthy for the fact that its encouragement of judicial intervention created confusion and conflicting rulings in the lower courts, the result of which is a seemingly inconsistent U.S. immigration policy.

Court promises to "Listen with Care." At issue in *Zadvydas* was the long-term detention of two criminal aliens who had been ordered deported. The Court heard both cases in the same hearing. Kestutis Zadvydas' criminal record included drug crimes, attempted robbery, attempted burglary, and theft. He also had a history of flight from both criminal and deportation proceedings. Kim Ho Ma was involved in a gang-related shooting and was convicted of manslaughter. Immigration officials could not find a country willing to receive the aliens within the statutory 90-day removal period. In continuing to detain the aliens after 90 days, the government invoked a statute that provides:

> "An alien ordered removed who is inadmissible [or] removable [as a result of violations of status requirements or entry conditions, violations of criminal law, or reasons of security or foreign policy] or who has been determined by the Attorney General to be a risk to the community or unlikely to comply with the order of removal, *may be detained beyond the removal period* and, if released, shall be subject to [certain] terms of supervision. ..."[73] (emphasis added).

In other words, Congress granted the Attorney General the authority to detain an alien beyond 90 days if he or she found it necessary to do so for public safety reasons or otherwise. It is not an unreasonable allowance considering that immigration authorities regularly detain dangerous individuals. It is even more understandable in light of the slow bureaucratic processes that make up our immigration system; 90 days is not always sufficient. The government argued that the decision "whether to continue to detain such an alien and, if so, in what circumstances and for how long" was up to the Attorney General, not the courts.[74]

But the high court did not agree with the government's interpretation of the statute and felt that, as applied, the statute violated the aliens' Constitutional rights to due process. The Court took issue with what it believed to be the "indefinite detention" of Zadvydas and Ma (despite the fact that the government continued to search for a place to deport the aliens during the post-90-day period). In a close 5-4 decision, the Court held that it could not find "any clear indication of congressional intent to grant the Attorney General the power to hold indefinitely in confinement an alien ordered removed."[75] The Court then decided to "construe the statute to contain an implicit 'reasonable time' limitation."[76] Clearly, on its face, the statute requires no such limitations. The Court explained their construction:

> "The government points to the statute's word, 'may.' But while 'may' suggests discretion, it does not necessarily suggest unlimited discretion. In that respect the word 'may' is ambiguous. Indeed, if Congress had meant to authorize long-term detention of unremovable aliens, it certainly could have spoken in clearer terms."[77]

Of course, one could argue that Congress could *not* speak more clearly and that such decisions were squarely within the discretion of the Attorney General. Nevertheless, in order to eliminate what it considered the "constitutional threat" of the potentially indefinite detention of deportable aliens, the Court held that "once removal is no longer reasonably foreseeable, continued detention is no longer authorized by statute."[78] The Court then arbitrarily decided that six months was all that was necessary for determining an alien's deportability:

> "After this six-month period, once the alien provides good reason to believe that there is no significant likelihood of removal in the reasonably foreseeable future, the Government must respond with evidence sufficient to rebut that showing. And for detention to remain reasonable, as the period of prior post-removal confinement grows, what counts as the 'reasonably foreseeable future' conversely would have to shrink. This six-month presumption, of course, does not mean that every alien not removed must be released after six months. To the contrary, an alien may be held in confinement until it has been determined that there is no significant likelihood of removal in the reasonably foreseeable future."[79]

Put simply, a reviewing court's definition of "reasonably foreseeable" will determine the release of deportable aliens back onto the streets. Put another way, the judicial branch rather than the political branches will have the final say on who is allowed into the country and who is required to leave. Of course, the lower courts had already begun taking control; before it went to the Supreme Court, Kim Ho Ma's lower court case was decided along with approximately 100 similar detention cases in a joint order.[80] It is unclear how many of these aliens in the lower proceeding were released back into our neighborhoods. Furthermore, before the decision in *Zadvydas*, the INS was holding approximately 3,000 individuals in what the Court would consider "indefinite detention." How many of these aliens were released as a result of the decision in *Zadvydas* is unclear. According to the Department of Justice, from January 2001 through September 2002, the INS reviewed 1,710 alien detention cases and released 1,034 (60 percent) of the aliens.[81]

The Court was well-aware that it was stepping on the political branches' toes and weakening congressional and executive plenary power over immigration. The majority acknowledged the "greater immigration-related expertise of the Executive Branch" and that "principles of judicial review in this area recognize primary Executive Branch responsibility."[82] Such realities, the Court noted, "require courts to listen with care" to the concerns of the Executive.[83] But such sentiment is hollow. The Court clearly moved from the "hands-off" approach articulated by the plenary power doctrine to a somewhat dismissive "listen with care" standard. The plenary power doctrine had seemingly yielded to judicial intervention. It is worth noting that although the decision in *Zadvydas* applied only to admitted aliens later determined to be deportable, a later case—*Clark v. Martinez* (2005)—extended these protections to removable aliens who have never been admitted into the country.[84]

Dissenting in Favor of the Plenary Power. The Court's dissenting justices felt that the case ultimately was about "a claimed right of release into this country by an individual who *concededly* has no legal right to be here" and argued that there is "no such constitutional right."[85] They also noted that the majority "offered no justification why an alien under a valid and final order of removal—which has *totally extinguished* whatever right to presence in this country he possessed—has any greater due process right to be released into the country than an alien at the border seeking entry."[86] This is a legitimate point: neither type of alien has a right to be in the United States, so why should one have a claim for release into the country? Such reasoning rests solely on the seemingly-arbitrary six-month time limit and, as the dissent noted, Zadvydas' case itself "demonstrates that the repatriation process may often take years to negotiate, involving difficult issues of establishing citizenship and the like."[87]

The dissenters also noted that the dangerousness of the alien and the risks he or she poses to society "do not diminish just because the alien cannot be deported within some foreseeable time."[88] Clearly, the dangerousness of an alien and the decision about whether to release him or her is a political question—a question that should be left up to politically-accountable actors who can be taken to task for making a faulty decision. By creating an arbitrary deadline for release, the ruling in *Zadvydas* arguably eliminates the type of accountability that can be corrected through elections: If a dangerous alien is released as a result of *Zadvydas*, executive branch officers can shrug their shoulders and point to the judiciary's demands, while lower court judges can shrug their shoulders noting that they have to abide by the Supreme Court's ruling.

But the dissenting justices' concerns went further than simply the release of dangerous aliens into U.S. society. For them, the larger concern was what they viewed as judicial intervention into a political process, something that upset the balance of powers. Although the majority claimed it was trying to avoid a constitutional question by deciding the case as it did, the dissent felt that the majority raised more constitutional questions than it avoided. In a scathing response, the dissenters laid out their case:

> "The Court says its duty is to avoid a constitutional question. It deems the duty performed by interpreting a statute in obvious disregard of congressional intent; curing the resulting gap by writing a statutory amendment of its own; committing

its own grave constitutional error by arrogating to the Judicial Branch the power to summon high officers of the Executive to assess their progress in conducting some of the Nation's most sensitive negotiations with foreign powers; and then likely releasing into our general population at least hundreds of removable or inadmissible aliens who have been found by fair procedures to be flight risks, dangers to the community, or both. Far from avoiding a constitutional question, the Court's ruling causes systemic dislocation in the balance of powers, thus raising serious constitutional concerns not just for the cases at hand but for the Court's own view of its proper authority. Any supposed respect the Court seeks in not reaching the constitutional question is outweighed by the intrusive and erroneous exercise of its own powers."[89]

Had the majority shown greater respect for the plenary power doctrine, and by consequence, greater deference to the political branches, none of these glaring concerns would have been raised. But in attempting to resolve the constitutional rights of the alien, it seems the majority raised numerous and arguably more significant constitutional conflicts.

Foreign Powers Controlling U.S. Immigration Policy? One of the arguments for the political branches' plenary power over immigration involves a focus on foreign affairs. That issue was a factor in the *Zadvydas* decision. Under the Constitution, it is the executive and legislative branches that direct foreign policy matters. This ensures that the U.S. relations with other countries are consistent and reliable. As explained by the dissenting justices in *Zadvydas*: "judicial orders requiring release of removable aliens, even on a temporary basis, have the potential to undermine the obvious necessity that the Nation speak with one voice on immigration and foreign affairs matters."[90] The problem is that the majority effectively empowered *foreign governments* to control U.S. immigration policy. The dissenting justices in *Zadvydas* explained:

> "The result of the Court's rule is that, by refusing to accept repatriation of their own nationals, other countries can effect the release of these individuals back into the American community. If their own nationals are now at large in the United States, the nation of origin may ignore or disclaim responsibility to accept their return. The interference with sensitive foreign relations becomes even more acute where hostility or tension characterizes the relationship, for other countries can use the fact of judicially mandated release to their strategic advantage, refusing the return of their nationals to force dangerous aliens upon us."[91]

Certainly, such political considerations are not on the average judge's radar, and they shouldn't be. Political issues are to be debated and resolved within the political branches. But the decision in *Zadvydas* arguably *requires* judges to involve the judiciary in foreign affairs. According to the dissenting justices:

> "One of the more alarming aspects of the Court's new venture into foreign affairs management is the suggestion that the district court can expand or contract the reasonable period of detention based on its own assessment of the course of negotiations with foreign powers. The Court says it will allow the Executive to perform its duties on its own for six months; after that, foreign relations go into judicially supervised receivership."[92]

By not adhering to the plenary power doctrine, the *Zadvydas* majority effectively relocates foreign policy considerations from experienced and accountable political actors to arguably less-politically astute judges while simultaneously politicizing the judiciary. The decision also puts foreign governments in the driver's seat.

The Political Branches Respond. Two months after the *Zadvydas* decision, the 9/11 terrorist attacks were perpetrated by 19 aliens. The Department of Justice was in the midst of updating its procedures to accommodate the Supreme Court ruling. While the provisions met the Court's requirements, they also narrowly defined the holding and carved out numerous exceptions. Specifically, the new provisions added immigration procedures for determining whether aliens with final orders of removal are likely to be removed within a reasonable amount of time and whether they should remain in government custody or be released into the United States pending their removal.[93] But the rule also set out a procedure for the *continued* detention of deportable aliens who are *not* likely to be removed in the reasonably foreseeable future. These involve aliens described by four special circumstances: (1) aliens who have highly contagious diseases that pose a danger to the public; (2) aliens who pose foreign policy concerns; (3) aliens who pose national security and terrorism concerns; and (4) aliens who are specially dangerous due to a mental condition or personality disorder (and have previously committed a crime of violence, and are likely to engage in acts of violence in the future).[94] These categories were not mentioned by the Court in *Zadvydas*, although the Court did state that its holding would be different if the case involved "terrorism or other special circumstances where special arguments might be made for forms of preventive detention and for heightened deference to the judgments of the political branches with respect to matters of national security."[95] The political branches have used this language to defend the new regulations and its plenary power over immigration regulation generally; the terms "special circumstances," "foreign policy concerns," "specially dangerous," and "matters of national security" offer some leeway in continuing the detention of many aliens.

The regulations add a handful of other tools that keep much control over immigration in the hands of the political branches. For example:

- Any alien released under supervised conditions due to a finding that there is no likelihood of removal in the reasonably foreseeable future must obey all laws, must continue to seek travel documents, must provide the immigration agency with all correspondence to and from foreign consulates, or face being placed back into detention. This might include a requirement of medical or psychiatric exams and attendance at any necessary rehabilitative programs.
- The government may revoke the alien's release if the government believes there are changed circumstances that create a significant likelihood of removal in the reasonably foreseeable future.
- The government is not required to grant employment authorization to a released inadmissible alien.
- Any alien denied a request for release must wait six months before submitting a new request for review of his detention.
- There is no administrative appeal from the immigration agency's finding of no likelihood of removal in the reasonably foreseeable future.[96]

In addition, the government has set high bonds as a means of keeping aliens detained longer. If the executive branch keeps a firm grasp on the process, all of these procedures give the political branches of the government greater control over immigration regulation than the ruling in *Zadvydas* might seem to allow.

Congress also crafted legislation aimed at weakening *Zadvydas*. Less than four months after *Zadvydas*, the "Uniting and Strengthening America by Providing Appropriate Tools Required to Intercept and Obstruct Terrorism Act" (the "PATRIOT Act") of 2001 was signed into law. It authorizes the continued detention of any alien whose removal is not reasonably foreseeable if the U.S. Attorney General has "reasonable grounds to believe" that the alien represents a security threat or has been involved in terrorist activities. Such detention is indefinitely renewable in six-month increments.[97] This act is viewed not only as a result of the 9/11 attacks, but also as a partial rebuke of the *Zadvydas* holding. Considering that the majority in *Zadvydas* justified the holding in that case by noting that Congress could have "spoken in clearer terms" on the issue of detaining aliens, the PATRIOT Act arguably gives the justices precisely what they wanted. The PATRIOT Act can properly be viewed as the political branches reasserting their control over part of the immigration system. In fact, a few years later, the Court seemed to specifically instruct Congress to reassert its plenary power over immigration in a 2005 immigration case when it noted the following: "The Government fears that the security of our borders will be compromised if it must release into the country inadmissible aliens who cannot be removed. If that is so, Congress can attend to it."[98] The Court then referred to the PATRIOT Act as evidence that the political branches can and have overcome some judicial regulation of immigration policy. Of course, the PATRIOT Act addresses terrorism-related concerns. If Congress wants to continue to reassert its authority over immigration in other areas, it could draft additional legislation aimed at non-terrorist aliens. While any such legislation may end up in court, the political branches are not without hope; the dissenting judges in the aforementioned 2005 case asserted that "*Zadvydas* was wrongly decided and should be overruled."[99]

A few years later, the REAL ID Act of 2005 was signed into law. Although the act was aimed at a variety of objectives, one provision focused specifically on the growth of judicial intervention in immigration regulation. Years before, in 2001, the Supreme Court held in *INS v. St. Cyr* that neither the Illegal Immigration Reform and Immigrant Responsibility Act of 1996 (IIRIRA) or the Antiterrorism and Effective Death Penalty Act of 1996 (AEDPA) deprived the federal district courts of jurisdiction over habeas corpus petitions filed by convicted criminal aliens challenging removal orders. Congress felt that this was a misreading of each act, that such aliens could only challenge their removal in appeals courts, and that the Court's holding would have the undesirable effect of "allowing criminal aliens to delay their expulsion from the United States for years."[100] In fact, Congress had originally written those two acts with the specific purpose of limiting judicial review of removal orders and also with the purpose of overcoming a judicially created rule on readmission (since abandoned) known as the "Fleuti Doctrine."[101] Seeing the need to reassert itself, Congress responded with the REAL ID Act and explicitly limited criminal alien habeas corpus review of removal orders to the Courts of Appeals. The committee report accompanying the REAL ID Act explains Congress' intent as follows:

> Under *St. Cyr*, "criminal aliens [were] able to begin the judicial review process in the district court, and then appeal to the circuit court of appeals. Criminal aliens thus [could] obtain review in two jurisdictional forums, whereas non-criminal aliens may generally seek review only in the courts of appeals... Not only is this result unfair and illogical...but it also wastes scarce judicial and executive resources."[102]

The committee report also noted that Congress' goal has long been to "abbreviate the process of judicial review of deportation orders and to eliminate the previous initial step in obtaining judicial review." In all, REAL ID was designed to put review of deportation, exclusion, and final orders of removal squarely within the Court of Appeals. It is important to remember that Congress is empowered to limit the district courts' jurisdiction.[103] So far, REAL ID has returned some power to the political branches, but it will take a few years to determine the act's full impact.

Ultimately, these examples show that the political branches can limit judicial intervention and assert authority over immigration regulation should Congress and executive branch officials decide to do so.

The Future of the Plenary Power

It is possible that the Supreme Court will take a more supportive position of the plenary power as a result of new appointments to the Court, and as a response to lower courts going too far in dismissing the power.[104] But if the political branches want to reassert their authority in the regulation of immigration, they will have to take the initiative by drafting focused legislation and vigorously enforcing existing immigration laws. Additionally, political branch attorneys should argue not only the substantive matters in immigration-related cases, but should also routinely challenge the courts on the ease with which they dismiss the plenary power. Two strategies might be useful in limiting judicial regulation of immigration policy: advocacy of the *Chevron* deference, and an expanded expedited removal process.

Chevron Deference. Immigration authorities should invoke the *Chevron* doctrine in court and argue that agencies are better equipped to handle immigration regulation than any judicial authority. In the 1984 case *Chevron, U.S.A., Inc. v. NRDC*, the Supreme Court held that when it comes to interpreting ambiguous statutory language, if the agency responsible for administering the statute at issue has rulemaking or adjudication authority, then courts should give deference to the agency's reasonable interpretation of the statute's language.[105] Specifically, the Court held:

> "When a court reviews an agency's construction of the statute which it administers, it is confronted with two questions. First, always, is the question whether Congress has directly spoken to the precise question at issue. If the intent of Congress is clear, that is the end of the matter; for the court, as well as the agency, must give effect to the unambiguously expressed intent of Congress. If, however, the court determines Congress has not directly addressed the precise question at issue, the court does not simply impose its own construction on the statute, as would be necessary in the absence of an administrative interpretation. Rather, if the statute is silent or ambiguous with respect to the specific issue, the question for the court is whether the agency's answer is based on a permissible construction of the statute."[106]

The Court also noted that the agency's interpretation need not be the only possible interpretation and that a court should not "substitute its own construction of a statutory provision for a reasonable interpretation made by the administrator of an agency." Only if an agency's interpretation of a statute is "arbitrary, capricious, or manifestly contrary to the statute" should courts intervene.[107] The logic is that the agency is staffed with individuals who are experts in the subject matter and more knowledgeable than a judge when it comes to interpreting and applying the statute. This is what has come to be known as the *Chevron* deference analysis. And for reasons outlined by the Supreme Court over the past century, immigration regulation is unquestionably deserving of such analysis. In fact, *Chevron* has been used by the Supreme Court as well as lower courts in the immigration context.[108] Ultimately, courts invoking *Chevron* are less likely to substitute an agency's interpretation and enforcement of immigration statutes for the court's own. This undoubtedly protects some authority of the political branches over immigration regulation. Of course, serious constitutional issues will not be overlooked by the courts, and the burden will remain on the immigration authorities to argue any such issues. And therein lies the weakness of the *Chevron* analysis: The anti-plenary crowd has been working overtime to grant all aliens the constitutional protections of U.S. citizens by interpreting many standard immigration issues as "constitutional" in nature, as explored earlier. The *Chevron* doctrine, then, works best on smaller, statutory issues that do not directly raise constitutional analysis. Finally, the doctrine's success will require Congress to draft immigration statutes in a way that clearly grants authority to the executive's immigration agencies.

Expedited Removal. A more promising strategy is the expansion of expedited removal. In 1996, the Illegal Immigration Reform and Immigrant Responsibility Act (IIRIRA) was signed into law. One component of the act was what has come to be known as "expedited removal."[109] The process generally allows federal agents to quickly remove any inadmissible alien who is without a valid claim of asylum. It results in a final order of removal and prohibits the alien from reentering the United States for a period of five years. Most significantly, it circumvents any judicial involvement from either the executive branch immigration courts or the judicial branch courts. In this sense, expedited removal keeps immigration regulation squarely within the political branches; immigration officers, rather than the courts, provide the alien his due process. In other words, expedited removal invokes the plenary power tenets as articulated by the Supreme Court at the doctrine's inception. As written into law, the policy applies to *any* illegal alien apprehended *anywhere* in the United States, provided the alien has not been continuously physically present in the country for longer than the two years preceding the determination of inadmissibility. For whatever reason, however, the executive branch has not taken full advantage of this authority. Both the Clinton and G.W. Bush Administrations have actually chosen to *limit* their authority; the Clinton White House implemented expedited removal only at a few ports of entry while the Bush White House has decided not to use the removal process for Mexican or Canadian aliens.[110] While there was some expansion of the program in the Bush administration since 9/11, it was minimal; the process is now being used at more ports of entry, but only on any alien apprehended within 100 miles of the borders, and only if the alien is apprehended within 14 days of entry.[111] The large majority of inadmissible aliens apprehended outside of these parameters will have access to the court system. Any future administration wishing to defend plenary power over immigration should expand expedited removal nationwide; Congress has obviously signaled its interest in reclaiming its influence over immigration enforcement by allowing expedited removal to apply nationwide. For the record, in Fiscal Year 2005, the Border Patrol detained over 18,000 aliens under the expedited removal program; over 14,500 of these aliens were removed.[112] The number would be much larger if implemented nationwide.

Conclusions

The plenary power doctrine has a lengthy history and serves the important purpose of keeping the regulation of immigration squarely within the control of politically accountable actors. The doctrine allows for informed deliberation of sensitive issues like foreign relations, national security, and other immigration-related policies. It also assures uniformity and efficiency within our immigration system. Ultimately, it allows citizens to decide the future of the United States through the political process. Should the doctrine be abandoned, the political branches will have their hands tied on the issue of who should be admitted and who should be required to leave. Unelected and largely unaccountable judges would become the nation's immigration gatekeepers. Of course, in order for this to happen, judges will have had to abandon *stare decisis*; unfortunately it is clear that many judges have already done so. If this trend continues, it is not unrealistic to suggest that some judges might make deportation a thing of the past; plenty of judges might have difficulty authorizing the deportation of aliens who, in their opinion, are not immediate threats to national security. And there are probably judges who could find reason to prevent the deportation even of an alien convicted of terrorism (i.e. "he claims he is reformed," "he has family here," etc.). Other justifications for excluding or deporting aliens may be abandoned: Excluding aliens because they might become public charges? Economic discrimination. Excluding aliens because they come from terrorist-sponsoring states? Nationality discrimination. Excluding aliens because they advocate the overthrow of the U.S. government? Viewpoint discrimination. In other words, the result could be effectively open borders, where no one is excluded. Such scenarios are less likely when immigration regulation is left to political actors who can be taken to task by constituents for faulty decisions.

Without the plenary power doctrine, the system of constitutional rights that has evolved to protect Americans from an overbearing government would instead operate to shield deportable aliens from basic enforcement of U.S. immigration law while subtly suggesting, incorrectly, that aliens have some "right" to immigrate here in the first place. Such an immigration system would no longer operate for the benefit of the American people as our immigration system always has; it would instead exist for the benefit of people around the globe. The entire notion of an immigration policy—a system that exists primarily for the benefit of the host country and secondarily for the alien—would be turned on its head.

The increasing complexity and unnecessary hair-splitting advanced by anti-plenary advocates has contributed to the perception that the nation's immigration system is broken. Yet despite their best efforts, the plenary power doctrine will not easily fade away. It is backed by decades of Supreme Court precedent that continues to be favorably cited by many courts. While it is undeniably true that the U.S. immigration system can be improved, the courtroom is not where this process can or should take place. This is not to suggest that the indefinite detention of aliens, for example, is necessarily good policy, but rather that the onus to improve the system should be placed on the political branches. Congress must make sure that immigration laws are clear and decisive as to the issue of authority, and the executive branch must vigorously defend its regulation and enforcement of those laws. Such sentiment must be regularly expressed by the political leadership within the first two branches of government in order to put a halt to judicial branch encroachment over immigration policy.

Notes

1. U.S. Const. art. I, § 8: "The Congress shall have power to... establish a uniform rule of naturalization ... [And] To make all laws which shall be necessary and proper for carrying into execution the foregoing powers."

2. This paper uses the term "plenary power" solely in the context of immigration powers; other plenary powers exist, such as Congress's plenary power over the regulation of interstate commerce, for example.

3. Mathews v. Diaz et al., 426 U.S. 67, 81 (1976).

4. *Id.* For example, when the Supreme Court was asked to expand welfare benefits to certain aliens in *Mathews v. Diaz* in 1976, the Court refused to do so and asserted the plenary power doctrine with the following words: "An unlikely, but nevertheless possible, consequence of holding that appellees are constitutionally entitled to welfare benefits would be a further extension of similar benefits to over 440,000 Cuban parolees... We decline the invitation."

5. Not all aliens facing removal are entitled to a day in immigration court; aliens subject to expedited removal, for example, are generally summarily removed by immigration law enforcement officers. Expedited removal, a way of avoiding anti-plenary courts, is discussed later in this report.

6. Interestingly, prior to 1983 the Immigration and Naturalization Service (INS) served the dual purpose of detaining aliens and conducting removal proceedings; after that date, enforcement and adjudication was separated.

7. Chae Chan Ping v. United States, 130 U.S. 581, 603 (1889).

8. *Id.* at 606.

9. *Id.* at 609.

10. Nishimura Ekiu v. United States, 142 U.S. 651 (1892).

11. *Id.* at 660. (Note: As to habeas corpus, a detained alien generally can apply for the writ in order to get the judicial branch involved only after he has exhausted all administrative remedies. If he does get to the judicial branch courts, the issue then turns to deference; courts supportive of the plenary power will generally uphold the administrative order by deferring to the agency decision-making. For more information on the relationship between habeas corpus and immigration law, *see generally* Hiroshi Motomura, *Immigration Law and Federal Court Jurisdiction Through the Lens of Habeas Corpus*, 91 Cornell L. Rev. 459 (2006)).

12. *Ekiu*, 142 U.S. at 660.

13. Fong Yue Ting v. United States, 149 U.S. 698 (1893).

14. *Id.* at 713.

15. *Id.* at 730 (Note: This reasoning is applicable only to an alien not claiming to be a citizen. A person claiming U.S. citizenship is entitled to due process—a judicial hearing—as deportation of a citizen does amount to deprivation of life, liberty, and property. *See, e.g.*, Ng Fung Ho v. White, 259 U.S. 276 (1922)); *see also, e.g.*, Carlson v. Landon, 342 U.S. 524 (1952) (affirming, along with many other cases, that "deportation is not a criminal proceeding and has never been held to be punishment. No jury sits. No judicial review is guaranteed by the Constitution.").

16. *See, e.g.*, Knauff v. Shaughnessy, 338 U.S. 537 (1950); *see also, e.g.*, Shaughnessy v. Mezei, 345 U.S. 206 (1953). Also of significance is *Yamataya v. Fisher*, 189 U.S. 86 (1903)—known as the "Japanese Immigrant Case"—in which the Supreme Court upheld the deportation of an illegal alien determined to be a likely public charge. Here, the Court did suggest that aliens facing deportation are entitled to some amount of due process. The administrative process provided by immigration officers seemed sufficient to meet constitutional requirements: "[T]his court has never held, nor must we now be understood as holding, that administrative officers, when executing the provisions of a statute involving the liberty of persons, may disregard the fundamental principles that inhere in 'due process of law' as understood at the time of the adoption of the Constitution. One of these principles is that no person shall be deprived of his liberty without opportunity, at some time, to be heard, before such officers, in respect of the matters upon which that liberty depends –not necessarily an opportunity upon a regular, set occasion, and according to the forms of judicial procedure, but one that will secure the prompt, vigorous action contemplated by Congress, and at the same time be appropriate to the nature of the case upon which such officers are required to act." at 100.

17. *See generally*, Steven H. Legomsky, Immigration and Refugee Law and Policy (4th ed. 2005).

18. *Knauff*, 338 U.S. 537.

19. *Id.* at 542 (citing both *Ekiu* and *Fong Yue Ting*).

20. *Id.* at 543.

21. *Id.* at 544.

22. *See generally,* Charles D. Weisselberg, *The Exclusion and Detention of Aliens: Lessons from the Lives of Ellen Knauff and Ignatz Mezei,* 143 U. Pa. L. Rev. 933 (1995)(discussing a detailed account of Knauff's immigration history).

23. Harisiades v. Shaughnessy, 342 U.S. 580 (1952)(upholding the retroactive application of a 1940 statute that made deportable any alien who had joined the Communist party after entering the United States).

24. *Id.* at 587.

25. *Id.* at 588.

26. *Id.* at 590.

27. *Id.* at 585.

28. *Id.* at 590. (Note: Some legal scholars argue that the Court's description of the threat of Communism in and of itself indicates a willingness on the part of the Court to address the "reasonableness" of immigration policy.)

29. *Id.* at 591.

30. *Id.* at 596-8.

31. Shaughnessy v. United States ex rel. Mezei, 345 U.S. 206 (1953).

32. United States ex rel. Mezei v. Shaughnessy, 195 F.2d 964 (1952).

33. *United States ex rel. Mezei,* 345 U.S. at 210.

34. *Id.* at 212.

35. *Id.* at 213.

36. For a detailed account of Mezei's immigration history, see generally Weisselberg, *supra* note 22.

37. Galvan v. Press, 347 U.S. 522 (1954).

38. Kleindienst v. Mandel et al., 408 U.S. 753 (1972); *see also* Boutilier v. INS, 387 U.S. 118 (1967).

39. *Mandel,* 408 U.S. at 766; *see also* Lem Moon Sing v. United States, 158 U.S. 538 (1895); *see also* Yamataya v. Fisher, 189 U.S. 86 (1903).

40. *Mandel,* 408 U.S. at 770.

41. *Diaz et al.,* 426 U.S. at 81.

42. *Id.* at 84.

43. *See, e.g.,* Ng Fung Ho v. White, 259 U.S. 276 (1922); *see also, e.g.,* Kwock Jan Fat v. White, 253 U.S. 454 (1912) (holding that decisions by immigration officials are "final, and conclusive upon the courts, unless it be shown that the proceedings were manifestly unfair, were such as to prevent a fair investigation, or show manifest abuse of the discretion committed to the executive officers by the statute, or that their authority was not fairly exercised, that is, consistently with the fundamental principles of justice embraced within the conception of due process of law.").

44. Hampton v. Mow Sun Wong et al., 426 U.S. 88 (1976)(holding unconstitutional a federal regulation that barred non-citizens from employment with the Civil Service Commission without due process of law.).

45. For an analysis of the judicial application of semi-constitutional norms to immigration cases, *see* Hiroshi Motomura, *Immigration Law After a Century of Plenary Power: Phantom Constitutional Norms and Statutory Interpretation*, 100 Yale L.J. 545 (1990).

46. For additional examples, *see* Bridges v. Wixon, 326 U.S. 135 (1945)(reversing deportation order of suspected Communist alien and calling deportation a "hardship" and an immigration statute "unconstitutional"); *see also* Woodby v. INS, 385 U.S. 276 (1966)(requiring more due process than would be normal in most civil proceedings –here, deportation –and substantially raising the burden of proof against the executive branch's wishes); *see also* the Woodby dissent (noting, "This is but another case in a long line in which the Court has tightened the noose around the Government's neck in immigration cases.").

47. Fong Haw Tan v. Phelan, 333 U.S. 6, 8 (1948) (Note: the crime of murder involves "moral turpitude").

48. Fong Haw Tan v. Phelan, 162 F.2d 663, 665 (1947).

49. *Fong Haw Tan*, 333 U.S. at 9. Interestingly, the appeals court predicted such a holding and explained why it would be problematic to do anything other than defer to the executive's interpretation of the statute: "By what formula shall the permissible lapse of time between crimes be measured? How closely must the crimes be related to each other? Must they derive from the same impulse? Do separate crimes of different natures committed to clear the way for a main objective come within the conclusion?" *Fong Haw Tan*, 162 F.2d at 665.

50. *Fong Haw Tan*, 333 U.S. at 10.

51. *See* cases cited *supra* note 15.

52. *See* Chanan Din Khan v. Barber, 147 F. Supp. 771, 773 (1957); *see also* 8 U.S.C. § 1227(a)(2)(A)(ii).

53. United States ex rel. Kwong Hai Chew v. Colding, 97 F. Supp. 592, 594 (1951).

54. *Id.* at 595 (Note: The court rendered its decision "with some reluctance, not because the court has not the power of judicial review under the statute, but rather...[because Kwong Hai Chew was] to be deported without knowing what charge as been levelled against him.").

55. United States ex rel. Kwong Hai Chew v. Colding, 192 F.2d 1009 (1951).

56. Louis Henkin, *The Constitution and United States Sovereignty: A Century of Chinese Exclusion and Its Progeny*, 100 Harv. L. Rev. 853, n.40 (1987) (Note: Columbia Law Professor Henkin also counts among these feats the anti-plenary cases of *Rosenberg v. Fleuti* (1963) and *Landon v. Plasencia* (1982), discussed later.)

57. See, Kwong Hai Chew v. Colding, 344 U.S. 590, 591 n.1 (1953). (Note: The statute allowed exclusion of aliens with membership in "a political organization associated with or carrying out policies of any foreign government opposed to the measures adopted by the Government of the United States in the public interest" or for aliens "engaged in organizing, teaching, advocating, or directing any rebellion, insurrection, or violent uprising against the United States," for example.)

58. *Id.* at 596.

59. Justice O'Connor describing the holding in *Kwong Hai Chew*: "[T]o avoid constitutional problems, we construed the regulation as inapplicable. Although the holding was one of regulatory interpretation, the rationale was one of constitutional law." Landon v. Plasencia, 459 U.S. 21, 33 (1982).

60. Interestingly, the Court reviewed a 1953 presidential commission report on immigration entitled, "Whom We Shall Welcome" in rendering its decision and noted that the commission "treats the provisions [above] as applicable to entrant and reentrant aliens but does not even suggest that they are applicable to aliens lawfully admitted to permanent residence and physically present in the United States ... [and it] does not...even suggest that the reentry doctrine attempts to limit the constitutional right to a hearing which resident aliens, in the status of [Kwong Hai Chew], may have under the Fifth Amendment." See Kwong Hai Chew, n.11. In other words, the commission did not speak to the situation at issue. Of course, one must ask: If the Court felt it reasonable to look to an executive branch report for help in resolving the case, why would the Court not defer to the executive branch officials who actually enforced the statute in the first place? Had the court done the latter, it would have been making use of the plenary power doctrine—a doctrine that is designed, in part, to resolve the very type of uncertainty found in *Kwong Hai Chew*. Instead, the Court created a legal fiction, applied a constitutional due process analysis, and abandoned decades of precedent.

61. *United States ex rel. Mezei*, 345 U.S. at 212.

62. *Id.* at 214.

63. The earliest Supreme Court case to actually strike down a federal statute involving the admission and expulsion of aliens was not until 1983 in INS v. Chadha et al., 462 U.S. 919. (Note: The case focused largely on separation of powers issues rather than the rights of individual aliens or the plenary power, however.)

64. Motomura, *supra* note 45, at 580.

65. Landon v. Plasencia, 459 U.S. 21, 23 (1982).

66. *Id.* at 24.

67. For example, an alien who loses in a deportation hearing can designate the country of deportation, depart voluntarily in order to avoid certain legal stigmas, and can seek suspension of deportation.

68. *Plasencia*, 459 U.S. at 25.

69. *Id.* at 34 (citing a case not immigration-related but nonetheless constitutionally-significant: Mathews v. Eldridge (1976)).

70. Motomura, *supra* note 64.

71. *Plasencia*, 459 U.S. at 34.

72. *See, e.g* Peter J. Spiro, *Explaining the End of Plenary Power*, 16 Geo. Immigr. L.J. 339 (2002).

73. Zadvydas v. Davis, 522 U.S. 678, 682 (2001); *see also* 8 U.S.C. § 1231(a)(6).

74. *Zadvydas*, 522 U.S. at 689.

75. *Id.* at 697.
76. *Id.* at 682.
77. *Id.* at 697.
78. *Id.* at 699.
79. *Id.* at 701.
80. *Id.* at 686.
81. The Immigration and Naturalization Service's Removal of Aliens Issued Final Orders, No. I-2003-004 (Dep't of Justice, Feb. 2003). Available at: http://www.usdoj.gov/oig/reports/INS/e0304/ background.htm
82. *Zadvydas*, 522 U.S. at 700.
83. *Id.* at 701.
84. Clark v. Martinez, 543 U.S. 371 (2005).
85. *Zadvydas*, 522 U.S. at 702-3.
86. *Id.* at 704.
87. *Id.* at 712-13.
88. *Id.* at 709.
89. *Id.* at 705.
90. *Id.* at 711.
91. *Id.*
92. *Id.* at 712.
93. Press Release, Dep't of Justice, "Justice Department Implements Zadvydas v. Davis Supreme Court Decision." (Nov. 14, 2001). Available at: http://www.usdoj.gov/opa/pr/2001/November/01_ins_595.htm.
94. *Id. See also* 18 U.S.C § 16 (listing crimes of violence in a finding of "specially dangerous"). For the last three types of aliens, there must also be no conditions of release that can reasonably be expected to prevent public danger.
95. *Zadvydas*, 522 U.S. at 696.
96. *See* 8 C.F.R. § 241.13,14; *see also* 8 U.S.C. § 1231(a)(3) (outlining post-release supervision requirements).
97. 8 U.S.C. § 1226a.
98. Clark v. Suarez Martinez, 543 U.S. 371, 386, n.8 (2005).
99. *Id.* at 388.
100. *See, e.g* Enwonwu v. Chertoff, 276 F. Supp. 2d 42, 82 (2005).

101. In the 1963 Supreme Court case *Rosenberg v. Fleuti*, the Court held that a Legal Permanent Resident (LPR) who took an "innocent, casual, and brief" trip outside the borders of United States could not be deemed to have "intended" to depart, and thus was not "entering" upon his return; the immigration service could not treat the LPR as if he was seeking admission. 374 U.S. 449. This judicially-created rule was replaced with Congress' own definition of admission when Congress wrote the IIRIRA; it allowed the immigration service to treat some LPRs as if they were seeking admission for the first time, even if they were outside the country for only a few hours. For a full explanation of these changes, see *In re Jesus Collado-Munoz*, 21 I. & N. Dec. 1061 (1998).

102. *Enwonwu*, 276 F. Supp. 2d at 82.

103. U.S. Const. art. III, § 1: "The judicial Power of the United States, shall be vested in one supreme Court, and in such inferior Courts as the Congress may from time to time ordain and establish."

104. Indeed, the Court already has brought order to inconsistent, anti-plenary power rulings in the lower courts in Demore v. Hyung Joon Kim, 538 U.S. 510 (2003). The Court overruled the idea that due process prohibited detention pending removal proceedings, absent some evidence of the aliens flight risk or danger to the community.

105. Chevron, U.S.A., Inc. v. NRDC, 467 U.S. 837 (1984).

106. *Id.* at 842.

107. *Id.* at 843-4.

108. *See, e.g.* INS v. Aguirre-Aguirre, 526 U.S. 415, 425 (1999): "[W]e have recognized that judicial deference to the Executive Branch is especially appropriate in the immigration context where officials exercise especially sensitive political functions that implicate questions of foreign relations." *See also* Malagon de Fuentes v. Gonzales, 462 F.3d 498, 502 (2006): "We subject the BIA's construction of the law it administers to a deferential review."

109. *See, e.g.* 8 U.S.C. §§ 1225, 1228.

110. Press Release, U.S. Customs and Border Protection, "DHS Expands Expedited Removal Authority Along Southwest Border." (Sept. 14, 2005)(noting, "ER provides DHS the authority to expeditiously return non-Mexican illegal aliens to his or her country of origin as soon as circumstances will allow."). Available at: http:// www.cbp.gov/xp/cgov/newsroom/news_releases/archives/2005_press_releases/092005/09142005.xml

111. Press Release, Dep't Homeland Security, "DHS Announces Expanded Border Control Plans." (Aug. 10, 2004). Available at: http://www.dhs.gov/xnews/releases/press_release_0479.shtm

112. Webpage, Immigration and Customs Enforcement, "FAQ–commonly asked questions about ICE." (Visited Aug. 26, 2008). Available at: http://www.ice.gov/about/faq.htm

DISCUSSION QUESTIONS

1. What are the justifications offered by Jon Feere as to why the courts have generally left addressing immigration issues to the political branches of government?

2. Summarize the Supreme Court cases *Shaughnessy v. United States ex rel. Mezei* and *Landon v. Plasencia*. To what degree did either case invoke the constitutional protection of due process? Why does Feere characterize the decision in *Plasencia* as the court turning "phantom constitutional norms into real immigration law"?

3. Explain the two strategies Feere says could be useful in limiting the judiciary's reach into immigration policy: deference to the Chevron doctrine and expedited removal.

4. What were the Chinese Exclusion Act cases? How did the Supreme Court, in affirming the constitutionality of these laws, provide precedent for government deportation actions after 9/11?

5. Explain the Supreme Court's decision in *Zadvydas v. Davis*. In what way does this decision change our understanding of the plenary powers of the executive branch regarding immigration? In what ways does the decision uphold the traditional view of executive plenary power?

6. What is "expedited removal" under the Illegal Immigration Reform and Immigrant Responsibility Act? In what way does this law represent a reclamation by Congress of its authority over immigration?

CHAPTER THREE

Legal Immigration

Visas, Green Cards, and Refugees

Introduction

In 2012, President Barack Obama instituted a policy, known as Deferred Action for Childhood Arrivals, or DACA, which relaxed immigration enforcement against undocumented aliens who came to the United States as children. Although their presence was illegal under the law, strictly speaking, President Obama exercised what he saw as his executive prerogative through this policy to end deportations of people who through no fault of their own wound up living in the United States during their childhood and who were now adults. These individuals were labeled "dreamers," in reference to proposed legislation known as the DREAM Act, which would have granted legal status to these individuals but failed to be enacted by Congress.

In 2014, President Obama announced an expansion of the DACA policy, along with a new policy that would permit illegal aliens who were parents of U.S. citizens or of legal residents to remain in the United States legally. This was a bridge too far for many states who carried much of the burden of expense associated with illegal immigration, including education and health care, and whose costs would dramatically increase with millions of new residents gaining legal status and therefore access to additional state-funded programs. Twenty-six states sued the Obama administration and secured an injunction prohibiting the expansion of DACA and the implementation of the new policy for parents. The injunction against expansion was ultimately left in place by the U.S. Supreme Court.

In September 2017, President Donald Trump announced he would be rescinding the Obama-era DACA policy. He gave Congress until March 2018 to craft a legislative solution to legalize dreamers currently in the country. In January 2018, President Trump proposed his own plan for Congress to consider. The plan contained four key prongs, one of which was a solution for DACA dreamers. The plan would grant 1.8 million people not only legal status, but a path to citizenship. This element of the plan was far more generous than the Obama policy. Democrats and some Republicans, however, found the other three prongs of the plan more objectionable. Those prongs included significant funding for a border wall (one of Trump's campaign promises), elimination of chain migration (which gives relatives of legal residents priority for legal immigration over others waiting in line to come to the United States), and elimination of the Diversity Visa Program, aka the "visa lottery" (which randomly selects immigration applicants from around the world for permanent residency and a path to citizenship without regard for their merit, education, skill sets, or how their presence might benefit the United States).

The political debate over immigration and border security—who should be allowed to immigrate to the United States, and under what conditions—has waged for decades without consensus or solution. And yet, there is a framework in place to serve as a starting point in the form of current federal laws on the books that govern immigration and naturalization. In this chapter, readers are presented with a piece that speaks to legal immigration and the laws and policies that govern it. The policy report, written by William Kandel of the Congressional Research Service, provides a primer on the topic. Written for legislative audiences, it provides an overview of immigration laws in the United States and the policies through which those laws are executed. The result is that readers will have an understanding of what constitutes legal immigration into the United States and how it occurs. This understanding is an important backdrop to the discussion of illegal immigration and immigration enforcement, as well as crime and other social problems fairly or unfairly associated with illegal immigration.

READING 3

Permanent Legal Immigration to the United States

Policy Overview

By William A. Kandel

Summary

The pool of people who are eligible to immigrate to the United States as legal permanent residents (LPRs) each year typically exceeds the worldwide level set by the Immigration and Nationality Act (INA). In an effort to process the demand for LPR visas fairly and in the national interest, LPR admissions are subject to a complex set of numerical limits and preference categories that give priority for admission on the basis of family relationships, needed skills, and geographic diversity. The INA further specifies that each year, countries are held to a numerical limit of 7% of the worldwide level of U.S. immigrant admissions, known as per-country limits or country caps.

In FY2013, just under 1 million aliens became U.S. legal permanent residents (LPRs). Of this total, 65.6% entered the United States on the basis of family ties. Other major categories of LPRs were employment-based (16.3%), refugees and asylees (12.1%), and diversity migrants (4.6%).

In FY2013, Mexico was the source country of 13.6% of LPRs who were admitted or who adjusted status. Other top countries were China (7.2%), India (6.9%), the Philippines (5.5%), and the Dominican Republic (4.2%). Rather than newly arriving from abroad, 53.6% (530,802) were adjusting to LPR status from a temporary (i.e., nonimmigrant) status within the United States.

There were 4.4 million approved LPR visa petitions pending with the National Visa Center at the end of FY2013 because of the numerical limits in the INA, most of which are family-based petitions. These data do not constitute a backlog of petitions to be processed; rather, these data represent persons who have been approved for visas that are not yet available due to the numerical limits in the INA. Visas are generally available for unmarried adult children of U.S. citizens who filed in FY2006, but there

William A. Kandel, "Permanent Legal Immigration to the United States: Policy Overview," pp. 1-13, 2014.

are even longer waits for unmarried adult children of U.S. citizens from Mexico and the Philippines. Prospective family-sponsored immigrants from the Philippines have the most substantial waiting times before a visa is scheduled to become available to them; consular officers are now considering the petitions of the brothers and sisters of U.S. citizens from the Philippines who filed almost 24 years ago.

Most agree that revision of the system of permanent legal immigration should be one of the major components of a comprehensive immigration reform (CIR) proposal, along with increased border security and enforcement of immigration laws within the U.S. interior, reform of temporary worker visas, and options to address the millions of unauthorized aliens residing in the country. Congress is considering proposals to alter the legal immigration system—either in the form of CIR or in the form of incremental revisions aimed at strategic changes.

Some are advocating for a significant reallocation of the visa categories or a substantial increase in legal immigration to satisfy the desire of U.S. families to reunite with their relatives abroad and to meet the labor force needs of employers hiring foreign workers. Yet, proponents of family-based migration maintain that any proposal to increase immigration should also include the option of additional family-based visas to reduce waiting times—currently up to years or decades—for those already "in the queue." Arguing against these competing priorities for increased immigration are those who favor reduced immigration, including proposals to limit family-based LPRs to the immediate relatives of U.S. citizens, to confine employment-based LPRs to highly skilled workers, and to eliminate the diversity visas.

Four major principles currently underlie U.S. policy on legal permanent immigration: the reunification of families, the admission of immigrants with needed skills, the protection of refugees, and the diversity of admissions by country of origin. These principles are embodied in federal law, the Immigration and Nationality Act (INA) first codified in 1952. The Immigration Amendments of 1965 replaced the national origins quota system (enacted after World War I) with per-country ceilings, and the statutory provisions regulating permanent immigration to the United States were last revised significantly by the Immigration Act of 1990.[1]

The critiques of the permanent legal immigration system today are extensive, but there is no consensus on the specific direction the reforms of the law should take. As the Congress considers comprehensive immigration reform (CIR), many maintain that revision of the legal immigration system should be one of the major components of a CIR proposal.[2] This primer on legal permanent immigration law, policies, and trends provides a backdrop for the policy options and debates that may emerge as Congress considers a revision of the legal immigration system.[3]

Introduction

The two types of legal aliens are *immigrants* and *nonimmigrants*. As defined in the INA, immigrants are synonymous with legal permanent residents (LPRs) and refer to foreign nationals who come to live lawfully and permanently in the United States. The other major class of legal aliens are nonimmigrants—such as tourists, foreign students, diplomats, temporary agricultural workers, exchange visitors, or intracompany business personnel—who are admitted for a specific purpose and a temporary period of time. Nonimmigrants are required to leave the country when their visas expire, though certain classes of nonimmigrants may adjust to LPR status if they otherwise qualify.[4]

The conditions for the admission of immigrants are much more stringent than nonimmigrants, and many fewer immigrants than nonimmigrants are admitted. Once admitted, however, immigrants are subject to few restrictions; for example, they may accept and change employment, and may apply for U.S. citizenship through the naturalization process, generally after five years.

The prospective immigrant must maneuver a multi-step process through federal departments and agencies to obtain LPR status. Petitions for immigrant (i.e., LPR) status are first filed with U.S. Citizenship and Immigration Services (USCIS) in the Department of Homeland Security (DHS) by the sponsoring relative or employer in the United States. If the prospective immigrant is already legally residing in the United States, USCIS handles most of the process, which is called "adjustment of status" in the INA because the alien is moving from a temporary category to LPR status.[5] If the prospective LPR has not established a lawful residence in the United States, the petition is forwarded to the Department of State's (DOS) Bureau of Consular Affairs in the home country after USCIS has approved it. The Consular Affairs officer (when the alien is coming from abroad) and USCIS adjudicator (when the alien is adjusting status in the United States) must be satisfied that the alien is entitled to the immigrant status. These reviews are intended to ensure that they are not ineligible for visas or admission under the grounds for inadmissibility spelled out in the INA.[6]

Many LPRs are adjusting status from within the United States rather than receiving visas issued abroad by Consular Affairs.[7] As discussed more fully in the Immigration Trends section below, 53.6% of all LPRs adjusted to LPR status in the United States rather than abroad in FY2013.

The INA specifies that each year countries are held to a numerical limit of 7% of the worldwide level of U.S. immigrant admissions, known as per-country limits. The actual number of immigrants that may be approved from a given country, however, is not a simple percentage calculation. Immigrant admissions and adjustments to LPR status are subject to a complex set of numerical limits and preference categories that give priority for admission on the basis of family relationships, needed skills, and geographic diversity.

Current Law and Policy

Worldwide Immigration Levels

The INA provides for a permanent annual worldwide level of 675,000 legal permanent residents (LPRs), but this level is flexible and certain categories of LPRs are permitted to exceed the limits.[8]

The permanent worldwide immigrant level consists of the following components: family immigration, including immediate relatives of U.S. citizens and family-sponsored preference immigrants (480,000 plus certain unused employment-based preference numbers from the prior year); employment-based preference immigrants (140,000 plus certain unused family preference numbers from the prior year); and diversity immigrants (55,000). Immediate relatives[9] of U.S. citizens as well as refugees and asylees who are adjusting status are exempt from direct numerical limits.[10]

The annual level of family-sponsored preference immigrants is determined by subtracting the number of immediate relative visas issued in the previous year and the number of aliens paroled[11] into the United States for at least a year from 480,000 (the total family immigration level) and—when available—adding employment preference immigrant numbers unused during the previous year. By law, the family-sponsored preference level may not fall below 226,000. As a consequence, the 480,000 level of family immigration has often been exceeded to maintain the 226,000 floor on family-sponsored preference visas, because the number of immediate relatives is greater than 254,000 annually.

Per-country Ceilings

As mentioned above, the INA establishes per-country levels at 7% of the worldwide level.[12] For a dependent foreign state, the per-country ceiling is 2%.[13] The per-country level is not a quota or set aside for individual countries, as each country in the world could not receive 7% of the overall limit. As the State Department describes, "(T)he country limitation serves to avoid monopolization of virtually all the annual limitation by applicants from only a few countries. This limitation is not a quota to which any particular country is entitled, however."[14]

Two important exceptions to the per-country ceilings were enacted in the past decade. Foremost is an exception for certain family-sponsored immigrants. More specifically, the INA states that 75% of the visas allocated to spouses and children of LPRs are not subject to the per-country ceiling.[15] Prior to FY2001, employment-based preference immigrants were also held to per-country ceilings. The American Competitiveness in the Twenty-First Century Act of 2000 (P.L. 106–313) enabled the per-country ceilings for employment-based immigrants to be surpassed for individual countries that are oversubscribed as long as visas are available within the worldwide limit for employment-based preferences. The impact of these revisions to the per-country ceilings is discussed later in this report. The actual per-country ceiling varies from year to year according to the prior year's immediate relative and parolee admissions and unused visas that roll over.

Family and Employment-Based Preferences

Within each family and employment preference, the INA further allocates the number of LPRs issued visas each year. The family preferences are based upon the closeness of the family relationship to U.S. citizens and LPRs.[16] The employment preferences are based upon the professional accomplishments and skills needed by U.S. employers. As Table 3.1 summarizes the legal immigration preference system,

Table 3.1 Legal Immigration Preference System

Category	Numerical limit
Total Family-Sponsored Immigrants	**480,000**
Immediate relatives — Aliens who are the spouses and unmarried minor children of U.S. citizens and the parents of adult U.S. citizens	Unlimited
Family-sponsored Preference Immigrants	**Worldwide Level 226,000**
1st preference — Unmarried sons and daughters of citizens	23,400 plus visas not required for 4th preference
2nd preference — (A) Spouses and minor children of LPRs; (B) Unmarried sons and daughters of LPRs	114,200 plus visas not required for 1st preference [77% are reserved for spouses and children of LPRs]
3rd preference — Married sons and daughters of citizens	23,400 plus visas not required for 1st or 2nd preference
4th preference — Siblings of citizens age 21 and over	65,000 plus visas not required for 1st, 2nd, or 3rd preference
Employment-Based Preference Immigrants	**Worldwide Level 140,000**
1st preference — Priority workers: persons of extraordinary ability in the arts, science, education, business, or athletics; outstanding professors and researchers; and certain multi-national executives and managers	28.6% of worldwide limit plus unused 4th and 5th preference
2nd preference — Members of the professions holding advanced degrees or persons of exceptional abilities in the sciences, art, or business	28.6% of worldwide limit plus unused 1st preference
3rd preference—skilled — Skilled shortage workers with at least two years training or experience, professionals with baccalaureate degrees	28.6% of worldwide limit plus unused 1st or 2nd preference
3rd preference—"other" — Unskilled shortage workers	10,000 (taken from the total available for 3rd preference)
4th preference — "Special immigrants," including ministers of religion, religious workers other than ministers, certain employees of the U.S. government abroad, and others	7.1% of worldwide limit; religious workers limited to 5,000
5th preference — Employment creation investors who invest at least $1 million (amount may vary in rural areas or areas of high unemployment) which will create at least 10 new jobs	7.1% of worldwide limit; 3,000 *minimum* reserved for investors in rural or high unemployment areas

Source: CRS summary of §§203(a), 203(b), and 204 of INA; 8 U.S.C. §1153.

Note: Employment-based allocations are further affected by §203(e) of the Nicaraguan and Central American Relief Act (NACARA), as amended by §1(e) of P.L. 105–139. This provision states that the employment 3rd preference "other workers" category is to be reduced by up to 5,000 annually for as long as necessary to offset adjustments under NACARA.

the complexity of the allocations becomes apparent. Note that in most instances unused visa numbers are allowed to roll down to the next preference category. Employment-based visa allocations not used in a given year roll-over to the family preference categories the following year, and vice versa.[17]

As part of the Immigration Act of 1990, Congress added a fifth preference category for foreign investors to become LPRs. The INA allocates up to 10,000 admissions annually and generally requires a minimum $1 million investment and employment of at least 10 U.S. workers. Less capital is required for aliens who participate in the immigrant investor pilot program, in which they invest in targeted regions and existing enterprises that are financially troubled.

Employers who seek to hire prospective employment-based immigrants through the second and third preference categories also must petition the U.S. Department of Labor (DOL) on behalf of the alien. The prospective immigrant must demonstrate that he or she meets the qualifications for the particular job as well as the preference category. If DOL determines that a labor shortage exists in the occupation for which the petition is filed, labor certification will be issued. If there is not a labor shortage in the given occupation, the employer must submit evidence of extensive recruitment efforts in order to obtain certification.[18]

Other Permanent Immigration Categories

There are several other major categories of legal permanent immigration in addition to the family-sponsored and employment-based preference categories. These classes of LPRs cover a variety of cases, ranging from aliens who win the Diversity Visa Lottery to aliens in removal (i.e., deportation) proceedings granted LPR status by an immigration judge because of exceptional and extremely unusual hardship.[19] Table 3.2 summarizes these major classes and identifies whether they are numerically limited.

Immigration Trends

Immigration Patterns, 1900–2013

Immigration to the United States is not totally determined by shifts in flow that occur as a result of lawmakers revising the allocations. Immigration to the United States plummeted in the middle of the 20th century largely as a result of factors brought on by the Great Depression and World War II. There are a variety of "push-pull" factors that drive immigration. Push factors from the immigrant-sending countries include such circumstances as civil wars and political unrest, economic deprivation and limited job opportunities, and catastrophic natural disasters. Pull factors in the United States include such features as strong employment conditions, reunion with family, and quality of life considerations. A corollary factor is the extent that aliens may be able to migrate to other "desirable" countries that offer circumstances and opportunities comparable to the United States.

Table 3.2 Other Major Legal Immigration Categories

	Non-preference Immigrants	Numerical Limit
Asylees	Aliens in the United States who have been granted asylum due to persecution or a well-founded fear of persecution and who must wait one year before petitioning for LPR status	No limits on LPR adjustments as of FY2005. (Previously limited to 10,000)
Cancellation of Removal	Aliens in removal proceedings granted LPR status by an immigration judge because of exceptional and extremely unusual hardship	4,000 (with certain exceptions)
Diversity Lottery	Aliens from foreign nations with low admission levels; must have high school education or equivalent or minimum two years of work experience in a profession requiring two years training or experience	55,000
Refugees	Aliens abroad who have been granted refugee status due to persecution or a well-founded fear of persecution and who must wait one year before petitioning for LPR status	Presidential Determination for refugee status, no limits on LPR adjustments
Other	Various classes of immigrants, such as Amerasians, parolees, and certain Central Americans, Cubans, and Haitians who are adjusting to LPR status	Dependent on specific adjustment authority

Source: CRS summary of §§203(a), 203(b), 204, 207, 208, and 240A of INA; 8 U.S.C. §1153.

The annual number of LPRs admitted or adjusted in the United States rose gradually after World War II, as Figure 3.1 illustrates. The DHS Office of Immigration Statistics (OIS) data present those admitted as LPRs or those adjusting to LPR status. The growth in immigration after 1980 is partly attributable to the total number of admissions under the basic system, consisting of immigrants entering through a preference system as well as immediate relatives of U.S. citizens, that was augmented considerably by legalized aliens.[20] The Immigration Act of 1990 increased the ceiling on employment-based preference immigration, with the provision that unused employment visas would be made available the following year for family preference immigration. In addition, the number of refugees admitted increased from 718,000 in the period 1966-1980 to 1.6 million during the period 1981–1995, after the enactment of the Refugee Act of 1980.

Many LPRs are adjusting status from within the United States rather than receiving visas issued abroad by Consular Affairs before they arrive in the United States. In the past decade, the number of LPRs arriving from abroad has remained somewhat steady, hovering between a high of 481,948 in FY2012 and a low of 358,411 in FY2003. Adjustments to LPR status in the United States have fluctuated

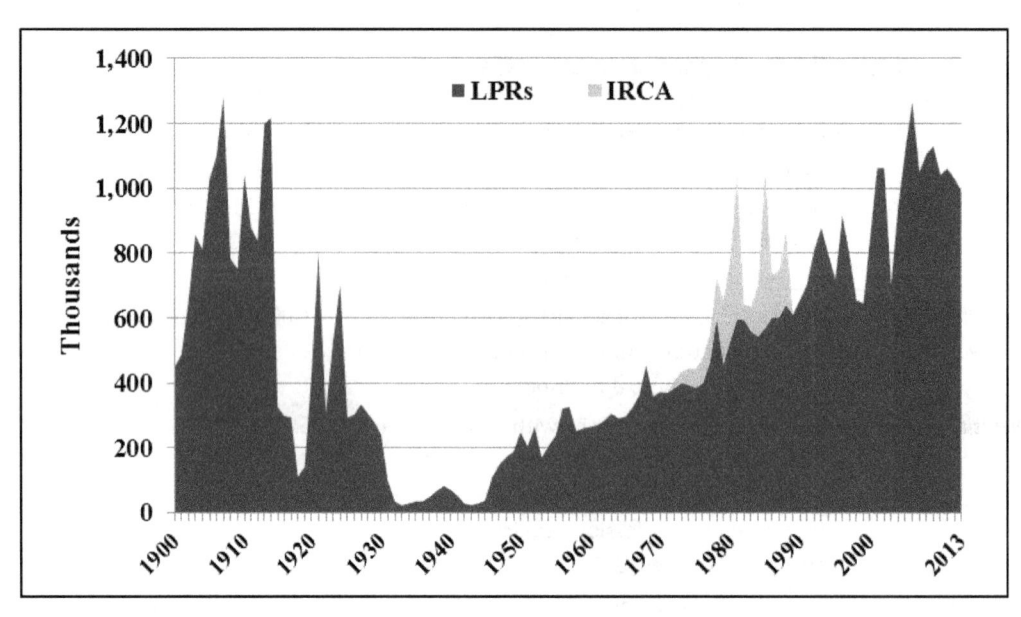

Figure 3.1 Annual LPR Admissions and Status Adjustments, 1900–2013

Source: Statistical Yearbook of Immigration, U.S. Department of Homeland Security, Office of Immigration Statistics, multiple fiscal years. Aliens legalizing through the Immigration Reform and Control Act (IRCA) of 1986 are depicted by year of arrival rather than year of adjustment.

over the same period, from a low of 244,793 in FY1999 to a high of 819,248 in FY2006. As Figure 3.2 shows, most of the variation in total number of aliens granted LPR status over the past decade is due to the number of adjustments processed in the United States rather than visas issued abroad.

In any given period of United States history, a handful of countries have dominated the flow of immigrants, but the dominant countries have varied over time. Figure 3.3 presents trends in the top immigrant-sending countries (together comprising at least 50% of the immigrants admitted) for selected decades. The figure illustrates that immigration at the close of the 20th century was not as dominated by 3 or 4 countries as it was earlier in the century. These data suggest that the per-country ceilings established in 1965 had some effect. As Figure 3.3 illustrates, immigrants from only three or four countries made up more than half of all LPRs prior to 1960. By the last two decades of the 20th century, immigrants from seven to nine countries comprised about half of all LPRs and this pattern has continued into the 21st century.

Although Europe was home to the countries sending the most immigrants during the early 20th century (e.g., Germany, Italy, Austria-Hungary, and the United Kingdom), Mexico has been a top sending country for most of the 20th century and into the 21st century. Other top sending countries from FY2001 through FY2010 are the Dominican Republic, El Salvador, Colombia and Cuba (Western Hemisphere) and the Philippines, India, China, South Korea and Vietnam (Asia).

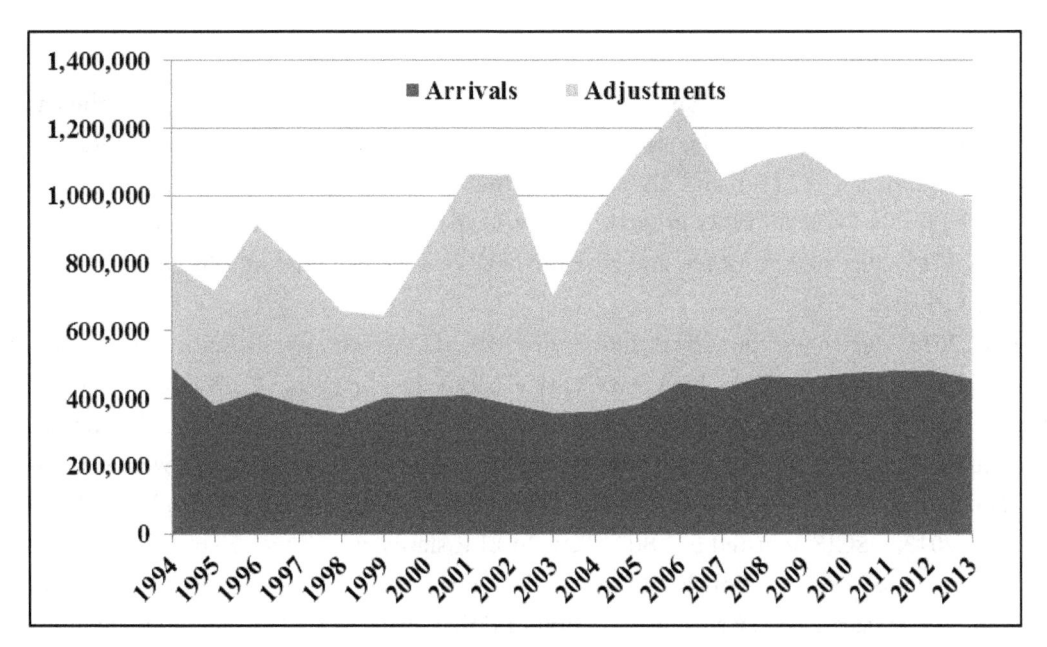

Figure 3.2 Legal Permanent Residents, New Arrivals and Adjustments of Status, FY1994–FY2013

Source: Statistical Yearbook of Immigration, U.S. Department of Homeland Security, Office of Immigration Statistics (multiple years).

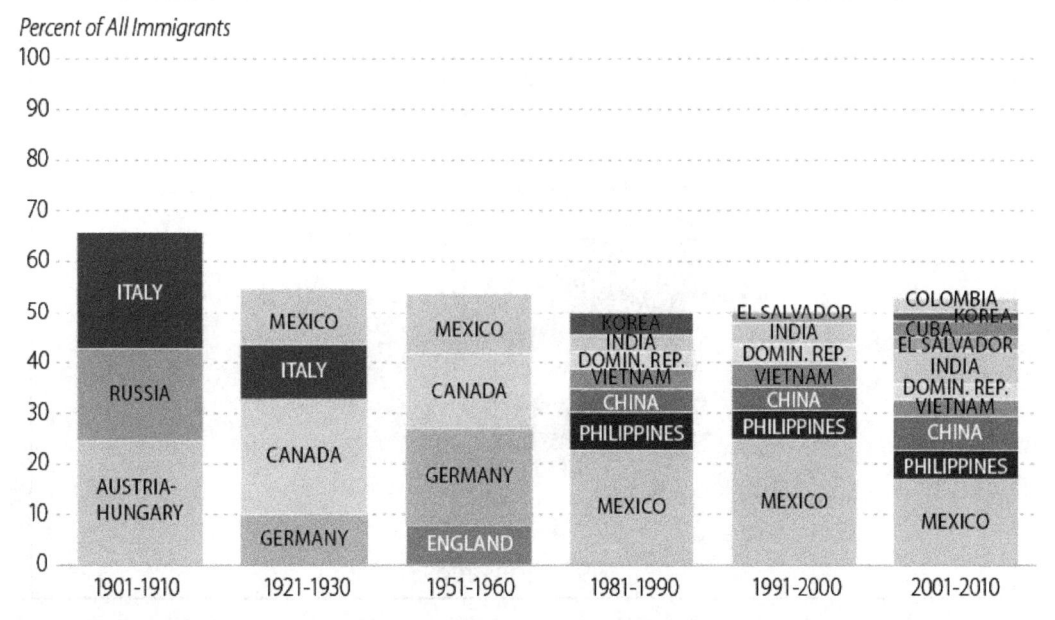

Figure 3.3 Top Sending Countries (Comprising at Least Half of All LPRs): Selected Periods

Source: CRS analysis of Table 2, *Statistical Yearbook of Immigration*, U.S. Department of Homeland Security, Office of Immigration Statistics, FY2010.

CHAPTER THREE Legal Immigration ♦ 85

FY2013 Admissions

In FY2013, just under 1 million aliens became LPRs. Of this total, 65.6% entered on the basis of family ties. As Figure 3.4 presents, other major categories were employment-based LPRs (16.3%), refugees and asylees (12.1%), and diversity migrants (4.6%). Immediate relatives of U.S. citizens accounted for 44.4% of all LPRs in 2013. More specifically, spouses of U.S. citizens were 25.1%, parents of U.S. citizens were 12.1%, and children of U.S. citizens (including adopted orphans) were 7.2% of LPRs.

In FY2013, Mexico was the source country of 13.6% of LPRs who were admitted or who adjusted status. Other top countries were China (7.2%), India (6.9%), the Philippines (5.5%), and the Dominican Republic (4.2%). These top five countries made up 37.4% of all LPRs who were admitted or who adjusted status in FY2013. Similarly, the leading regions of birth for LPRs in FY2013 were Asia (40.4%) and North America[21] (31.9%), accounting for almost three quarters of the LPRs in FY2013.[22]

In FY2013, USCIS adjusted 530,802 aliens to LPR status, which was 53.6% of all LPRs. The lowest number of foreign nationals adjusted in the United States was in FY2003, when USCIS was just standing up as an agency after the creation of DHS. Most (86.9%) of the employment- based immigrants adjusted to LPR status within the United States in FY2013. Half (52.8%) of the immediate relatives of U.S. citizens also did so that year. Only 10.4% of the other family- preference immigrants adjusted to LPR status within the United States in FY2013.[23]

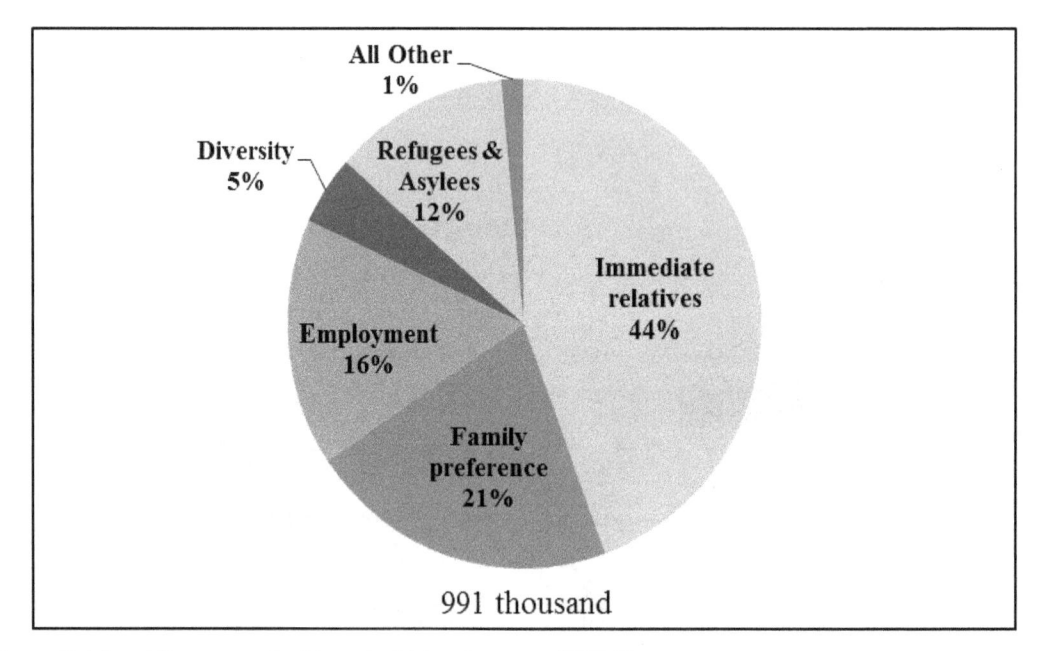

Figure 3.4 Legal Permanent Residents by Major Category, FY2013

Source: U.S. Department of Homeland Security, Office of Immigration Statistics, *U.S. Legal Permanent Residents: 2013*, 2014.

Approved Visa Petitions Pending

The pool of people who are eligible to immigrate to the United States as LPRs each year typically exceeds the worldwide level set by U.S. immigration law. At the end of each fiscal year, the Department of State publishes a tabulation of approved visa petitions pending with the National Visa Center.[24] These data do not constitute a backlog of petitions to be processed; rather, these data represent persons who have been approved for visas that are not yet available due to the numerical limits in the INA. The National Visa Center caseload is the data that drive the priority dates published in the *Visa Bulletin* each month.[25]

The family-based preference categories dominate the approved visa petitions pending. Figure 3.5 presents approved petitions for the 4.4 million LPR visas pending with the National Visa Center at the end of FY2013, by preference category.[26] Over half (57%) of all approved petitions pending were 5th preference (i.e., brothers and sisters of U.S. citizens). Children of U.S. citizens with approved LPR visas pending totaled 24% (i.e., 6% unmarried and 18% married). Family members of LPRs totaled 16% of the 4.4 million approved visa petitions pending.

As Figure 3.5 indicates, the employment-based preferences account for only 3% (111,604) of the 4.4 million LPR visas pending with the National Visa Center as of November 1, 2013. This figure of 111,604 reflects persons registered under each respective numerical limitation (i.e., the totals represent not only principal applicants or petition beneficiaries, but their spouses and children entitled to derivative status under the INA).

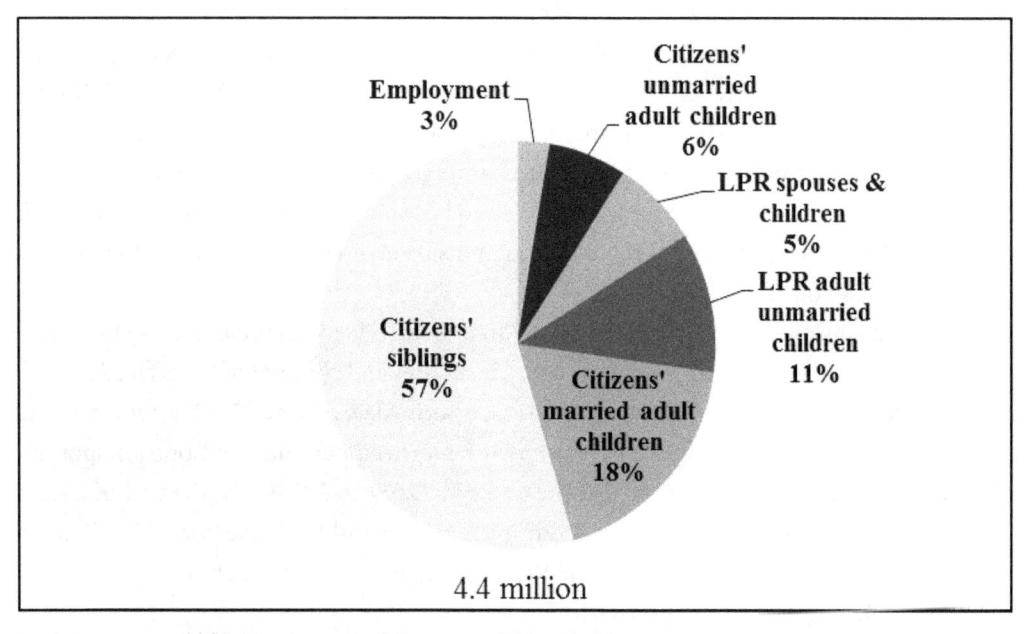

Figure 3.5 Approved LPR Visa Petitions Pending November 2013

Source: U.S. Department of State, *Annual Report of Immigrant Visa Applicants in the Family-Sponsored and Employment-Based Preferences Registered at the National Visa Center as of November 1, 2013.*

Caveat on the Queue

Trends in applications for immigration benefits drawn from USCIS' Performance Reporting Tool (PRT) suggest that USCIS has not yet forwarded a substantial portion of the LPR caseload to the National Visa Center.[27] Similarly, the I-485 Inventory that USCIS maintains on all employment—based adjustment of status cases pending suggests that there might be a significant number of employment-based LPR petitions that are in the "pipeline."[28] USCIS does not formally report how many LPR petitions are awaiting approval and how many approved LPR petitions are pending.[29]

Visa Processing Dates

According to the INA, family-sponsored and employment-based preference visas are issued to eligible immigrants in the order in which a petition has been filed. Spouses and children of prospective LPRs are entitled to the same status, and the same order of consideration as the person qualifying as principal LPR, if accompanying or following to join (referred to as derivative status). When visa demand exceeds the per-country limit, visas are prorated according to the preference system allocations (detailed in Table 3.1) for the oversubscribed foreign state or dependent area.[30]

Family-Based Visa Priority Dates

As Table 3.3 evidences, relatives of U.S. citizens and LPRs are waiting in backlogs for a visa to become available. Brothers and sisters of U.S. citizens now can expect to wait over 12 years, with even longer waits for siblings from Mexico and the Philippines. "Priority date" means that unmarried adult sons and daughters of U.S. citizens who filed petitions on June 8, 2007, are now being processed for visas (with older priority dates for certain countries as noted in Table 3.3). Married adult sons and daughters of U.S. citizens who filed petitions over 10 years ago (December 8, 2003) are now being processed for visas. Prospective family-sponsored immigrants from the Philippines have the most substantial waiting times before a visa is scheduled to become available to them; consular officers are now considering the petitions of the brothers and sisters of U.S. citizens from the Philippines who filed over 23 years ago.[31]

Amidst these long queues, the spouses and children of LPRs (second preference A) have the most recent priority date: March 1, 2013. Ten years ago, the spouses and children of LPRs faced a four- year queue. Two years ago, that preference category had a priority date of June 15, 2010, which amounted to almost a two and-a-half-year wait. The number of approved pending petitions for spouses and children of LPRs dropped from 332,636 at the end of FY2011 to 238,417 at the end of FY2013. It is unclear whether this decline represents a diminishing demand for these visas, USCIS delays in submitting approved petitions to the National Visa Center, or a backlog of petitions in the "pipeline" that have yet to be processed and approved.

Table 3.3 Priority Dates for Family Preference Visas, as of November 2014

Category	Worldwide	China	India	Mexico	Philippines
Unmarried sons and daughters of citizens	June 6, 2007	June 8, 2007	June 8, 2007	July 8, 1994	Nov. 1, 2004
Spouses and children of LPRs	Mar. 1, 2013	Mar. 1, 2013	Mar. 1, 2013	Sep. 22, 2012	Mar. 1, 2013
Unmarried sons and daughters of LPRs	Jan. 1, 2008	Jan. 1, 2008	Jan. 1, 2008	Sep. 8, 1994	Jan. 1, 2004
Married sons and daughters of citizens	Dec. 8, 2003	Dec. 8, 2003	Dec. 8, 2003	Nov. 1, 1993	June 8, 1993
Siblings of citizens age 21 and over	Feb. 8, 2002	Feb. 8, 2002	Feb. 8, 2002	Feb. 15, 1997	May 1, 1991

Source: U.S. Department of State, Bureau of Consular Affairs, *Visa Bulletin* for November 2014.

Employment-Based Visa Priority Dates

As of November 2014, the priority workers (i.e., extraordinary ability) visa category is current, as Table 3.4 presents. The advanced degree visa category is current worldwide, but those seeking advanced degree visas from China have a priority date of December 8, 2009, and from India have a February 15, 2005, priority date. Visas for professional and skilled workers have a worldwide priority date of June 1, 2012, except for those workers from India and the Philippines, who have longer waits.[32]

Table 3.4 Priority Dates for Employment Preference Visas, as of November 2014

Category	Worldwide	China	India	Mexico	Philippines
Priority workers	current	current	current	current	current
Advanced degrees/exceptional ability	current	Dec. 8, 2009	Feb. 15, 2005	current	current
Skilled and professional	June 1, 2012	Jan. 1, 2010	Nov. 3, 2003	June 1, 2012	June 1, 2012
Unskilled	June 1, 2012	July 22, 2005	Nov 22, 2003	June. 1, 2012	June 1, 2012
Special immigrants	current	current	current	current	current
Investors	current	current	current	current	current

Source: U.S. Department of State, Bureau of Consular Affairs, *Visa Bulletin* for November 2014.

Concluding Observations

Most agree that revision of the system of permanent legal immigration should be one of the major components of a CIR proposal, along with increased border security and enforcement of immigration laws within the U.S. interior, reform of temporary worker visas and options to address the millions of unauthorized aliens residing in the country. Congress is considering proposals to alter the legal immigration system—either in the form of CIR or in the form of incremental revisions aimed at strategic changes. The Senate passed a CIR bill, S. 744, in June 2013 that would make significant changes to the system of permanent legal immigration.[33] The House Committee on the Judiciary has ordered to be reported legislation (H.R. 2131) that also would revise the allocation of LPR visas. [34]

Some are advocating for a significant reallocation of the visa categories or a substantial increase in legal immigration to satisfy the desire of U.S. families to reunite with their relatives abroad and to meet the labor force needs of employers hiring foreign workers. Some favor a reallocation toward employment-based immigration to help U.S. employers compete for the "best and the brightest," including foreign professional workers in science, technology, engineering, or mathematics (STEM) fields.[35] Yet, proponents of family-based migration maintain that any proposal to increase immigration should also include the option of additional family-based visas to reduce waiting times—currently up to years or decades—for those already "in the queue."

Arguing against these competing priorities for increased immigration are those who favor reduced immigration, including proposals to limit family-based LPRs to the immediate relatives of U.S. citizens, to confine employment-based LPRs to highly skilled workers, and to eliminate the diversity visas.

Acknowledgment

This report was authored by Ruth Ellen Wasem, Specialist in Immigration Policy, who is on leave from CRS until October 1, 2015.

Notes

1. Congress has significantly amended the INA numerous times since 1952. Other major laws amending the INA are the Refugee Act of 1980, the Immigration Reform and Control Act of 1986, and the Illegal Immigration Reform and Immigrant Responsibility Act of 1996. 8 U.S.C. §1101 et seq.

2. Other major components of CIR that are commonly mentioned are: increased border security and enforcement of immigration laws within the U.S. interior; reform of temporary worker visas; and options to address the millions of unauthorized aliens residing in the country.

3. For a discussion of the legislation under consideration, see CRS Report R43320, *Immigration Legislation and Issues in the 113th Congress*, coordinated by Andorra Bruno.

4. Nonimmigrants are often referred to by the letter that denotes their specific provision in the statute, such as H-2A agricultural workers, F-1 foreign students, or J-1 cultural exchange visitors. CRS Report RL31381, *U.S. Immigration Policy on Temporary Admissions*, by Ruth Ellen Wasem.

5. INA §245 details the circumstances under which an alien can change from a nonimmigrant or other temporary status to legal permanent resident status without leaving the United States to apply for the LPR visa.

6. These include criminal, national security, health, and indigence grounds as well as past violations of immigration law. Section 212(a) of INA. CRS Report R41104, *Immigration Visa Issuances and Grounds for Exclusion: Policy and Trends*, by Ruth Ellen Wasem.

7. For background and analysis of visa issuance and admissions policy, see CRS Report R41104, *Immigration Visa Issuances and Grounds for Exclusion: Policy and Trends*, by Ruth Ellen Wasem.

8. §201 of INA; 8 U.S.C. §1151.

9. "Immediate relatives" are defined by the INA to include the spouses and unmarried minor children of U.S. citizens, and the parents of adult U.S. citizens.

10. Refugees are admitted to the United States as such and then may adjust to LPR status after one year. Asylees are foreign nationals who request and receive asylum after they have entered the United States. They too, can adjust to LPR status after one year. CRS Report RL31269, *Refugee Admissions and Resettlement Policy*, by Andorra Bruno.

11. "Parole" is a term in immigration law which means that the alien has been granted temporary permission to be present in the United States. Parole does not constitute formal admission to the United States and parolees are required to leave when the terms of their parole expire, or if otherwise eligible, to be admitted in a lawful status.

12. §202(a)(2) of the INA; 8 U.S.C. §1151.

13. Macau, the former Portuguese colony that became a special administrative region of the Peoples' Republic of China in 1999, would be considered a dependent foreign state.

14. Bureau of Consular Affairs, *Operation of the Immigrant Numerical Control Process*, U.S. Department of State, undated, p. 3, located at http://travel.state.gov/content/visas/english/law-and-policy/bulletin.html.

15. §202(a)(4) of the INA; 8 U.S.C. §1151.

16. For a complete discussion and analysis, see CRS Report R43145, *U.S. Family-Based Immigration Policy*, by William A. Kandel.

17. Employment-based allocations are further affected by §203(e) of the Nicaraguan and Central American Relief Act (NACARA), as amended by §1(e) of P.L. 105-139. This provision states that when the employment 3rd preference "other worker" (OW) cut-off date reached the priority date of the latest OW petition approved prior to November 19, 1997, the 10,000 OW numbers available for a fiscal year are to be reduced by up to 5,000 annually beginning in the following fiscal year. This reduction is to be

made for as long as necessary to offset adjustments under NACARA. Since the OW cut-off date reached November 19, 1997, during FY2001, the reduction in the OW limit to 5,000 began in FY2002.

18. See CRS Report RL33977, *Immigration of Foreign Workers: Labor Market Tests and Protections*, by Ruth Ellen Wasem.

19. CRS Report R41747, *Diversity Immigrant Visa Lottery Issues*, by Ruth Ellen Wasem; and, CRS Report R42477, *Immigration Provisions of the Violence Against Women Act (VAWA)*, by William A. Kandel.

20. The Immigration Reform and Control Act of 1986 legalized 2.7 million aliens residing in the United States without authorization.

21. North America includes the Caribbean and Central America as well as Mexico and Canada.

22. DHS Office of Immigration Statistics, *Yearbook of Immigration Statistics: 2013*, Table 10.

23. DHS Office of Immigration Statistics, *Yearbook of Immigration Statistics: 2013*, Table 7.

24. U.S. Department of State, *Annual Report of Immigrant Visa Applicants in the Family-Sponsored and Employment—Based Preferences Registered at the National Visa Center as of November 1, 2013*.

25. For further specifications of the data that DOS factors into the visa priority dates, see U.S. Department of State, Visa Office, *Annual Numerical Limits for Fiscal Year 2014*, located at http://travel.state.gov/content/visas/english/law-and-policy/statistics/immigrant-visas.html.

26. U.S. Department of State, *Annual Report of Immigrant Visa Applicants in the Family-Sponsored and Employment- Based Preferences Registered at the National Visa Center as of November 1, 2013*.

27. The Performance Reporting Tool (PRT) is the USCIS System for capturing and reporting field office and service center performance data. It is comparable to the Performance Analysis System (PAS) used by the former Immigration and Naturalization Service. For an example, see http://www.uscis.gov/sites/default/files/USCIS/Resources/ Reports%20and%20Studies/N-400%20and%20Application%20for%20Benefits/applications-for-benefits-2013-june.pdf

28. The USCIS maintains a system of approved employment-based I-485 petitions, (i.e., the Application to Register Permanent Residence or Adjust Status) that are pending, which provides another source of data on the number of approved employment-based LPRs. Known as the I-485 Inventory, these data are available by preference category and by top countries. These I-485 data include the employment-based petitioners who plan to adjust status within the United States. http://www.uscis.gov/sites/default/files/files/nativedocuments/EB_I-485_Pending_Inventory_as_October_01-2013.pdf

29. For further discussion and analysis on numerical limits and backlogs, see CRS Report R42048, *Numerical Limits on Employment-Based Immigration: Analysis of the Per-Country Ceilings*, by Ruth Ellen Wasem; and congressional distribution memorandum, Approved Legal Permanent Resident Petitions Pending for 2012, by Ruth Ellen Wasem, May 2, 2012, available upon request.

30. Bureau of Consular Affairs, *Visa Bulletin For November 2014*, U.S. Department of State, No. 74, Vol. IX, 2014.

31. For more analysis of the family-based visa queue, see CRS Report R43145, *U.S. Family-Based Immigration Policy*, by William A. Kandel.

32. For more analysis of the factors driving the employment-based visa queue, see CRS Report R42530, *Immigration of Foreign Nationals with Science, Technology, Engineering, and Mathematics (STEM) Degrees*, by Ruth Ellen Wasem.

33. For a full discussion of S. 744 as passed, see CRS Report R43097, *Comprehensive Immigration Reform in the 113th Congress: Major Provisions in Senate-Passed S. 744*, by Ruth Ellen Wasem.

34. CRS Report R43320, *Immigration Legislation and Issues in the 113th Congress*, coordinated by Andorra Bruno.

35. CRS Report R42530, *Immigration of Foreign Nationals with Science, Technology, Engineering, and Mathematics (STEM) Degrees*, by Ruth Ellen Wasem.

DISCUSSION QUESTIONS

1. In your own words, explain the Legal Immigration Preference System as presented by William Kandel. To what extent do you agree or disagree with the primacy of the preferences articulated in that system?

2. Consider the patterns of immigration to the United States since 2000. Do you believe the numbers of immigrants, across categories, is too high, too low, or about right? Explain your answer.

3. How have immigrants' countries of origin changed over the years since 1900? Are there any patterns or other observations you find interesting with regard to the leading countries of origin for immigrants at any particular time in history? Explain.

4. President Trump and others supporting a change to current immigration policies argue for prime consideration to be given to the "best and the brightest," which is generally understood to mean highly educated people, particular in the science, technology, engineering, and mathematics (STEM) fields. Would you favor emphasizing this type of background for immigrants, even if it would mean some current immigrant residents separated from family members abroad may not be able to bring them to the United States for permanent residency? Discuss.

5. How important is it that the United States be willing to take in refugees and political asylum seekers? Explain. Also, what are the humanitarian reasons for receiving refugees and asylum seekers? What are the practical reasons? What are the concerns of doing so?

CHAPTER FOUR

Immigration and Federal Law Enforcement

Introduction

Federal law enforcement in the United States has a storied history that goes all the way back to the nation's founding in the late 18th century. Immigration and naturalization enforcement have been a part of the federal law enforcement mission for almost that long. One of the early acts of Congress was passage of the Judiciary Act of 1789. That law, among other things, created the Office of the United States Marshal in each federal judicial district. U.S. marshals, and their deputies, served in many respects much as a federal sheriff—executing court orders, apprehending fugitives, and performing other law enforcement tasks in the absence of other properly designated officials. U.S. marshals were called upon to enforce the Alien Act of 1798 and other immigration laws. The Alien Act of 1798 required that foreigners in the country deemed to be dangerous were to be arrested and deported.

Over the years, the federal law enforcement community expanded as the nation expanded. Early federal law enforcement included the U.S. marshals, postal inspectors, customs inspectors, and constables protecting government property. The Secret Service came along in 1865 to confront the scourge of counterfeit currency and fraud against the government. Law enforcement rangers protecting forests and national parks were authorized in 1905 and 1916, respectively. The Justice Department's Bureau of Investigation (later renamed the Federal Bureau of Investigation) was created in 1908. The Internal Revenue Service's Intelligence Unit—from which many later agencies ultimately emerged, including the Internal Revenue Service Criminal Investigation Division (IRS-CID), the Bureau of Alcohol, Tobacco, Firearms, and Explosives (ATF), and the Drug Enforcement Administration (DEA)—was formed in 1919. In 1925, the U.S. Border Patrol was established as a part of the Bureau of Immigration, which was then housed in the Department of Commerce. Prior to that time, immigration enforcement had been part of the mission of the Treasury Department. In 1933, the function of immigration enforcement and the law enforcement officials assigned to that task were relocated under the Department of Labor, and the Immigration and Naturalization Service (INS) was created to house them. In 1940, the INS was moved to the Department of Justice.

Fast-forward to March 2003. The Department of Homeland Security (DHS) was established as a result of the Homeland Security Act of 2002 in the wake of the 9/11 terror attacks. The DHS was created by the merger of 22 existing agencies, pulled from across the landscape of the federal government. Indeed, creation of the DHS was the largest reorganization of the federal government since creation of the Defense Department in 1949. Among the agencies moved over to DHS were the U.S. Secret Service (from Treasury), the U.S. Coast Guard (from Transportation), the U.S. Customs Service (from Treasury), and the Immigration and Naturalization Service (from Justice). In the new cabinet-level department, criminal investigative and uniformed elements of the U.S. Customs Service and INS were combined into the Bureau of Immigration and Customs Enforcement (ICE) and the Bureau of Customs and Border Protection (CBP). Today, ICE and CBP play the primary roles in immigration enforcement and border protection. They perform their roles along the borders, at aviation and maritime ports of entry, and in the interior of the country.

Within ICE, there are two operational divisions that contribute to the federal effort of enforcing immigration laws: Homeland Security Investigations (HSI) and Enforcement and Removal Operations (ERO). ICE-HSI special agents investigate a wide array of federal criminal offenses related to customs and immigration laws. These include smuggling, cybercrime, human trafficking, trade violations, and immigration and employment violations. Officers from ICE-ERO primarily investigate the presence and whereabouts of criminal aliens—particularly those who have committed violent crimes—and captures them so they might be deported.

While plainclothes investigators and special agents dominate ICE, uniformed officers are the mainstay of Customs and Border Protection. The U.S. Border Patrol employs roughly 20,000 uniformed agents to do just that—patrol along the United States border with the goal of apprehending those entering the country illegally and thwarting human trafficking, drug smuggling, and the smuggling of other contraband. In addition, there are about 21,000 CBP uniformed officers who work the ports of entry and the border entry stations to inspect those entering and leaving the country. Finally, CBP includes both air and marine divisions, which interdict violators who use aircraft or watercraft to enter the country. The air and marine divisions also provide operational support to the other CBP elements.

In this chapter, Tonya Golash-Boza presents a critical view of the way in which DHS, and ICE in particular, has conducted itself in past years pursuant to its mission of border and interior enforcement of immigration laws. The author laments the militarized posture of DHS elements and the aggressiveness of ICE in going after illegal immigrants working in the United States without documentation or authorization. Although this piece was published in 2012, it remains timely today. Many politicians and other public figures have stepped up their criticism of ICE, particularly during the Trump administration, claiming that ICE all too often sweeps up undocumented aliens and their families who pose no danger to the community. Critics, however, cannot dispute ICE's authority to do so, as the presence of undocumented aliens is *prima facia* illegal and therefore subject to enforcement. ICE can certainly be said to be between a rock and a hard place as it seems that performing its very mission, which it is uniquely authorized to do, makes it subject to the criticism presented here by Golash-Boza. For many critics, only the standing down of ICE altogether appears sufficient to mollify them.

READING 4

The Department of Homeland Security and the Immigration Enforcement Regime of the Twenty-First Century

By Tanya Maria Golash-Boza

For most of the twentieth century, immigration enforcement in the United States focused primarily on the U.S./Mexico border. In the last decade of the twentieth century, the process of border militarization accelerated. Presidents ordered walls to be built and fortified. Thousands of Border Patrol agents were stationed along the southern border. The Border Patrol placed a variety of technological innovations designed to detect unauthorized migrants at strategic locations near the border (Andreas 2000). Ground troops were deployed to assist police in the southern border region (Dunn 2001). Despite criticism from immigrant advocates and researchers, border militarization continues apace.

In addition to border militarization, we are now witnessing an unprecedented surge in interior enforcement. Whereas *border militarization* refers to the use of military-style techniques along the border to prevent the entry of undocumented migrants, *interior enforcement* describes policing strategies designed to find undocumented migrants within the borders of the United States. The only time we have seen such large-scale enforcement of immigration laws within the borders of the United States was during the Great Depression when the United States engaged in a mass repatriation of Mexicans.

In 1930, there were about 1.5 million Mexicans and Mexican-Americans in the United States (as compared to nearly 30 million today). Balderrama and Rodríguez (2006) estimate that the majority of the 1.5 million people of Mexican origin residing in the United States were deported in the 1930s; as many as one million Mexicans and their children were repatriated to Mexico in this decade. This repatriation has been heavily criticized. In 2003, for example, the California Senate Select Committee on Citizen Participation held hearings on the repatriation, and the California legislature passed a

Tanya Maria Golash-Boza, "The Department of Homeland Security and the Immigration Enforcement Regime of the Twenty-First Century," *Immigration Nation: Raids, Detentions, and Deportations in Post 9/11 America*, pp. 45-79, 175-178. Copyright © 2012 by Taylor & Francis Group. Reprinted with permission.

bill that authorized the creation of a commission to explore and document the repatriation. The bill never became law, however, due to a veto by Governor Arnold Schwarzenegger (Johnson 2004). In recent years, advocates have demanded an apology at the national level for the inhumanity of these mass deportations.[1]

In the first decade of the twenty-first century, DHS deported more than two and a half million people, and nearly three-quarters of them were Mexican.[2] The current era of mass deportation remarkably has led to more deportations than the mass repatriation of the 1930s. The mass repatriation of Mexicans in the 1930s is different from the current era, however, in two ways. First, it accounted for a much larger portion of the Mexican population. Second, many more legally present Mexicans and even U.S. citizens of Mexican descent were deported as a matter of course. Today, most Mexican deportees are undocumented, and citizens are only rarely deported, usually due to bureaucratic errors. This mass repatriation of people of Mexican origin in the 1930s is similar to the current era of deportation insofar as it was accomplished through raids that terrorized communities. Unfortunately, this aspect of the story has not changed, to any great extent, in the twenty-first century.

An examination of what happens during immigration raids and inside immigrant detention facilities reveals startling results regarding the human consequences of the increases in U.S. interior enforcement. The escalation of raids and detentions has worsened the lot of noncitizens in the United States. Immigration raids terrify communities. For instance, the day after a large-scale immigration raid in Postville, Iowa, half of the children did not report to school. It took weeks for normal school attendance to resume. Many noncitizens have undergone brutal mistreatment in immigrant detention facilities, and many more have faced verbal abuse, neglect, and illness.

Although the assumed goal of immigration raids is to target noncitizens, they also affect citizens. Jeffrey Abram Hernandez, for example, was born in the United States in 2005, and he now lives in Xicalcal, Guatemala with his parents, Viviana and Filiberto. They live with Filiberto's mother, sisters, and brothers because they cannot afford a place of their own. Since their return to Guatemala in late 2007, Filiberto has not been able to find work, and the family struggles to survive. Although Jeffrey is a U.S. citizen, his parents entered the country illegally and were deported after a raid at the Michael Bianco Inc. factory in New Bedford, Massachusetts.[3] Jeffrey is one of many children whose, as a migrant mother adeptly put it, "wings have been cut"[4] due to immigration policy. Their lives have been severely and often irreparably affected by raids carried out by the U.S. Immigrations and Customs Enforcement (ICE). In Guatemala, Jeffrey will not find the same educational opportunities that he would have in the United States. Although he will have the right to return to the United States when he is able to do so, on his own, he most likely will have to enter the low-wage sector of the economy, because his chances for getting beyond the sixth grade are slim.

Raiding Our Communities

Immigration raids are one of the most visible aspects of the increases in immigration enforcement. These raids lead to the *de facto* deportation of U.S. citizens and wreak havoc on immigrant communities by creating a fearful and distrusting climate. A de facto deportation of a U.S. citizen occurs when a noncitizen parent or spouse of a U.S. citizen is deported, and the U.S. citizen's best or only alternative for survival is to accompany this person back to his homeland.

Worksite and home raids have occurred with growing frequency over the past few years, despite limited evidence of their efficacy at removing dangerous people or reducing the numbers of undocumented employees in the United States. In fiscal year (FY) 2002, worksite raids led to just over 485 arrests; in 2007, they led to 5,184. To achieve such marked escalation, ICE has had to implement a sixfold increase in the number of officers it employs to carry out worksite operations.[5] These new tactics were put into place in 2006 and continued throughout 2007 and 2008, with devastating effects on immigrant communities.

Such massive immigration law enforcement efforts have been possible because of an enormous infusion of money, in recent years, into both the established and newly created agencies. In the aftermath of the terrorist attacks of September 11, 2001, the U.S. government's launch of the "war on terror," with its mission to prevent such attacks in the future, created the Department of Homeland Security (DHS) in 2003. This new government agency was specifically designed to subsume all aspects of homeland security. DHS took over all the operations of the Immigration and Naturalization Service (INS) as well as those of other agencies, including the Federal Marshall Service, the Secret Service, and the U.S. Coast Guard, that were not part of the INS. The creation of such an overarching and broad-based agency as DHS was the most significant transformation of the U.S. government's security structure in over a half-century. For immigration policy, the transfer of immigration law enforcement from the Department of Justice (DOJ) to the DHS was a critical moment; the policy took on new meaning when it became central to the United States' efforts in fighting terrorism.

The DHS has a much bigger budget, being a much larger agency than its predecessor, the INS. Moreover, this budget has steadily increased since its creation in 2003—from $31.2 billion to $50.5 billion in 2009.[6] Of the $50.5 billion DHS budget for FY 2009, about $10.9 billion went to Customs and Border Patrol (CBP), $5.7 billion to ICE, and $2.7 billion to Citizenship and Immigration Services (USCIS). ICE's budget of $5.7 billion means that unprecedented amounts of money are put into interior enforcement. ICE's budget alone is now larger than the entire budget of the INS. In 2002, the last full year of the existence of the INS, its budget was at an all-time high of $6.2 billion, up from $1.5 billion in 1993. Based on the dollar value of that year, this represented a growth of 223 percent.[7] In the early 1990s, less than 10 percent of the INS budget was dedicated to interior enforcement.[8] Now that the DHS has replaced the INS, 10 percent of the much larger DHS budget goes to interior enforcement. This budget is used for home and worksite raids as well as a variety of other enforcement operations.

Home Raids

ICE agents use home raids to go into private homes in search of suspected undocumented migrants or "criminal aliens." The agents typically conduct the raid in the following format. Early in the morning, when most occupants are sleeping, the agents surround a house and pound on the door and windows. If the occupant opens the door, the agents enter the home, frequently without properly identifying themselves or gaining the consent of the occupant. Once the agents enter the house, they order all the occupants—including children and the elderly—to a central location. Although the agents are often looking for a particular person who is suspected to be a fugitive or criminal alien, they frequently interrogate all occupants of the house and arrest anyone who they suspect is unlawfully present in the United States. Such an act is roughly equivalent to police agents entering a house where a suspected robber lives, finding the robber does not live there, yet arresting other people in the house, simply because they are suspected of having the same criminal tendencies. ICE refers to these literally "unwarranted" arrests of suspected undocumented migrants as *collateral arrests*. Because you cannot tell whether someone is undocumented simply by looking at them, many U.S. citizens and legally present people of Latin American origin have been arrested in these raids (Azmy, Farbenblum, Michelman, et al. 2008).

ICE home raids, over the past decade, have involved a series of violations both of people's constitutional rights and of ICE's own policies. According to a recent report, aptly titled "Constitution on ICE," ICE agents routinely fail to observe constitutional rights during home raids. The Fourth Amendment to the Constitution implicitly protects citizens and noncitizens from unreasonable searches and seizures. When ICE agents with an administrative warrant enter a person's home without consent, they are violating that person's constitutional rights, as well as ICE's own guidelines. Chiu et al. (2009) point out that ICE's Field Manual is clear in its stipulation that administrative warrants do not grant officers the authority to enter private homes without consent and that ICE agents are also not allowed to arrest people without probable cause. However, according to a vast amount of evidence—including eyewitness accounts of home raids, lawsuits, media reports, and ICE's own documentation—these rights are violated on a consistent basis.

Attorneys, from the Seton Hall School of Law, filed a civil rights action in which the plaintiffs claimed they were victims of unconstitutional practices in the course of several home raids. Some of the plaintiffs were U.S. citizens or lawful residents. They reported that ICE agents gained unlawful entry to their homes through deceit or force and detained the occupants of the home without a judicial warrant. One of the plaintiffs in this case, Maria Argueta, had valid Temporary Protection Status (TPS), which allowed her to remain lawfully in the United States. Maria reported that around 4:30 a.m. on January 29, 2008, ICE agents banged loudly on the doors and windows of her home. When she opened the door, they told her they were police agents (which is inaccurate) and that they were looking for a certain man who Maria did not know. Although she told them she did not know the man, and the officers did not have a search warrant, they proceeded to search her entire apartment. After not finding the man in question anywhere in her apartment, they asked Maria about her immigration status. She told them about her TPS and that she was waiting to receive her card in the mail. Despite producing a letter that indicated her card would arrive soon, the ICE agents seized her passport and arrested her. She was placed in detention where she remained for 36 hours before being released. In FY 2007, similar operations resulted in 2,079 arrests in New Jersey alone. Fewer than 15 percent of these arrestees had any criminal history, even though these raids are designed to find criminal fugitives (Azmy, Farbenblum, Michelman, et al. 2008).

Maria Argueta's home raid was part of the National Fugitive Operations Program (NFOP), an initiative led by ICE that has come under harsh criticism for its inefficacy. NFOP is intended to enhance national security by finding and deporting dangerous "fugitive aliens." A *fugitive alien*, as defined by the NFOP, is a noncitizen who has been ordered to be deported yet has not left the country. NFOP's budget has increased dramatically since its inception in 2003—from $9 million to $218 million in FY 2008. A recent report by the Migration Policy Institute criticizes the program, primarily because of its failure to arrest dangerous fugitives—"NFOP has failed to focus its resources on the priorities Congress intended when it authorized the program. In effect, NFOP has succeeded in apprehending the easiest targets, not the most dangerous fugitives" (Mendelson, Strom, and Wishnie 2009: 2). Although NFOP is designed to deport dangerous criminals, nearly three-quarters of the people they apprehended through February 2008 had no criminal records. In 2007, with a $183 million budget, NFOP arrested only 672 fugitive aliens that ICE considered to be dangerous. The other 30,000 arrested were people with deportation orders (15,646), undocumented migrants (12,084), or noncitizens who had been convicted of nonviolent crimes, such as shoplifting (2,005). Mendelson et al. of the Migration Policy Institute point out that "the number of fugitive aliens with criminal convictions arrested ... remained relatively constant between FY 2004 and FY 2008. Congressional allocations to NFOP, by contrast, grew 17-fold over the same period" (2009: 15).

NFOP has been given the money and the authority by Congress to search homes for dangerous criminal and fugitive aliens who threaten national security. However, in FY 2007, 40 percent of people arrested by these agents were ordinary undocumented migrants who were neither fugitive aliens nor convicted criminals. These noncitizen arrests occurred even though there was no warrant for their arrest, nor were they given a hearing before an immigration judge.

Such arrests happened because the executive branch has given ICE agents the authority to enforce immigration law, and they do not need a warrant to arrest noncitizens. Although it seems improbable that lawmakers in the United States Congress would approve legislation that permitted federal agents to roam the streets in search of immigration status violators because of the civil rights implications of such practices, this is, in effect, what NFOP has done (Mendelson, Strom, and Wishnie 2009).

Despite criticism from legal advocates and immigrant rights organizations, these practices continue. I learned firsthand the effects of these home raid practices when, in February 2010, I spoke with "Maximo," a Dominican citizen who lived in Puerto Rico. Maximo shared an apartment in San

Juan with two other men—a Venezuelan and a Puerto Rican. Early one morning in January 2010, they heard loud banging on the door. Maximo tried to sleep through it, but the banging got louder. Finally, he got up to answer the door. Just before he reached the door, the people knocking decided to break down the door. Maximo found himself surrounded by several officers, some of whom had jackets with *ICE* stamped on them. The agents did not indicate that they had a warrant for the arrest of a specific person. Instead, they demanded to see all occupants of the house, pointed guns at them, and ordered them to sit on the floor. Finally, they gave Maximo his clothes and allowed him to get dressed. When they asked him for identification, he gave them his Dominican passport. They asked if he was in the country illegally, and he said he was.

Once the search was over, Maximo was arrested and taken to an immigration detention center. He signed a voluntary departure form and was deported to Santo Domingo two days later. From Maximo's recounting of the story, it would seem his constitutional rights against search and seizure were violated. By law, immigration agents have administrative warrants that do not permit them to enter houses without the consent of the occupants. They definitely were not looking for Maximo, as he had never had previous encounters with immigration agents, and thus could not have had a deportation order. He just happened to be there and was arrested when he revealed that he was undocumented. Maximo's arrest is one of the many collateral arrests made by ICE agents during home raids. These sorts of arrests account for a substantial portion of arrests during home raids. Apart from reports by human rights advocates, these home raids have not received much national attention. In contrast, worksite raids or *worksite enforcement operations,* as ICE calls them, were something of a media spectacle between 2006 and 2008.

Worksite Raids

The stated goals of worksite enforcement operations are to ensure fair labor standards and eliminate the "job magnet": the existence of jobs that attract undocumented labor migrants to the United States. ICE has a goal or internally set quota of 18,000 arrests per year through these raids. Each year, Congress appropriates billions of dollars for worksite raids. In this type of raid, hundreds of ICE agents descend on a workplace and inspect the documents of the workers present to determine who should be taken into custody. This process often takes several hours, and normal operations of the workplace are stopped. These raids are intrusions to workflow. Those that are on a larger scale have immediate effects on the entire community. When word gets out that a raid is taking place, community members assemble outside of the plant or other site to find out if their loved ones are being apprehended or if they will be released. A general sense of panic and fear pervades the community, because many in the community are either undocumented or have family members or friends who are.

Once ICE officials have determined which of the workers they will take into custody, the workers are put onto buses and taken to an ICE processing facility. Some of these workers agree to be deported immediately without a hearing (voluntary departure), some are put into detention facilities, others are referred to federal or state authorities for criminal charges, and some are released on their own recognizance pending an immigration hearing. Those workers who are not immediately deported are eventually allowed to stay in the United States legally or are formally deported later, depending on the outcome of their immigration trial.

To shed light on this particular era of immigration law enforcement, it is useful to take a close look at four highly publicized raids—Greeley, Colorado; New Bedford, Massachusetts; Little Village, Chicago; and Postville, Iowa. The raid in Greeley, Colorado, in December 2006 marked the beginning of this era of ICE raids, and the raid in Postville, Iowa, marks the end. These are four of the largest raids in the history of immigration law enforcement. Although these raids represent less than 1 percent of all people deported during this time period, they received substantial media attention and came under harsh criticism for human rights violations; fortunately, these types of raids seem to have come to an end.

Greeley, Colorado—December 12, 2006

On a cold morning in December, workers at Swift Meatpacking Co. got up early and went to work as they did every morning, where they earned between $10 and $15 per hour for full-time work and had health and other benefits. At 7:25 a.m., shortly after everyone had begun to carry out their daily tasks, ICE agents surrounded the plant and sealed all the exits. When the heavily armed agents stormed into the plant, many of the workers were frightened; some even threw themselves into the cattle pens. All of the workers were led into the cafeteria and separated into two groups—those who claimed to have the proper documents to work and those who did not. Workers, both men and women, were frightened, and many were reduced to tears (Bacon 2007; Capps et al. 2007).

Word about the raid spread quickly to the community, and family and community members massed around the gates of the plant. Some people brought their family members' documents to the plant for them, while others shouted at the ICE agents not to take away their loved ones. Onlookers screamed that children were crying in school for their parents, that they were not terrorists, simply workers. Outside the factory gates, a priest led a vigil, as was particularly appropriate, because this was the day of the Virgin of Guadalupe.[9] Some high school students learned about the raids via their mobile phones and left school to come to the factory to find out what was happening to their parents (Capps et al. 2007).

ICE processing of the nearly 3,000 employees took about four hours. By 11:30 a.m., ICE agents had arrested 262 Swift employees. By noon, the ICE agents left the plant, with 262 people boarded onto buses to be taken into custody (Bacon 2007). As the buses rolled away, one young woman watching the bus leave wiped away her tears and asked who was going to care for her and her three-month old daughter. The woman said she did not want to go on welfare to support her family.[10]

The arrestees were given the option of signing voluntary departure orders. Of the 128 Mexican arrestees, 86 signed voluntary departure orders and were sent to Mexico within two days. The deportation of Mexicans is the easiest because of the country's proximity to the United States. Of those who did not sign voluntary departure orders, some were released on their own recognizance; some were released with bail; and others remained in ICE detention. Those who were released the quickest were people who were the sole caregivers for minors and those who had authorization to work but could not prove it at the time of the raid (Capps et al. 2007).

Lucia, from Guatemala, was among those detained. She was taken to Texas and then to New Mexico, where she was in jail for more than a month. During that time, she worried a great deal about her minor son, who was left alone. After being released on bond, Lucia was concerned that she would be deported to Guatemala, where she did not expect to be able to find work to support herself and her son.[11]

ICE had warrants to search the plant for people charged with identity theft. A lengthy investigation had shown that twenty-five people were using other people's social security numbers. ICE obtained the warrants to look for those people. In the course of the raid, ICE agents arrested eighteen people who they suspected of identity theft and fraud. Later, eleven of those people were charged, and seven had their charges dismissed (Bacon 2007). Although the raid took the workers by surprise, the owners of Swift had been informed by ICE that such an operation was imminent. Swift tried to prevent the raid, citing its potential losses (Dyer 2006).The raid on the Swift plant greatly affected the workers' children and families as well. Many workers who were deported or detained were the sole breadwinners for families. For many families, this meant not only sparse pickings on Christmas day, but also not having money to meet their basic needs for months to come. Helen Somersall, of Catholic Charities in Greeley, reported having helped 109 households with basic needs. In these households were more than 250 children, many of whom were U.S. citizens (Capps et al. 2007).[12] With the primary breadwinner gone, many of these families were not sure where their next meal would come from. The children began to eat less, especially because they could not have the foods to which they were accustomed. In addition, many of these families faced severe emotional distress, especially in those families where the sole caregiver of children was not able to return immediately. Family members and friends stepped in to care for children when parents did not return from work after the raid; some children remained in these situations for several months. The raids created an atmosphere of fear in Greeley, even among kids whose parents were not arrested (Capps et al. 2007).

In sum, ICE officials obtained warrants to arrest 25 people and thus were able to conduct this raid on Swift Meatpacking Co. In the course of this operation, they verified the documentation of more than 3,000 workers and arrested 262 people. As a result, they were able to deport 132 people, and 11 faced criminal charges. In addition, this raid had substantial economic and emotional impacts on Greeley.

According to a recent report, there have been upwards of eight million cases of identity theft in the United States since 2005.[13] Another report indicates that there were seven million undocumented workers in the United States in 2006 (Passel 2006). Thus, this operation surely was not intended to put a dent in either identity theft or in the use of undocumented labor. It was meant to serve as a deterrent to both of these activities. The cost, however, has been borne by many more than those who are the targets of ICE strategies. The affected include the family members of the workers, the twenty-eight hundred workers who were in the plant at the time of the raid, community workers and leaders, and immigrants and families across the country who live more fearfully every day as a result of these scare tactics.

New Bedford, Massachusetts—Tuesday, March 6, 2007

Just before dawn on Tuesday, March 6, 2007, 300 heavily armed ICE agents stormed into Michael Bianco, Inc., a leather factory, demanding to see the work documents of all 500 employees. All the machines were turned off. Panicking, people began to run and hide. ICE agents ran after people, shouting at them to sit down. The agents then proceeded to handcuff the workers (Bacon 2007). Reports indicate that some employees became ill and vomited. Others testified that they were mistreated and abused both at the factory and later during detention.[14]

After screening each of the employees, the agents determined that 361 of them were to be placed in ICE custody. These 361 workers were handcuffed and taken to Fort Devens, in Ayer, Massachusetts for processing around 3pm. The following day, sixty of these workers were released for humanitarian reasons; ninety were sent to a detention center in Harlingen, Texas, thousands of miles away. On March 8, another 116 workers were flown to a detention center in El Paso, Texas. Over the next few days, 31 more workers were released from Texas for humanitarian reasons, primarily because they are the sole caregivers of children.[15]

As a result of this raid, many children spent at least one night without their parents. Since many of the children were in the same childcare setting, family and community members took charge of those children whose parents did not come to pick them up.[16] At least one mother was not able to convince ICE that she had a toddler, and thus was not released until late at night. About twenty other parents were flown to Texas and waited several days before they could be reunited with their children (Capps et al. 2007). Among these was Marta Escoto, the mother of two young children. Both Daniel, 2, and Jessie, 4, were born in the United States and were in day care when their mother was arrested. Jessie suffers from a debilitating illness and cannot walk. Marta's sister, Andrea, heard of the raid, and was able to care for Marta's children in her absence. On Wednesday, March 14, over a week after the raid, Marta was released pending her trial and was flown back to Massachusetts to care for her children.[17]

Another woman who is a sole caregiver reported that ICE agents in the factory and in the detention center in Massachusetts would not listen to her when she insisted that she had a daughter and that she was the sole caregiver. Upon being sent to Texas with the other detainees, she was able to explain that she has a six-year old daughter who was ill and had to be taken to the doctor the next week. On her second day in Texas, she was permitted to contact her babysitter, who did not know what had become of the mother. Her daughter was worried about her mother's whereabouts and told her mother she was going to kill herself if she didn't come home. On Monday, the woman was released.

This woman reported that she had experienced minor mistreatment but was particularly disturbed by the treatment of the breastfeeding mothers. She reported that women who said that they were breastfeeding had to prove it by showing the milk secretions. She said that the guards made fun of the women when the milk was excreted, by laughing and asking other guards to bring out the Oreo cookies.[18] At least one of the breastfeeding mothers' babies was hospitalized as a result of dehydration. Her eight-month old child could not be convinced to take a bottle in her absence and was taken the hospital to be treated for dehydration.[19]

Mistreatment in immigrant detention facilities is known to be widespread, as detailed in the next section. Detainees from the New Bedford raids reported abusive treatment. Some detainees testified that they were given dirty clothes and were not given proper medical attention.[20] Others claimed that they were treated badly by the prison guards in El Paso. One woman reports that the guards threw bags of food at them when it was time to eat.[21] The stress of the detention has had long-term effects, especially for those people who had to wear ankle bracelets when released, which further enhances their status as criminals. It also causes financial stress, as many detainees had to borrow several thousands of dollars to pay bail.[22]

Two months after the raid in New Bedford, 42 of the workers had been deported, 181 had been released pending their immigration hearings, and 137 remained in detention.[23] One year after the raid, only one worker remained in detention, and 165 of the detainees had been deported.[24] The remaining workers had been released pending their trials. Hector Mendez, for example, spent three months in prison before he was released upon borrowing $10,000 to post bail. When released, Mendez saw his wife and three children for the first time in three months.[25] Immigration attorneys expect that many of those awaiting trial will be granted stays of deportation, because they have unearthed stories of rapes and killings that occurred in the civil wars in Guatemala and El Salvador. Women who experienced sexual violence during these conflicts may be eligible for refugee status under the Violence Against Women Act (VAWA). Ten arrestees have been allowed to stay in the United States thus far under these and other provisions in immigration law.[26]

Little Village, Chicago—April 24, 2007

Shortly before 2 p.m., hundreds of heavily armed federal agents, dressed in bulletproof vests, descended on the Little Village Discount Mall in a predominantly Mexican neighborhood in Chicago. On most weekday afternoons, this mall is frequented by mothers of small children, the elderly, and others who live in the vicinity and are in need of any of the wide variety of things sold here—from quinceañera gowns to cowboy boots, and from roast chicken to *pan dulce*. On April 24, 2007, agents from ICE, the FBI, and the Secret Service closed off all the exits to the mall and proceeded to search for suspects in a fraudulent ID ring that allegedly was being run out of the mall. All the shoppers and workers had to show their IDs to prove they were not the suspects. Once that was established, they were allowed to leave the mall. Those who did not have IDs were detained and questioned.

Women in the health clinic with small children reported that armed federal agents stormed in, yelling at people and terrifying everyone—especially the children. Others testified that agents stormed into bathrooms and instilled fear in the shoppers and workers. A beauty salon owner reported that innocent people were placed in handcuffs. Word got out quickly about the raid, and community members and activists soon showed up. Over two hundred people staged a protest in front of the mall that lasted until around 11:00 p.m.[27]

Community members came out to the mall to protest what many perceived to be an attack on the Mexican community in Chicago. ICE officials threw men, women, and children on the ground and pushed others onto fences. The use of force and the large weaponry instilled fear in people in the mall, in those who were looking on, and even in those who heard about the event later. At a one-year anniversary of the raid, one speaker said that she would never forget the day that the *migra* intimidated her community.[28]

At the time of the raid, not even the local police were aware of why the raid was taking place. At a press conference the next day, however, Patrick Fitzgerald, from the Chicago U.S. attorney's office, announced that the raid was designed to arrest an identity-theft ring that operated in this mall. For many years, a crime ring sold fake driver's licenses and "green cards" to people who needed them. Undocumented people require proof of legal status for most jobs and thus rely on places such as these to secure fake "green cards" to work.

In conjunction with the raid at the mall, ICE agents raided two other houses that were connected with the making of the false identifications. On April 24, they were able to arrest twelve people; the other ten people named in the investigation remained at large. Elissa Brown, from ICE, insisted that similar measures would have been taken, were this illegal activity to have been taking place on State Street, in downtown Chicago, but many Latino leaders and activists in Chicago found this implausible and decried ICE's actions as a direct attack on the Latino community in Chicago.

The purpose of this raid was not to find undocumented workers, but to arrest the perpetrators in an international crime ring. ICE had the names of the suspects and had been studying the organization for years. Their main targets were the leaders of the ring. Nevertheless, ICE chose the strategy of closing off the entire mall, using heavy weaponry, and instilling fear in the hearts of the shoppers at the mall, many of whom were young children. ICE reports describe the raid as an operation directed at one photo shop in the mall—Nuevo Foto Muñoz—that was suspected of producing false identification documents.[29]

The raid in Little Village was not designed to reduce the pull of the "job magnet," but to find people who produce false identification documents. This operation was successful at finding many of the ringleaders of this particular crime ring, both in the United States and in Mexico. Nevertheless, as argued in a recent *Newsweek* article, the availability of false documentation in Chicago or other cities around the nation has not declined.[30] Furthermore, judging from the widespread community protests in the wake of the raid, the raid was interpreted by many locals as an attack on their community.

Postville, Iowa: Monday, May 12, 2008

In December 2006, federal agents began to plan a worksite enforcement operation in Postville, Iowa, a town with 2,273 inhabitants, 968 of whom worked at the Agriprocessors slaughterhouse. On Monday, May 12, 2008, the federal plan became a reality and 900 agents descended on Postville, armed with warrants for nearly 700 workers. This worksite raid led to a humanitarian and economic disaster for the town and for much of the region. The raid led to the closing of Agriprocessors, Inc., a kosher meat processing plant, which had a ripple effect throughout the region for its suppliers and within Postville for local stores that sold products to its former employees (Camayd-Freixas 2008; Grey, Devlin, and Goldsmith 2009).

The ICE raid in Postville, Iowa, was an enormous undertaking that involved the cooperation of several federal and local agencies. It was the largest raid that ICE had carried out, in the largest meatpacking plant in Northeastern Iowa. In all, 389 immigrant workers were arrested at the Agriprocessors plant on a Monday in the middle of May. The following day, Tuesday, half of the school system's 600 students were absent because their parents were in hiding or had been arrested (Hsu 2008).

Around 10 a.m. on Monday morning, dozens of helicopters, buses, and vans began to encircle the western edge of town. Within ten minutes, hundreds of agents surrounded the plant (Hsu 2008). One Postville worker reported that agents entered the plant with their guns drawn, shouting, "Don't run, because we are going to chase you like rats!" The armed agents called the workers donkeys and other names.[31] Within a couple of hours, 313 male suspects were taken to the National Cattle Congress grounds in Waterloo, Iowa, for processing. The 76 female suspects were taken to local jails. 290 of the arrestees were Guatemalan. The remaining included 93 Mexicans, 2 Israelis, and 4 Ukranians (Hsu 2008).

What differentiates this raid from previous ICE raids is the decision of ICE officials to work with the DOJ to pursue criminal charges against nearly all the detainees. In previous raids, ICE charged most of the workers with administrative violations, and the workers were placed in deportation proceedings. In Postville, nearly all the workers were charged with aggravated identity theft and placed in criminal proceedings. These charges were not because the workers had done things any differently in Postville than in the other sites of the worksite raids, but because ICE decided to pursue a new strategy. This new strategy, however, came under great scrutiny. The scrutiny and negative attention caused ICE to decide not to continue this tactic of criminally charging undocumented workers, at least for the time being.

The decision to pursue criminal charges was made well in advance of the raid at Postville. Through a lengthy investigation, ICE officials learned that the majority of workers at the Agriprocessors plant did not have the right to work legally in the United States and had used fraudulent documents to gain employment at the plant. Thus, ICE was able to obtain a criminal search warrant for evidence related to identity theft and fraudulent use of social security numbers, and a civil search warrant to arrest people illegally present in the United States (U.S. House of Representatives 2008c).

On the day of the raid, 83 of the employees were arrested for immigration violations, and 306 were detained on criminal charges (U.S. House of Representatives 2008c). After placing the employees under arrest, ICE transported them to a fairground in Waterloo, about two hours away from Postville. As mandated by law, ICE had only 72 hours to press charges against all 306 people. To avoid having to release detainees, ICE created a new system called *fast-tracking*. In this system, ICE offered the same plea agreement to all the detainees and told them they had to accept or reject it fully. The plea agreement offered to drop the charge of aggravated identity theft and for the detainees to serve only five months of the six-month sentence of Social Security fraud. In exchange, the detainee would agree to be deported from the United States. Because of the short time period and the complicated nature of immigration law, many of the detainees and their criminal defense lawyers were unaware that "accepting a plea for a felony involving fraud has immense immigration consequences, most notably that the detainee can never become a U.S. citizen" (Peterson 2009: 334).

In all, there were 18 defense attorneys for the 306 defendants. Most of the 306 workers faced charges of aggravated identity theft because the social security numbers they had been using belonged to someone else. Aggravated identity theft carries a two-year prison sentence. The workers were offered a plea bargain where they could plead guilty to a lesser charge, not have a jury trial, and spend five months in jail. Subsequent to serving their sentences, they would be deported. They were given seven days to make a decision (U.S. House of Representatives 2008c).

After consulting with their attorneys, 233 defendants pled guilty to the use of false identification to obtain employment, 30 pled guilty to false use of a social security number, and 8 pled guilty for illegal reentry to the United States. These 271 defendants were sentenced to five months in prison and three years of supervised release. Two other defendants were sentenced to twelve months in prison for using false identification to obtain employment. Twenty-seven defendants were sentenced to five years of probation for using social security numbers that did not actually belong to any one, or for illegal reentry (U.S. House of Representatives 2008c).

The way this raid was handled led to a public outcry, and eventually a Congressional hearing. Lawyers, human rights activists, immigrant rights activists, and others decried the way that the criminal cases were handled. These claims of injustice result from the government officials' treatment of the slaughterhouse workers. Government bureaucrats in Washington, DC, decided, before the raid began, that the workers would be charged with aggravated identity theft. This federal offense (U.S. 18: I: 47 § 1028) involves knowingly using a false identification with the intent to commit an unlawful act. The undocumented workers were given the option to plea to a lesser charge—using a false social security number—which carries a sentence of 0 to 6 months. Prosecutors offered the workers five months in jail in exchange for the plea—hardly a bargain (Peterson 2009).

Erik Camayd-Freixas, a federally certified interpreter who was present for much of the criminal proceedings, contends that these court proceedings constituted a tremendous travesty of justice. His reasons are compelling.[32] Camayd-Freixas argues that, because most of the workers did not know what a social security number actually was, and because obtaining work is not unlawful activity, it is extraordinarily unlikely that a grand jury would find probable cause of identity theft. "But with the promise of faster deportation, their ignorance of the legal system, and the limited opportunity to consult with counsel before arraignment, all the workers, without exception, were led to waive their 5th Amendment right to grand jury indictment on felony charges" (Camayd-Freixas 2008: 15).

In the aftermath of the raid, allegations surfaced that an Agriprocessors supervisor had charged plant employees $220 for work authorization, which turned out to include a fake "green card." Legal scholar Peterson argues that, "ICE's fast-tracking model cut off the need to determine whether the detainees knowingly used the identification of another person in the Postville cases, because almost all of the detainees accepted the plea agreement" (2009: 341).

On May 4, 2009, nearly a year after the raid, the U.S. Supreme Court decided that defendants must know that a social security number belongs to another person to be charged with identity theft.[33] The Court argued that the distinction between using an invalid social security number and one that belonged to an actual person was meaningless, and that the charge of identity theft does not apply to workers using false social security numbers. However, this decision came too late for the majority of the Postville arrestees, who had long since served their sentences and been deported (Chaudry et al. 2010).

This raid provides a prime example of how the current enforcement regime threatens the balance of powers—a pillar of our democracy. Executive branch officials—primarily from DHS and the DOJ—were the main decision-makers in this case. They decided beforehand to use an "inflated charge" to have more "bargaining leverage" (Camayd-Freixas 2008: 14). The fast-tracking system not only left the defendants with little choice but to plead guilty, it also took away the decision-making authority from the judge. The inflated charge "reduced the judges to mere bureaucrats ... [with] absolutely no discretion or decision-making power. ... When the executive branch forces the hand of the judiciary, the result is abuse of power and arbitrariness, unworthy of a democracy founded upon the constitutional principles of checks and balances" (Camayd-Freixas 2008: 14).

The defendants in this trial were not fully accorded the rights we normally ensure criminal defendants—adequate access to legal counsel, the presumption of innocence, and judicial review. The workers' inadequate access to legal counsel was exacerbated by their complete lack of access to immigration counsel. David Wolfe Leopold of the American Immigration Lawyers Association, who testified at the same hearing as Camayd-Freixas, argued that the criminal defense attorneys were not aware of the immigration consequences of the guilty pleas they advised their clients to accept (U.S. House of Representatives 2008a).

Some of the workers may have been eligible for legalization. For example, if the workers had a U.S.-citizen spouse or child, they may have been eligible for legalization under immigration laws that take family ties into account. If the workers had been in the United States for more than ten years, they may have been eligible for a cancellation of their deportation order on the basis of the needs of a U.S.-citizen family member. Finally, the workers may have been eligible for asylum, based on humanitarian concerns in their countries of origin. The workers were not able to pursue any of these options because pleading guilty to a crime of fraud rendered all the workers ineligible for any of these paths to legalization. The lack of immigration counsel combined with the speed with which they had to make decisions left the defendants without the opportunity to benefit from any of the provisions in immigration law (U.S. House of Representatives 2008a).

The Social Costs of Worksite Raids

The raid in Greeley, Colorado, marked a new era for DHS in general, and ICE in particular—one in which large-scale raids would become a major part of their public identity. The raid in New Bedford attracted even more attention largely because of its proximity to Boston, a city with a vocal progressive population. Activists in Boston were able to use their access to multimedia equipment and the Internet to make public the abuses detainees endured and the inhumane nature of the raid. The raid in Little Village was in the heart of the Latino community of a major city and thus struck a chord with people who may have thought that raids were restricted to rural meatpacking factories. The Postville operation seems to have been the apex of ICE's inventive tactics. The huge outcry with regard to the criminalization of migrants and the Congressional hearing on raids appears to have convinced ICE officials not to pursue criminal prosecution of undocumented workers. In raids since the Postville operation, ICE agents have not brought in the DOJ to prosecute workers.

The intensification of efforts to deport, detain, and terrify immigrants in the United States has not led to a mass exodus of undocumented immigrants. These large scale raids have, however, had the effect of drawing media attention and making it seem as though the government is doing what it can to crack down on undocumented migration. The cost of these raids is the devastation of communities, the tearing apart of families, and the promotion of a culture of fear and terror. The intensification of raids in recent years means that undocumented migrants experience a growing sense of fear of detention and deportation. Millions of U.S.-citizen spouses, children, and siblings of undocumented immigrants have to worry each day about the possibility that their loved ones and their breadwinners will be taken away from them (Pew Hispanic Center 2007).

This change of strategy to focus on interior enforcement has been done in the name of national security. These massive budget increases have been possible because the DHS presents its needs in the context of national security. Although there are no clear connections between protecting the nation from terrorism and removing workers from meatpacking plants, ICE has capitalized on fears of terrorism to request funding for workplace raids. In turn, these raids serve as media spectacles that make it seem as though ICE is doing its part to protect the nation.

The raid in Postville provides a case in point. ICE had warrants for nearly 700 people. They arrested fewer than 400. No efforts were made in the aftermath of the raid to find the remaining 300 people. ICE had the option of turning over those warrants to the local police department, but they did not.

Had ICE perceived those undocumented migrants to be a threat to society, it seems reasonable that they would pursue the remaining 300 migrants, or at least allow the local police to do so. However, they did not (Peterson 2009). One could interpret their failure to follow up with the remaining warrants as an indication that the Postville raid was primarily a spectacle—meant to send a message, and not intended to "protect the nation from dangerous people."

Subsequent to the Postville raid in May 2008, ICE seems to have scaled back its worksite enforcement operations. As of this writing in March 2011, there have been no major worksite raids since the arrest of 28 workers in Bellingham, Washington in February 2009. The public outcry in the aftermath of the Postville and the other raids seems to have led ICE to pursue other strategies in recent years. Immigrant detention, in contrast, shows no signs of abating.

Immigrant Detention

People arrested during immigration raids often are placed in immigrant detention facilities. Noncitizens can also be placed in these facilities after being arrested by ICE agents, encountered by Border Patrol agents, or released from incarceration by state or local jails and prisons. The arrival of thousands of Cubans and Haitians in the early 1980s led to a surge in immigrant detention, reversing the policy enacted in 1954 to detain only migrants who were clearly dangerous (Dow 2004). Ellis Island, renowned as a dismal penitentiary for arriving migrants, was closed in 1954 when the INS announced that it would no longer detain migrants who were not clearly dangerous. The U.S. Attorney General, Herbert Brownell, Jr., declared on November 12, 1954:

> In all but a few cases, those aliens whose admissibility or deportation is under study will no longer be detained. Only those deemed likely to abscond or those whose freedom of movement could be adverse to the national security or the public safety will be detained. All others will be released on conditional parole or bond or supervision, with reasonable restrictions to insure their availability when their presence is required by the Immigration and Naturalization Service (*New York Times*, 11/12/1954: Page 14).

Over the next three decades, relatively few immigrants were detained. However, racism infused the immigration debates from the beginning of the twentieth century to its end. In 1980, 125,000 Cubans and 15,000 Haitians arrived by sea to Miami. The Cubans were the infamous "Marielitos," poorer and darker than their compatriots who had arrived in the 1950s and 1960s. The Haitians, who were even darker and poorer, were not made to feel welcome by the local or federal governments. In response to the arrival on the shores of South Florida of a tide of brown and black migrants, the INS reversed its policy of thirty years of nondetention (Dow 2004). On July 1, 1981, the attorney general insisted in a

Congressional hearing that migrants should be detained as they wait for their exclusion hearings. The following day, the INS announced its new detention policy, which mandated the detention of most Haitians and some Cubans—mainly those found to have had criminal records in Cuba. The decision to detain Haitian asylees was taken primarily to deter more Haitians from attempting to come to the United States to request asylum. Prior to 1981, Cubans and Haitians usually were paroled into the community and were given a date to come back to have their asylum cases heard. The mass detention of Haitians in prisons and camps caused some public outcry, yet the policy of detaining asylees has remained in place ever since. These changes in INS detention practices marked a new era in INS policy—that of a consistently expanding jail complex (Stewart 1986; Dow 2004).

Over the past thirty years, ICE has gone from a policy of presuming that non-citizens do not present a threat to society to a policy of assuming they do present a threat, and only releasing migrants who can prove otherwise. This has translated into a dramatic surge in the number of detainees. The first notable increase came with mass Cuban and Haitian immigration in the early 1980s. The second, more substantial, increase occurred after the passage of the Illegal Immigration Reform and Immigrant Responsibility Act of 1996 (IIRIRA) (Dow 2004; Welch 2002). This law required the detention of legal permanent residents convicted of an array of crimes and expanded the grounds on which asylum seekers were to be detained (Morawetz 2000). The third dramatic surge came with the creation of the DHS in 2003. The infusion of money into DHS has allowed it to enforce immigration laws more aggressively and to house more detainees. In 1973, the INS detained a daily average of 2,370 migrants. By 1980, this had gone up to 4,062. By 1994, the daily average was 5,532; it was about 20,000 in 2001; and, in 2008, ICE detained an average of 33,400 migrants a day (Dow 2004: 8–9; Immigration and Customs Enforcement 2008b; Kerwin and Lin 2009).

Some of the migrants detained by ICE are detained at ICE facilities, others at private prisons, and still others at county and state jails. People detained by ICE include asylum seekers, long-term permanent residents, and undocumented migrants (United Nations Human Rights Council 2008). More than two-thirds of ICE detainees are in county or local jails.[34] The time that immigrants spend in detention has also increased dramatically, from an average of four days in 1981 to an average of 54 days by 1994 (Welch 2002: 107). ICE reports indicate that the average time in detention had gone down to 37.6 days in 2007, due to an increase in expedited removals. However, snapshot data from January 25, 2009, reveal that of the 32,000 people in ICE custody on that day, the noncriminal detainees had been detained for an average of 65 days, as compared to 121 days on average for detainees with criminal convictions.[35] Lengthy stays in detention are particularly pernicious for people with medical issues. These issues often go unattended, primarily because detention is designed for short-term stays. Detention centers are not equipped with the necessary medical facilities (Seattle University School of Law 2008).

Francisco Castañeda was thirty-five years old when he entered ICE custody in March 2006, after spending four months in prison on a drug charge. He had come to the United States from El Salvador when he was ten years old. At the time of his detention, he had a fourteen-year-old U.S.-citizen daughter. While he was detained, Castañeda complained to ICE officials of painful lesions on his penis. He was sent to specialists, each of whom determined that he needed a biopsy to tell whether he had penile cancer. The U.S. Public Health Service and the Division of Immigration Health Services, however, denied him the biopsy, on the grounds that it was an elective procedure. Despite excessive bleeding, he was given only ibuprofen for pain. After suffering in custody for eleven months, he was released and went to the hospital. In February 2007, he was diagnosed with penile cancer and had nearly his entire penis removed. Although he received chemotherapy upon his release, Mr. Castañeda passed away on February 16, 2008, leaving his daughter fatherless (Patel and Jawetz 2007).[36] This is one example, albeit extreme, of the systematic denial of health care to immigrant detainees. I have chosen it for its impact, but many lesser examples of health care denial to immigrant detainees occur every day and contribute to not only health problems for the detainees and their families, but also added costs and administrative challenges to the enforcement agencies.

The United States detained mostly southern and eastern Europeans in the late nineteenth and early twentieth centuries. Today, most detainees hail from Latin America and the Caribbean. As of January 2007, the countries that were most represented in ICE detention facilities were Mexico, El Salvador, Guatemala, Honduras, the Dominican Republic, and Haiti.[37] In a 2009 report, researchers found that 37 percent of detainees were from Mexico, 28 percent from Central America, 7 percent from the Caribbean, and 6 percent from South America—accounting for 78 percent of all 177 countries from which detainees come (Kerwin and Lin 2009). Although many migrants come from Europe and Asia, these migrants are much less likely to end up in detention facilities. One reason for this is a change in laws in 2004 that allows immigration inspectors to detain any undocumented migrant apprehended within 14 days of entry and 100 miles of the border. Because Latin Americans are more likely to enter across the southern border, they are more likely to be detained under these provisions (Seattle University School of Law 2008). Another reason for the preponderance of Latin Americans in detention centers is related to racial profiling of noncitizens (Aldana 2008). Although Asians account for 25 percent of undocumented migrants, they are less likely to be targets of immigration enforcement actions, likely for reasons detailed above where ICE agents have substantial discretionary power in arrests.

Detention Practices Today

Immigrant detention centers in the United States have come under severe criticism from human rights organizations, nongovernmental organizations (NGOs), the United Nations, and the inspector general. Some of the major concerns are the prevalence of physical and verbal abuse of detainees, inadequate medical care, insufficient food, lack of phone and library access, lack of access to religious counsel, overcrowding, and inadequate access to legal counsel. Many of these problems are compounded by the fact that some detainees remain in detention for several months.

In the United States, people charged with a criminal offense have the right to legal counsel, regardless of their ability to pay for it. People in immigrant detention facilities, however, do not have this right to legal counsel, as they face immigration charges, not criminal charges. Individuals who face immigration charges may obtain legal counsel, but the government doesn't provide it. Immigrant detention centers are holding cells for noncitizens awaiting trial or deportation. Because they have not been charged with a crime, they do not have the legal right to access to legal counsel. Many detainees, however, would benefit greatly from access to immigration lawyers who may be able to prevent them from being deported or allow them to be released from detention. Most detainees are unable to afford legal counsel. Those who are able to afford a lawyer or who are lucky enough to find a lawyer who will work *pro bono* often have difficulties being represented. In a recent report by the Seattle University School of Law (2008), researchers pointed to several barriers to legal counsel. First, there was inadequate access to private meeting rooms. Second, staff at the facility opened confidential legal correspondence sent to detainees. Third, lawyers often had to wait for hours to see detainees. Finally, detainees could be transferred without notice at any time. All of these factors present obstacles to providing detainees with effective legal counsel.

This lack of access to legal counsel results in people being deported who may have a good case for remaining in the United States. The deplorable conditions in these facilities combined with the lack of access to counsel may lead detainees who are eligible for asylum based on mistreatment in their country of origin, or permanent residence based on family ties in the United States, to agree to be deported. Faced with a choice between spending several months or years in a detention facility and agreeing to be deported, many migrants choose this latter option, even if they have a good case for remaining in the United States. The issues surrounding the process of deportation will be addressed more fully in the next chapter.

A 2006 Office of the Inspector General (OIG) study confirmed many of the complaints activists have been making for years with regard to detention facilities. According to the OIG's December 2006 report, the five facilities visited were out of compliance with ICE detention standards. For example, these standards mandate that detainees be given a physical exam within 14 days of their arrival. At the Corrections Corporation of America (CCA) San Diego facility, 11 of the 19 detainees they audited had not undergone this required physical exam. In addition, at three of the five detention centers they visited, 196 of 481 medical requests were not responded to in the required time frame (OIG 2006). These oversights have had grave consequences in recent years, including the death of 66 detainees between 2004 and 2007 (Bernstein 2008). A report released in July 2009 by the National Immigration Law Center and the ACLU, titled "A Broken System: Confidential Reports Reveal Failures in U.S. Immigrant Detention Centers," indicates that ICE has not improved the facilities in response to these complaints (Tumlin, Linton, and Natarajan 2009).

The lack of sufficient medical attention is corroborated by reports of immigrant advocates. For example, one detainee reported it took two months from the time he broke his nose at a detention facility for him to be taken to the local hospital. In another case, a woman from Liberia was detained at a CCA facility in Arizona from November 2005 to April 2006; although she complained of physical pain on several occasions to the staff at the facility, she was not taken to the hospital for several months, although the facility's records show that she likely required medical attention. When she was finally taken, the hospital doctors determined that she had a cyst the size of a five-month-old fetus and required immediate surgery. ICE then released her from detention on medical parole to avoid having to pay for the surgery (Patel and Jawetz 2007).

A report issued on March 29, 2010 revealed that mentally ill residents of the United States are often detained and deported. People who have been declared mentally incompetent to stand criminal trial in the United States have been processed by immigration judges and ordered deported. For example, a fifty-year-old legal permanent resident who had lived in the United States since 1974 was declared incompetent by a New York criminal court and ordered to serve ninety days in a mental institution. Before the order was implemented, he was transferred to an immigration detention facility, where he was not given proper medical treatment. This legal permanent resident was able to gain release and avoid deportation because of the active intervention of his mother and his criminal defense lawyer—but not without the stress of being detained and denied proper medication—which could have been devastating for someone such as him with severe schizophrenia (Texas Appleseed 2010).

In addition to these extreme abuses, detainees often live in unsanitary conditions with inadequate food and cleaning services. At the Hudson County Correction Center (HCCC) in Kearny, New Jersey, the OIG report found that clothes are washed only once or twice a week, and socks and undergarments are not exchanged on a daily basis. The report further found that at Berks County Prison (BCP) in Leesport, Pennsylvania, detainees are given only one uniform and must sit around in their undergarments for two to six hours when they send their uniform in for washing (Office of Inspector General 2006). In addition, detainees were not given sufficient outdoor recreation time; they were generally allowed outside only three days a week (Office of Inspector General 2006).

ICE has detention standards that mandate the way detention centers should be operated. However, a 2009 report by the National Immigration Law Center, based on a system-wide analysis of ICE's compliance with its own standards, reveals "substantial and pervasive violations of the government's minimum standards for conditions at immigration detention facilities" (Tumlin, Linton, and Natarajan 2009: 7). For example, the report cites a United Nations Human Rights Council (UNHCR) study that found that one facility had neither indoor nor outdoor recreation programs for detainees, even though ICE regulations mandate that detainees be provided with at least one hour of recreation each day, and that efforts be made to ensure that recreational activities be held outdoors. When ICE has reviewed its own facilities, it does not always hold them to their own standards. For example, ICE reviewers rated facilities with no outdoor programs as acceptable for the recreation standard (Tumlin, Linton, and Natarajan 2009).

ICE's violation of its own policies sometimes has deadly consequences, as seen in the case of Yusif Osman, who never received the mandatory entrance medical exam. Osman is one of eighty-three immigrant detainees who died in or soon after their detention between 2002 and 2007, thirty-two of whom were younger than forty (Priest and Goldstein 2008: A01). Yusif Osman, a native of Ghana and a legal permanent resident of the United States, was detained by immigration authorities for crossing the border with a conational who used a false identification card. Osman had gone to Mexico for a visit. On the way back, he gave a ride to another Ghanaian. Osman's passenger was using a fake identification to enter the United States, and Osman was arrested for transporting an undocumented person across the border. Upon entering into ICE custody in March 2006, Osman was not given the requisite entrance medical exam. As a result, it was not noted that he had a heart problem that required treatment. When he collapsed on the floor of his cell three months after being taken into custody, it took the staff nearly an hour to get to him. By that time, it was too late for thirty-four-year-old Osman, who died because his heart suddenly stopped. *The Washington Post* reports that his death likely could have been avoided with "timely treatment, perhaps as basic as an aspirin."

Children and Families in Detention

The abysmal conditions in which migrant detainees are held become even more abhorrent when we consider that many detainees are children. Migrant children who are asylum seekers, undocumented, or charged with crimes are held in juvenile facilities, shelters, adult jails and prisons, and newer family detention centers. In 1998, Human Rights Watch conducted an investigation of the Berks County Youth Detention Center, where many minor immigrant detainees were held.[38] At this facility, migrant children are detained in both a secure-detention facility, where children who have been charged with crimes are held, and in a shelter care facility where children who are in the custody of child welfare authorities are held. In the secure detention facility, migrant detainees comingle with children convicted of serious crimes. The Human Rights Watch report indicates that those children in the shelter care facility had few complaints, except for issues related to language barriers. In contrast, those children in the secure detention facility were much less satisfied with their conditions. Spanish and Chinese speaking juveniles, for example, reported that they were punished for speaking in their own languages, and disciplinary measures, such as doing pushups, for these perceived violations were frequent.[39]

According to this report, very few children had adequate legal counsel, since the government does not pay for attorneys for immigration cases. However, since the law does not permit local immigration judges to hear cases from children without a lawyer or a family member present, many children's cases were simply not heard, thus prolonging their detention. This situation is exacerbated both by the relative isolation of the facility and the transfers of children to other facilities without notification.[40]

The Human Rights Watch report also found that some children were detained unnecessarily. For example, a child from China was detained for one year at the Berks facility despite the fact that her uncle had agreed to take custody of her. She told the researchers that she cried every day that she was in secure detention. Also, four Pakistani children were held in secure detention for three months, although they each had relatives in New York with guardianship papers.[41]

The most notorious family detention center is the T. Don Hutto Center in Texas, a former prison operated by CCA. Hutto has come under the scrutiny of a number of journalists and human rights agencies, despite the fact that no reporters have been admitted to Hutto since a single-day group media tour in February 2007. Even Jorge Bustamante, the U.N. Special Rapporteur on the Human Rights of Migrants, was denied the opportunity to visit Hutto during his visit to the United States. Bustamante was scheduled to tour the facility in May 2007, as part of a fact-finding mission on migrants in the United States. However, just days before his scheduled visit, DHS announced that he would not be granted access, due to the fact that "Hutto was subject to 'pending litigation'" (Gupta and Graybill 2008: 27).

At Hutto, families were detained together but often slept in separate cells. Only very young children were allowed to sleep with their mothers, and fathers slept in separate quarters. In addition, children were not allowed to have stuffed animals, crayons, pencils, or pens in their cells. Moreover, if children woke up during the night upset or ill, only staff members could attend to them; their parents were not allowed to go to their rooms at night, nor were children allowed to leave their rooms (Talbot 2008).

Many detainees housed at the T. Don Hutto Center complained that they did not have adequate food. Families were given twenty to twenty-five minutes to eat. However, this included the time that they had to get their food and sit down. Thus, a pregnant woman with two children said that she often was hungry because she did not have enough time both to eat for herself and to feed her two young children. This was compounded by the fact that she was not allowed to take food out of the cafeteria to eat later. She also complained that only children were given milk; thus, despite her doctor's order to drink milk, she was unable to do so. This same woman shared a twin bed with her two children, as they had only a bunk bed and were scared to sleep alone.[42] According to an investigation carried out at Hutto by the Women's Commission for Refugee Women and Children and Lutheran Immigration and Refugee Service, women and children were often denied sufficient and appropriate medical attention. They found that detainees' complaints were ignored, that the pulling out of teeth was the only dental treatment available, and that potentially serious medical cases were ignored.

At the Hutto facility, children and adults were allowed one hour of recreation each day. This is the only time that children had access to age-appropriate toys, as they were not allowed to have toys in their rooms. One can imagine that small children grew anxious in these circumstances. When children misbehaved, the staff often threatened them with separation from their parents. The same report indicates that, at Hutto,

> staff members encourage parents to keep their children quiet and get children to behave by telling children and their parents that if the child does not do what they are told to do by staff they will be taken away. Nelly, a 9-year-old girl

detained with her 3-year-old sister and her mother, who is applying for asylum, told us that if she misbehaved she would be separated from her mother.... All those we interviewed expressed frustration that children are punished for what is normal behavior for young children like running around, making noise, and climbing on the couches.

This disciplinarian approach is particularly disconcerting when we consider that families, especially asylum seekers, are often detained for several months. For these and other reasons, Michelle Brame, the author of the "Locking Up Family Values" report, recommends that the family detention facilities be closed and alternatives to detention be used in place of this. Alternatives to detention include placing migrants on house arrest and using ankle bracelets to keep track of migrants awaiting immigration trials. In response to complaints by immigration advocates and media attention to the T. Don Hutto Facility, in 2009, ICE decided to stop detaining families in the facility. In September 2009, they released the last family from Hutto and began the process of transforming the facility into a detention center for female detainees.[43]

Indefinite Detention

In early 2009, there were 4,154 people in ICE detention who had been detained for six months or longer. There were 1,312 who had been in ICE detention for more than one year (Kerwin and Lin 2009). Some of these detainees were fighting their cases; others were awaiting removal; still others had been ordered deported, but there was no country to which they could return. People in this latter group are referred to as *indefinite detainees*. Some of these people have been convicted of crimes in the United States and have served their sentences. Others have not been charged or convicted of crimes, such as asylum seekers who have not been granted refugee status. One example is Salim Y., a twenty-six-year-old Palestinian. He stowed away on a ship bound for the United States and sought asylum once he arrived. An immigration judge denied his petition for asylum in 2001. He was then placed in detention while awaiting deportation. Since Salim was born in Gaza and lived most of his life in a refugee camp in Libya, there is no country to which he can be deported—Israel does not recognize Palestinians born in Gaza as their citizens.[44] Salim Y. languished in detention for four years until a judge finally ruled that he was to be released, because there was no country to which he could be deported and because indefinite detention is not permitted under U.S. laws. In a more recent case, an entire Palestinian family was detained in Texas, because there was no country to which they could be returned. The family included Salaheddin Ibrahim, his pregnant wife, Hanan, and four of their five children.[45]

Farouk Abdel-Muhti spent two years in ICE detention, without ever being charged with a crime. Farouk was born in Palestine, and thus, like Salim Y., could not be deported. He was arrested for being undocumented and spent two gruesome years in county jails and immigrant detention centers prior to being released. Abdel-Muhti died of a heart attack two months after his release in 2004. He was fifty-seven years old when he died while giving a speech at the Ethical Society in Philadelphia. His early death was likely related to the lack of medical attention and poor conditions during his two-year stay in detention (Fernandes 2006).

People cannot be deported to countries with which the United States has no official diplomatic ties. These countries include Cambodia, Cuba, Iran, Iraq, Laos, Vietnam, former satellites of the Soviet Union, and Gaza. In a Supreme Court decision in 2001, *Zadvydas v. Davis,* the Supreme Court mandated that immigrants who had been legally admitted to the United States could not be subjected to indefinite detention when their deportation was not foreseeable.

This case revolved around the situation of Kestutis Zadvydas, who had been born in a displaced persons camp in Germany in 1948 to parents believed to be Lithuanian. He came to the United States when he was eight years old with his parents and other family members and subsequently became a legal permanent resident. After being convicted of possession with intent to distribute cocaine and serving his sentence in prison, Zadvydas was ordered deported. However, Germany would not accept him because he was not a citizen, and Lithuania refused because he was unable to establish citizenship there. The INS also tried, to no avail, to deport him to his wife's country of origin, the Dominican Republic. Based on this case, the Supreme Court decided that detainees must be conditionally released if there is no significant likelihood that they will be deported in the foreseeable future. It is noteworthy that Mr. Zadvydas was chosen as the test case for indefinite detention, because the majority of the indefinite detainees were Cubans, and few were European. Perhaps the attorneys thought the judge would be more sympathetic to a white defendant.

The *Zadvydas v. Davis* (2001) case applied only to migrants who had been lawfully admitted to the United States.[46] This outcome did not bode well for those Cubans who came to the United States in 1980 and 1981 on the so-called "Mariel Boatlift." These Cubans had not been formally admitted into the United States. Instead, they were only paroled into the United States. This meant that, in legal terms, they were not considered to have been formally admitted, and therefore, the Zadvydas case did not apply to them. As a consequence, many Mariel Cubans spent decades in prison for relatively minor offenses. Omar Rodriguez, for example, spent two years in prison in Texas for possessing two ounces of marijuana. He was released in 1984, but found himself in jail soon after, again for possession of marijuana. The second time, he was sentenced to four months in prison, and, upon his release from prison, he was taken into INS custody. In 2004, twenty years after completing his sentence, he remained in INS detention (Dow 2004). In May 2004, the Tenth Circuit U.S. Court of Appeals heard the case of Guillermo Borges-Brindis, another Cuban who arrived in 1980 on the Mariel boatlift. In his first five years in the United States, Borges-Brindis was convicted of unlawfully possessing a weapon, assault and battery, selling a controlled substance, and first degree manslaughter. He was sentenced to prison, where he served time until 1991. Upon his release, the INS took him into custody and ordered him deported. Although he was still in custody thirteen years after having completed his sentence, the Court of Appeals found that he did not merit release, and denied his appeal.[47]

In 2005, indefinite detention came to the attention of the Supreme Court again. This time the Supreme Court decided in the *Clark v. Martinez* case that the provisions of Zadvydas should extend to all migrants in the United States. As a result of this decision, migrants can be detained indefinitely only if they pose an immediate threat to national security or to the safety of the community or any person.[48] Despite these Supreme Court rulings, some detainees continue to serve indefinite sentences for two reasons. Either a judge determines that they continue to be a threat to society, or they are lost in bureaucratic proceedings and do not have the opportunity to see a judge.

Attorneys from the Catholic Legal Immigration Network (CLINIC) conducted a study between March 2004 and September 2005 and found that there were still about twelve hundred indefinite detainees. And, in 2007, the ACLU and the Special Rapporteur Jorge Bustamante found that migrants continued to be found in indefinite detention. According to the CLINIC report, many migrants remain in detention because they are not given the mandatory local reviews every ninety days. And, if they have the ninety-day review but are not released, most detainees have to resort to filing suit to have their cases heard again, even though they are entitled to a review every ninety days.[49]

When the OIG of the Department of Homeland Security conducted its own investigation in 2007, it found that 20 percent of detainees were not released or reviewed within the mandatory ninety days. The OIG reviewed a selective sample of 210 files and found that 14 had not received the mandatory ninety-day review, and 3 had not received a review after 180 days. Overall, of the 8,6ninety noncitizens with final deportation orders in March 2006, 1,725 were still in detention in June 2006, and 428 remained in detention as of February 2007. Many of these people were from countries that did not cooperate with U.S. officials. For example, of the 246 people from China who were ordered deported, only 90 were deported within ninety days; 120 were deported within 180 days, and 32 remained in detention after 360 days. In the case of China, the detainees are not released because DHS determines these detainees will eventually be deported. Although the process can be lengthy for Chinese immigrants, the United States has diplomatic ties with China, and the deportations can be processed. In contrast, because the United States has no diplomatic ties with Cuba, Laos, Cambodia, or Vietnam, most noncitizens from these countries are released because DHS recognizes that they cannot actually be deported. Nevertheless, in 2007, eight Vietnamese and two Cubans were not released after one year, and between 10 and 25 percent of the detainees from these countries remained in detention for more than the maximum allotted time of ninety days.[50]

Asylum Seekers

Asylum seekers, essentially, are people who flee persecution in their home country and seek protection in other countries. The right to seek and enjoy asylum is enshrined in Article 14 of the Universal Declaration of Human Rights (UDHR). In the United States, asylum-seekers must prove that they have a well-founded fear that, if returned to their home country, they will be persecuted based on their race, religion, nationality, membership in a particular social group, or political opinion. Noncitizens may apply for asylum at the port of entry, after arriving in the United States, or when they are facing deportation. In 2003, about a third of all asylum-seekers were granted asylum, with the remaining cases denied (Congressional Research Services 2005). There is quite a bit of contention around the issue of asylum-seeking. Immigration rights activists argue that asylum-seekers often have to leave their country quickly and thus are unable to produce evidence of their persecution. Detractors point out that asylum-seekers may be economic refugees or, in the worst case, potential terrorists.

Under the 1996 laws, applicants for asylum must convince the receiving border inspector that they have a credible fear of persecution. Otherwise, they face expedited deportation. This process has been criticized by refugee advocates, because border inspectors are not fully trained for the interview process. If refugees pass the credible fear of persecution test conducted by the border inspector, they are usually placed in detention while their applications are being processed. Some are detained for a few days, yet others are detained for years while awaiting trial. The UDHR states that "the right to seek and enjoy asylum is a basic human right; individuals must never be punished for seeking asylum." The DHS, however, maintains that detention is not punishment; it is a security measure to ensure that people report to their trial. In 2002, 9,260 of the 9,749 people who were found to have a credible fear of persecution were detained by the INS. Their average stay in detention was 43.5 days (Frelick 2005).

In many cases, after being detained for days, months, or years, an immigration judge determines that the asylum-seeker has a well-founded fear of persecution and is granted asylum. The fact that many petitioners are eventually granted asylum causes critics to question why asylum seekers are treated like criminals and housed in prison facilities, often along with people who have been convicted of crimes. Applicants for asylum face mandatory detention, often after having committed no crime.

Orbelina Brisuela and her son Fredy, age eleven, came to the United States to apply for asylum. A trained asylum officer found that they had a credible fear of persecution. They were ordered to be detained while they awaited their hearing. Despite the acknowledgement that they likely had experienced persecution, they faced further indignities at the hands of immigration agents. When they arrived at the detention facility, T. Don Hutto, a guard, interrogated them from 10 p.m. to 5 a.m. And Fredy was issued "torn, stained, and yellowed clothing and underwear upon his arrival" (ACLU 2007).

Many people who face persecution are denied asylum by border inspectors. In one case, a twenty-eight-year-old woman came to the United States from Albania, after having been gang-raped by armed gunmen. She feared facing such violence again and was stigmatized in her conservative community for having been raped. Her brother-in-law obtained a false passport for her, and she fled to the United States. The INS officials realized her passport was fake and ordered her deported when she arrived. She tried to apply for asylum but was reluctant to reveal all the details of having been gang-raped to the border inspector; therefore, she did not pass the credible fear test. Her case came to the attention of refugee rights' lawyers, and she successfully appealed her case. She was eventually allowed to return to the United States and was granted asylum (from Welch 2002: 88–89; source: ACLU).

For some asylum seekers, detention can be deadly. An elderly Haitian minister, Joseph Dantica, had been to the United States many times during his long life. In 2004, Dantica planned a trip to the United States to see his dying brother. He had his tourist visa and ticket ready and was awaiting the day of his departure. At the last minute, he was forced to flee from the church he had preached in for more than three decades. During that time in Haiti, UN troops and Haitian police were involved in an operation to root out local gangs. Dantica allowed United Nations troops to enter his church. Really, he had no choice, because they entered the premises with machine guns. However, when the UN troops shot local gang members from Dantica's premises, the gang leaders vowed that Dantica would pay for this (Danticat 2007).

Dantica found himself fleeing from his town, disguised as a woman so that the gang members would not recognize him. After several days of hiding out, the day of his departure finally came and Joseph Dantica and his son Maxo boarded a plane for Miami, where his niece lived (Danticat 2007). When Dantica arrived at the Miami airport, instead of showing his valid tourist visa, he told the CBP agent that he would like to apply for temporary asylum, because he feared for his life in Haiti. It is likely that he knew he would be staying longer than the 30 days his visa allowed and did not want to misrepresent himself to the agent (Danticat 2007). Unfortunately, Dantica's request for asylum meant that he was placed in detention at Miami's infamous Krome detention center (Fernandes 2006).

At Krome, the staff took Dantica's medicine and gave him replacements. On his second day there, Dantica began to experience stomach pains and complained to the officials. They initially dismissed his claims and denied his requests to see his family in Miami. The ninety-one-year-old Joseph Dantica began to have a seizure. Vomit shot out of his mouth and his eyes rolled back into his head. Dantica's lawyer was present and requested a humanitarian parole so that he could be taken to a hospital and be with his family. The medic from Krome responded that he thought that Dantica was faking. He nevertheless allowed Dantica to be taken to the hospital, in shackles (Danticat 2007).

Twenty-four hours after arriving in the emergency room, Joseph Dantica was seen by a physician. At 8:46 p.m., he was pronounced dead. His family's pleas to see him at Krome and at the hospital were denied, and Dantica died alone, five days after having arrived in the United States. The autopsy report showed that he "died from acute and chronic pancreatitis, ... for which he was never screened, tested, diagnosed, or treated while he was at Jackson Memorial Hospital" (Danticat 2007: 247).

Since September 11, 2001, asylum seekers are increasingly likely to be placed in detention. Asylum seekers are detained if they are unable to prove that they have community ties. Many are detained despite having such ties, as was Joseph Dantica, who had a niece in Miami. With the beginning of the war with Iraq, DHS initiated a program called Operation Liberty Shield, which requires mandatory detention for asylum seekers from thirty-three countries where Al Qaeda has been known to operate (Welch and Schuster 2005: 336). Although the DHS maintains that detention is not punishment, most detainees find it difficult to believe that being shackled, locked up, and treated without dignity is anything but punishment. As Dantica's case shows, detention can be an unforgettable punishment, for the detainees and their loved ones.

Protecting the Nation?

The high human cost of the surge in interior enforcement renders it necessary to consider the benefits of the enforcement regime. Why has this strategy been implemented? Looking through DHS documents for an explanation of why we have seen an increase in interior enforcement, the most frequently cited explanation is national security—the core of the DHS mission. The first priority of the DHS is to protect the nation from dangerous people. In Secretary Michael Chertoff's statement in support of the 2009 budget request, he stated:

> We will continue to protect our nation from dangerous people by strengthening our border security efforts and continuing our efforts to gain effective control of our borders. The Department's main priority is to prevent additional terrorist attacks against our country.

In this introductory statement, Secretary Chertoff confounds border security with terrorist prevention. He continues to do this in the statement. When he lists DHS's key accomplishments, the first accomplishment is "More Fencing at the Border." He lauds the fact that, by the end of 2008, U.S. CBP will have erected 670 miles of fencing along the border.

As Chertoff continues to praise DHS's accomplishments in terms of protecting the nation, he cites their "Record-Breaking Law Enforcement." He points out that ICE removed about 240,000 "illegal aliens, made 863 criminal arrests, and fined or seized more than $30 million following worksite investigations." In this statement, Chertoff is celebrating the fact that arrests in worksite enforcement operations increased ninefold between 2003 and 2008. Chertoff makes a direct connection between raids and national security. He cites the arrest and removal of 4,077 undocumented workers in worksite enforcement operations under the goal of protecting the nation from dangerous people.

There is no evidence to suggest that the undocumented workers removed from meatpacking plants are dangerous people. Moreover, the fact that most were removed on administrative and not criminal grounds is clear evidence that they had no criminal records. The vast resources that ICE has poured into these worksite enforcement operations has been possible due to the unwarranted conflation of national security with the removal of undocumented migrants. The same could be said for mandatory detention, especially the detention of asylum seekers.

Asylum seekers have to undergo lengthy investigations into their past. The in-depth nature of the probe into their lives makes asylum requests a highly unlikely route for potential terrorists to enter the country. The detention of children and families is also highly questionable as a strategy to protect the nation from dangerous people. Overall, it does not seem to be the case that the increase in interior enforcement of immigration laws is making the United States a safer place. It is clear, however, that these actions are causing harm to immigrants, their families, and their communities.

It may be the case that DHS officials are well aware that home and worksite raids are not making the United States a safer place, yet they use this rhetoric strategically to request budgetary allocations from Congress. Members of Congress may also be aware of the ineffectiveness of these strategies in terms of fighting terrorism but are unwilling to vote against anything that promotes fighting terrorism. Perhaps this is the best we can expect from bureaucrats and lawmakers in the current context of the war on terror. In that case, it is up to the citizenry to insist on the implementation of measures that actually enhance national security, not that simply claim to do so. It is also up to the citizenry to speak up against these sorts of policies that do little to make the country safer but do worlds of harm to communities and families.

To gain a full picture of the effects of the current enforcement regime, it's important to look at another aspect of interior enforcement—the rise in deportations, particularly the deportation of long-term residents of the United States. The stories and data in the next chapter shed further light on the dire human consequences that are the result of the existing enforcement regime.

Notes

1. "U.S. Urged to Apologize for 1930s Deportations." April 5, 2006. *USA TODAY*. Wendy Koch. http://www.usatoday.com/news/nation/2006-04-04-1930s-deportees-cover_x.htm. Accessed January 21, 2009.

2. Office of Immigration Statistics, Department of Homeland Security, Table 38. "Aliens Removed by Criminal Status and Region and Country of Nationality: Fiscal Years 2000 to 2009."

3. Evans, Becky. 2008. "In a Remote Guatemalan Village, Links to New Bedford Abound." *South Coast Today*. March 5. http://www.southcoasttoday.com/apps/pbcs.dll/article?AID=/20080306/NEWS/803060348/-1/special21. Accessed July 15, 2009.

4. Fieldnotes, April 24, 2008. Our Lady of Tepeyac Social Club. Chicago, Illinois.

5. "Worksite Enforcement Overview." April 30, 2009. Immigration and Customs Enforcement. http://www.ice.gov/pi/news/factsheets/worksite.htm. Accessed July15, 2009.

6. "Homeland Security: Budget in Brief. Fiscal Year 2005." Department of Homeland Security. http://www.dhs.gov/xlibrary/assets/FY_2005_BIB_4.pdf. Accessed July 15, 2009.

7. "Immigration and Naturalization Service Budget 1975–2003." Department of Justice. http://www.usdoj.gov/archive/jmd/1975_2002/2002/html/page104-108.htm. Accessed July 15, 2009.

8. "Immigration Enforcement Spending Since IRCA." 2005. Migration Policy Institute. http://www.migrationpolicy.org/ITFIAF/FactSheet_Spending.pdf. Accessed July 15, 2009.

9. "A Day to Remember." Shadowblogger YouTube Video. 2006. http://www.youtube.com/watch?v=QvRh-hAQorPw. Accessed July 15, 2009.

10. Ibid.

11. "Swift Justice" 2007. LittleVoiceProd. http://www.youtube.com/watch?v=YXztFiLq148. Accessed July 15, 2009.

12. "Ice Raids—One Year Later: Interview with Helen Somersall of Catholic Charities Northern." December 12, 2007. Chris Casey. *The Tribune.* http://www.greeleytrib.com/article/20071212/NEWS/112120110. Accessed July 15, 2009.

13. "Federal Trade Commission 2006 ID Theft Report." 2007. Synovate. http://www.ftc.gov/os/2007/11/SynovateFinalReportIDTheft2006.pdf. Accessed July 15, 2009.

14. "Testimony of Women Detained by ICE." NewBedfordRelief. 2007. YouTube video. http://www.youtube.com/watch?v=qADLyZctfok&feature=related. Accessed July 15, 2009.

15. "Immigration Matters: The Anatomy of an Immigration Raid." New America Media, News Analysis, Mary Holper, Posted: May 21, 2007. http://news.newamericamedia.org/news/view_article.html?article_id=f9a8d584602ed96b1602b 54ce054a550. Accessed July 15, 2009.

16. "New Bedford." NewBedfordRelief. 2007. YouTube video. http://www.youtube.com/watch?v=a-8ke8gd60g. Accessed July 15, 2009.

17. "Immigration Raid Rips Families: Illegal Workers in Massachusetts Separated from Children." Robin Shulman, Washington Post Staff Writer. March 18, 2007; Page A06. http://www.washingtonpost.com/wp-dyn/content/article/2007/03/17/AR2007031701113.html. Accessed July 15, 2009.

18. "New Bedford Detainee Testimony." NewBedfordRelief. 2007. YouTube video. http://www.youtube.com/watch?v=2qG6FZbr9rM&feature=related. Accessed July 15, 2009.

19. "New Bedford." NewBedfordRelief. 2007. YouTube video. http://www.youtube.com/watch?v=a-8ke8gd60g. Accessed July 15, 2009.

20. "Timeline of the New Bedford Raid." 2007. *The Boston Globe.* http://www.boston.com/news/local/articles/2007/03/15/timeline_of_the_new_bedford_raid/. Accessed July 15, 2009.

21. "New Bedford Detainee Testimony." NewBefordRelief. 2007. YouTube video. http://www.youtube.com/watch?v=2qG6FZbr9rM&feature=related. Accessed July 15, 2009.

22. "Testimony of Woman Detained by ICE" NewBedfordRelief 2007. YouTube video. http://www.youtube.com/watch?v=qADLyZctfok Accessed 15 July 2009.

23. "Fight to Free Bianco Workers Dominates Mayan Ceremony." Becky Evans. Standard-Times staff writer. October 01, 2007. http://www.southcoasttoday.com/apps/pbcs.dll/article? AID=/20071001/NEWS/710010333. Accessed July 15, 2009.

24. "A Year After Raid, Immigration Cases Drag On for Many." Maria Sacchetti. *Boston Globe.* March 6, 2008. http://www.boston.com/news/local/articles/2008/03/06/a_year_after_raid_immigration_cases_drag_on_for_many/. Accessed July 15, 2009.

25. "Illegal Immigrant Father Reunited with Family." Becky Evans. *Standard-Times,* June 06, 2007. http://www.southcoasttoday.com/apps/pbcs.dll/article?AID=/20070606/NEWS/706060363. Accessed July 15, 2009.

26. "A Year After Raid, Immigration Cases Drag On for Many." Maria Sacchetti. *Boston Globe.* March 6, 2008. http://www.boston.com/news/local/articles/2008/03/06/a_year_after_raid_immigration_cases_drag_on_for_many/. Accessed July 16, 2009.

27. "ICE Raids Chicago Neighborhood—Again." World War IV Report. September 20, 2008. http://www.ww4report.com/node/6052. Accessed July 16, 2009.

28. Fieldnotes. April 24, 2008. Our Lady of Tepeyac Social Club. Chicago, Illinois.

29. "Operator of a Chicago 'Little Village' Photo Shop—Nuevo Foto Muñoz—Charged with Participating in Fraudulent Identification Document Conspiracy." U.S. ICE May 30, 2007. http://www.ice.gov/pi/news/newsreleases/articles/070530chicago.htm. Accessed March 3, 2010.

30. "ID Bust: A Woman's Terror Fears Have Taken Down One of the Largest Fake Document Rings in the U.S." Joe Contreras. *Newsweek.* February 29, 2008. http://www.newsweek.com/id/117121. Accessed July 16, 2009.

31. "Guatemalan Natives Talk About Postville Immigration Raid." GazetteOnline May 14, 2008. http://www.youtube.com/watch?v=b1IUTdU9IF8. Accessed July 16, 2009.

32. Although Camayd-Freixas is an interpreter and not a lawyer or a social scientist, his recounting is unique and important insofar as he had privileged access to the proceedings. Others, such as anthropologist Mark Grey and public health professor Michele Devlin, recount that they were not able to gain access to the Waterloo Cattle Congress, and thus also have to rely on Camayd-Freixas's account of the proceedings.

33. Flores-Figueroa v. United States. Certiorari to the United States Court of Appeals for the Eighth Circuit No. 08–108. Argued February 25, 2009—Decided May 4, 2009. http://www.supremecourtus.gov/opinions/08pdf/08-108.pdf. Accessed March 11, 2010.

34. "About the U.S. Detention and Deportation System." http://www.detentionwatchnetwork.org/aboutdetention. Accessed March 23, 2009.

35. "Alien Detention Standards: Telephone Access Problems Were Pervasive at Detention Facilities; Other Deficiencies Did Not Show a Pattern of Noncompliance." GAO. June 6, 2007. http://www.gao.gov/htext/d07875.html Accessed 16 July 2009 and "Immigrant Detention: Can ICE Meet Its Legal Imperative and Case Management Responsibilities?" Donald Kerwin and Serena Yi-Ying Lin. September 2009. Migration Policy Institute. http://www.migrationpolicy.org/pubs/detentionreportSept1009.pdf. Accessed March 2010.

36. October 4, 2007. Francisco Castaneda's testimony before Congress. http://www.aclu.org/images/asset_upload_file841_32062.pdf and United States District Court Central District of California Francisco

Castaneda, Plaintiff, Case No. CV 07-07241 DDP (JCx) Amended Order Denying Motion to Dismiss. http://www.cacd.uscourts.gov/CACD/RecentPubOp.nsf/bb61c530eab0911c882567cf005ac6f9/6d9b8d3d3142d7be8825740b0053dbdc/$FILE/CV07-07241DDP.pdf. Accessed July 15, 2009.

37. Ibid.

38. "Detained and Deprived of Rights: Children in the Custody of the U.S. Immigration and Naturalization Service." Human Rights Watch. 1998. http://www.hrw.org/reports98/ins2/. Accessed July 16, 2009.

39. Ibid.

40. Ibid.

41. Ibid.

42. "Locking Up Family Values: The Detention of Immigrant Families." 2007. Women's Commission for Refugee Women and Children and Lutheran Immigration and Refugee Service. http://www.womenscommission.org/pdf/famdeten.pdf. Accessed July 16, 2009.

43. "ICE Detention Reform: Principles and Next Steps: Secretary Napolitano Announces New Immigration Detention Reform Initiatives." DHS. October 9, 2009. http://www.docstoc.com/docs/12873022/ICE-detention-reform. Accessed March 11, 2010.

44. "Urge Release of Palestinian Salim Y." CLINIC. July 12, 2004. http://www.lifeorliberty.org/action_alerts/urge_release_of_palestinian_sa.html. Accessed July 17, 2009.

45. "Systemic Problems Persist in U.S. Ice Custody Reviews for "Indefinite" Detainees." 2005. Kathleen Glynn and Sarah Bronstein. CLINIC. http://idc.rfbf.com.au/wp-content/uploads/2009/06/clinicindefinitereport-final.pdf. Accessed July 17, 2009; "Palestinian Children Living in Detention: Family in U.S. Illegally Can't Stay, Can't Go Home." January 31, 2007. Paul Meyer and Frank Trejo. *The Dallas Morning News.* http://www.dallasnews.com/sharedcontent/dws/news/localnews/stories/020107 dnmetpalfamily.3b835587.html. Accessed August 25, 2009.

46. Zadvydas v. Davis. http://supct.law.cornell.edu/supct/html/99-7791.ZO.html.

47. *Borjes-Brindis v. Gunja and Ashcroft.* U.S. Tenth Circuit Court of Appeals. May 26, 2004. http://ca10.washburnlaw.edu/cases/2004/05/03-1447.htm.

48. "§ 1226a. Mandatory detention of suspected terrorists; habeas corpus; judicial review." http://www.law.cornell.edu/uscode/8/usc_sec_08_00001226---a000-.html. Accessed May 11, 2011.

49. "Systemic Problems Persist in U.S. Ice Custody Reviews for "Indefinite" Detainees." 2005. Kathleen Glynn and Sarah Bronstein. CLINIC. http://idc.rfbf.com.au/wp-content/uploads/2009/06/clinicindefinitere-portfinal.pdf. Accessed July 17, 2009.

50. "ICE's Compliance with Detention Limits for Aliens with a Final Order of Removal from the United States." Office of Inspector General. OIG-07-28. 2007. http://www.dhs.gov/xoig/assets/mgmtrpts/OIG_07-28_Feb07.pdf. Accessed July 17, 2009.

Bibliography

ACLU. 2007. "Family Profiles in the ACLU's Challenge to the Hutto Detention Center." 3.6.07. http://www.aclu.org/immigrants-rights/family-profiles-aclus-challenge-hutto-detention-center. Accessed October 18, 2010.

Aldana, Raquel. "Of Katz and 'Aliens': Privacy Expectations and the Immigration Raids." *UC Davis Law Review* 41 (2008): 1081–1136.

Andreas, Peter. *Border Games: Policing the U.S.-Mexico Divide.* Ithaca: Cornell University Press, 2000.

Azmy, Baher, Bassina Farbenblum, Scott Michelman, R. Scott Thompson, Scott L. Walker, and Heather C. Bishop 2008. First Amended Complaint in Argueta et al. vs Meyers et al. http://law.shu.edu/ProgramsCenters/PublicIntGovServ/CSJ/upload/amended_complaint.pdf. Accessed October 18, 2010.

Bacon, David. "The Real Political Purpose of the ICE Raids." *New America Media.* March 30, 2007. http://news.newamericamedia.org/news/view_article.html?article_id=e5a3be40ba1f338650f2c0f793d11c3d. Accessed October 10, 2008.

Balderrama, Francisco, and Raymond Rodríguez. *Decade of Betrayal: Mexican Repatriation in the 1930s (Second Edition).* Albuquerque, NM: University of New Mexico Press, 2006.

Bernstein, Nina. "Few Details on Immigrants Who Died in Custody." *New York Times.* May 5, 2008. http://www.nytimes.com/2008/05/05/nyregion/05detain.html. Accessed October 28, 2010.

Camayd-Freixas, Erik. 2008. "Statement of Dr. Erik Camayd-Freixas, Federally Certified Interpreter at the US District Court for the Northern District of Iowa Regarding a Hearing on 'The Arrest, Prosecution, and Conviction of 297 Undocumented Workers in Postville, Iowa from May 12 to 22, 2008' before the Subcommittee on Immigration, Citizenship, Refugees, Border Security, and International Law." July 24, 2008.

Capps, Randy, Rosa Maria Castañeda, Ajay Chaudry, and Robert Santos. "Paying the Price: The Impact of Immigration Raids on America's Children." Report for the Urban Institute for the National Council of La Raza. 2007. http://www.urban.org/UploadedPDF/411566_immigration_raids.pdf. Accessed December 2, 2008.

Chaudry, Ajay, Randy Capps, Juan Manuel Pedroza, Rosa Maria Castañeda, Robert Santos, and Molly M. Scott. "Facing Our Future: Children in the Aftermath of Immigration Enforcement." Report for the Urban Institute. April 7, 2010. http://carnegie.org/fileadmin/Media/Publications/facing_our_future.pdf. Accessed October 28, 2010.

Chiu, Bess, Lynly Egyes, Peter L. Markowitz, and Jaya Vasandani. 2009. Constitution on ICE: A Report on Immigration Home Raid Operations Cardozo Immigration Justice Clinic. http://www.cardozo.yu.edu/uploadedFiles/Cardozo/Profiles/immigrationlaw-741/IJC_ICE-Home-Raid-Report%20Updated.pdf. Accessed November 11, 2010.

Congressional Research Services. "U.S. Immigration Policy on Asylum Seekers." Updated May 5, 2005. Ruth Ellen Wasem. http://www.fas.org/sgp/crs/misc/RL32621.pdf. Accessed April 2, 2011.

Danticat, Edwidge. *Brother, I'm Dying.* New York: Alfred A. Knopf, 2007.

Dow, Mark. *American Gulag.* Berkeley: University of California Press, 2004.

Dunn, Timothy. "Border Militarization via Drug and Immigration Enforcement: Human Rights Implications." *Social Justice* 28, no. 2 (2001): 7–30.

Dyer, Joel. "Meatpacking Industry Has a Long History of Reliance on Immigrant Labor." *The Fort Collins Weekly,* 2006. http://www.greeleytribune.com/article/20061226/NEWS/112230087. Accessed April 6, 2010.

Evans, Becky. "In a Remote Guatemalan Village, Links to New Bedford Abound." *South Coast Today,* Bedford, Massachusetts. March 5, 2008. http://www.southcoasttoday.com/apps/pbcs.dll/article?AID=/20080306/NEWS/803060348/-1/special21. Accessed July 11, 2008.

Fernandes, Deepa. *Targeted: Homeland Security and the Business of Immigration.* New York: Seven Stories Press, 2006.

Frelick, Bill. "US Detention of Asylum Seekers and Human Rights." *Migration Policy Institute.* March, 2005. http://www.migrationinformation.org/Feature/display.cfm?ID=296. Accessed April 6, 2010.

Grey, Mark, Michele Devlin, and Aaron Goldsmith. *Postville U.S.A.: Surviving Diversity in Small Town America.* Boston: Gemmamedia, 2009.

Gupta, Vanita, and Lisa Graybill. "Justice Denied: Immigrant Families Detained at Hutto" in *Human Rights Begins at Home* ed. ACLU 23–28. 2008. http://www.udhr60.org/justice_denied.pdf. Accessed April 6, 2010.

Hsu, Spencer. "Immigration Raid Jars a Small Town: Critics Say Employers Should Be Targeted." *Washington Post Sunday.* May 18, 2008. http://www.washingtonpost.com/wp-dyn/content/article/2008/05/17/AR2008051702474.html. Accessed April 6, 2010.

Immigration and Customs Enforcement 2008b. "ICE Fiscal Year 2007 Annual Report." http://www.ice.gov/doclib/about/ice07ar_final.pdf. Accessed July 11, 2008.

Johnson, Kevin. *The 'Huddled Masses' Myth: Immigration and Civil Rights.* Philadelphia: Temple University Press, 2004.

Kerwin, Donald, and Serena Yi-Ying Lin. "Immigrant Detention: Can ICE Meet Its Legal Imperatives and Case Management Responsibilities?" Migration Policy Institute. 2009. http://www.migrationpolicy.org/pubs/detentionreportSept1009.pdf. Accessed November 12, 2010.

Mendelson, Margot, Shayna Strom, and Michael Wishnie. 2009. "Collateral Damage: An Examination of ICE's Fugitive Operations Program." Migration Policy Institute. http://www.migrationpolicy.org/pubs/NFOP_Feb09.pdf. Accessed April 6, 2010.

Morawetz, Nancy. "Understanding the Impact of the 1996 Deportation Laws and the Limited Scope of Proposed Reforms." *Harvard Law Review* 113, 8 (2000): 1936–1962.

Office of Inspector General, Department of Homeland Security. "Treatment of Immigration Detainees at Immigration and Customs Enforcement Facilities." December 2006. http://www.dhs.gov/xoig/assets/mgmtrpts/OIG_07-01_Dec06.pdf. Accessed November 12, 2010.

Passel, Jeffrey. "The Size and Characteristics of the Unauthorized Migrant Population in the US Estimates Based on the March 2005 Current Population Survey." Pew Hispanic Center. 2006. http://pewhispanic.org/files/execsum/61.pdf. Accessed October 10, 2008.

Patel, Sunita, and Tom Jawetz. 2007. "Conditions of Confinement in Immigration Detention Facilities." Briefing Materials. http://www.aclu.org/pdfs/prison/unsr_briefing_materials.pdf. Accessed October 10, 2008.

Peterson, Cassie L. "An Iowa Immigration Raid Leads to Unprecedented Criminal Consequences: Why ICE Should Rethink the Postville Model." *Iowa Law Review* 95, no. 1 (2009): 323–346.

Pew Hispanic Center. "2007 National Survey of Latinos: As Illegal Immigration Issue Heats Up, Hispanics Feel a Chill." Washington, DC, December 2007. http://pewhispanic.org/reports/report.php?ReportID=84. Accessed April 1, 2011.

Priest, Dana, and Amy Goldstein. "System of Neglect: As Tighter Immigration Policies Strain Federal Agencies, The Detainees in Their Care Often Pay a Heavy Cost." *Washington Post.* Page A1; May 11, 2008. http://www.washingtonpost.com/wp-srv/nation/specials/immigration/cwc_d1p1.html. Accessed April 2, 2011.

Sacchetti, Maria. "A Year After Raid, Immigration Cases Drag On for Many." *Boston Globe.* March 6, 2008. http://www.boston.com/news/local/articles/2008/03/06/a_year_after_raid_immigration_cases_drag_on_for_many/. Accessed July 11, 2008.

Seattle University School of Law. 2008. "Voices from Detention: A Report on Human Rights Violations at the Northwest Detention Center." http://www.law.seattleu.edu/documents/news/archive/2008/DRFinal.pdf. Accessed April 7, 2010.

Shulman, Robin. "Immigration Raid Rips Families: Illegal Workers in Massachusetts Separated from Children." *Washington Post.* March 18, 2007. http://www.washingtonpost.com/wp-dyn/content/article/2007/03/17/AR2007031701113.html. Accessed July 11, 2008.

Stewart, Elizabeth. "International Human Rights Law and the Haitian Asylum Applicant Detention Cases." *Virginia Journal of International Law* 26 (1986): 173–218. http://heinonline.org/HOL/Page?handle=hein.journals/vajint26&id=1&collection=journals&index=. Accessed October 8, 2008.

Talbot, Margaret. "The Lost Children: What Do Tougher Detention Policies Mean for Illegal Immigrant Families?" *The New Yorker.* March 3, 2008.

Texas Appleseed. 2010. "Justice for Immigration's Hidden Population: Protecting the Rights of Persons with Mental Disabilities in the Immigration Court and Detention System." March 2010.

Tumlin, Karen, Joaquin Linton, and Ranjana Natarajan. 2009. "A Broken System: Confidential Reports Reveal Failures in U.S. Immigrant Detention Centers." National Immigration Law Center. ACLU of Southern California. Holland & Knight.

United Nations Human Rights Council. 2008. "Promotion and Protection of All Human Rights, Civil, Political, Economic, Social and Cultural Rights, Including the Right to Development: Report of the Special Rapporteur on the Human Rights of Migrants. Jorge Bustamante. Addendum Mission to the United States of America. March 5, 2008.

U.S. House of Representatives. 2008a. Committee on the Judiciary. Subcommittee on Immigration, Citizenship, Refugees, Border Security, and International Law. "Statement of David Wolfe Leopold on Behalf of the American Immigration Lawyers Association Before the Subcommittee on Immigration, Citizenship, Refugees, Border Security, and International Law, Committee on the Judiciary, United States House of Representatives 'Hearing on the Arrest, Prosecution, and Conviction of Undocumented Workers in Postville, Iowa from May 12 to May 22, 2008.'" David Wolfe Leopold, Washington, D.C., July 24, 2008.

U.S. House of Representatives. 2008c. Committee on the Judiciary. Subcommittee on Immigration, Citizenship, Refugees, Border Security, and International Law. "Statement of Deborah Rhodes, Senior Associate Deputy Attorney General, United States Department of Justice Before the United States House of Representatives Committee on the Judiciary, Subcommittee on Immigration, Citizenship, Refugees, Border Security, and International Law. Hearing Entitled 'Immigration Raids: Postville and Beyond.'" Deborah Rhodes, Washington, D.C., July 24, 2008.

Welch, Michael. *Detained: Immigration Laws and the Expanding I.N.S. Jail Complex* Philadelphia: Temple University Press, 2002.

DISCUSSION QUESTIONS

1. What is meant by "border militarization"? What are the arguments for and against border militarization? What is your view of such a posture on the border with Mexico? With Canada?

2. According to Golash-Boza, how have immigration raids by Department of Homeland Security officials sometimes affected American citizens?

3. What are the social costs of large-scale ICE raids, according to the author?

4. Discuss how immigration detention practices have changed over time. What are the arguments for aggressive immigration detention? What arguments might critics of immigration detention put forth against the practice?

5. Golash-Boza notes that many officials in the Homeland Security community, including former Secretary of Homeland Security Michael Chertoff, conflate border security and immigration enforcement with undermining terrorism and violent crime. In your view, does the author have a point? Explain.

CHAPTER FIVE

Immigration and State/Local Law Enforcement

Introduction

In 2010, Arizona Governor Jan Brewer signed into law the "Support Our Law Enforcement and Safe Neighborhoods Act," commonly known by its Arizona state Senate bill number, SB 1070. There were several provisions in this legislation. For one, it made it a state crime to be within the boundaries of Arizona while in the United States illegally. It also made it a state crime—a misdemeanor—to work or seek work in Arizona without federal authorization to do so. Immigrants were required under SB 1070 to carry documentation of their legal status. Also, law enforcement officers in Arizona were given expanded powers to detain individuals if the officers had reasonable suspicion that an individual was undocumented. If that reasonable suspicion developed into probable cause, officers could make a warrantless arrest of the suspected illegal immigrant for the violation of state law. The person's status would then need to be confirmed by federal immigration officials. As police under the law were required to stop and detain those suspected of being in the country illegally, the law overrode individual department and/or municipal and county policies that limited or forbad the involvement of police officers and sheriff's deputies in immigration enforcement.

Shortly after the law's enactment, SB 1070 was challenged in court by the U.S. Department of Justice under President Barack Obama. The Obama administration argued that immigration enforcement was the sole province of the federal government, and only the federal government should engage in it (even if the feds weren't doing so at a level deemed satisfactory by an affected state). The case ultimately made its way to the U.S. Supreme Court (*Arizona v. United States*), which rendered a decision in 2012. The Supreme Court found that some aspects of SB 1070 were unconstitutional as they interfered with the federal government's prerogative in immigration enforcement, including the state's criminalization of one's undocumented immigration status, the requirement to carry immigration papers, and the authorization to arrest individuals based on probable cause that those arrested are in the United States illegally. But the requirement that law enforcement officers make a reasonable attempt to determine the immigration status of arrestees was upheld. State and local law enforcement in Arizona could indeed assist federal immigration officials in enforcement by sharing information with federal authorities and turning over immigration violators to the federal government who were in custody for non-immigration offenses.

While the state of Arizona, in 2010, sought to expand the ability of local law enforcement to contribute to the fight against illegal immigration, and hopefully dent the rates of other crimes the state determined were associated with large numbers of illegal immigrants in some of its communities, other state and local government entities have gone out of their way to limit the ability of the police to even cooperate with federal immigration agents, much less do their job for them. This phenomenon is explored further in the next chapter (Chapter 6), which deals with sanctuary jurisdictions. In the present chapter, the author of the piece clearly takes a position that the use of local police resources in immigration enforcement is, at best, misguided.

Although the Supreme Court struck down Arizona's attempt to craft for itself an immigration enforcement role under state law, the Court has not struck down the federal government's authority to invite states to assist in immigration enforcement. In the later situation, the federal government's authority isn't interfered with, but rather voluntarily delegated. The primary tool for doing this is found in Section 287g of the Immigration and Nationality Act. This section of federal law permits the Department of Homeland Security to essentially deputize local law enforcement so that it may enforce immigration laws. This actually isn't without historical precedent. For much the 19th and early 20th century, local law enforcement officers were contracted by the federal government to perform immigration and customs enforcement duties at the ports of entry and along the border. The 287g program, which was added to the Immigration and Nationality Act under President Bill Clinton in 1996 but only became operational under President George Bush after the 9/11 attacks, is something of a return to historical immigration enforcement practices.

One of the primary criticisms of using local law enforcement assets to assist federal immigration enforcement is that doing so affects public safety at the local level. The argument is that undocumented persons who are victims of crime or witnesses to crime will be less likely to report what they know to the police if they believe the police will refer them to immigration officials. In other words, communication and cooperation between local law enforcement and the undocumented segments of the community will erode; the consequence will be that crime in those communities is neither thwarted nor solved.

In the article below by Radha Vishnuvajjala, an argument is presented backing up this concern. In particular, the author examines the issue of domestic violence among undocumented immigrant women and explores how programs and policies promoting the deliberate involvement of local law enforcement officers in immigration enforcement contribute to crimes going unreported and victims remaining in peril. Domestic violence is just one example of a category of crime which victims and witnesses may choose to live with rather than risk deportation after reporting incidents to the police. As you read the article, consider the benefits and pitfalls of greater or lesser degrees of cooperation between local, state, and federal law enforcement authorities where immigration matters are concerned.

READING 5

Insecure Communities

How an Immigration Enforcement Program Encourages Battered Women to Stay Silent

By Radha Vishnuvajjala

Introduction

When Maria Bolanos called the police during a fight with her partner, she never imagined that a call for help could lead to her own deportation.[1] A police officer responded to the call from the twenty-eight-year-old Salvadoran undocumented immigrant, but ended up charging her with illegally selling a phone card to a neighbor.[2] The police later dropped the charge, but not before fingerprinting Bolanos.[3] Under the Secure Communities program, officers cross-referenced her fingerprints with a federal immigration database maintained by Immigration and Customs Enforcement (ICE).[4] Because Bolanos had been previously fingerprinted after customs officials caught her illegally entering the United States, she was flagged for deportation.[5]

Secure Communities was designed to improve public safety by identifying and removing criminal aliens.[6] ICE claims that Secure Communities "prioritiz[es] the removal of criminal aliens, those who pose a threat to public safety, and repeat immigration violators," but Bolanos' current predicament may prove otherwise.[7] Even though police later dropped the phone card charge, Bolanos' fingerprints were the first step toward deportation proceedings.[8] Bolanos' story demonstrates how Secure Communities not only removes dangerous criminals from communities, but also is used as a widespread immigration enforcement tool.[9]

Using Secured Communities as a broad enforcement mechanism undermines the relationship between undocumented immigrants and local law enforcement by making victims of crime hesitant to ask for help.[10] In instances of domestic violence, the risk of contacting the police is further compounded by barriers of language, culture, and dependency on documented, abusive partners.[11] Undocumented domestic violence victims—mostly women—are less likely to report abuse than documented or non-immigrant victims because they fear being reported to immigration authorities.[12]

Radha Vishnuvajjala, "Insecure Communities: How an Immigration Enforcement Program Encourages Battered Women to Stay Silent," *Boston College Journal of Law & Social Justice*, vol. 32, no. 1, pp. 185-213. Copyright © 2012 by Berkeley Electronic Press. Reprinted with permission. Provided by ProQuest LLC. All rights reserved.

Undocumented women are especially vulnerable when their abusive partners are documented because a documented abuser has no fear of deportation and therefore has another element of power.[13] Abusers may exert their control by threatening deportation or blocking their victims from obtaining lawful status.[14]

This Note argues that Secure Communities should only crosscheck fingerprints of those accused of serious crimes, thereby preserving the relationship between police and undocumented victims of domestic violence.[15] Part I describes the problem of domestic violence against undocumented immigrants, the importance of trust between law enforcement and the immigrant community, and language barriers that immigrants face in seeking assistance. Part II describes the Secure Communities program, including the history of collaboration between local and federal law enforcement and the impetus for the program. Finally, part III argues that ICE must decisively reform the Secure Communities program to protect those victims of domestic violence by using a proposed three-step process.

I. Domestic Violence, Undocumented Immigrants, and Local Law Enforcement

Undocumented women face barriers in the form of society at large, the culture and customs of their native countries, and often times their inability to communicate effectively in the English language.[16] These barriers can create a rift between law enforcement officials and the undocumented immigrant community that they serve.[17] These factors, in combination with a fear of deportation, make undocumented women reluctant to ask for help.[18]

A. Domestic Violence Perpetrated Against Immigrant Women

Immigrants, especially those perceived to be undocumented, are frequently victims of crime.[19] Undocumented immigrants are easy prey because they are reluctant to report crimes to police.[20] Therefore, criminals perceive them as having no source of protection and they are likely to be repeatedly victimized.[21]

This police-averse mentality also enters the home, where domestic violence against undocumented immigrants often goes unreported and unresolved.[22] Domestic violence is an increasingly pervasive problem in American society—"a woman is assaulted by her partner every fifteen seconds and each year 1500 women are killed as a result of domestic violence."[23] These numbers, however, only reflect reported domestic violence incidents.[24]

Domestic violence statistics show a stark divide when examined by immigration status.[25] Immigrant women are the most vulnerable group among victims of domestic violence.[26] Estimates show that nearly sixty percent of married immigrant women are in abusive relationships.[27] They are also less likely to report abuse than documented or non-immigrant women.[28] While fifty-five percent of all domestic violence victims report their abuse to law enforcement officials, only thirty percent of documented immigrants turn to law enforcement for help and the number drops to fourteen percent for undocumented women.[29] Many undocumented victims indicate that fear of being reported to immigration authorities is one of their primary reasons for remaining in an abusive relationship.[30]

1. Social Barriers

Abusive partners often tend to socially isolate their undocumented victims from society.[31] An undocumented woman is especially vulnerable when her abusive partner is documented because her immigration status then becomes another form of leverage that abuser may use to isolate her.[32] Abusers frequently exploit their partners' immigration status to exert further control by threatening deportation or creating barriers during victims' attempts to gain lawful status.[33] Undocumented victims may then feel reliant on abusers, especially when American laws are difficult to comprehend and victims do not know of, understand, or trust legal aid programs.[34]

Abusers often prohibit contact with friends and family or forbid the victim to work or attend school.[35] Isolation furthers domestic violence because the undocumented victim is cut off from potential sources of support and assistance.[36] For example, a woman named Luisa came to the United States illegally from Mexico.[37] She initially had the support of her friends and family, but this changed after she married her husband, who was a U.S. citizen.[38] He became abusive and possessive, causing her to feel isolated from the community and unable to seek help.[39]

Although abuse initially causes the isolation, friends and family may worsen a situation by warning victims not to leave abusive partners because life would be too hard as a single, undocumented immigrant.[40] For example, another undocumented and abused woman, Leticia, found herself in a social network comprised entirely of her husband's friends and relatives with no support of her own.[41] Her mother-in-law exacerbated the situation by threatening to call the police and have her deported if she complained about her husband's violence.[42]

An undocumented immigrant from El Salvador was so desperate to leave her abusive boyfriend that she tried to jump out of a moving car.[43] He then grabbed her and beat her in the street, but she never reported the incident because of her illegal status.[44] One undocumented woman from Mexico married a U.S. citizen and spent five years in an abusive relationship with him.[45] Her husband repeatedly raped her and even threatened to kill their two children, but she failed to report the abuse in fear of deportation.[46] Without support outside of abusive relationships, many undocumented victims remain unaware that domestic violence is a crime in the United States or that there are services available.[47]

2. Cultural Barriers

In addition to the social barriers that isolate undocumented domestic violence victims, there are also cultural barriers—norms and customs—that discourage women from standing up to domestic violence.[48]

In many Asian cultures, society is centered around groups.[49] Families are the most important social units, and members of many Asian communities are expected to put the needs of the family above their own.[50] Traditionally, many Asian cultures consider women secondary to men, as evidenced by marriage customs.[51] Women would stay at home while men worked to support the family, thereby merging a woman's identity with that of her family.[52]

When this subordinate role persists in modern times, women may be reluctant to break out of the traditional family unit in an effort to stop domestic violence.[53] These norms make women feel that they must protect the family reputation at their own expense because one family member's guilt or shame extends to the rest of the family.[54] One example of this strong sense of family reputation is the story of Kim Seng, a Cambodian woman murdered by her abusive husband.[55] Just one week before the murder, Seng's family organized an intervention to ask her husband to stop his beatings and encourage them to stay together.[56] Seng's mother later admitted, "'I didn't sense the danger because I was so focused on the shame my daughter's actions would bring in the Cambodian community'. ... 'And I was thinking about my daughter's children and the importance of their having a family.'"[57] This same family-centric culture precludes the option of divorce because it would break up the family unit and bring shame to the family.[58]

Similarly powerful social norms about how a wife and mother should behave exist in the Latino immigrant community.[59] This dynamic can be illustrated by one commentator's description:

> Within the Latino community, Latinas' identities are defined on the basis of their roles as mothers and wives. By encouraging definitions of Latinas as interconnected with and dependent upon status within a family unit structure, the Latino patriarchy denies Latinas individuality on the basis of gender. For Latinas, cultural norms and myths of national origin intersect with these patriarchal notions of a woman's role and identity. The result is an internal community-defined role, modified by external male-centered paradigms.[60]

These cultural norms, even without considering the possibility of deportation, can make women increasingly reluctant to report violence.[61] In a survey of battered Latina immigrant women, 48.2% chose to stay with their abusers in fear of losing their children, 41.2% did not want to separate their children from their father, 18.8% cited the perception that a good wife and mother does not leave her family, and 18.8% would not leave for religious reasons.[62] Each of these cultural norms about the role of a woman as a wife and mother create a barrier between battered women and the assistance they need.[63]

3. The Language Barrier

Battered women may also be unable to seek help from abusive relationships when a language barrier hinders effective communication with law enforcement officers.[64] When an officer cannot understand the victim and either ignores or fails to resolve her underlying issue, she may be less likely to seek help in the future.[65] A language barrier prevents police from effectively protecting the entire community.[66] This creates a danger of marginalizing entire immigrant populations.[67] For example, according to one study, seventy-two percent of foreign-born Latinos in the United States consider Spanish their dominant language, while only twenty-four percent consider themselves bilingual.[68] Additionally, fifty-five percent of foreign-born Latinos have less than a high school education, thereby making communication of complex legal procedures even more difficult.[69]

Likewise, law enforcement agencies do not always have bilingual staff sufficient to serve those lacking proficiency in English—especially outside of large metropolitan areas.[70] Therefore, when police cannot communicate with domestic violence victims, they may instead interview others at the scene.[71] Without direct communication with the victim, however, officers will likely be confronted with the cultural barriers that cause witnesses to downplay or deny abuse.[72] Law enforcement efficacy further deteriorates when only the abuser speaks English, as he is not likely to incriminate himself.[73] Furthermore, if the police do not arrest the abuser, he may retaliate against the victim after the police leave.[74]

For example, one survey of Latino domestic violence victims reported that in nearly one third of domestic violence police responses, officers did not speak directly to the victim.[75] Furthermore, eleven percent of respondents indicated that police only spoke to the abuser, and thirty-four percent said an officer spoke to them in Spanish.[76] Overall, less than one quarter of respondents could communicate in English and over twenty-five percent stayed with their abusers because of their inability to speak English.[77] These results are not unique to the Latino community and are likely attributable to the language barrier between victims and police officers, too few of whom are bilingual.[78]

This communication hindrance can lead to the police arresting the victim instead of the abuser.[79] For example, an Asian immigrant named Ling called the police when her husband attacked her with a chair.[80] She used a fish knife to defend herself and her husband cut himself on the knife while attacking her—when the police arrived, Ling's husband accused her of attacking him.[81] He spoke English well but she did not, and the language barrier ultimately resulted in the police arresting Ling instead of her attacker.[82] In these situations, the language barrier is even more harmful to the victim because the police may be more likely to believe the party with more proficiency in the English language.[83]

Language barriers also negatively affect immigrant domestic violence victims when they seek social services or legal protection.[84] Victim advocates may not be able to effectively convey concepts of confidentiality or even indicate what services are available to domestic violence victims.[85] The resulting feeling of hopelessness, coupled with a fear of revealing illegal immigration status, creates an atmosphere where victims are unlikely to seek help.[86]

B. The Relationship Between Undocumented Immigrants and Law Enforcement

These social, cultural, and language barriers make it especially important that immigrant victims of domestic violence have trust in local law enforcement.[87] Cultural notions of authority and fear of deportation may weaken the relationship between law enforcement officers and the community they police.[88] Conversely, certain law enforcement initiatives, such as community policing and noncooperation policies, may strengthen the relationship.[89]

1. A Weakened Relationship Between Police and the Community

Some refugees and other recent immigrants may distrust U.S. law enforcement officers by equating them with the corruption, brutality, and insensitivity of police in their native countries.[90] For example, Mexico, the former home of many U.S. immigrants, ranked 72nd out of 180 in the 2008 Corruption Perception Index.[91] One survey shows that four out of five Mexicans believe police are generally corrupt and take advantage of citizens.[92] Also, many Mexican parents teach their children not to trust the police, and television programs in Mexico portray police "as corrupt and incompetent oafs or sinister antagonists."[93] In cases where the victims are women and children, such as domestic violence, Mexicans generally believe authorities are more willing to protect perpetrators than victims.[94]

These perceptions of law enforcement may stay with immigrants as they enter the United States, especially the undocumented immigrants who may already be distrustful from fear of deportation.[95] Those undocumented immigrants predisposed to alienation may further distrust law enforcement officers who openly collaborate with federal immigration enforcement agencies.[96] Undocumented immigrants are unlikely to cooperate in criminal investigations or report crimes if they believe doing so would subject them to deportation.[97] The end result may be to undermine community safety through the added difficulty in charging criminals or obtaining convictions.[98] Therefore, communities are best served by encouraging communication between undocumented immigrants and local law enforcement officers.[99]

2. Strengthening Relationships Between Police and the Community

Local governments have tried to increase communication and trust between immigrant communities and law enforcement by enacting noncooperation policies.[100] These policies limit the local government's relationship with federal law enforcement, usually by ensuring that local law enforcement agents do not inquire into immigration status or withholding immigration information from federal authorities.[101] Some such policies, however, have been preempted by federal statute, making some cooperation with federal enforcement officials compulsory.[102]

Alternatively, community policing programs are an effective way to strengthen the relationship between law enforcement officers and the community.[103] Community policing often relies on traditionally marginalized groups, such as the immigrant community, to report crimes and other problems.[104] The public helps law enforcement by looking for suspicious behavior, being aware of empty homes, and learning how to handle different emergencies.[105] Programs are tailored to the needs of each particular community, but the underlying goal is to create a relationship that helps identify and stop crime and disorder.[106]

Community policing occurs incrementally by increasing a community's trust in law enforcement.[107] Law enforcement officers build trust not only with victims, but also with their social peers so that friends and family members will encourage victims to seek help.[108] Local police departments may also develop stronger relations with communities by meeting with various immigrant groups to discuss their needs and issues.[109] Because leaders of immigrant community groups are predominantly male, law enforcement officials may also need to contact women's or domestic violence victim's organizations in an attempt to learn the needs of those communities.[110]

II. Cooperation Between Federal and State Law Enforcement

The federal government controls immigration law in the United States.[111] Section 287(g) of the Immigration and Nationality Act (INA), however, allows federal law enforcement to enter into agreements with local law enforcement to enforce federal immigration law.[112] Such agreements have strained the relationship between undocumented immigrants and community police officers, especially since the implementation of the Secure Communities program.[113]

A. History of Cooperation Between Federal and Local Law Enforcement

Immigration in the United States is controlled by the federal government and, as the Supreme Court has recognized, regulation of immigration is "'unquestionably exclusively a federal power.'"[114] Therefore, states and localities are limited in their abilities to regulate immigration matters, though they may enforce criminal provisions of federal immigration laws.[115] Congress may, however, authorize state officers to enforce immigration laws.[116] Congress may not compel states or commandeer state officers to enforce such laws, but it can prevent states from refusing to share immigration information with federal authorities.[117]

Section 287(g) of INA expressly authorizes the Secretary of Homeland Security to enter into agreements with states and localities to enforce federal immigration law.[118] These agreements must dictate the specific functions state or local officers are required or allowed to perform.[119] Section 287(g) agreements are limited to investigation, arrest, and detention; they do not authorize removal.[120] Between the enactment of section 287(g) in 1996 and December of 2009, ICE "signed sixty-three memoranda of agreement (MOAs) with state and local law enforcement agencies."[121]

Many of these agreements are limited in scope and only allow jail officials to report immigration violators to ICE.[122] Others are broader, allowing local law enforcement officers to directly enforce immigration laws after a specified training period.[123] Allegations surfaced, however, claiming that law enforcement officers were arresting immigrants solely to initiate investigations and removal proceedings.[124] In 2009, Department of Homeland Security (DHS) Secretary Janet Napolitano responded to those allegations by announcing that law enforcement agencies acting pursuant to 287(g) agreements must pursue all criminal charges originally causing an immigrant's arrest.[125]

B. Secure Communities

Local enforcement of federal immigration laws has strained the relationship between undocumented immigrants and community police officers.[126] Section 287(g) agreements are one cause of this tension, but the Secure Communities program has further exacerbated the problem since its implementation.[127] Secure Communities is a formal program where state and local governments sign MOAs with ICE, agreeing to cross-check fingerprints against a federal database in an attempt to identify undocumented immigrants.[128] Secure Communities began in 2008 under President George W. Bush, funded through DHS.[129] Initially, the program focused on removable noncitizens in prisons and jails, charging state and local officials with identifying them by running fingerprint data against DHS's immigration databases.[130] Secure Communities soon expanded, "ma[king] the identification and removal of criminal aliens a top priority. ..."[131] Although intended to identify and remove dangerous criminals, participating agencies screen all arrested immigrants regardless of whether they are ultimately convicted.[132] For example:

> In December, Mesa police arrested Roberto Gonzalez-Corona, 42, a Mexican immigrant, on a disorderly-conduct charge. He was booked into the Mesa jail, where his fingerprints were run through the criminal and immigration databases.
> The checks showed that Gonzalez-Corona had been removed from the United States nine times. Gonzalez-Corona also had numerous misdemeanor and felony convictions in California on charges related to drug possession and grand-theft auto.
> After being verified by an ICE center in Vermont, which can take several hours, the information was sent electronically through a secure law-enforcement network to ICE's field office in Phoenix. By then, Mesa police had released Gonzalez-Corona after charging him with disorderly conduct.
> But ICE agents tracked him down with information received from Mesa police. ICE agents arrested him on Jan. 27. Gonzalez-Corona is now being held in federal custody facing felony charges of illegally re-entering the United States.[133]

The Secure Communities program is extensive and rapidly growing: by November 2009, ninety-five cities and counties in eleven states were participants.[134] As of September 2011, 1595 jurisdictions in forty-four states and territories were participants.[135] Nationally, "5.6 million people have been screened, resulting in the deportation of more than 21,500 immigrants convicted of major crimes, or about 26 percent of the 81,489 immigrants deported overall."[136] ICE plans to require every jurisdiction in the country to participate in the program by 2013.[137]

Several local governments have questioned the Secure Communities program's negative impact on community relations.[138] Localities are concerned that Secure Communities will put an extra burden on local police departments that are already working with limited funds.[139] Local government officials have also questioned the program because it may target both legal and undocumented immigrants.[140] Secure Communities may negatively impact the number of immigrants reporting crimes or seeking medical attention, thereby endangering public safety.[141] The association between local law enforcement and immigration officials can discourage community cooperation and undermine cooperative community policing programs.[142]

Immigrant advocacy groups have also criticized Secure Communities because it fails to prioritize Level 1 offenders—those convicted of serious drug offenses or violent crimes.[143] Data supports this concern, as most of the immigrants who have been removed through Secure Communities are low-level offenders.[144] Of all Secure Communities jurisdictions, Maricopa County, Arizona has the highest number of immigrants both arrested and deported.[145] Sixty-six percent of Maricopa County deportees, however, are either low-level criminals or have no criminal history at all.[146] Nationally, sixty percent of Secure Communities deportees are low-level criminals or have no criminal history.[147]

Secure Communities has broadened far beyond its mission of identifying and deporting dangerous criminals.[148] It may empower law enforcement officers to act as deportation agents by making pre-textual arrests just to obtain fingerprints.[149] This was the case for Maria Bolanos, who police arrested but never prosecuted for illegally selling a phone card to a neighbor.[150]

Despite these criticisms, DHS Secretary Janet Napolitano announced in 2010 that communities would not be able to opt-out of the program.[151] This, however, is a departure from Napolitano's prētions statements that participation is optional.[152] ICE planned to achieve uniform participation by isolating and pressuring communities that objected to the program.[153] ICE initially advertised the program as 'Voluntary," but actually only intended for one narrow provision of the program to be voluntary.[154] In April of 2010, the National Day Labor Organizing Network, the Center for Constitutional Rights, and the Immigration Justice Clinic of the Benjamin N. Cardozo School of Law filed a complaint for the release of ICE documents to clarify the scope and enforceability of Secure Communities.[155] Then, in the fall of 2010, ICE clarified its compliance requirements, thereby dispelling community perceptions that they could opt-out of sharing fingerprints.[156]

The 2010 clarification came after several months of vague and contradictory statements from ICE about the program.[157] For example, in July 2010, a regional coordinator for the Secure Communities program sent an e-mail to the New York State Division of Criminal Justice Services ("the Division") that said [n]o jurisdiction will be activated if they oppose [Secure Communities].. and that ICE would "'do everything [it] can to work with a N.Y law enforcement agency to satisfy its concerns but at the end of the day, if they are opposed, [it] won't go forward.'"[158] A spokesman for the Division stated several days later that he learned it was "'the position of the federal government that it can require participation.'"[159]

ICE then publicly announced in June 2011 that Secure Communities would be mandatory and universally implemented by 2013.[160] ICE also acknowledged that "some of [its] past public statements led to confusion about whether state and local jurisdictions can opt out of the program."[161] This change began through the abolition of state MOAs—the agreements setting forth the bounds of Secure Communities in each locality.[162] Communities therefore lost the little bargaining power afforded by MOAs that allowed them to tailor Secure Communities to their needs.[163]

III. A Proposed Solution for ICE

Secure Communities undermines protections for domestic violence victims by encouraging silence through fear of deportation.[164] Because domestic violence perpetrators often use their partners' undocumented status as a means of control, victims will be less likely to call for help if they know that police will share their biometric data with immigration enforcement.[165] Undocumented women are further deterred from calling for help because any arrest, regardless of whether the charge is later dropped, may allow local law enforcement to obtain their fingerprints.[166]

ICE should therefore modify Secure Communities to allow for adequate protections of domestic violence victims in three distinct steps.[167] First, the program should mandate delayed reporting until after those arrested during domestic violence incidents are convicted.[168] Second, ICE should limit the program to sharing only those fingerprints obtained through felony charges and misdemeanor convictions.[169] Finally, ICE should encourage local officials to communicate these changes to the public.[170]

The benefits to these changes are two-fold: protecting vulnerable women from violence and preserving the relationship between undocumented immigrants and local police.[171] The Bolanos incident, like others, underscores how the program has departed from its alleged original intent of removing dangerous criminals from communities.[172] ICE and the states should narrowly tailor Secure Communities to protect victims of domestic violence while still removing dangerous criminals.[173]

A. ICE's Attempt to Acknowledge the Problem

ICE changed Secure Communities in the summer of 2011.[174] John Morton, the Director of ICE, sent a memorandum to Field Office Directors, Special Agents in Charge, and Chief Counsel to outline the revised policy on prosecutorial discretion.[175] In his memorandum, Morton sets forth a new policy regarding prosecutorial discretion in "cases involving the victims and witnesses of crime, including domestic violence. ..."[176] Morton claims:

> The vast majority of state and local law enforcement agencies do not generally arrest victims or witnesses of crime as part of an investigation. However, ICE regularly hears concerns that in some instances a state or local law enforcement officer may arrest and book multiple people at the scene of alleged domestic violence. In these cases, an arrested victim or witness of domestic violence may be booked and fingerprinted and, through the operation of the Secure Communities program or another ICE enforcement program, may come to the attention of ICE.[177]

Morton then advises officers, agents, and attorneys "to exercise all appropriate discretion on a case-by-case basis when making detention and enforcement decisions in the cases of victims of crime. ..."[178]

While attempting to recognize the domestic violence issue, this aspirational memorandum does not ensure that immigrant victims of domestic violence will not be subjected to racial profiling or subsequent removal proceedings.[179] ICE justifies Secure Communities by noting that the lack of discretion protects the community from racial profiling.[180] Because police lack discretion, many consider Secure Communities a better alternative to an Arizona-like law that allows police to choose whom to ask for proof of citizenship.[181] Because Secure Communities applies to all fingerprints, the police do not have to decide who might be an undocumented immigrant and unfair implementation is a non-issue.[182] ICE's memorandum, however, contradicts its attempt to be fair, instead using prosecutorial discretion as protection from racial profiling and pretextual arrests.[183] ICE should therefore establish clear guidance to fully protect victims of domestic violence because, without it, "prosecutorial discretion" may further enable pretextual arrests.[184]

B. A Three-Step Process to Protecting Victims of Domestic Violence and Increasing Community Safety

Discretion alone will likely not solve the problem of pretextual arrests that prevent abused women from calling for help.[185] Instead, ICE should implement three specific changes to protect victims of domestic violence.[186] First, ICE should modify Secure Communities to specify that reporting of arrestees pursuant to domestic violence incidents is not required until conviction.[187] Second, ICE should limit the program to felony charges and misdemeanor convictions.[188] Third, ICE should work with states and localities to implement a public relations campaign that communicates these changes.[189] This final step would ensure that all residents—documented and undocumented—understand the program's scope and that they can contact law enforcement without fear of deportation.[190]

Colorado's former MOA had already implemented a framework similar to this first step, specifying that reporting is not required until conviction for those arrested as a result of a domestic violence incident.[191] It did this by specifically referencing Colorado statutory language that mirrored this first step.[192] Furthermore, Colorado's MOA stated that "ICE offers protection and assistance to victims of trafficking and violence, regardless of their immigration status. This protection or assistance applies to those who might have been arrested for a crime and subsequently determined to be a victim, not a perpetrator."[193]

ICE should implement this first step because, as it already acknowledges, police sometimes arrest both domestic violence victims and perpetrators.[194] Because Secure Communities requires local police to send all fingerprint data to ICE before conviction, those victims who are arrested but not charged or prosecuted still face the risk of deportation.[195] A decisive policy against reporting fingerprint data before conviction, however, may protect domestic violence victims.[196]

Then, ICE should implement the second step of limiting the program to felony charges and misdemeanor convictions.[197] This step would prevent situations like that of Maria Bolanos—charged but never tried for selling phone cards without a license.[198] Doing this would act to return Secure Communities to its original purpose while protecting undocumented women who call for help from being charged pretextually with a misdemeanor.[199]

The Colorado Hispanic Bar Association (CHBA) detailed its concerns about Secure Coimnunities's implementation in Colorado.[200] Though targeted at Colorado, these concerns may be applicable to other communities, and addressing them may in turn help prioritize the targeting of dangerous criminals while protecting more victims.[201] CHBA criticized the ability of law enforcement officials to make pretextual arrests solely to obtain fingerprints that are then checked against the federal immigration database.[202] The Bolanos case arguably gives credibility to these concerns, as her arrest may have been pretextual.[203]

Restricting Secure Communities to felony charges and misdemeanor convictions may also help strengthen community policing programs.[204] When immigrants no longer fear calling the police, they may be more willing to communicate with police about crimes to which they are witnesses.[205]

Modifying Secure Communities, however, may not be enough if victims do not know they can call the police without fear of that call leading to deportation.[206] Therefore, ICE should implement the third step of working with state and local authorities to communicate these changes to the immigrant communities.[207] Communication would help ensure that residents understand how the program is implemented and that they may contact law enforcement without fear of deportation.[208] Without this, undocumented residents may continue to be cautious and hesitant to contact law enforcement.[209] This phenomenon of hesitance already occurs in communities with unpublicized noncooperation agreements that limit communication with federal law enforcement.[210]

An effective communication campaign would ensure that victims can find resources in their native languages so as to mitigate the effect of language barriers.[211] In addition to communicating these changes, police departments should educate the public that domestic violence is a crime.[212] This may also help alleviate some of the social and cultural pressure women face and make them more comfortable with seeking help.[213]

Proponents of Secure Communities might argue that its scope is irrelevant and that undocumented immigrants should be deported regardless of their crime's severity.[214] A narrow scope for the program, however, gives it legitimacy and community support.[215] Immigrants and non-immigrants alike do not wish to live among violent criminals and drug dealers.[216] Limiting the scope of Secure Communities would likely sharpen its focus and effectiveness, thereby removing those criminals that no community wants in its midst.[217]

Conclusions

Domestic violence perpetrated against undocumented women is a pervasive problem. Many undocumented victims of domestic violence indicate that fear of immigration authorities is their primary reason for remaining in abusive relationships. Language and cultural barriers only compound these difficulties by preventing women from seeking assistance outside the home. Trust in local law enforcement facilitates solving the problem of domestic violence against undocumented immigrants.

These severe problems illustrate a need for change in the way ICE operates the Secure Communities program. There have been many documented instances of abuse of Secure Communities, especially as it affects victims of domestic violence. Therefore, ICE should implement a three-step reform: requiring delay of reporting until conviction for domestic violence arrestees; limiting the program to felony charges and misdemeanor convictions; and working with states and localities to notify immigrant communities of these changes.

Notes

1. Shankar Vedantam, *Destined for Deportation? Salvadoran Woman Targeted by Program Designed to Catch Undocumented Criminals*, Wash. Post, Nov. 1, 2010, at B1.

2. *Id.*; Erin Pangilinan, *Domestic Violence Victim Calls Out ICE Assistant Director on her Deportation*, Change.org (Nov. 29, 2010), http://news.change.org/stories/domestic-violence-victim-calls-out-ice-assistant-director-on-her-deportation.

3. Vedantam, *supra* note 1.

4. *Id.*; Erin Pangilinan, *Mother Battles Secure Communities and Deportation*, Change.org (Dec. 29, 2010), http://news.change.org/stories/mother-battles-secure-communities-and-deportation.

5. Vedantam, *supra* note 1.

6. *See id.*; *Secure Communities*, U.S. Immigr. & Customs Enforcement, http://www.ice.gov/secure_communities (last visited Nov. 1, 2011).

7. *Secure Communities*, *supra* note 6; *see* Vedantam, *supra* note 1.

8. Vedantam, *supra* note 1.

9. *See id.*

10. *See* Katerina Shaw, Note, *Barriers to Freedom: Continued Failure of U.S. Immigration Laws to Offer Equal Protection to Immigrant Battered Women*, 15 Cardozo J.L. & Gender 663, 678 (2009); Sarah M. Wood, Note, *VAWA's Unfinished Business: The Immigrant Women Who Fall Through the Cracks*, 11 Duke J. Gender L. & Pol'y 141, 151–52 (2004); Vedantam, *supra* note 1. Strong relationships between police officers and the communities they are in charge of protecting are necessary for effective law enforcement. *See* Jason G. Idilbi, *Local Enforcement of Federal Immigration Law: Should North Carolina Communities Implement 287(g) Authority?*, 86 N.C. L. Rev. 1710, 1728–29 (2008). Not only does the community depend on the police for protection, but the police depend on the community to report crimes and serve as witnesses. *Id.* at 1728; *see* David Hench, *Building Trust vs. Checking for Visas: Making Police Enforce Immigration Laws Could Actually Detract from Crime Fighting, Some Officials Say*, Portland Press Herald, Mar. 29, 2004, at 1B.

11. *See* Lee J. Teran, *Barriers to Protection at Home and Abroad: Mexican Victims of Domestic Violence and the Violence Against Women Act*, 17 B.U. Int'l L.J. 1, 12 (1999). One study indicated that among immigrant Latina women in Washington, D.C., seventy-seven percent were victims of abuse. *Id.*; *see* H.R. Rep. No. 103-395, at 26–27 (1993). Immigrant women, and especially undocumented women, are at particular risk for violence because they already face language and cultural barriers to receiving social services. Teran, *supra*, at 12; *see* Leslye E. Orloff et al., *With No Place to Turn: Improving Legal Advocacy for Battered Immigrant Women*, 29 Fam. L.Q. 313, 316–17 (1995); Susan Girardo Roy, Note, *Restoring Hope or Tolerating Abuse? Responses to Domestic Violence Against Immigrant Women*, 9 Geo. Immigr. L.J. 263, 267 (1995) (citing Christine Whalen & Martha King, *Abuse in a New Land: Immigrant Wives Often Isolated, Vulnerable*, Seattle Times, Aug. 8, 1994, at A1). Undocumented women are especially deterred from seeking help from law enforcement because they lack "the legal status or the employment authorization necessary to support themselves and their children." Teran, *supra*, at 12; *accord* H. Rep. No. 103-395, at 26–27. Undocumented women also face threats of deportation from their partners and loss of child custody, making them less likely to seek help from law enforcement regarding an abusive partner. Teran, *supra*, at 12; *see* H.R. Rep. No. 103-395, *supra*, at 26–27.

12. Molly Dragiewicz & Yvonne Lindgren, *The Gendered Nature of Domestic Violence: Statistical Data for Lawyers Considering Equal Protection Analysis*, 17 Am. U. J. Gender Soc. Pol'y & L. 229, 256 (2009); Mary Ann Dutton et al., *Characteristics of Help-Seeking Behaviors, Resources and Service Needs of Battered Immigrant Latinas: Legal and Policy Implications*, 7 Geo. J. on Poverty L. & Pol'y 245, 293 (2000); Nat Stern & Karen Oehme, *Increasing Safety for Battered Women and Their Children: Creating a Privilege for Supervised Visitation Intake Records*, 41 U. Rich. L. Rev. 499, 501 n.11 (2007); Teran, *supra* note 11, at 12; Shaw, *supra* note 10, at 678; Juliette Terzieff, *More Services Reach Abused Immigrant Women*, Women's eNews, 1, 3 (Aug. 11, 2005), http://www.ncdsv.org/images/moreservicesreachabuseimmigrantwomen.pdf. In one study, sixty-five percent of battered immigrant women reported that their batterer had threatened them with deportation. Shaw, *supra* note 10, at 666; *see* Giselle Aguilar Hass et al., *Battered Immigrants and U.S. Citizen Spouses*, Legal Momentum, 1, 3 (Apr. 24, 2006), http://www.legalmomentum.org/assets/pdfs/wwwbatteredimmsanduscspouses.pdf.

13. *See* Teran, *supra* note 11, at 12. If the man is documented and the woman is not, she may perceive him to be less resistant to calling immigration authorities because he would have no fear of deportation himself. *See* Hass et al., *supra* note 12, at 3–4.

14. Idilbi, *supra* note 10, at 1732 n.125; Hass et al., *supra* note 12, at 3; *see* Gail Pendleton, *Local Police Enforcement of Immigration Laws and Its Effects on Victims of Domestic Violence*, A.B.A. Commission on Domestic Violence, 1, 1, http://www.nationalimmigrationproject.org/legal_archives/Archive_Local%20 Enforcement%20and%20Domestic%20Violence-1.doc (last visited Sept. 26, 2011).

15. This Note focuses on domestic violence in heterosexual relationships, where women tend to be victims and men their abusers. This is not always the case, but studies show that women are at greater risk of violence from male partners than men are from their female partners. Dragiewicz & Lindgren, *supra* note 12, at 256; Stern & Oehme, *supra* note 12, at 501 n.11. There are relatively few cases involving men as victims with women as perpetrators and, in those cases, "much of female violence is committed in self-defense and inflicts less injury than male violence." Stern & Oehme, *supra* note 12, at 502 n.11; *accord* Dragiewicz & Lindgren, *supra* note 12, at 256.

16. *See* Karin Wang, *Battered Asian American Women: Community Responses from the Battered Women's Movement and the Asian American Community*, 3 Asian L.J. 151, 162–63 (1996); Shaw, *supra* note 10, at 665; Wood, *supra* note 10, at 150–52; *see* Idilbi, *supra* note 10, at 1728–29.

17. *See* Wang, *supra* note 16, at 162–63.

18. *See* Dutton et al., *supra* note 12, at 293; Idilbi, *supra* note 10, at 1728–29.

19. Orde F. Kittrie, *Federalism, Deportation, and Crime Victims Afraid to Call the Police*, 91 Iowa L. Rev. 1449, 1450–55 (2006); Christopher Carlberg, Note, *Cooperative Noncooperation: A Proposal for an Effective Uniform Noncooperation Immigration Policy for Local Governments*, 77 Geo. Wash. L. Rev. 740, 748 (2009); Wang, *supra* note 16, at 162–63; Shaw, *supra* note 10, at 665; Wood, *supra* note 10 at 150–52; *see, e.g.*, Matt Hughes, *Leaders: Learn from Hate*, Times Leader, Jan. 29, 2011, at 1A (describing the 2008 beating that led to the death of an undocumented Mexican immigrant); Sarah Netter, *Hating Hispanics: Has Arizona Ignited Firestorm After Decade of Simmering Tension?*, ABC News (July 19, 2010), http://abcnews.go.com/US/hating-hispanics-arizona-ignited-firestorm-decade-simmering-tension/story?id =11179708; *Staten Island Teen to Serve Time for Attack on Mexican Immigrant*, NY1 News, http://www.ny1.com/content/top_stories/134218/staten-island-teen-to-serve-time-for-attack-on-mexican-immigrant (last updated Feb. 18, 2011, 5:44PM).

20. Kittrie, *supra* note 19, at 1451–52; Carlberg, *supra* note 19, at 748.

21. *See* Carlberg, *supra* note 19, at 748–49.

22. *See id.*; *see, e.g.*, Laura Jontz, Note, *Eighth Circuit to Battered Kenyan: Take a Safari—Battered Immigrants Face New Barrier When Reporting Domestic Violence*, 55 Drake L. Rev. 195, 196 (2006).

23. Jontz, *supra* note 22, at 196–97.

24. *Id.* According to one 2009 report, twenty-seven percent of domestic violence victims in the prior year did not report the incident to police. Ramsey Hanafi, *Over One-Fourth of Domestic Violence*

Incidents Go Unreported, Legal Match (Apr. 22, 2009), http://lawblog.legalmatch.com/2009/04/22/over-one-fourth-of-domestic-violence-incidents-go-unreported. Accurate statistics, however, are difficult to obtain. *See* C. J. Newton, *Domestic Violence Statistics: Prevalence and Trends*, FindCounseling.com (Feb. 2001), http://www.findcounseling.com/journal/domestic-violence/domestic-violence-statistics.html.

> The precise incidence of domestic violence in America is difficult to determine for several reasons: it often goes unreported, even on surveys; there is no nationwide organization that gathers information from local police departments about the number of substantiated reports and calls; and there is disagreement about what should be included in the definition of domestic violence. "One study estimated that more than 3% (approximately 1.8 million) of women were severely assaulted by male partners or cohabitants over the course of a year, while other studies indicate the percentage of women experiencing dating violence ... ranges as high as 65%.

Id. (quoting Joy D. Osofsky, *The Impact of Violence on Children*, 9 Future of Child., Winter 1999, at 33, 34).

25. *See* Shaw, *supra* note 10, at 663.
26. Kerry Abrams, *Immigration Law and the Regulation of Marriage*, 91 Minn. L. Rev. 1625, 1696 (2007); Shaw, *supra* note 10, at 663; *see* Hass et al., *supra* note 12, at 3.
27. Jontz, *supra* note 22, at 197.
28. Shaw, *supra* note 10, at 678.
29. *Id.*
30. Dutton et al., *supra* note 12, at 293 (stating that 21.7% of the surveyed battered immigrant women listed fear of being reported to immigration officials as one of their primary reasons for remaining in the abusive relationship).
31. *See* Margot Mendelson, *The Legal Production of Identities: A Narrative Analysis of Conversations with Battered Undocumented Women*, 19 Berkeley Women's L.J. 138, 163 (2004).
32. *See* Shaw, *supra* note 10, at 665.
33. Hass et al., *supra* note 12, at 3.
34. Mendelson, *supra* note 31, at 183. This lack of education tends to persist until a woman receives legal status because many undocumented women are too afraid to enroll in school and feel uncomfortable dealing with people outside their homes. *Id.* The legal system, and immigration law in particular, is very complex. Linda Kelly Hill, *The Right to Be Heard: Voicing the Due Process Right to Counsel for Unaccompanied Alien Children*, 31 B.C. Third World L.J. 41, 62 (2011). This complexity seriously undermines the ability of unrepresented individuals to navigate the system. *Id.* When litigants must rely on attorneys, immigrants who do not speak English are at an even greater disadvantage than other unrepresented persons. *See id.*
35. Leslye E. Orloff et al., *Battered Immigrant Women's Willingness to Call for Help and Police Response*, 13 UCLA Women's L.J. 43, 81 (2003); *see* Shaw, *supra* note 10, at 665.
36. Orloff et al., *supra* note 35, at 81.

37. Mendelson, *supra* note 31, at 163.
38. *Id.*
39. *Id.*
40. *Id.* at 164–65.
41. *Id.* at 164.
42. Mendelson, *supra* note 31, at 164.
43. Jontz, *supra* note 22, at 196.
44. *Id.*
45. *Id.*
46. *Id.*
47. *See, e.g.*, Wang, *supra* note 16, at 162–63.
48. *See id.* at 168–72; Wood, *supra* note 10, at 151–52.
49. Wang, *supra* note 16, at 168.
50. Evelyn Lee, *Overview: The Assessment and Treatment of Asian American Families*, *in* Working with Asian Americans: A Guide for Clinicians 7 (Evelyn Lee ed., 1997); Tam B. Tran, *Using DSM-IV to Diagnose Mental Illness in Asian Americans*, 10 J. Contemp. Legal Issues 335, 342–43 (1999); Wang, *supra* note 16, at 168–69; *see* Carolyn Jin-Myung Oh, *Questioning the Cultural and Gender-Based Assumptions of the Adversary System: Voices of Asian-American Law Students*, 7 Berkeley Women's L.J. 125, 167 (1992).
51. Wang, *supra* note 16, at 169. In many Asian cultures, marriages "were frequently prearranged [and] often involved an exchange of money from the groom's family to the bride's family," much like in a sale, indicating that the wife would be subject to the will of the husband. *Id.*; *see* Christine K. Ho, *An Analysis of Domestic Violence in Asian American Communities: A Multicultural Approach to Counseling*, 9 Women & Therapy 129, 131 (1990). Although these traditions seem outdated, they still exist to some extent in modern times in the United States. *See* Ho, *supra*, at 136–37; Wang, *supra* note 16, at 169 n.105. "In a study in Seattle on domestic violence, Vietnamese men expressed a sense of ownership over their wives and Vietnamese, Laotian, and Khmer women all said that they could not refuse their husbands' requests for sex without a good excuse." Wang, *supra* note 16, at 169 n.105; *see* Ho, *supra*, at 141.
52. Nilda Rimonte, *A Question of Culture: Cultural Approval of Violence Against Women in the Pacific-Asian Community and the Cultural Defense*, 43 Stan. L. Rev. 1311, 1318 (1991); Wang, *supra* note 16, at 169.
53. Wang, *supra* note 16, at 169–72.
54. Ho, *supra* note 51, at 134; Wang, *supra* note 16, at 169.
55. Geeta Anand, *Mother's Regret Raises Abuse Issue*, Bos. Globe, May 8, 1994, at 29.
56. *Id.*

57. *Id.*

58. *See* Wang, *supra* note 16, at 170.

59. Orloff et al., *supra* note 35, at 82; Jenny Rivera, *Domestic Violence Against Latinas by Latino Males: An Analysis of Race, National Origin, and Gender Differentials*, 14 B.C. Third World L.J. 231, 240–41 (1994); Wood, *supra* note 10, at 151.

60. Rivera, *supra* note 59, at 241; *accord* Wood, *supra* note 10, at 151–52.

61. *See* Orloff et al., *supra* note 35, at 82; Wood, *supra* note 10, at 151–52.

62. Orloff et al., *supra* note 35, at 82 (citing Dutton et al., *supra* note 12, at 245 (discussing a study conducted from 1992 to 1995)).

63. *Id.*

64. *Id.* at 75; Wood, *supra* note 10, at 150. Foreign languages are often spoken at home, and one study on Asian-American immigrant communities indicates that over seventy-five percent speak their native language at home. Wang, *supra* note 16, at 164. A 1993 book, commissioned by the Social Science Research Council's National Committee for Research on the 1980 Census, reports that 79.5% of Chinese immigrants, 63.8% of Filipino immigrants, 76.8% of Korean immigrants, 60.1% of Asian Indian immigrants, and 83.4% of Vietnamese immigrants speak their native language at home. Herbert R. Barringer et al., Asians and Pacific Islanders in the United States 187 (1995); Wang, *supra* note 16, at 164.

65. Orloff et al., *supra* note 35, at 75.

66. *Id.*; Carlberg, *supra* note 19, at 742; *see, e.g.*, Mendelson, *supra* note 31, at 170; *infra* notes 87-110.

67. *See* Orloff et al., *supra* note 35, at 75.

68. Wood, *supra* note 10, at 150–51.

69. *See id.* at 151.

70. *Id.*

71. *See* Orloff et al., *supra* note 35, at 90–91.

72. *See id.*

73. *See id.* at 54 n.51.

74. *See id.*

75. *Id.* at 90–91. The survey was a large-scale research project conducted from 1992 to 1995 and participants were immigrant Latinas in the Washington, D.C. metropolitan area. *Id.* (citing Dutton et al., *supra* note 12, at 245 (discussing the study conducted from 1992 to 1995)).

76. Orloff et al., *supra* note 35, at 90–91.

77. *Id.* at 82–83. In the survey, 93.8% of the battered immigrant women requesting police assistance experienced "severe physical abuse." *Id.* at 71. Additionally, all respondents reported injury at the time of the

call and nearly sixty percent had visible injuries when police arrived. *Id.* Over half reported physical evidence of domestic violence present on the crime scene—property in disarray, torn clothing, and violence or threats of abuse in the presence of police. *Id.*

78. *See id.* at 74, 90–91 ("The need for bilingual police officers and/or interpreters working with police forces in communities with significant immigrant populations has long been recognized."); Wang, *supra* note 16, at 164; *supra* note 64.

79. Wang, *supra* note 16, at 165.

80. *Id.* at 162.

81. Margaretta Wan Ling Lin & Cheng Imm Tan, *Holding Up More Than Half the Heavens: Domestic Violence in Our Communities, A Call for Justice, in* The State of Asian America: Activism and Resistance in the 1990s, at 321, 327 (Karin Aguilar-San Juan ed., 1994); Wang, *supra* note 16, at 162, 164–65.

82. Lin & Tan, *supra* note 81, at 327; Wang, *supra* note 16, at 162–63.

83. *See* Wang, *supra* note 16, at 164–65; *see, e.g.*, Lin & Tan, *supra* note 81, at 323.

84. *See* Orloff et al., *supra* note 35, at 71.

85. *See* Wood, *supra* note 10, at 151. Furthermore, the myriad public and private agencies devoted to helping victims of domestic violence can be so daunting that a woman may decide to not bother contacting each organization because, by contacting multiple agencies for different services, she could potentially reveal her immigration status to multiple people. *See* Orloff et al., *supra* note 35, at 90–91. Examples of public and private domestic abuse victim advocacy agencies include medical facilities, counseling centers, shelters, and hotlines. Wang, *supra* note 16, at 165.

86. Wang, *supra* note 16, at 165.

87. Orloff et al., *supra* note 35, at 46–47; Wang, *supra* note 16, at 172–73; *see, e.g.*, Mendelson, *supra* note 31, at 170.

88. Orloff et al., *supra* note 35, at 46–47; Wang, *supra* note 16, at 172–73; *see, e.g.*, Mendelson, *supra* note 31, at 170.

89. *See* Dan M. Kahan, *Reciprocity, Collective Action, and Community Policing*, 90 Calif. L. Rev. 1513, 1513 (2002); Orloff et al., *supra* note 35, at 85; Carlberg, *supra* note 19, at 742.

90. Ki-Taek Chung & Nadja Zalokar, U.S. Comm'n on Civil Rights, Civil Rights Issues Facing Asian Americans in the 1990s 53 (1992), *available at* http://www.eric.ed.gov/PDFS/ED343979.pdf; Police Exec. Research Forum, Community Policing: The Past, Present, and Future 134 (Lorie Fridell & Mary Ann Wycoff, eds., 2004), *available at* http://www.policeforum.org/library/community-policing/CommunityPolicingReduced.pdf; Orloff et al., *supra* note 35, at 47. United States law enforcement officers, too, are not always trustworthy: in 1991, New York City traffic police severely beat a Chinese immigrant because he misunderstood a request for his registration and got out of his car. Chung & Zalokar, *supra*, at 53. Police insensitivity also took root in 1989 in a small California town through "a general pattern of harassment

of Filipino" youth, where officers frequently searched their car trunks and asked them if they were members of gangs. *Id.* at 54.

91. Luz E. Nagle, *Corruption of Politicians, Law Enforcement, and the Judiciary in Mexico and Complicity Across the Border*, 21 Small Wars & Insurgencies 95, 97 (2010). Mexico was given a "weak" rating in 2007 by Global Integrity, a non-profit organization that tracks corruption trends. *See Global Integrity Report: Mexico: 2007*, Global Integrity, http://report. globalintegrity.org/Mexico/2007 (last visited Oct. 27, 2011). In 2009, Mexico's Global Integrity rating rose to the level of "moderate." *Global Integrity Report: Mexico: 2009*, Global Integrity, http://report.globalintegrity.org/Mexico/2009 (last visited Oct.. 27, 2011).

92. *See* Nagel, *supra* note 91, at 99.

93. *Id.*

94. *Id.* at 100.

95. *See, e.g.*, Idilbi, *supra* note 10, at 1731; Nagle, *supra* note 91, at 99; Wang, *supra* note 16, at 173. For example, one undocumented woman spent eight years living in fear of deportation and would not even leave her own house lest she be arrested and deported. Mendelson, *supra* note 31, at 170. For that reason, she did not call the police when her husband violently abused her. Mendelson, *supra* note 31, at 170.

96. *See, e.g.*, Mendelson, *supra* note 31, at 170.

97. Carlberg, *supra* note 19, at 741, 749; *see, e.g.*, Mendelson, *supra* note 31, at 170.

98. Carlberg, *supra* note 19, at 741–42; *see, e.g.*, Mendelson, *supra* note 31, at 170. Domestic violence can increase in frequency and severity over time, making it especially important that law enforcement officials and courts respond forcefully after an initial incident. *See* Deborah Epstein, *Effective Intervention in Domestic Violence Cases: Rethinking the Roles of Prosecutors, Judges, and the Court System*, 11 Yale J.L. & Feminism 3, 7 (1999); Julia Weber, *Domestic Violence Courts: Components and Considerations*, 2 J. Center for Families, Child. & Courts 23, 24 (2000).

99. Carlberg, *supra* note 19, at 741–42.

100. *Id.* at 742.

101. *Id.*

> In 1989, the Mayor of New York City, Edward Koch, issued Executive Order No. 124, which prohibited any city employee from reporting the immigration status of any individual to federal authorities, unless: (1) it was required by law, (2) the individual authorizes the immigration information to be transmitted to federal authorities, or (3) the individual had been engaging in criminal behavior.
>
> *Id.* at 747; *accord* City of N.Y., Exec. Order No. 124 (Aug. 7, 1989), *available at* http://courts.state.ny.us/library/queens/PDF_files/Orders/ord124.pdf; *see also* City of New York v. United States, 179 F.3d 29, 31–32 (2d Cir. 1999). Similarly, Maine passed a noncooperation law that provides for disclosure of immigration status to federal authorities only if:

i. the individual to whom such information pertains is suspected ... of engaging in illegal activity, other than mere status as an undocumented alien; or ii. the dissemination of such information is necessary to apprehend a person suspected of engaging in illegal activity, other than mere status as an undocumented alien; or iii. such disclosure is necessary in furtherance of an investigation of potential terrorist activity; or iv. such disclosure is required by law.

John E. Baldacci, Governor of Maine, *An Order Concerning Access to State Services By All Entitled Maine Residents* (Apr. 9, 2004), *available at* http://www.maine.gov/portal/government/governor (select the "Policy Initiatives" hyperlink, then select the "Executive Orders" hyperlink, then select the "Executive Order Archive" hyperlink, then select "An Order Concerning Access to State Services By All Entitled Maine Residents" hyperlink); Carlberg, *supra* note 19, at 752.

102. *City of New York*, 179 F.3d at 36–37; Carlberg, *supra* note 19, at 746. In 1996, Congress enacted section 434 of the Personal Responsibility and Work Opportunity Reconciliation Act and section 642 of the Illegal Immigration Reform and Immigrant Responsibility Act, which were enacted to prevent localities from enacting their own noncooperation laws. Carlberg, *supra* note 19, at 746; *see* H.R. Rep. No. 104-725, at 383 (1996) (Conf. Rep.); Huyen Pham, *The Constitutional Right Not to Cooperate?: Local Sovereignty and the Federal Immigration Power*, 74 U. Cin. L. Rev. 1373, 1374–76 (2006). In *City of New York v. United States*, the Second Circuit explained that "the City [did] not dispute that Congress has plenary power to legislate on the subject of aliens." 179 F.3d at 34. The City therefore challenged the statutes on both the Tenth Amendment and the Guarantee Clause of the U.S. Constitution. *Id.* at 34, 36. The court, however, found that the statutory interference with New York's executive order was permissible and upheld the statutes. *Id.* at 37.

103. See Kahan, *supra* note 89, at 1513; Orloff et al., *supra* note 35, at 85.

104. *See* Kahan, *supra* note 89, at 1513–15.

105. *Understanding the Responsibilities of an Officer and the Rights of a Civilian*, Community-Policing.org, http://www.communitypolicing.org/officers-and-civilians (last visited Oct. 27, 2011) [hereinafter Community Policing].

106. Suzanne Meiners, Comment, *A Tale of Political Alienation of Our Youth: An Examination of the Potential Threats on Democracy Posed by Incomplete "Community Policing" Programs*, 7 U.C. Davis J. Juv. L. & Pol'y 161, 170 (2003); Community Policing, *supra* note 105.

107. *See* Orloff et al., *supra* note 35, at 85.

108. *Id.* at 85–86.

109. *Id.* at 85.

110. *See id.*

111. Yule Kim, *The Limits of State and Local Immigration Enforcement and Regulation*, 3 Al-bany Gov't L. Rev. 242, 244 (2010); *see* Fong Yue Ting v. United States, 149 U.S. 698, 705 (1893); Chy Lung v. Freeman, 92 U.S. 275, 280 (1875); Henderson v. Mayor of New York, 92 U.S. 259, 270 (1875).

112. Immigration and Nationality Act § 287(g), Public Law No. 82-414, 8 U.S.C. § 1357 (2006); Kim, *supra* note 111, at 251.

113. *See* Jennifer M. Chacón, *A Diversion of Attention? Immigration Courts and the Adjudication of Fourth and Fifth Amendment Rights*, 59 Duke L.J. 1563, 1584–85; *see, e.g.*, Morgan John-son, *New Police Chief Named After Immigration Policy Dispute*, Brown Daily Herald, Mar. 10, 2011, at 12 (quoting Providence, Rhode Island Public Safety Commissioner Steven Pare in discussing the implementation of the Secure Communities program in Providence).

114. Kim, *supra* note 111, at 244 (quoting DeCanas v. Bica, 424 U.S. 351, 354 (1976)); *see Fong Yue Ting,* 149 U.S. at 705; *Chy Lung,* 92 U.S. at 280; *Henderson,* 92 U.S. at 270.

115. *See* Gonzales v. City of Peoria, 722 F.2d 468, 474–75 (9th Cir. 1983); Kim, *supra* note 111, at 244–45, 247–48.

116. Kim, *supra* note 111, at 251.

117. City of New York v. United States, 179 F.3d 29, 32–33 (2d Cir. 1999); *Gonzales, 722* F.2d at 474–75; H.R. Rep. No. 104-725, at 383. Local governments are also restricted by federal statute in their discretion to use information that their officers collect regarding an individual's immigration status. *City of New York,* 179 F.3d at 32–33.

118. Kim, *supra* note 111, at 251; Immigration and Nationality Act § 287(g).

119. *See* Kim, *supra note* 111, at 252.

120. *Id.*

121. Chacón, *supra* note 113, at 1582.

122. *Id.* at 1583–84; *see also Memorandum of Agreement,* U.S. Immigr. & Customs Enforcement, at 21, http://www.ice.gov/doclib/detention-reform/pdf/287g_moa.pdf.

123. Chacón, *supra* note 113, at 1584; *Memorandum of Agreement, supra* note 122, at 4. The sample MOA on the ICE website includes a section on training for performance of immigration officer functions. *Memorandum of Agreement, supra* note 122, at 4, 17.

124. *Id.*

125. Chacón, *supra* note 113, at 1584–85.

126. *See id.;* Johnson, *supra* note 113.

127. *See* Chacón, *supra* note 113, at 1584–85. In a letter to ICE, the Providence, Rhode Island Public Safety Commissioner, Steven Pare, wrote, "The Secure Communities program will create fear and mistrust between the community and law enforcement—thus undermining our community policing model and risking the public safety of our capital city." Johnson, *supra* note 113.

128. Chacón, *supra* note 113, at 1595.

129. *Id.*

130. *Id.*

131. *Testimony of David Venturella, Executive Director, Secure Communities, Immigration and Customs Enforcement, Before the House Appropriations Committee Subcommittee on Homeland Security, "Priorities Enforcing Immigration Law,"* U.S. Department Homeland Security, http://www.dhs.gov/ynews/testimony/testimony_1239800126329.shtm (last visited Oct. 30, 2011); *see* Chacón, *supra* note 113, at 1595-96.

132. Chacón, *supra* note 113, at 1595–96; *More Questions Than Answers About the Secure Communities Program,* Nat'l Immigr. L. Center 1, 1-2 (Mar. 2009), http://www.nilc.org/immlawpolicy/LocalLaw/secure-communities-2009-03-23.pdf; *Secure Communities: Get the Facts,* U.S. Immigr. & Customs Enforcement, www.ice.gov/secure_communities/get-the-facts.htm (last visited Oct. 30, 2011).

133. Daniel González, *ICE Project Mainly Nets Low-Level Criminals,* Ariz. Republic, Mar. 9, 2011, at Al.

134. Chacón, *supra* note 113, at 1596.

135. *Activated Jurisdictions,* ICE Secure Communities, http://www.ice.gov/doclib/secure-communities/pdf/sc-activated.pdf (last visited Oct. 30, 2011).

136. González, *supra note* 133.

137. Julia Preston & Kirk Semple, *U.S. Hardens Its Stance on an Immigrant Policy,* N.Y. Times, Feb. 18, 2011, at A20; *see Activated Jurisdictions, supra* note 135.

138. *See* Shankar Vedantam, *Reversals by Immigration Officials Are Sowing Mistrust,* Wash. Post, Nov. 22, 2010, at A4.

139. Ken Green, *Denver Mayor Candidate Mejia Joins Linkhart in Opposing 'Secure Communities,'* Examiner.com, Feb. 17, 2011, http://www.examiner.com/top-news-in-denver/denver-mayor-candidate-mejia-joins-linkhart-opposing-secure-communities.

140. Gloria Pazmiño & Debralee Santos, *Opposition Grows Against Secure Communities Immigration Program,* Manhattan Times, Nov. 23, 2010, http://www.manhattantimesnews.com/2010/opposition-grows-against-secure-communities-immigration-program.html.

141. *Id.*

142. *See* Pazmiño & Santos, *supra* note 140; Carlberg, *supra* note 19, at 741–42.

143. Pazmiño & Santos, *supra* note 140; Preston & Semple, *supra* note 137; Michele Waslin, *The Secure Communities Program: Unanswered Questions and Continuing Concerns,* Immigr. Pol'y Center, Nov. 2009, at 3–4, *available at* http://www.immigrationpolicy.org/sites/default/files/docs/Secure_Communities_112309.pdf. Level 1 offenders are "[i]ndiv duals who have been convicted of major drug offenses and violent offenses such as murder, manslaughter, rape, robbery, and kidnapping." Waslin, *supra,* at 3. Level 2 offenders are "[i]ndividuals who have been convicted of minor drug offenses and property offenses such as burglary, larceny, fraud, and money laundering." *Id.* Level 3 offenders are "[i]ndividuals who have been convicted of other offenses." *Id.*

144. *See* Preston & Semple, *supra* note 137. From the time of the program's inception until November 2009, Secure Communities had identified over 111,000 criminal aliens in local custody. Waslin, *supra* note

143, at 4. Of those, "more than 11,000 were charged with or convicted of Level 1 crimes, while more than 100,000 had been convicted of Level 2 and 3 crimes." *Id.*

145. Gonzalez, *supra* note 133.

146. *Id.*

147. *Id.*

148. *Id.; Secure Communities: Get the Facts, supra* note 132.

149. Waslin, *supra* note 143, at 4. "[T]he program has come under increasing criticism from immigrant advocates who say it also encourages police to engage in unconstitutional racial profiling and discriminatory arrests so they can run fingerprints through the immigration databases as part of Secure Communities." González, *supra* note 133.

150. Vedantam, *supra* note 1; *see* Waslin, *supra* note 143, at 4.

151. Vedantam, *supra* note 138; *see* Suzanne Gamboa, *'Voluntary' Immigration Program Not so Voluntary,* MSNBC (Feb. 16, 2011 1:50:56 PM), http://www.msnbc.msn.com/id/41625585/ns/us_news-security; Preston & Semple, *supra* note 137.

152. Vedantam, *supra* note 138; *see* Gamboa, *supra* note 151; Preston & Semple, *supra* note 137. In September of 2010, United States Secretary of Homeland Security Janet Napolitano sent a letter to Zoe Lofgren, Chairwoman of the Subcommittee on Immigration, Citizenship, Refugees, Border Security, and International Law of the House Judiciary Committee, stating that "[a] local law enforcement agency that does not wish to participate in the Secure Communities deployment plan must formally notify the Assistant Director for the Secure Communities program" and that "[i]f a local law enforcement agency chooses not to be activated in the Secure Communities deployment plan, it will be the responsibility of that agency to notify its local ICE field office of suspected criminal aliens." Letter from Janet Napolitano, Sec'y, U.S. Dep't of Homeland Sec., to The Honorable Zoe Lofgren, Chairwoman, Subcomm. on Immigration, Citizenship, Refugees, Border Sec., & Int'l Law (Sept. 7, 2010), *available at* http://www.nilc.org/immlawpolicy/LocalLaw/s-comm-opt-out-ltrs-USDOJ-DHS-2010-09-08.pdf; *accord* Vedantam, *supra* note 138.

153. Preston & Semple, *supra* note 137. One such method of pressure involves creating a ring around the resistant jurisdiction by bringing all nearby communities into the program. *Id.*

154. *Preliminary Briefing Guide: Newly Pwleased Documents Chronicle Agency's Deception About Opting-Out of "Secure Communities" Program,* Center for Constitutional Rights, http:// ccrjustice.org/files/foiabrief.pdf [hereinafter *Preliminary Briefing Guide*]; *see Secure Communities: Get the Facts, supra* note 132.

> A jurisdiction may choose not to receive the identifications that result from processing the fingerprints through DHS's biometric system that are provided to the local ICE field office. In the past, this option has been mischaracterized as a mechanism for a jurisdiction to opt out of the program. In fact, a jurisdiction's decision not to receive this information directly does not affect whether the local ICE field office in that jurisdiction will or will not take enforcement action based on those results.

Secure Communities: Get the Facts, supra note 132.

155. Complaint for Declaratory and Injunctive Relief at 1, 25, Nat'l Day Laborer Org. Network v. Immigration & Customs Enforcement, (S.D.N.Y filed Apr. 27, 2010) (No. 10 Civ. 3488), *available at* http://ccrjustice.org/files/SC_Complaint_REAL_FINAL.pdf.

156. Preston & Semple, *supra* note 137; Kirk Semple, *Program to Have Police Spot Illegal Immigrants Is Mired in Confusion,* N. Y. Times, Nov. 10, 2010, at A26; *Preliminary Briefing Guide, supra* note 154.

157. Vedantam, *supra* note 138; Semple, *supra* note 156.

158. Semple, *supra* note 156.

159. *Id.* Several organizations sought documents pursuant to a Freedom of Information Act (FOIA) request that highlight the internal confusion and deception regarding the availability of an opt-out option for states and localities. Press Release, Ctr. for Constitutional Rights, Newly Released Secure Cmtvs. Documents Signal Opening for Local Opt-Out (Feb. 16, 2011), *available at* http://ccrjustice.org/newsroom/press-releases/newly-released-secure-communities-documents-signal-opening-local-opt-out; *Preliminary Briefing Guide, supra* note 154. This confusion was ongoing in the aftermath of the release of information pursuant to the FOIA request. *See* Letter from Chris Newman, Legal Director, National Day Laborer Organizing Network, to Deval Patrick, Governor, Commonwealth of Massachusetts (Mar. 21, 2011), *available at* http://ndlon.org/pdf/patrickletter.pdf. In March 2011, legal advocates from the National Day Laborer Organizing Network, the Center for Constitutional Rights, and the Cardozo Immigrant Justice Clinic advised Massachusetts Governor Deval Patrick that he could prevent statewide participation in Secure Communities. *Id.*

160. *Preliminary Briefing Guide, supra* note 154.

161. *Secure Communities: Get the Facts, supra* note 132.

162. Leslie Berestein Rojas, *The Letter from ICE Terminating 'Alt Existing' S-Comm Agreements,* Multi-American, Aug. 5, 2011, http://multiamerican.scpr.org/2011/08/the-letter-from-ice-terminating-all-existing-secure-communities-moas.

163. *Id.* "In order to clarify that a memorandum of agreement between ICE and a state is not required to operate Secure Communities for any jurisdiction, today, ICE Director John Morton sent a letter to Governors terminating all existing Secure Communities MOAs to avoid further confusion." Leslie Berestein Rojas, *ICE Rescinds Secure Communities MOAs, Program Continues,* Multi-American, Aug. 5, 2011, http://multiamerican.scpr.org/2011/08/ice-rescinds-secure-communities-moas-allowing-controversial-program-to-continue (quoting statement of Nicole Navas, ICE spokeswoman) (emphasis omitted).

164. *See* Vedantam, *supra* note 1; *Fact Sheet: Intersection of Domestic Violence & The Secure Communities Program,* Colo. Coalition Against Domestic Violence, http://www.leg.state.co.us/CLICS/CLICS2011A/commsumm.nsf/b4a3962433b52fa787256e5f00670a71/b95c4f7f94 5 b961c8725783700727d81/%-24FILE/0214HseLocalAttachH.pdf (last visited Oct. 30, 2011) [hereinafter *Fact Sheet*].

165. *Fact Sheet, supra* note 164.

166. *See* Vedantam, *supra* note 1; Waslin, *supra* note 143; *Fact Sheet, supra* note 164.

167. *See* Orloff et al., *supra* note 35, at 84 (discussing the importance of communicating the availability of battered women's services to immigrant populations); Tim Hoover, *May OK Illegal-Immigrant Checks*, Denver Post, Jan. 4, 2011, at 3B; *States Without "Secure Communities" Already Face Problems with Police-ICE Collaboration,* Deportation Nation, Dec. 7, 2010, http:// www.deportationnation.org/2010/12/states-withont-secure-communities-already-face-problems-with-police-ice-collaboration [hereinafter *States Without "Secure Communities"*]; *Updated: Colorado May Limit Immigrants Targeted by "Secure Communities,"* Deportation Nation, Jan. 4, 2011, http://www.deportationnation.org/2011/01/colorado-may-limit-immigrants-targeted-by-secure-communities [hereinafter *Updated: Colorado]* (giving suggestions for an MOA that would be sensitive to domestic violence issues).

168. *See* Colo. Rev. Stat. Ann. §29-29-103 (West 2011); *Updated: Colorado, supra* note 167.

169. See Hoover, *supra* note 167; Letter from Damian J. Arguello, President, Colo. Hispanic Bar Ass'n, to Honorable Bill Ritter, Jr., Governor, State of Colo., (Aug. 4, 2010), *available at* https://crocodoc.com/yuGJ2i [hereinafter CHBA letter].

170. *See* Orloff et al., *supra* note 35, at 84 (discussing the importance of communicating the availability of battered women's services to immigrant populations).

171. *See* Kittrie, *supra* note 19, at 1482–83; Carlberg, *supra* note 19, at 741–42.

172. *Secure Communities: Get the Facts, supra* note 132; *see, e.g.,* Vedantam, *supra* note 1. In addition to Bolanos, Prince George's County Police officers arrested Florinda Faviola Lorenzo-Desimilian for the same crime, namely selling phone cards without a license. Pangilinan, *supra* note 4. Lorenzo-Desimilian entered the country legally, but then overstayed her work visa. *Id.*

173. *See* Carlberg, *supra* note 19, at 742; *Secure Communities: Get the Facts, supra* note 132; *see, e.g.,* Hoover, *supra* note 167.

174. Memorandum from John Morton, Dir., ICE, to All Field Office Dirs., All Special Agents in Charge, & All Chief Counsel, ICE (June 17, 2011), *available at* http://www.ice. gov/doclib/secure-communities/pdf/domestic-violence.pdf [hereinafter Morton Memorandum]; Elise Foley, *Secure Communities Agreements Canceled, Participation Still Required,* Huffington Post (Aug. 5, 2011), http://www.huffingtonpost.com/2011/08/05/secure-communities-update-department-of-homeland-security_n_919651.html.

175. *See generally* Morton Memorandum, *supra* note 174.

176. *Id.*

177. *Id.*

178. *Id.*

179. *See* CHBA letter, *supra* note 169, at 1; Morton Memorandum, *supra* note 174.

180. *See* Morton Memorandum, *supra* note 174; *Secure Communities: Get the Facts, supra* note 132.

181. Jefferson Dodge, *Crackdown: 'Dragnet' May Fend Off Arizona-Style Immigration Law,* Boulder Wkly., Jan. 27, 2011, http://www.boulderweekly.com/article-4298-i-support-the-states-participation-of-secure-comm.html; *Secure Communities: Benefitting Law Enforcement Throughout the United States,* U.S. Immigr. & Customs Enforcement, http://www.ice.gov/doclib/secure-communities/pdf/lea-benefits.pdf (last visited Oct. 30, 2011) (justifying the Secure Communities program because it gives police less discretion, thereby reducing the possibility of racial profiling). Arizona's immigration program, S.B. 1070, became law in 2010. David A. Selden et al., *Placing S.B. 1070 And Racial Profiling into Context, and What S.B. 1070 Reveals About the Legislative Process in Arizona,* 43 Ariz. St. L.J. 523, 526 (2011). The law requires police officers who have a reasonable suspicion that someone is in the country illegally to stop, detain, or arrest that person to check immigration status. *Id.* at 525; *see* Ariz. Rev. Stat. Ann. § 11-1051 (2010), *invalidated by* United States v. Arizona, 641 F.3d 339, 354 (2011).

182. Dodge, *supra* note 181, at 14; *Secure Communities: Benefitting Law Enforcement Throughout the United States, supra* note 181; *Secure Communities: Get the Facts, supra* note 132.

183. *See* Morton Memorandum, *supra* note 174; Dodge, *supra* note 181, at 14; *Secure Communities: Benefitting Law Enforcement Throughout the United States, supra* note 181; *Secure Communities: Get the Facts, supra* note 132.

184. *See* Dodge, *supra* note 181, at 14; CHBA Letter, *supra* note 169; Morton Memorandum, *supra* note 174; *Secure Communities: Benefitting Law Enforcement Throughout the United States, supra* note 181; *Secure Communities: Get the Facts, supra* note 132.

185. *Compare* Dodge, *supra* note 181, at 14 (noting that reducing police discretion may reduce racial profiling), *with* Morton Memorandum, *supra* note 174, (advocating for discretion as a means to protect victims). *See also Secure Communities: Benefitting Law Enforcement Throughout the United States, supra* note 181 (claiming that Secure Communities "reduces the possibility for allegations of racial or ethnic profiling because the fingerprints of every individual arrested . . . are checked against immigration records"); *Secure Communities: Get the Facts, supra* note 132 ('Under Secure Communities, the fingerprints of every single individual arrested and booked into custody, including U.S. citizens and legal permanent residents, are checked against immigration records—reducing the risk of discrimination or racial profiling.").

186. *See* Orloff et al., *supra* note 35, at 84; Hoover, *supra* note 167; *States Without "Secure Communities," supra* note 167; *Updated: Colorado, supra* note 167.

187. *See* Colo. Rev. Stat. Ann. § 29-29-103 (West 2011); Hoover, *supra* note 167; *Updated: Colorado, supra* note 167.

188. *See* Hoover, *supra* note 167; CHBA letter, *supra* note 169.

189. *See* Kahan, *supra* note 89, at 1525 (explaining that trust in law enforcement depends on the public's perception of the fairness and legitimacy of police procedures); Orloff et al., *supra* note 35, at 84-85; Carlberg, *supra* note 19, at 755; *see, e.g.,* Vedantam, *supra* note 1 (publicizing the ill effects of Secure Communities on domestic violence victims).

190. *See* Kahan, *supra* note 89, at 1525; Orloff et al., *supra* note 35, at 84–85; Carlberg, *supra* note 19, at 755; *see, e.g.,* Vedantam, *supra* note 1.

191. *See* Memorandum of Agreement between U.S. Dep't of Homeland Sec. Immigration & Customs Enforcement and Colo. Dep't of Public Safety 3 (Jan. 6, 2011), *available at* http://www.ice.gov/doclib/foia/secure_communities-moa/colorado-sc-moa.pdf [hereinafter *Colorado MOA*]; *Updated: Colorado, supra* note 167.

192. Colo. Rev. Stat. Ann. §§ 18-6-800.3, 29-29-103; *Colorado MOA, supra* note 191, at 3. The following is Colorado's statute regarding reporting when the arrestee is charged with a domestic violence offense:

> (I) A peace officer who has probable cause that an arrestee for a criminal offense is not legally present in the United States shall report such arrestee to the United States immigration and customs enforcement office if the arrestee is not held at a detention facility. If the arrestee is held at a detention facility and the county sheriff reasonably believes that the arrestee is not legally present in the United States, the sheriff shall report such arrestee to the federal immigration and customs enforcement office.
>
> (II) This subsection (2) shall not apply to arrestees who are arrested for a suspected act of domestic violence as defined by section 18-6-800.3, C.R.S., until such time as the arrestee is convicted of a domestic violence offense.

Colo. Rev. Stat. Ann. § 29-29-103(2) (a).

193. *Colorado MOA, supra* note 191, at 3.

194. *See* CHBA Letter, *supra* note 169; Morton Memorandum, *supra* note 174.

195. *See, e.g.,* Vedantam, *supra* note 1; CHBA letter, *supra* note 169.

196. *See* Colo. Rev. Stat. § 29-29-103; Hoover, *supra* note 167; *Updated: Colorado, supra* note 167.

197. *See* Hoover, *supra* note 167; CHBA letter, *supra* note 169.

198. *See* Hoover, *supra* note 167; Vedantam, *supra* note 1; CHBA letter, *supra* note 169.

199. *See* Hoover, *supra* note 167; Pangilinan, *supra* note 2.

200. CHBA letter, *supra* note 169.

201. *See* Chacón, *supra* note 113, at 1596; Vedantam, *supra* note 1; CHBA letter, *supra* note 169.

202. CHBA letter, *supra* note 169.

203. *See* Pangilinan, *supra* note 2; Vedantam, *supra* note 1; CHBA letter, *supra* note 169.

204. *See* Kahan, *supra* note 89, at 1513; Orloff et al., *supra* note 35, at 85; Vedantam, *supra* note 1.

205. *See* Kahan, *supra* note 89, at 1513; Orloff et al., *supra* note 35, at 85; Vedantam, *supra* note 1 (quoting Maria Bolanos as saying, "You would have to be crazy to call the police. ... I would never call the police again.").

206. *See* Kahan, *supra* note 89, at 1525; Orloff et al., *supra* note 35, at 84–85; Carlberg, *supra* note 19, at 755.

207. *See* Kahan, *supra* note 89, at 1525; Orloff et al., *supra* note 35, at 87; Carlberg, *supra* note 19, at 755.

208. *See* Kahan, *supra* note 89, at 1525; Orloff et al., *supra* note 35, at 87; Carlberg, *supra* note 19, at 755.

209. Orloff et al., *supra* note 35, at 87; Carlberg, *supra* note 19, at 755.

210. Kittrie, *supra* note 19, at 1483 (noting that "victimized unauthorized aliens who are confused as to how the policy in their jurisdiction operates are likely to play it safe and not report the crime"); Carlberg, *supra* note 19, at 755–56.

211. *See* Orloff et al., *supra* note 35, at 74; Wang, *supra* note 16, at 162–63.

212. *See* Orloff et al., *supra* note 35, at 84.

213. *See id.* at 84–85.

214. *See* Vedantam, *supra* note 1 (quoting ICE spokesman Brian Hale as saying that "ICE cannot and will not turn a blind eye to those who violate federal immigration law. ... While ICE's enforcement efforts prioritize convicted criminal aliens, ICE maintains the discretion to take action on any alien it encounters.").

215. *See Secure Communities: Benefitting Law Enforcement Throughout the United States*, *supra* note 181.

216. *See* Chacón, *supra* note 113, at 1596; *Secure Communities: A Modernized Approach to Identifying and Removing Criminal Aliens*, U.S. Immigr. & Customs Enforcement, *available at* http://www.ice.gov/doclib/secure-communities/pdf/sc-brochure.pdf (last visited Oct. 30, 2011).

217. *See* Chacón, *supra* note 113, at 1596; *Secure Communities: A Modernized Approach to Identifying and Removing Criminal Aliens*, *supra* note 216. *But see* CHBA Letter, *supra* note 169.

DISCUSSION QUESTIONS

1. Briefly summarize what happened to Maria Bolanos as reported in the article's introduction. Is what happened to Bolanos after calling police a problem? Explain.

2. What barriers exist which make undocumented women especially unlikely to report abuse by their partners to the police?

3. According to Vishnuvajjala, is community policing compatible with local-federal immigration enforcement cooperative efforts? Why?

4. What is the Secure Communities Program? Describe the program. Do you believe the program is beneficial to public safety? Why or why not?

5. What three steps does Vishnuvajjala propose as a solution to the problem of domestic violence among the undocumented in localities participating in the Secure Communities Program? Do you agree with these proposed steps? Could they be implemented for undocumented victims of other types of crime?

CHAPTER SIX

Sanctuary Cities/ Counties

Introduction

In 2013, California enacted a state law that banned state and local law enforcement agencies from cooperating with U.S. Immigration and Customs Enforcement. The effect of the law was that local agencies would not hand over offenders in their custody to ICE agents without a judicial warrant (as opposed to an ICE detainer, which is an administrative hold request). This policy was always controversial, but it became a heated point of national debate with the killing in San Francisco of Kate Steinle by Francisco Sanchez in 2015. Sanchez had been in ICE custody for deportation but was turned over to the San Francisco County Sheriff's Department on an outstanding marijuana warrant. ICE put a detainer on Sanchez, thereby letting San Francisco County know that ICE wanted him back when the county was through with him. About this time, San Francisco decided to no longer prosecute minor marijuana cases, so Sanchez was let go rather than turned over to ICE. On July 1, 2015, Sanchez shot and killed Kate Steinle with a stolen gun he claimed to have found under a bridge. Steinle was unknown to Sanchez and was simply a bystander strolling nearby when Sanchez fired the weapon. Sanchez claimed it was an accident and was eventually acquitted of murder charges, but was found guilty of being a felon in possession of a gun. Critics of policies that prohibit local law enforcement's cooperation with ICE point to the Steinle case, among many others, as examples of what goes wrong when local governments practice political correctness in protecting illegal immigrants rather than enforcing the law.

A few states and dozens of local jurisdictions have adopted similar "sanctuary policies." No other state, however, has gone as far as California did in in 2017 when it passed a law barring private employers from cooperating with federal immigration officials. Under the law, private businesses can be fined up to $10,000 for each occurrence of providing ICE officers with any more information about their employees than is required by federal law. In fact, ICE officers may not even be invited into areas of the business that is not available to the public at large. California has truly set out to be a sanctuary for undocumented aliens. It is quite open about it. The state claims that by protecting illegal immigrants from federal authorities, their relationship as a community with local law enforcement and other government agencies is improved and enhanced.

ICE officials have lamented this posture of California and other sanctuary jurisdictions. According to ICE, these policies have the unintended consequences of creating dangerous encounters for its agents and also the increased apprehension of nonviolent illegal aliens who happen to be around when the targeted offenders are arrested. If ICE has to go out into the community to arrest priority-target illegal aliens, rather than arrest them in the safety of the local jail, then there is a greater danger of resistance and force being used. There is also the greater likelihood that other illegal aliens will be present, and ICE is not able to ignore those.

While the previous chapter reading raised concerns over the use state and local police agencies as tools of immigration enforcement, this chapter's reading challenges the other extreme—that state and local communities can wall themselves off as bulwarks, or sanctuaries, from the reach of federal immigration enforcement through noncooperation and the placement of obstacles. The reading is a product of the Center for Immigration Studies (CIS), a nonprofit think tank and public affairs advocacy organization that supports stricter controls on legal and illegal immigration. The CIS article here makes the argument that sanctuary cities and counties are potentially unlawful and certainly harmful to public safety.

READING 6

Tackling Sanctuaries

By Dan Cadman and Jessica Vaughan

Key Findings

This report examines the justifications given by sanctuary jurisdictions for their policies, and finds them to be largely unfounded:

- Cooperation with immigration enforcement has not been shown to undermine community trust nor cause immigrants to refrain from reporting crimes; there are better ways to address issues of access to police assistance without obstructing enforcement;

- Simply cooperating with federal immigration agencies does not turn local officers into de facto immigration officers, because federal officers make the decisions on which aliens are targeted for deportation;

- Such cooperation is not very costly for local jurisdictions because the removal of criminal aliens spares future victims and saves future supervision, incarceration, and social services costs to criminal aliens. In addition, cooperative localities can receive partial reimbursement for their incarceration costs.

- Claims by some local law enforcement agencies that they need a warrant in order to hold aliens for ICE are dubious but can be accommodated by the issuance of ICE administrative warrants.

The Trump administration has a number of tools available at its disposal and within the confines of executive authority to address the problem of sanctuaries and the public safety problems they create.

Dan Cadman and Jessica Vaughan, "Tackling Sanctuaries." Copyright © 2016 by Center for Immigration Studies.

Here's how to do so:

- Rescind the Obama administration actions and policies that encourage and enable sanctuaries, including clarifying that local agencies are expected to comply with detainers;
- Cut federal funding to sanctuaries;
- Initiate civil litigation to enjoin state or local laws and policies that egregiously obstruct enforcement of federal immigration laws and regulations;
- Selectively initiate prosecution under the alien harboring-and-shielding statute, which is a federal felony; and
- When requested, issue administrative warrants to accompany detainers as a reasonable accommodation to state or local concerns. Negotiating over which aliens will be subject to detainers, as is current policy, is not a reasonable accommodation.
- Direct ICE to begin publishing a weekly report providing the public with information on all criminal aliens released by the sanctuaries.

Introduction and Background

View Map of Sanctuary Cities

In the past several years, a "sanctuary" movement has arisen in various states and political subdivisions around the country. This movement intends to, and does in fact, obstruct the efforts of federal officers to enforce immigration laws, substituting instead the views of the state or local jurisdiction over how or whether immigration laws will be enforced within its boundaries.

The Center for Immigration Studies has tracked the movement, repeatedly spoken out against it,[1] and watched as it has grown under the policies of the Obama White House, whose aims have more closely mirrored those of open borders advocates than those of an administration constitutionally charged with faithfully executing the laws of the United States.[2] There are now more than 300 state and local governments with laws, rules, or policies that impede federal efforts to enforce immigration laws.[3]

Donald Trump began his dark horse presidential candidacy by campaigning to restore respect for America's borders and its immigration laws. Included in his platform was the message that sanctuaries which flouted those laws would not be tolerated. In his immigration policy speech in Phoenix in August, Trump said:

> "Block funding for sanctuary cities ... no more funding. We will end the sanctuary cities that have resulted in so many needless deaths. Cities that refuse to cooperate with federal authorities will not receive taxpayer dollars, and we will work with

Congress to pass legislation to protect those jurisdictions that do assist federal authorities."

Mr. Trump's platform resonated with voters and he is now president-elect.

Reacting to Trump's election, a number of sanctuary cities have declared that they will not retreat from their existing policies. The statements from Mayors Rahm Emanuel of Chicago and Bill DeBlasio of New York, as well as a number of others, have had a particular "throw down the gauntlet" tone to them.[4] Several police chiefs have taken a similar approach,[5] and one governor has threatened to sue the federal government if it withholds funds from sanctuaries.[6]

In addition, the students and faculty at a number of colleges and universities nationwide have demanded that administrators declare their campuses to be sanctuaries.[7] A publicly supported university in Oregon has done this,[8] as have the private Wesleyan and Columbia Universities. Meanwhile these schools collect millions of dollars in federal research funds and are the happy beneficiaries of additional millions from students using federal Pell grants and federally-subsidized student loans to pay for their tuition.[9]

But even many of those institutions which do not declare themselves sanctuaries already openly accept illegal alien students, in flagrant disregard of the immigration laws, and offer them in-state tuition rates. Ironically, this includes the University of California system, whose president is Janet Napolitano, former secretary of the Department of Homeland Security (DHS) under the Obama administration. The UC system goes so far as to provide an online Undocumented Student Resources guide, declaring that "Undocumented students of all ethnicities and nationalities can find a safe environment and supportive community at the University of California ... UC campuses offer a range of support services—from academic and personal counseling, to financial aid and legal advising ..."[10]

The purpose of this paper is to consider the means available to the Trump administration to confront and dissuade sanctuaries and diminish their ability to impede enforcement of federal immigration laws.

What is a "Sanctuary"?

Different people and groups may have different definitions of a sanctuary, and there is a spectrum of such policies across the nation. For our purposes, a sanctuary is a jurisdiction that has a law, ordinance, policy, practice, or rule that deliberately obstructs immigration enforcement, restricts interaction with federal immigration agencies, or shields illegal aliens from detection. In addition, federal law includes two key provisions that forbid certain practices: one that forbids policies restricting communication and information sharing (8 U.S.C. Section 1373) and one that forbids harboring illegal aliens or shielding them from detection (8 U.S.C. Section 1324).

Information exchanges. 8 U.S.C. 1373 states:

> "a Federal, State, or local government entity or official may not prohibit, or in any way restrict, any government entity or official from sending to, or receiving from, [federal immigration authorities] information regarding the citizenship or immigration status, lawful or unlawful, of any individual."

A recent report from the Department of Justice's Office of Inspector General (DOJ OIG)[11], requested by Rep. John Culberson (R-Texas), who chairs the appropriations committee in charge of the DOJ budget, determined that sanctuary policies which prohibit local officers from communicating or exchanging information with ICE are "inconsistent" with federal law. Sanctuary jurisdictions do this by ignoring immigration detainers, which are filed by Immigration and Customs Enforcement (ICE) agents to signal their intent to take custody of aliens for purposes of removal, once state or local justice system proceedings are concluded. Some jurisdictions go further by prohibiting communication to advise or even acknowledge to ICE agents that the alien has been arrested. They also sometimes prevent ICE agents from access to the alien to conduct interviews.

The OIG report investigated the policies of 10 jurisdictions and found that they did indeed limit cooperation with ICE in an improper way:

> "[E]ach of the 10 jurisdictions had laws or policies directly related to how those jurisdictions could respond to ICE detainers, and each limited in some way the authority of the jurisdiction to take action with regard to ICE detainers ... We also found that the laws and policies in several of the 10 jurisdictions go beyond regulating responses to ICE detainers and also address, in some way, the sharing of information with federal immigration authorities."

Harboring Aliens in Violation of Law. 8 U.S.C. 1324 states:

> "Any person who ... knowing or in reckless disregard of the fact that an alien has come to, entered, or remains in the United States in violation of law, conceals, harbors, or shields from detection, or attempts to conceal, harbor, or shield from detection, such alien in any place, ...; encourages or induces an alien to come to, enter, or reside in the United States, knowing or in reckless disregard of the fact that such coming to, entry, or residence is or will be in violation of law; or engages in any conspiracy to commit any of the preceding acts, or aids or abets the commission of any of the preceding acts, shall be. ... fined under title 18, imprisoned not more than 5 years, or both ..."[12]

Much of the sanctuary movement seems to be centered on shielding from federal action deportable aliens who have been arrested and charged with various crimes. But other jurisdictions have more expansive policies aimed at shielding some or all illegal aliens, including the so-called Dreamers and their families, from enforcement action.

What are the Arguments Made by Sanctuary Advocates?

The arguments have several distinct but interrelated themes:

- Police cooperation with immigration agents erodes trust between immigrants and authorities, and causes immigrants to refrain from reporting crimes;
- We don't want to act as immigration agents;
- We don't get reimbursed for incarceration costs;
- Cooperation is voluntary;
- Detainers must be accompanied by warrants;
- States are sovereign entities that have the right to make their own decisions on immigration.

In our view, when examined critically none of these arguments holds water, except for the one having to do with warrants, and that argument holds only to a certain degree, which we will discuss further below.

Police cooperation compromises community trust and safety. One of the most common reasons offered for non-cooperation policies is that they are needed so that immigrants will have no fear of being turned over for deportation when they report crimes. This frequently-heard claim has never been substantiated, and in fact has been refuted by a number of reputable studies. Not a shred of evidence of a "chilling effect" on immigrant crime reporting when local police cooperate with ICE exists in federal or local government or police data or independent academic research.

It is important to remember that crime reporting can be a problem in any place, and is not confined to any one segment of the population. In fact, most crimes are not reported, regardless of the victim's immigration status or ethnicity. According to the Bureau of Justice Statistics (BJS), in 2015, only 47 percent of violent victimizations, 55 percent of serious violent victimizations, were reported to police. In 2015, the percentage of property victimizations reported to police was just 35 percent.[13] These rates have been unaffected, either by changes in the level of interaction between local and federal enforcement from 2009-2012 (which coincides with the implementation of the Secure Communities biometric matching program) or by the spread of sanctuary policies since 2014.

Data from BJS show no meaningful differences among ethnic groups in crime reporting. Overall, Hispanics are slightly more likely to report crimes than other groups. Hispanic females, especially, are slightly more likely than white females and more likely than Hispanic and non-Hispanic males to report violent crimes.[14] This is consistent with academic surveys finding Hispanic females to be more trusting of police than other groups.[15]

A multitude of other studies refute the notion that local-federal cooperation in immigration enforcement causes immigrants to refrain from reporting crimes:

- A major study completed in 2009 by researchers from the University of Virginia and the Police Executive Research Forum (PERF) found no decline in crime reporting by Hispanics after the implementation of a local police program to screen offenders for immigration status and to refer illegal aliens to ICE for removal. This examination of Prince William County, Virginia's 287(g) program is the most comprehensive study to refute the "chilling effect" theory. The study also found that the county's tough immigration policies likely resulted in a decline in certain violent crimes.[16]

- The most reputable academic survey of immigrants and crime reporting found that by far the most commonly mentioned reason for not reporting a crime was a language barrier (47 percent), followed by cultural differences (22 percent), and a lack of understanding of the U.S. criminal justice system (15 percent)—not fear of being turned over to immigration authorities.[17]

- The academic literature reveals varying attitudes and degrees of trust toward police within and among immigrant communities. Some studies have found that Central Americans may be less trusting than other groups, while others maintain that the most important factor is socio-economic status and feelings of empowerment within a community, rather than the presence or level of immigration enforcement.[18]

- A 2009 study of calls for service in Collier County, Fla., found that the implementation of the 287(g) partnership program with ICE enabling local sheriff's deputies to enforce immigration laws, resulting in significantly more removals of criminal aliens, did not affect patterns of crime reporting in immigrant communities.[19]

- Data from the Boston, Mass., Police Department, one of two initial pilot sites for ICE's Secure Communities program, show that in the years after the implementation of this program, which ethnic and civil liberties advocates alleged would suppress crime reporting, showed that calls for service decreased proportionately with crime rates. The precincts with larger immigrant populations had less of a decline in reporting than precincts with fewer immigrants.[20]

- Similarly, several years of data from the Los Angeles Police Department covering the time period of the implementation of Secure Communities and other ICE initiatives that increased arrests of aliens show that the precincts with the highest percentage foreign-born populations do not have lower crime reporting rates than precincts that are majority black, or that have a smaller foreign-born population, or that have an immigrant population that is more white than Hispanic. The crime reporting rate in Los Angeles is most affected by the amount of crime, not by race, ethnicity, or size of the foreign-born population.[21]

- Recent studies based on polling of immigrants about whether they might or might not report crimes in the future based on hypothetical local policies for police interaction with ICE, such as one recent study entitled "Insecure Communities", by Nik Theodore of the University of Illinois, Chicago, should be considered with great caution, since they measure emotions and predict possible behavior, rather than record and analyze actual behavior of immigrants.[22] Moreover, the Theodore study is particularly flawed because it did not compare crime reporting rates of Latinos with other ethnic groups.

For these reasons, law enforcement agencies across the country have found that the most effective ways to encourage crime reporting by immigrants and all residents are to engage in tried and true initiatives such as community outreach, hiring personnel who speak the languages of the community, establishing anonymous tip lines, and setting up community sub-stations with non-uniform personnel to take inquiries and reports—not by suspending cooperation with federal immigration enforcement efforts. Proposals to increase ICE-local cooperation, such as the Davis-Oliver Act, which was passed by the House Judiciary Committee in 2015, enjoy strong support among law enforcement leaders across the country. These leaders—sheriffs, police, and state agency commanders—routinely and repeatedly express concern over crime problems associated with illegal immigration and routinely and repeatedly express their willingness to assist ICE, and that it is their duty to assist ICE.[23] The National Sheriffs Association and numerous individual sheriffs and police chiefs have endorsed the Davis-Oliver Act.

Instead of pushing sanctuary policies, advocates for immigrants in the community should be stressing that victims and witnesses are never targets for immigration enforcement (unless they, too, are criminals). If immigrant advocates would help disseminate this message, instead of spreading the myth that immigrants have something to fear from interaction with local police, then everyone in the community would be safer. It is important to remember that much of the crime inflicted on aliens comes from other aliens—for instance, coyotes, drug dealers, gangbangers and other career criminals—who prey on their own communities. When this is the case, alien victims and witnesses, significantly including aliens illegally in the United States, have every reason to want them plucked out of their midst by local law enforcement and removed by ICE.

What is more, aliens tend to be very familiar with the workings of immigration law, much more so than the average citizen, because it is in their interest to do so. As such, while they may not be able to cite specific visa categories, they are quite likely to know that immigration law and policy actually contain provisions to protect victims and witnesses from removal actions so that they can provide key information to police and prosecutors. If police officers want to be able to help immigrants who are victimized to take advantage of these programs, they need to have a good working relationship with ICE—and they also need to be allowed to inquire about immigration status so that they can offer this protection.

Lastly, we should point out that while state and local governments can't point to any credible studies to support their argument that cooperation with ICE diminishes trust levels in ethnic and alien communities, there is plenty of empirical, and powerful anecdotal, evidence which shows the damage done to communities when alien offenders are inappropriately released back to the street, whether by state and local police or by ICE, rather than being detained and removed from the United States for their offenses.[24] There have been so many victims of criminal behavior by illegal aliens that surviving family members of those killed have banded together to draw attention to their plight, and to the danger posed by sanctuary policies.[25] The families of these victims have been steadfastly ignored by law enforcement organizations and governments engaged in sanctuary policies, and they were ignored by the Democratic party during the presidential campaign. (Even before that, one Democratic representative went so far as to refer to the murder of a young woman by a multiply deported illegal alien felon as "a little thing".[26]) But the families of the victims were not ignored by presidential candidate Trump; he embraced them publicly, and they appeared frequently with him on the campaign trail as he promised to address the problem of sanctuaries if elected.

Refusal to act as immigration agents. Much of the controversy surrounding sanctuary policies has to do with state and local law enforcement agencies refusing to honor immigration detainers filed by ICE agents against aliens arrested for criminal offenses, aliens whom the agents have determined to be deportable and intend to take custody of, once state or local criminal justice proceedings are done. The detainer is a notification to the arresting/holding agency of ICE's intention to assume custody.[27]

Many state and local agencies complain that by being asked to honor the detainer, they are being forced to act as surrogate immigration officials. This belies the fact that when ICE agents file detainers against an individual in police custody, they have already made determinations about his alienage and deportability. They are not asking the police either to render that judgment on their own, or to second-guess their decision-making. For this reason, state and local agencies are not being asked to act as immigration agents; they are simply expected to tender to the federal authorities the individual identified in the detainer.

What is more, the reality of sanctuaries is that there are many variations on the theme: a number of jurisdictions make decisions about whether to honor a detainer based on the crimes for which an alien has been charged or convicted. When they do this, they are effectively substituting their judgment for federal statutes which make clear the offenses that render an alien to be deportable, and so it is dishonest and deceptive for such jurisdictions to complain about acting as surrogates. They have already done so—and done it in a way that is contrary to law.

Reimbursement for incarceration costs. Many jurisdictions complain that it costs them hundreds of thousands (sometimes millions) of dollars each year arresting, prosecuting, and incarcerating deportable aliens, or holding them for additional time (up to 48 hours) on an ICE detainer. They charge that, in turn, they get reimbursed for only a portion of those costs, usually via the State Criminal Alien Assistance Program (SCAAP). They ask, then, why they should honor immigration detainers. It is worth observing, though, that the amounts being disbursed are significant. In 2015 more than $165,342 million was disbursed to state, county, and city law enforcement entities—*including* to sanctuary cities that thumb their nose at federal immigration agents and provide no cooperation whatever, or actively impede enforcement efforts.[28]

But putting aside the millions of dollars being disbursed, there are at least three additional, obvious, flaws in this train of logic.

- First, although control of immigration is in fact a federal responsibility—and one which the Obama administration has been notoriously reluctant to embrace—it does not follow that the federal taxpayer should be on the hook for the entire cost of locking up aliens who are arrested and charged with state crimes, especially if state or local policies encourage or tolerate illegal settlement.

- Second, if the complaint of non-cooperating jurisdictions is that the federal government has substantially failed in its job of keeping aliens from illegally crossing the border and in preventing aliens from overstaying their visas, thus resulting in increased numbers of alien criminals and heavier burdens for state and local law enforcement, then how does it follow that the solution is to release these aliens onto the street and back into the community rather than give custody of them over to federal agents to remove them, once the state criminal justice proceedings have concluded? Where is the logic in that?

- Third, many state and local law enforcement agencies report that cooperating in the removal of criminal aliens actually saves the community significant sums of money. As is the case with other offenders, criminal aliens are prone to re-offend (at rates comparable to native-born criminals). When criminal aliens are removed instead of returned to the community, the community is spared the cost of their future crimes and the associated costs of incarceration and supervision, not to mention the pain and trauma of future victims.

The previously-referenced OIG report mentioned ICE's view that, until there is further clarification that cooperation with federal immigration authorities is obligatory, then state and local governments can get away with refusing cooperation on budgetary grounds. Indeed, many of the sanctuary policies specify that no funds may be expended to assist the federal government in immigration enforcement. Yet in some cases, notably Cook County, Illinois, when ICE has offered to repay the cost of any additional time in custody for the criminal alien, the county did not accept the offer, which makes clear that cost was not the real reason for the sanctuary policy.

Cooperation is voluntary. This argument is closely aligned with the prior discussion about detainers, as well as the discussion that follows regarding states' rights. The "cooperation is voluntary" argument suggests that state and local agencies may choose whether or not they cooperate with federal immigration authorities—usually, in relation to ICE and its detainers. The Obama administration has given power to this argument by public pronouncements to this effect from one of its senior ICE officials; pronouncements made, we note, with no legal justifications to support them that we can determine.[29] Moreover, the Priority Enforcement Program (PEP) implemented in November 2014 as part of a large set of executive actions explicitly allows local jurisdictions to ignore ICE attempts to gain custody of a criminal alien in their custody, and allows local jurisdictions to dictate to ICE which criminal aliens will be subject to enforcement.[30]

When considering the validity of the pronouncement that honoring of detainers is voluntary, it is well to keep in mind that the Obama administration made a similar argument about whether or not state and local governments were obliged to cooperate with the biometric matching that forms the heart of the successful Secure Communities program—an argument it was later forced to admit was untrue and which had no factual basis in the law, although it repeatedly made the assertion until events forced them to backtrack on their prior assertion.[31]

What is more, the suggestion that honoring detainers is voluntary, or in some way optional, defies the ordinary practices, procedures, and expectations of all other federal, state, and local agencies where detainers are concerned. When other agencies file detainers, they fully expect them to be honored. Imagine, if you will, the United States Marshals Service suggesting that a detainer which it files with state or local law enforcement agencies is "voluntary"—it's unthinkable.

Some have said that the fundamental difference is because immigration detainers are issued by administrative authorities, as opposed to judges. This flies in the face of reality: parole boards are administrative authorities, yet parole officers routinely file detainers to take back into custody parole violators, which detainers are uniformly honored. So, too, with military police authorities who file detainers to take into custody soldiers or sailors who have deserted or are absent without leave, when they are arrested by police? Should these detainers be rejected by state or local governments because, hypothetically, they disagreed with laws under which the offender was convicted and paroled, or with the federal government's wars in Iraq or Afghanistan? Again, unreasonable.

In any case, questioning the issuing authorities is beyond the purview of state or local officials. Immigration officials who issue detainers (and, in fact, even warrants for the arrest of aliens in removal proceedings) are indeed administrative officials—but so are immigration judges who hear the deportation cases. All of them are the individuals who have been given the authority under the laws passed by Congress and signed into law by various presidents which, under the federal preemption and supremacy doctrines (discussed below), puts them uniquely within the purview of the federal government. That state and local governments like or agree with the statutory scheme is neither here nor there.

Detainers must be accompanied by warrants. Several sanctuary jurisdictions have indicated that they will honor detainers only when accompanied by warrants. The nature of the warrant has not been specified in many jurisdictions, but a few have been clear that what they are looking for is a judicial warrant.

The argument behind this approach is that a detainer, in and of itself, does not reflect the probable cause needed to justify detention and arrest.[32] We believe that this argument is beyond the scope of state or local jurisdictions to assert, because it is not their business to stand behind immigration agents looking over their collective shoulder, rendering legal determinations on the adequacy of their work—such a notion flies in the face of federal supremacy in the matter of immigration (see our discussion below, under "States rights").

What is more, federal law very clearly provides for arrest of an alien believed to be illegally in the United States without warrant by a federal officer when "he has reason to believe that the alien so arrested is in the United States in violation of any such law or regulation and is likely to escape before a warrant can be obtained for his arrest".[33] Often when immigration agents file detainers with police, sheriffs, and jails, they don't know how quickly the alien may be released from custody on bond or on order of a presiding judge or magistrate, and time is of the essence. The exigency will depend in large measure on how many hours have elapsed between the initial arrest of the alien by police and when ICE officers become cognizant of the arrest. If it has been a substantial period of time, they may seek to stay that release with a detainer long enough to be able to follow up afterward with additional charging documents, such as a warrant of arrest in immigration proceedings, and ultimately assume custody.

However, we understand that open borders and migrant advocacy groups have been aggressively litigious in recent years, and that the Obama administration has exhibited a disturbing tendency to leave its "law enforcement partners", as they are wont to describe state and local enforcement agencies, in the lurch when lawsuits over detainers have been filed[34] (something we believe is less likely to occur with a President Trump and an Attorney General Sessions in office).

For this reason, there is the potential for compromise within certain boundaries, where jurisdictions insist on warrants. But to be specific, the warrants we describe are not judicial warrants. *There are no judicial warrants available to immigration agents when seeking to arrest an alien and charge him in removal proceedings for being in the United States in violation of law.*

The only judicial warrants available to immigration agents would be those obtained to criminally prosecute an alien, for instance if he has unlawfully reentered the United States after deportation, or if he has committed some kind of fraud, or the like. Thus when sanctuary jurisdictions demand a judicial warrant to accompany a detainer filed in civil removal proceedings, they either have no idea what they are insisting upon—or they do, and they know such a demand, being impossible to meet, will obstruct the arrest and deportation of illegal aliens, including aliens who have been arrested, prosecuted, and convicted by state and local authorities for crimes. Of course, this results in such criminals being released back into the community to reoffend, often with horrendous consequences.

When state or local jurisdictions ask ICE to accompany detainers with copies of a warrant, but don't insist on it being a judicial warrant, this is the area in which compromise is possible. The Immigration and Nationality Act provides that "On a warrant issued by the [Secretary of Homeland Security], an alien may be arrested and detained pending a decision on whether the alien is to be removed from the United States".[35]

To be clear, this provision of law refers to a civil warrant issued by federal immigration officers who have been delegated authority flowing from the Secretary. Thus, when jurisdictions seek to protect themselves from the possibility of tort litigation by asking for warrants then, absent exigent circumstances, the prevailing ICE policy should be to accommodate the request by concurrently filing with the detainer an administrative warrant (form I-200) or, if the alien is already a fugitive from deportation proceedings against whom a final order of removal is outstanding, then a warrant of removal (form I-205).

However, it is important to emphasize that decisions about which deportable aliens to take custody of and initiate deportation proceedings against must always be a federal decision and not left to the discretion of state and local governments, which have no constitutional role in that process.

The Suffolk County Solution. The practice of issuing administrative warrants along with the detainer is precisely the solution that has been worked out in Suffolk County on Long Island, New York. In September of 2014, Sheriff Vincent DeMarco was told by county officials that the county would no longer indemnify his department against lawsuits instigated by anti-enforcement advocacy groups if he continued to comply with ICE detainers.

Following the deployment of Secure Communities fingerprint-matching in Suffolk County in February of 2011, ICE had been able to increase the deportations from Suffolk County jails by 60 percent. Suffolk County cases represented nearly 20 percent of the criminal alien deportation workload for the New York City ICE field office, so this was a hard blow to immigration enforcement in the area, not to mention its detrimental effect on community safety.

The enforcement disruption came just at the time when communities in Suffolk County had begun to experience the arrival of hundreds of illegal alien youths from Central America, including many who were involved with MS-13, the violent transnational street gang dominated primarily, but not exclusively, by members from El Salvador.

Despite pressure from advocacy groups to bar ICE from the jail and cease communicating with ICE, Sheriff DeMarco continued to cooperate with them in other ways, and complied with all ICE requests for notification of the release of any deportable aliens in custody at the jail. Still, a number of criminal aliens fell through the cracks and had to be released instead of being held and turned over to ICE for deportation proceedings.

Inexplicably, while this was playing out, ICE failed to inform Sheriff DeMarco that the Supreme Courts of New York, sitting in two neighboring counties, had decided in two different cases in 2014 and 2015 (People vs. Xirum and Josue Chery v Sheriff of Nassau) that holding an alien on an ICE detainer after a finding of probable cause is entirely permissible and is not a violation of the alien's civil rights. Said the court in *Xirum*:

> "this court cannot say that under a Fourth Amendment analysis it is unreasonable for the [county Department of Corrections] to further hold a defendant for at most 48 hours as requested in the Detainer after the conclusion of the state case in order to give DHS an opportunity to seize the subject of the deportation order."

Further:

> "Similar to the fellow officer rule that permits detention by one police officer acting on probable cause provided by another, the DOC had the right to rely upon the very federal law enforcement agency charged under the law with 'the identification, apprehension, and removal of illegal aliens from the United States.'"

Meanwhile, the number of new illegal alien youth arrivals from Central America doubled, and violence attributed to MS-13 and some of the youths affiliated with the gang significantly escalated. Since 2014, there have been at least seven murders attributed to MS-13 in just one Suffolk County town (Brentwood), including the slaying of two 16 year-old girls not involved with the gang.[36]

After meeting with local lawmakers concerned about the public safety implications of the forced sanctuary policy, and after learning that New York courts had held that there were no legal obstacles to a fully cooperative policy, Suffolk County reversed its position. Sheriff DeMarco was able to secure an agreement from ICE to issue administrative warrants of arrest or removal to accompany the detainers, and announced an end to the sanctuary policy on December 5, 2016.

States have the sovereign right to choose sanctuary policies. Much of the argument devolving around the obligation to honor immigration detainers, and otherwise cooperate with federal immigration authorities surrounds the issue of states' rights. This argument derives from the Tenth Amendment to the Constitution, which states that "The powers not delegated to the United States by the Constitution, nor prohibited by it to the States, are reserved to the States respectively, or to the people."[37]

It is true that the Constitution preserves only a select few powers to the federal government—powers which, if left to the states, might very result in an unraveling of our republic. However, among those reserved powers are foreign policy, interstate and foreign commerce and, most specifically relevant to the issue at hand, immigration.[38] This fundamental fact would seem to foreclose the argument that states (or their political subdivisions) can pick and choose from among the federal immigration statutes they wish to see enforced, while frustrating the remainder by refusal to cooperate with federal efforts.

Imagine, if you will, a state insisting that it had the right to establish its own foreign policy and decided to initiate "diplomatic" ties with North Korea. Or imagine that a state or one of its political subdivisions decided that it could not support a trade embargo established by the federal government, and therefore began trade negotiations with the renegade nation? Is there any doubt that the federal government would squelch any such an initiatives at their first inception and land on the backs of the intransigent state and local officials with very heavy boots? Yet this is exactly what has transpired with immigration law and policy in the last few years.

Many readers are probably aware that "states' rights" as embodied by the Tenth Amendment (the argument being used by sanctuary apologists today) was one of the principle arguments made by rebellious states which attempted to secede from the Union to form the Confederacy.[39] We are neither the first nor the only ones to note that irony.[40] There is something perverse about so-called progressives using a neo-Confederate states' rights argument to avoid meeting their responsibilities under the law, which includes acknowledging federal supremacy on the subject of immigration. Some on the ultra left have even gone so far as to urge California's secession from the United States (often referred to as "Calexit").[41]

Make no doubt, we believe in states' rights—the right, for instance, of individual states to enact laws that support, and are consonant with, federal efforts at controlling illegal immigration in order to safeguard their own communities and preserve their limited resources for persons lawfully present. But in the topsy-turvy world of the Obama administration, those were the efforts that resulted in lawsuits and injunctions, while sanctuary jurisdictions have been left untouched to fester and grow.

We see sanctuary policies as nothing more, and nothing less, than a "nullification of law" effort much akin to past attempts by some states to defy federal integration policies in the field of civil rights—only this time, because the policy underlying the nullification argument is fashionable among open borders elitists, they choose to clothe it in other garb. This is unconscionable, and it is a situation that Donald Trump has vowed to change.

How can the New Administration Tackle Sanctuaries?

There are a number of options available to the new administration in order to begin the process of dismantling sanctuaries and restoring a clear understanding of federal supremacy in immigration matters, where state and local governments, and even universities public or private, are concerned:

- Rescinding "prosecutorial discretion" and "priority enforcement program" policies;
- Restoring effective alien criminal identification programs and technology;
- Defunding of federal monies now pouring into sanctuary states and local governments;
- Decertifying various authorizations, such as the ability to enroll foreign students on campuses that declare themselves to be sanctuaries;
- Initiating civil litigation to enjoin obstructive laws or policies;
- Criminally prosecuting the most egregious cases of harboring and shielding criminal illegal aliens from ICE by state or local government agencies; and
- Issuing administrative warrants to accompany detainers.

It's important to recognize that dismantling state and local government sanctuaries also requires attending to, and eliminating, those factors at the federal level that have contributed to the creation and expansion of sanctuaries during the last several years.

Rescinding "prosecutorial discretion" and "priority enforcement program" policies. In the past several years, the Obama administration has overseen the implementation of a significant number of policy memoranda and binding guidance that tie the hands of immigration agents and trial attorneys trying to go about the business of arresting, litigating against, and removing illegal aliens, including most especially alien criminals.[42]

All of these policy documents have been based on the argument that finite resources require prioritizing which aliens merit investigative and prosecutorial attention. But what they have actually done is effectively eviscerate immigration enforcement by virtually any measure one might choose to use: the number of detainers permitted to be filed against aliens in police custody; the number of aliens arrested by ICE; the incredible number of aliens inappropriately released and now on the streets of American cities, many of them under unexecuted final orders of removal; and historic lows in the number of removals.

When we hear of the "broken immigration system" we are repeatedly reminded that it is dysfunctional in great measure because this administration has willfully and deliberately chosen to undermine it. In our view, the first order of business for the new leadership at DHS must be to rescind these policies and make clear that ICE agents and prosecutors are free within the boundaries of the law to pursue their mission.

Restoring effective criminal alien identification programs and technology. When DHS secretary Jeh Johnson issued his series of November 2014 executive actions, which significantly impinged on the already weakened interior enforcement structure, he directed the end of the Secure Communities (SC) program, which had proven itself an effective and efficient means of obtaining near-realtime information about criminal arrests of aliens nationwide, so that agents could follow up by filing detainers and taking custody of the aliens at the earliest opportunity. He substituted instead the Priority Enforcement Program (PEP), which has proven itself a failure by even further hamstringing the agents.[43] PEP must be rescinded and SC reinstituted.

Even before that, DHS and ICE leaders had taken steps to cripple another extremely successful enforcement program called "287(g)" after the provision in the INA on which it is based. The 287(g) program provides for delegation of authority to state and local enforcement officers so that if, in the course of their own patrol or jail duties, they encounter situations having obvious immigration implications (for instance, state police encountering alien smuggling loads on interstate highways), they could act as immigration officers in order to secure the aliens, transport them, and even process them if needed, until ICE agents could arrive.[44] Importantly, the 287(g) program also provided those state and local officers with immunity to the same extent as is enjoyed by federal officers. The 287(g) program should be resuscitated and invigorated so that there are the greatest possible number of state and local agencies participating nationwide.

Taking the above steps will go far toward restoring a balance in tone and approach on the part of the federal government clearly reflecting its own commitment to fair but vigorous enforcement in the interior of the United States.

From here on, we focus on what actions may be taken against state and local sanctuary governments. Although they may be perceived as a hierarchy of actions that rise in level of severity, it's important to note that nothing requires them to be used sequentially; they could potentially be used all at once, or in any combination, as the occasion, jurisdiction, or circumstance require.

Publish Information on Criminal Releases. One of the Trump administration's first moves to address the sanctuaries should be to provide the public with more information on the practical effect of these policies. ICE should be directed to publish a weekly list of details about the criminal aliens who are freed by the sanctuaries, including criminal histories. In addition, where possible, the victims should also be notified.

The list should be known as "Denny's List," named for Dennis McCann, who was killed by an illegal alien in Chicago in 2011, who ran over him while driving drunk, just months after completing probation for a prior aggravated drunk driving conviction. The illegal alien, Saul Chavez, was released within weeks after Cook County adopted one of the most extreme sanctuary policies in the country. Chavez fled to Mexico and has never faced charges for McCann's death.

Defunding. One of the quickest, most obvious ways to get the attention of state and local authorities is via the power of the purse. Tens of millions of dollars are given away in various grant programs yearly. Withholding of these funds would make a serious dent in the budgets of state and local agencies. This can, for the most part, be done without the need for new legislation because federal rules already require that grant funding applicants be in conformance with all federal laws before they can be found eligible to receive funds. As discussed above, the most applicable and relevant section of the law is 8 U.S.C. 1373.[45]

This was always a tool available to the Obama administration, which opted not to use it until recently when Rep. Culberson made clear that he would hold back Department of Justice (DOJ) funding unless DOJ, in turn, began forcing compliance and withholding Bureau of Justice Assistance (BJA) monies from sanctuary jurisdictions. That, of course, got the attention of the attorney general.[46]

On July 7, 2016, DOJ released updated guidelines that disqualify sanctuary jurisdictions from receiving DOJ law enforcement funding if they are found to be in violation of 8 U.S.C. 1373, among other laws. All state and local agencies were told that they would have to attest to compliance with the law as a part of the application process. According to the revised guidance:

> "If the applicant is found to be in violation of an applicable federal law by the OIG, the applicant may be subject to criminal and civil penalties, in addition to relevant OJP programmatic penalties, including suspension or termination of funds, inclusion on the high risk list, repayment of funds, or suspension and debarment."

The affected programs administered by BJA include SCAAP, and Byrne JAG and possibly other grants. They were told that they had until June 30, 2017 to change their sanctuary policies to avoid running afoul of federal law.

Nonetheless the 10 jurisdictions investigated by the Inspector General still received about $96 million in grants for 2016. It remains to be seen whether they will change their position by the looming deadline or new policies or actions to be taken by the Trump administration. So far, Philadelphia, Chicago, and New York City, among others, have announced that they intend to keep their sanctuary policies despite notification from DOJ that they are inconsistent with the law.

The table below lists the 10 jurisdictions that are on notice and the amount of funding that they could potentially have to return if they are found to be non-compliant.

Jurisdiction	Byrne/JAG and SCAAP Grants Received (FY16)	Byrne/JAG and SCAAP Grants Received (FY06–FY15)
State of Connecticut	$2,722,870	$66,933,068
State of California	$68,844,210	$1,237,605,093
Orleans Parish, Louisiana	$265,832	$5,325,650
New York, New York	$14,849,269	$211,537,308
Philadelphia, Pennsylvania	$1,677,937	$36,147,315
Cook County/City of Chicago, Illinois	$3,671,202	$91,246,038
Miami-Dade County, Florida	$1,445,347	$11,586,407
Milwaukee, Wisconsin	$989,025	$17,611,261
Clark County, Nevada	$1,634,341	$25,692,240
TOTAL	**$96,100,033**	**$1,703,684,380**

There are additional programs containing substantial pots of money that could be withheld from obstructionist jurisdictions, such as the various homeland security grant programs administered by DHS, which are provided to state, county, and city governments all over the nation (in 2015, DHS disbursed more than $1.044 billion to state and local jurisdictions under its extensive grant programs[47]). DHS is, after all, the primary cabinet department charged with defending America's borders and enforcing its immigration laws. Why should it continue to provide funds to scofflaw governments who by their sanctuary actions make the country, and their own communities, significantly less safe?

Another area ripe for consideration is the Department of Defense program which provides military surplus vehicles, equipment, and supplies to state and local law enforcement agencies for little or nothing.

Depending on the level of intransigence, a Trump administration might even consider withholding community development and community services block grants to sanctuary jurisdictions. These are programs administered by the federal Departments of Housing and Urban Development and Health and Human Services, respectively.

Such a move could be justified on the grounds that sanctuary policies encourage illegal settlement, thereby increasing the number of people who need costly social and educational services and who are not contributing significantly to tax revenues.

Decertification. Almost all public and private universities seek approval from DHS to permit foreign students and exchange visitors to attend their institutions. This permits them to issue the forms that potential students and exchange scholars need to present to American consular officers in order to obtain the required visas for entry.[48] They do this for reasons of prestige and, not least, money: foreign students are a ready source of revenue because they usually pay much higher tuition rates than citizen or resident alien students. Such a constant and reliable stream of money can make the difference between solvency and the need to raise tuition rates across the board.

It is an irony that even as most institutions of higher learning seek and obtain DHS approval to enroll the foreign students and exchange visitors, many have a policy of permitting illegal aliens to attend classes, often at subsidized in-state tuition rates or with targeted scholarship or tuition waiver programs, even if they don't make any public announcements that they are pursuing official sanctuary non-cooperation policies, such as the University of California system we described earlier.

The answer to this conflicting and oxymoronic policy is self-evident. DHS need only implement a policy to decertify any and all institutions with sanctuary policies, official pronounced or not, and deny them the opportunity to enroll foreign students and exchange visitors until they mend their ways.

Decertifying sanctuary institutions from the list of schools approved to receive foreign students should also be coupled with a loss of research and other federal funding dollars, such as the university-based centers of excellence administered by DHS[49], or the Department of Education's Fund for the Improvement of Post-Secondary Education (FIPSE). The denial of such grants has been used in the past to incentivize certain behavior; for instance, schools that bar military recruiters from campus are prohibited from receiving FIPSE awards. It seems to us appropriate to take the same course of action to curb obstruction of federal immigration laws.

The Trump administration may also wish to initiate the practice of refusing to provide Pell grant or other tuition monies to students who enroll in sanctuary institutions, thus forcing them to choose schools whose policies are more in line with the requirements of federal immigration law.

Civil Litigation. The Trump administration should consider filing lawsuits against sanctuary jurisdictions and seek to enjoin laws, regulations, policies, and operating instructions in those jurisdictions that obstruct proper and effective enforcement of the nation's immigration laws. We recognize that even the federal government has finite resources and not all sanctuary governments will likely be sued, no matter how richly deserving, but the obvious place to start would be the most egregious, perhaps defined as the jurisdictions that free the most criminal aliens who are subject to ICE detainers. Reportedly, the following five large sanctuary jurisdictions are refusing to cooperate with ICE in any way whatsoever: San Francisco, California; Cook County, Illinois; Contra Costa County, California; Santa Clara County, California; and King County, Washington.

The previously-mentioned provisions of federal law that proscribe any government entity from prohibiting or impeding communication of its employees to or from federal authorities regarding an alien's status in the United States is a good starting point to initiate such injunctive action. It's worth noting that while these provisions are particularly pertinent to exchanges of information between ICE and state and local law enforcement agencies for the purpose of identifying and apprehending alien criminals, on their face they apply to any government agency, including for instance state motor vehicle departments, as well as state-supported university and college systems.

Criminal Prosecution. Several sanctuary jurisdictions appear to us to have crossed the line with their conduct and activities into criminal behavior, as well as potentially leaving themselves open to civil lawsuits filed by victims or surviving family members of individuals killed or harmed by illegal aliens.[50]

The murder of Kate Steinle in San Francisco is one example. In that case, the multiply-deported alien criminal was actually turned over to local enforcement authorities by ICE after having been apprehended by its agents. He was tendered to local authorities on the basis of an outstanding criminal warrant, which was later dismissed by the District Attorney. The San Francisco County Sheriff, however, refused to return custody of the alien to ICE, citing sanctuary noncooperation policies as his rationale—even though he had received the prisoner from ICE to begin with. Instead, the alien was released onto the streets of the community, only to murder Ms. Steinle a short time afterward. While the sheriff later lost his reelection bid, it seems to us that he ought to have been prosecuted for his actions. Equally outrageous, though, was the inexplicable Obama White House assertion that Steinle's death could have somehow been avoided had "comprehensive reform" (meaning a general amnesty) been enacted.[51]

The relevant law is a federal felony statute that prohibits "harboring and shielding from detection" aliens in the U.S. in violation of law. The statute applies to governmental officials as readily as it does to employers, private citizens or even corporations.[52] Using this criminal statute seems to us an appropriate remedy in egregious cases such as that of Ms. Steinle (and, frankly, a host of others that have occurred in recent years, the stories of many of whom can be found on the Remembrance Project website previously mentioned) to ensure that state and local officials understand the seriousness with which the federal government is going to take their intransigence and obstruction.

Using the harboring and shielding statute as a tool to dismantle sanctuaries was item 50 in the series of recommendations we at the Center made in a backgrounder published this past April, "A Pen and a Phone: 79 immigration actions the next president can take."[53]

Conclusions

Mr. Trump has announced that he would nominate Senator Jeff Sessions as his attorney general. During his tenure in the Senate, Mr. Sessions has been an unapologetic advocate of immigration enforcement, and a steadfast believer that immigration policies should serve the national interest and the interests of ordinary Americans. As the attorney general, Sen. Sessions, working with the new DHS secretary, will have the legal mechanisms at his disposal to tackle sanctuaries on every front.

It is clear that a showdown is coming. What form it will take remains to be seen.

Notes

1. See, for instance, Mark Krikorian, "No Sanctuary for Sanctuary Cities", Center for Immigration Studies (CIS) blog, Feb. 25, 2009; http://cis.org/krikorian/no-sanctuary-sanctuary-cities and W.D. Reasoner, "Which Way, New York?" CIS blog, Oct. 2011. http://cis.org/nyc-local-interference

2. Article II, Section 3 of the United States Constitution requires that "[The President] shall take Care that the Laws be faithfully executed. ..." See, e.g.,"The Heritage Guide to the Constitution" http://www.heritage.org/constitution/articles/2/essays/98/take-care-clause.

3. For an interactive map of existing sanctuary locations, see Bryan Griffith and Jessica Vaughan, "Map: Sanctuary Cities, Counties, and States: Sanctuary Cities Continue to Obstruct Enforcement, Threaten Public Safety" CIS backgrounder, orig. Jan. 2016, updated Aug. 31, 2016. http://cis.org/Sanctuary-Cities-Map

4. Associated Press, "Mayor Rahm Emanuel says Chicago will remain sanctuary city for immigrants" The Herald News, Nov. 14, 2016 http://www.theherald-news.com/2016/11/14/mayor-rahm-emanuel-says-chicago ...; David Goodman, " 'The Ball's in His Court,' Mayor de Blasio Says After Meeting With Trump", New York Times, Nov. 16, 2016 http://www.nytimes.com/2016/11/17/nyregion/donald-trump-mayor-bill-de-bl ...; Neil W. McCabe, "Mayor Trolls President-elect Trump: Take Our Federal Funds, We Will Stay a Sanctuary City Forever", Breitbart.com, Nov. 21, 2016. http://www.breitbart.com/big-government/2016/11/21/mayor-trolls-presiden ... take-our-federal-funds-we-will-stay-a-sanctuary-city-forever/

5. See, for example, the statements made by the Los Angeles Police Department Chief: "Chief Beck: LAPD Will Not Aid Trump Deportation Efforts", Police Magazine, Nov. 15, 2016. http://www.policemag.com/channel/patrol/news/2016/11/15/chief-beck-lapd-will-not-aid-trump-deportation-efforts.aspx

6. Mark Davis, "Malloy says he'll sue if Trump attempts to punish 'Sanctuary City' New Haven", News8 WTNH online, Nov. 22, 2016. http://wtnh.com/2016/11/22/malloy-says-hell-sue-if-trump-attempts-to-pun...

7. Edmund Kozak, "Students Rage for 'Sanctuary' Campuses: Fearful of Trump, college agitators demand colleges become safe spaces for illegal aliens" Lifezette online magazine, updated Nov. 17, 2016. http://www.lifezette.com/polizette/students-rage-sanctuary-campuses/ and John Binder, "Vanderbilt Students Demand 'Sanctuary Campus'", Breitbart.com, Nov. 28, 2016. http://www.breitbart.com/texas/2016/11/28/vanderbilt-students-demand-san...

8. "President Wim Wiewel declares PSU a sanctuary university", press announcement, Portland State University website, Nov. 18, 2016. http://www.pdx.edu/news/president-wim-wiewel-declares-psu-sanctuary-univ...

9. Blake Neff, "Columbia University Declares Itself a Sanctuary Campus for Illegal Immigrants", The Daily Caller, Nov. 21, 2016. http://dailycaller.com/2016/11/21/columbia-university-declares-itself-a-...

10. "Undocumented Student Resources", University of California website, accessed on December 2, 2016. http://undoc.universityofcalifornia.edu/

11. Memorandum from Michael E. Horowitz, Inspector General, "Department of Justice Referral of Allegations of Potential Violations of 8 USC 1373 by Grant Recipients," May 31, 2016, https://oig.justice.gov/reports/2016/1607.pdf.

12. With regard to the potential penalty, note, though, that the statute says, "in the case of a violation ... resulting in the death of any person, be punished by death or imprisoned for any term of years or for life, fined under title 18, or both." An extreme reading of the statute might lead one to conclude that the actions of the San Francisco sheriff in releasing a multiply-deported alien felon which in turn led him to murder of Kate Steinle (discussed later in the body of this report) would subject him not only to prosecution but punishment under this enhancement of the available penalties.

13. Jennifer Truman, Ph.D., Lynn Langton, Ph.D., and Michael Planty, Ph.D., Bureau of Justice Statistics, "Crime Victimization 2012," http://www.bjs.gov/content/pub/pdf/cv12.pdf.

14. See additional data from the National Crime Victimization Survey here: http://www.bjs.gov/content/pub/pdf/cvus0805.pdf.

15. Lynn Langton, Marcus Berzofsky, Christopher Krebs, and Hope Smiley-McDonald, Bureau of Justice Statistics report, "Victimizations Not Reported to the Police, 2006–2010," http://www.bjs.gov/content/pub/pdf/vnrp0610.pdf.

16. Evaluation Study of Prince William County's Illegal Immigration Enforcement Policy: FINAL REPORT 2010, http://www.pwcgov.org/government/dept/police/Documents/13185.pdf.

17. Robert C. Davis, Edna Erez and Nancy Avitabile, "Access to Justice for Immigrants Who are Victimized. The Perspectives of Police and Prosecutors" Criminal Justice Policy Review, 12(3): 183–196, 2001.

18. Menjivar, Cecilia and Cynthia L. Bejarano, "Latino Immigrants' Perceptions of Crime and Police Authorities in the United States: A Case Study from the Phoenix Metropolitan Area," Ethnic and Racial Studies 27(1): 120–148, 2004.

19. Commander Michael Williams, Collier County (Fla.) Sheriff's Office, as reported here: http://cis.org/files/articles/2009/leaps/index.htm.

20. Boston Police Department report on calls for service by precinct provided by Jessica Vaughan.

21. Los Angeles Police Department annual Statistical Digest, available at www.lapdonline.org.

22. Nik Theodore, "Insecure Communities: Latino Perceptions of Police Involvement in Immigration Enforcement", College of Urban Planning & Public Affairs, University of Illinois at Chicago, May 1, 2013. https://greatcities.uic.edu/2013/05/01/insecure-communities-latino-perce...

23. See for example, the remarks of sheriffs at these events by the Center for Immigration Studies: http://cis.org/Videos/Sanctuary-Cities-Panel, http://cis.org/Videos/Panel-Crime-Challenges, and http://cis.org/vaughan/sheriffs-skeptical-chilling-effect-secure-communi...

24. Jessica Vaughan, "The Non-Departed: 925,000 Aliens Ordered Removed Are Still Here" CIS backgrounder, June 30, 2016. http://cis.org/vaughan/non-departed-925000-aliens-ordered-removed-are-st …

25. See http://www.theremembranceproject.org/.

26. Mark Krikorian, "Kate Steinle Day", CIS blog, July 1, 2016, http://cis.org/krikorian/kate-steinle-day

27. For an in-depth discussion of detainers, see Dan Cadman and Mark Metcalf, "Disabling Detainers", CIS Backgrounder, Jan. 2015. http://cis.org/disabling-detainers

28. A spreadsheet of yearly SCAAP disbursements to each receiving location can be found on the Department of Justice Bureau of Justice Assistance website, by clicking on the "Archives" tab in the SCAAP section: https://www.bja.gov/ProgramDetails.aspx?Program_ID=86#horizontalTab8

29. Cadman and Metcalf, op. cit.

30. Jessica Vaughan, "Public Safety Impact of the Obama Administration's Priority Enforcement Program," testimony before the Texas Senate Subcommittee on Border Security, Mar. 23, 2016, http://cis.org/Testimony/Vaughan-Public-Safety-Impact-of-the-Obama-Admin. …

31. See, for example, "ICE: Secure Communities program not optional", Homeland Security News Wire, Mar. 7, 2011. http://www.homelandsecuritynewswire.com/ice-secure-communities-program-n…

32. The very reference to "probable cause" as the legal standard for arrests pursuant to civil removal proceedings is mistaken, because that is not the standard at play. This insistence itself reflects the many misunderstandings that prevail when state and local authorities start substituting their judgment for that of the officials responsible for enforcing the federal scheme of immigration control.

33. 8 U.S.C. Sec. 1357(a)(2). https://www.law.cornell.edu/uscode/text/8/1357

34. W.D. Reasoner, "Leaving a Local Law Enforcement Partner in the Lurch: With Friends Like ICE, Who Needs Enemies?", CIS blog, Sep. 4, 2012.http://cis.org/reasoner/leaving-local-law-enforcement-partner-lurch-friends-ice-who-needs-enemies

35. 8 U.S.C. Sec. 1226(a). https://www.law.cornell.edu/uscode/text/8/1226

36. Joseph J. Kolb, "Brentwood, NY Consumed by MS-13 Crime Wave," CIS backgrounder, Nov. 2016, http://cis.org/Brentwood-NY-Consumed-by-MS-13-Crime-Wave.

37. The Legal Information Institute of Cornell University Law School phrases it this way: "The Tenth Amendment helps to define the concept of federalism, the relationship between Federal and state governments. As Federal activity has increased, so too has the problem of reconciling state and national interests as they apply to the Federal powers to tax, to police, and to regulations such as wage and hour laws, disclosure of personal information in recordkeeping systems, and laws related to strip-mining." https://www.law.cornell.edu/constitution/tenth_amendment

38. Article 1, Section 8, Clause 4 states, "The Congress shall have Power … To establish an uniform Rule of Naturalization[.] http://www.usconstitution.net/xconst_A1Sec8.html The Supreme Court has ruled the federal preeminence in naturalization matters to include not just naturalization, but immigration

generally, since entry of an alien into, and residence within, the United States are the precursor steps to naturalization.

39. For a topical treatment of the subject, see "States' Rights: The Rallying Cry of Secession", The Civil War Trust, http://www.civilwar.org/education/history/civil-war-overview/statesright...

40. See Victor Davis Hanson, "Enemies of Language", National Review Online, Nov. 24, 2016. http://www.nationalreview.com/article/442459/language-police-liberals-se...

41. Austin Yack, "California's Secession Movement Gains Traction After Trump's Victory, National Review Online, Nov. 10, 2016 http://www.nationalreview.com/corner/442096/california-secession-trumps-...; and Joel B. Pollak, "Calexit: Leftists File Papers to Secede, Form New Confederacy", Breitbart.com, Nov. 22, 2016. http://www.breitbart.com/california/2016/11/22/calexit-leftists-file-pap...

42. An exhaustive list of the various prosecutorial discretion policy memoranda, which increasingly inhibited the ability of ICE agents to initiate arrests, and of trial attorney prosecutors to pursue removal cases can be found in an online article by Van Esser titled, "Executive Amnesty Review Promises More Twists and Turns (of the Law)", Numbers USA, March 20 2014. The article also provides hotlinks to the documents themselves. https://www.numbersusa.com/content/nusablog/van-esser/march-20-2014/exec...

43. Vaughan, op. cit., Texas testimony.

44. Jessica Vaughan and James R. Edwards, Jr., "The 287(g) Program, Protecting Home Towns and Homeland", CIS backgrounder, Oct. 2009. http://cis.org/287greport.

45. In addition to the prohibition against impeding communication with federal immigration authorities found in 8 U.S.C. 1373, https://www.law.cornell.edu/uscode/text/8/1373 there is a second, similar provision to be found at 8 U.S.C. 1644, https://www.law.cornell.edu/uscode/text/8/1644 although it is not cited as frequently when discussing state or local intransigence.

46. Jessica Vaughan, "House Appropriations Boss Initiates Crackdown on Sanctuaries", CIS blog, Feb. 1, 2016 http://cis.org/vaughan/house-appropriations-sanctuaries ; and "Justice Department Agrees to End Subsidies for Sanctuaries" Feb. 25, 2016. http://cis.org/vaughan/justice-department-agrees-end-subsidies-sanctuaries

47. Archived records relating to the various programs and amounts for 2015 can be found online at https://www.fema.gov/media-library-data/1438021101390-ce3bbdde8b84b174b8 ... and a list of the various Homeland Security grants that were available in FY 2016 can be found at https://www.fema.gov/fiscal-year-2016-homeland-security-grant-program.

48. The responsibility for oversight of foreign students and exchange visitors, as well as approval, denial, or withdrawal of approval (decertification) of schools and institutions of learning seeking permission to enroll them, is handled by the Student Exchange Visitor Program (SEVP) at Immigration and Customs Enforcement. For 18, grounder, Jan. 2015. http://cis.org/disabling-detainers Sanctuaries" Feb. 25, 2016. http://cis.org/vaughan/justice-department-agrees-end-subsidies-sanctuaries

49. The DHS Centers of Excellence homepage can be found at https://www.dhs.gov/science-and-technology/centers-excellence. Within that web page, one can then click on the tab labeled "Office of University Programs" for more information about the interconnection between DHS and institutions of higher

learning. A glance at current and "emeritus" centers of excellence include universities that are already or contemplating becoming, sanctuaries.

50. Dan Cadman, "Hammering Sanctuaries with Lawsuits", CIS blog, Jul. 24, 2015. http://cis.org/cadman/hammering-sanctuaries-with-lawsuits

51. Dan Cadman, "Rending the Fabric of Truth in the Steinle Case", CIS blog, Jul. 9, 2015, http://cis.org/cadman/rending-fabric-truth-steinle-case

52. The statute can be found at 8 U.S.C. § 1324. https://www.law.cornell.edu/uscode/text/8/1324 For more information on its potential application, see W.D. Reasoner, "Looking to One's Own Backyard", CIS blog, Jan. 2, 2012. http://cis.org/reasoner/looking-to-ones-own-backyard

53. "A Pen and a Phone: 79 immigration actions the next president can take". CIS backgrounder, April 2016. http://cis.org/A-Pen-and-a-Phone-79-immigration-actions-the-next-preside…

DISCUSSION QUESTIONS

1. What does federal law say about harboring illegal aliens? Can sanctuary policies be construed to be in violation of federal law? If so, would you support prosecuting state and local officials who pass or implement sanctuary policies?

2. What is the State Criminal Alien Assistance Program? What arguments does the CIS article offer to rebut the claims of state and local agencies that it is too expensive to detain illegal immigrants for ICE?

3. What is the difference between a detainer and a judicial warrant? What authority does ICE have to arrest aliens without a court-issued warrant? Why is it not possible in most cases for ICE agents to obtain a judicial warrant when taking an illegal alien into custody?

4. According to Dan Cadman and Jessica Vaughn, how are sanctuary polices enacted by state and local governments an attempt to nullify federal law? Can one be supportive of states' rights and federalism and still be against the right of states and local communities to become sanctuary jurisdictions? Explain.

5. What recommendations does the CIS article make for the Trump administration to consider? With which of these recommendations do you agree? With which do you disagree? Explain.

CHAPTER SEVEN

Immigration and Crime

Introduction

On January 20, 2017, President Donald Trump delivered his State of the Union Address to Congress and, through television, to the nation. As has been customary of State of the Union addresses in the past, President Trump in his speech highlighted the stories of guests who were present in the gallery. At one point in his speech, while talking about immigration and border security, the president introduced the parents of Kayla Cuevas and Nisa Mickens, two teenage girls from Long Island, NY, who were murdered by members of the violent Latino gang MS-13, in 2016. Six members of the gang were charged with the murders. The president, in his remarks, said those charged with the murders had entered the country illegally or otherwise took advantage of lax immigration policies in the United States.

MS-13 is an especially violent and brutal gang. It was started in Los Angeles in the 1980s by young immigrants who came to the United States as refugees from Central America—particularly El Salvador, but also Honduras and Guatemala. The U.S. Department of Justice estimates there are more than 10,000 members of the gang throughout the United States today. The gang has grown in membership by continuing to draw in immigrant and second-generation youths—often through coercion. The gang is involved in multiple criminal activities, including human trafficking and sex crimes, drug trafficking, and gunrunning. Their acts of murder tend to be especially brutal, often hacking victims to death with edged weapons.

Murders committed by members of MS-13, especially when they are in the country illegally, grab news headlines and make people understandably upset. After all, each one of these murders is one that wouldn't have occurred were these people not in the country. For the family members of Kayla Cuevas and Nisa Mickens, whose stories were highlighted in the president's State of the Union address, or the family members of Kate Steinle discussed in the previous chapter, these killings were completely avoidable and shouldn't have happened—indeed, couldn't have happened—but for poor immigration enforcement. For them, immigrants who were in the United States, lawfully or unlawfully, chose to engage in criminal activity that cost the lives of these families' loved ones. The connection between immigration and crime is a real one for them.

More broadly, however, there is earnest and ongoing public policy debate about the links, if there are any, between immigration and crime. Intuitively, one would expect that immigrant communities—especially from poor or developing countries—would reflect greater propensities for committing crime and becoming victims of crime, given the inherent structural disadvantages of living in the United States near or below the poverty line, often having limited English communication skills, and few marketable or educational attributes that might otherwise result in gainful, well-paying and benefited employment. Interestingly, the intuitive expectation isn't always borne out. Many studies have shown that immigration populations in the United States are less likely than native-born ones to commit crimes. This lower rate of crime, relative to the rest of the population, tends to disappear with the second and third generations of immigrant families as they become assimilated with and acculturated to American society.

On the other hand, there have also been reports and studies that show an overrepresentation of immigrants, especially illegal immigrants and their children, among violent and property offenders in states such as Arizona, California, and New York. Immigrants are also disproportionately represented in federal prisons. A 2006 Migration Policy Institute (MPI) report found that while lower crime rates are prevalent among first- and second-generation immigrants, there tend to be higher crime rates among third-generation immigrants, especially from Latin America.[1] Consequently, the MPI surmises, the long-term intergenerational assimilation process tends to stall in the third generation.

In this chapter, Vincent Ferraro walks readers through the theoretical framework for understanding immigration and crime. He explores historical theories that might be used to explain links between immigration and crime, but he also introduces readers to newer theoretical paradigms and studies that undermine the earlier theories. In the end, readers of the Ferraro piece will have a solid understanding of the classical and contemporary criminological literature regarding immigration, criminal offenders, and crime victims. This theoretical grounding is useful when evaluating the broader significance and contribution of immigration enforcement to crime control and law enforcement generally.

READING 7

Divergent Perspectives
Social Disorganization and Segmented Assimilation

By Vincent A. Ferraro

Sociological theories of immigrant criminality have tended to flow from the dominant conception of immigrants' broader integration into the host society, pointing to the role that the larger socioeconomic structure plays in determining outcomes. For the better part of the last century, the guiding lens through which scholars understood the structural connection between immigration and crime was social disorganization theory, which was rooted in a particular view of the process of incorporation: traditional, or straight-line, assimilation theory. In the last few decades, owing to the legal, political, and economic changes discussed in the previous chapter, researchers have noted that contemporary immigration no longer appears to follow this traditional pattern; nor do the tenets of social disorganization seem as applicable as they once did. In the sections that follow, traditional and contemporary theories of immigrant incorporation are reviewed, as are their correlates for interpreting the link between immigration and crime.

Immigrant Incorporation

The Traditional Assimilation View

Traditional assimilation theory developed out of the early Chicago school in the first few decades of the last century. Park and Burgess (1924) termed the process through which ethnic minorities become incorporated into mainstream culture, assimilation. Park viewed it as the final stage of a process that begins with "the breakdown of social order ... initiated by the impact of an invading population, and completed by the contact and fusion of native with alien peoples" (Park 1928: 885). The process, as Park envisions it, can be viewed as a *necessary blending* of sorts. It is a diffusion from high pressure to low, wherein the dominant and more pervasive host culture, which surrounds the

---

Vincent A. Ferraro, "Divergent Perspectives: Social Disorganization and Segmented Assimilation," *Immigrants and Crime in the New Destinations*, 1st ed., pp. 57-92, 205-227. Copyright © 2014 by LFB Scholarly Publishing. Reprinted with permission.

newcomers, leaks into their way of life, transforming them from Italians to Italian-Americans, from Irish to Irish Americans, and so on.

In more direct terms, this process plays out as a product of the newcomers' differentness. For example, to the degree that they lack proficiency in the English language, immigrants are precluded from employment positions that require direct communication between workers, most notably managerial positions, and are more likely to find employment in positions where this is not an essential feature of the job, such as manufacturing. In other words, lack of English language proficiency prevents access to higher paying, higher status positions. Over time, however, the skill is developed either formally, via enrollment in local schools or the taking of formal classes in programs like English for Speakers of Other Languages (ESOL)[2], or informally, through repeated interactions with native-born acquaintances and the institutions of the host country, including the police, banks, markets, all of which the immigrants may at times need to avail themselves. This development enables entry into those higher paying positions. The acquisition of language has been shown particularly easy among children, one of the key reasons for the pattern of increasing generational attainment. As newcomers adopt the host language and assume roles within the host employment structure, they begin more and more to "look like" the native-born, in the sense that their daily routines become similarly patterned around work, they speak the same language, and may come to value the same things. As they and their children gain access to higher paying positions, income and wealth may grow, enabling many to purchase items like new cars, and importantly, "nice" new homes outside of their initial place of settlement. For many immigrants, and many students of immigration and assimilation, this major step of moving to the suburbs has been a key indicator of "making it," whether envisioned as the attainment of socioeconomic parity or simply a parity of status—the transition from outsider to insider.

The above is an oversimplification of a very complex process and language is only one factor of many that affects the flow from contact to assimilation. And the above presents the situation as the inevitable outcome of a largely *structural* process, when in fact the choices, actions, and reactions made by both the native-born and newcomers greatly impact the end result. Two crucial phenomena are left out: native racism and immigrant isolationism. Their omission has received notable attention in recent years, posing a significant challenge to the early assimilation theory. Nonetheless, Park's "race-relations cycle" of contact, competition, accommodation and ultimately assimilation set the foundation for much work to come. Importantly, Park and Miller (1921) note that the assimilation process entails significant within-group variation, meaning that, for example, the amount of time between *contact* and *assimilation* will vary not only across different nationalities but also for different individuals and families of the same nationality.

Warner and Srole (1945) pick up on the theme of intragroup variation, noting that the process of assimilation will vary from group to group based on characteristics of the newcomers, including their skin color, language of origin, and religion. For Warner and Srole, these factors combine with socioeconomic status to determine the speed of assimilation. While these authors recognize variability in the process, they also ultimately accept Park's version of inevitable assimilation. Milton Gordon (1964) further extends assimilation theory by distinguishing between what he calls *structural assimilation* and *acculturation*. The former refers to immigrants' entry into primary group relations with members of the dominant group, while the latter refers to immigrants' adoption of the dominant group's cultural patterns. For Gordon, structural assimilation is the key to attaining full assimilation. Acculturation, while certainly not irrelevant, is inevitable in Gordon's view, given enough time in the host society, and in itself is not necessary for assimilation. Together, these early works share two key hypotheses that form the bulk of traditional assimilation theory: first, that integration into primary group relations with the majority group drives full assimilation and upward mobility, and second, that intergenerational change—the tendency for successive generations to more quickly adopt the lifestyles of the native-born—precipitates the process (Morenoff and Astor 2006). In this way, each generation moves one step closer toward the majority group.

A contemporary variant of traditional assimilation theory is spatial assimilation theory (Alba and Nee 1997; Massey and Denton 1985). Spatial assimilation theory combines the status attainment perspective with an ecological model (Massey and Denton 1985), and views residential proximity to whites "as a key indicator of, and in some cases precursor to, more general processes of assimilation" (South, Crowder, and Chavez 2005: 497; see also Alba and Nee 1997). Increasing residential proximity to native whites is seen as an indicator of both a decline in the insularity of ethnic enclaves and an acceptance of the minority group by the majority; conversely, rejection by the majority would be manifested in what has been termed "white flight." In essence, the more the residences of the foreign-born and their children are embedded among native communities, the more *blended* are they with the host. Close proximity to the majority enables interethnic relationships, friendships and marriages, via shared businesses, workplaces and schools, which are exactly the types of primary group relationships that fuel assimilation (South et al. 2005; South and Messner 1986; Massey and Denton 1985). As with traditional assimilation theory, spatial assimilation theory assumes a generational component, whereby successive generations should experience increasing proximity to the white majority.

Research on spatial assimilation has found that it is positively correlated with socioeconomic status (Massey and Denton 1985), English language proficiency (South, et al. 2005; Alba, Logan, and Stults 2000; Alba and Nee 1997), and generational change (South, et al. 2005). As income and education increase, minority group members are more likely to have greater contact with native-born whites. As immigrants' grasp of the English language increase, they are more likely to move into neighborhoods with greater proportions of white residents. Lastly, as South, et al. (2005) note, for Mexicans and Latinos more generally, the 1.5 generation (i.e., foreign-born children who immigrated before age 11) and later ones are more likely than their parents to move to increasingly Anglo neighborhoods.

Traditional assimilation theory, and those theories which stemmed from it, was the accepted version of events for earlier waves of immigrants primarily from southern and eastern Europe arriving in the

19th and early 20th centuries. Research on immigration and its effects dwindled in the middle of the 20th century due in part to restrictive immigration policies (Martinez 2006), the absence of recorded data on ethnicity in official statistics (Morenoff and Astor 2006), and challenges from cultural theories whose findings defied the "straight-line" path of immigrants (Bursik 2006; cf. Whyte 1943). The passage of the 1965 Hart-Cellar Immigration Reform Act made immigration from non-European countries easier, resulting in an influx of Asian and Latino immigrants. The last few decades have witnessed a return to importance for the study of immigration, and findings from that research have suggested for some that the experiences of the "new immigrants" (those arriving after 1965) differ markedly from their European counterparts in the earlier wave. Consequently, many believe the notion of a straight-line assimilation to "the mainstream" is no longer the appropriate way of understanding the process of immigration.

The Segmented Assimilation View

The most articulated challenge to traditional assimilation theory has come from those embracing the idea of segmented assimilation. In one sense, it is quite similar to traditional assimilation theory, which accepts that incoming groups over time become more like members of the host society. Segmented assimilation theory acknowledges that this is the case *for some immigrants*, though not for all. It holds that *under certain conditions* incoming groups can adapt to the host society by acculturating to dominant norms and becoming economically integrated in such a way as to enable upward mobility, that is, to structurally assimilate. Where it differs from traditional assimilation theory is in rejecting, or rather problematizing, what the latter takes for granted. The question for segmented assimilation theorists becomes, "assimilated *to what*"? Implicit in traditional assimilation theory is the notion of a unified "middle ground," a middle class that is not only economically homogenous but culturally as well.[3] This is the straight-line (or as Gans [1992] has re-envisioned it, "the bumpy-line") approach. Yet scholars of the new immigration point out that in an increasingly pluralistic society, the idea of a singular core culture is unlikely, as is the incorporation of immigrants into it. Depending on a number of factors, newcomers may find their way to this preferred structural location, or they may find themselves someplace else.

In their introductory piece on segmented assimilation, Portes and Zhou (1993) note that the experiences of new immigrants—again, those arriving after the 1965 Immigration Act—differ markedly from the previous wave of mass immigration—occurring from the late 19th to the early 20th centuries—for two reasons: skin color and fundamental changes to the national and global economies. European immigrants predominated in the last wave and, while in some cases slightly darker in complexion than the native population, their skin color created no lasting barriers. This is not the case for recent immigrants, who tend to come from Latin America, Asia, Africa, and the West Indies. The second factor has been the shift of the U.S. economy from industrial-manufacturing to service-oriented. While the former may not have made immigrant workers wealthy, it at least provided steady pay for those without technical skill sets and the promise of employment for their children as well. The loss of manufacturing has led to a restructuring of employment opportunities and the creation of a two-tiered or "hourglass economy," with high skill, high wage jobs, typically requiring college degrees, at the top and low skill, low-wage positions at the bottom (Crutchfield 1989; Bluestone 1970; Piore 1970).

According to segmented assimilation theory, the new immigrants exhibit three distinct patterns of adaptation to American society. First is *upward assimilation*, akin to the traditional view, in that growing acculturation is accompanied by integration into the white middle class. The second pattern, often termed *downward assimilation*, involves immigrants' acculturation to and integration into what Wilson (1987) has termed the underclass. The third pattern entails rapid economic advancement and the intentional preservation of ethnic identity, values, and solidarity. To put this in Gordon's terms, it is essentially structural assimilation without—or with a delayed or lagged—acculturation. As mentioned, while Gordon viewed acculturation as unnecessary for assimilation, he nevertheless viewed it as inevitable given time in the host society. As recent research suggests, some immigrant groups, including those who have had established residence in the U.S. for several decades, continue to retain their ethnic identity and culture (for discussions of Miami's insular Cuban population, see Martinez and Nielsen 2006; Nielsen and Martinez 2006; Velez 2006; Lee, et al. 2001; Portes and Zhou 1993). While traditional assimilation theory suggests that the maintenance of ethnic identity should serve as an obstacle to advancement—most notably by marking the newcomer as an outsider and potentially inviting discrimination—researchers have pointed to a number of benefits offered by such maintenance. In particular, a strong established ethnic community offers economic opportunities to newly arrived immigrants and the children of immigrants that don't require college degrees but still offer the potential for upward mobility (Portes and Rumbaut 2006; Zhou 1997; Portes and Zhou 1993). Strong co-ethnic communities can also offer educational support in the form of access to college grants and the presence of a private school system, which works to reinforce ethnic values and parental views and insulate youth from oppositional cultures (Portes and Zhou 1993). Lastly, strong ties to one's home culture can aid in enforcing norms against divorce and family disruption, as well as reinforcing parental authority over children, particularly important in cases of *dissonant acculturation*, Portes and Rumbaut's (2006) term for challenges to parental authority that occur when children's learning of English and American customs is faster than or conflicts with their parents'.

The path of adaptation taken is the result of individual and family characteristics as well as contextual factors like the political relations between the sending and receiving country, the nature of the host country's economy, and the size and structure of preexisting co-ethnic communities[4]. Portes and Rumbaut (2006; see also Portes and Zhou 1993) offer the concept of *modes of incorporation* to describe how the host country accepts newcomers. These modes are the result of the interactions of a complex of variables: the policies of the host government (whether receptive, indifferent, or hostile), the values and prejudices of the host society (whether primarily prejudiced or not), and the characteristics of the co-ethnic community (whether its organization is weak or strong). Three features of the contexts into which newcomers settle can increase the likelihood of downward assimilation. The first is skin color. Generally, the darker the skin color of the incoming group, the more likely it is that members will be ascribed a lower social status. Second is location. Specifically, residential concentration in urban areas puts the immigrant group in contact with native-born minorities, which leads the majority white population to identify one with the other and potentially exposes children of immigrants to an oppositional youth subculture. Third is the lack of mobility ladders in an increasingly bifurcated employment structure (Crutchfield, Matsueda, and Drakulich 2006), which impels adult immigrants to try to bridge the wide gap from entry-level to professional positions in one generation, in order to afford sending their children to competitive colleges and show them that hard work can yield success (Portes and Zhou 1993). Not surprisingly, many are unable to do so. Segmented assimilation theory suggests, then, that immigrants who enter this country possessing darker skin, who settle in our inner cities, and who lack either access to or the skills required for the primary employment sector, are likely to experience downward assimilation or what Gans (1992) has termed "second-generation decline," whereby rather than reaping gains in human and financial capital across generations, groups experience loss. This *segment* of the immigrant population—rather than all or even most immigrants, as traditional assimilation suggests—are more susceptible to criminal involvement precisely because of their economic marginalization.

Immigration and Crime

As mentioned, theories of the link between immigration and crime have tended to flow from our understanding of the process by which the foreign-born are incorporated into the host society. The sections that follow review the classic and emergent contemporary theories of this link and locate the theories within their larger respective theoretical frameworks.

Social Disorganization Theory

With respect to crime, the dominant theoretical view of the link to immigration has remained Shaw and McKay's (1942) social disorganization theory, which drew heavily from the assimilation perspective developed by Park and Burgess (1924). As Bursik (2006) notes, Shaw and McKay likely even borrowed the term, *social disorganization* from Thomas and Znaniecki's (1918) much earlier work on the experiences of polish immigrants in America. Not surprisingly, then, discussions of immigration and crime have tended to accept the view that immigrants are more prone to engage in crime than the native population. Shaw and McKay's theory posits that the criminogenic effects of immigration stem from structural factors rather than qualities of racial and ethnic groups themselves, as is often posited by theories of the cultural deficiencies of minority groups.[5] In their analysis, those authors indicate that no matter from where the immigrant groups travel, their experiences will be similar and crime will be an option for many, again not because of innate dispositions, but rather a lack of viable legitimate alternatives.[6] What is key is that Shaw and McKay accepted that assimilation was a largely uniform process, rather than segmented, and that most immigrants would experience it in the same way and have similar outcomes. Their study was one of the first ecological analyses of crime in America, and in mapping rates of juvenile delinquency in Chicago, offered a number of key findings.[7] First, rates of delinquency varied inversely to the distance from the center of the city and inversely to socioeconomic status. Second, delinquency persisted despite changes to the racial and ethnic composition of a community. Third, in slum conditions, the researchers found gangs to be natural responses to the living conditions, rather than a collection of innate deviants. Finally, and most importantly, Shaw and McKay found no direct correlations between immigration status and crime *or* between poverty and crime. Rather immigration status and poverty each worked indirectly through residential instability and population turnover to produce a socially disorganized community, no longer able to enforce norms against crime and delinquency.[8]

According to this school of thought, large scale processes of rapid industrialization, urbanization, and immigration result in a heterogeneous population that is residentially unstable. Heterogeneity and instability undermine a community's formal and informal sources of *social control*, which Bursik and Grasmick (1993: 15) define as the "effort of the community to regulate itself and the behavior of residents and visitors to the neighborhood." Communication between neighbors becomes difficult as they lack linguistic, cultural, or historic commonalities. Community members' familiarity with each other and attachment to local institutions and organizations are consequently weakened. Essentially, it is no longer possible to know everyone. Residents begin to treat one another with indifference, creating an environment wherein informal controls are ineffective, leading to a greater reliance and eventual strain on formal social control in the form of police or other official agents.

The micro-social process leading to crime, particularly among young people, may go something like the following: in disorganized communities, the family breaks down as an agent of social control, putting added pressure on schools and the police who must then do double duty, carrying out their assigned tasks—education and rule enforcement, respectively—as well as socializing youth into dominant norms. Schools experience their own unique problems. Large numbers of new and different students—students with different languages, ways of learning, cultural and social capital, perhaps learning disabilities, education levels, and so on—that similarly make communication and familiarity difficult. Further, in areas that experience rapid increases in population size, due for example to immigration, the influx of students puts a strain on the resources of school systems. Many students in such schools are pushed to the margins; their different forms of knowledge and expression having no conversion value within their new schools (Fordham 1996). Consequently, they are viewed as inferior by the grading standards of the school, which are typically slow to adapt (Carter 2005; Hargreaves 1967). Precisely because they are overburdened and their resources to educate and indoctrinate are spread thin, schools can respond to delinquent behavior with only the limited (official) sanctions available to them: detention, suspension, and expulsion. As these approaches fail to address the underlying causes of delinquent behavior—the inability to communicate needs and have needs met and the devaluation of students' social and cultural capital—they do little to curb the undesired behavior and in fact may foster a mistrust of the school among the students and ultimately may alienate those youth further (Carter 2005; Vigil 2002).

As they enter adulthood, these alienated youth stand greater risk of involvement with the last agent of community social control, the police, for two reasons. First, alienated youth may come to reject school, start skipping classes or drop out altogether. Second, youth who are alienated but who do not drop out, will likely have much difficulty in school, experience a reduction in academic success and ultimately in occupational achievement. Due to racism, many will be met with blocked opportunity upon graduation, and be subject to the social strain that motivates so many to engage in illegitimate opportunities (Martinez 2002; Vigil 2002; MacLeod 1987).

Sampson, Morenoff, and Earls (1999) offer as well a model for the ways in which the structural factors of social disorganization play out at the micro level in their concept of *collective efficacy*. In their view, three aspects of neighborhood social (dis)organization affect the criminal involvement of youth. First, *intergenerational closure* is the degree to which different age groups—juveniles, young adults, adults and elderly—are linked and interact. Second, *reciprocal exchange* is the degree of interfamily and adult interaction with respect to child rearing. Third, *mutual support of children* is the degree to which neighborhood residents can and will intervene on behalf of children. These factors are found in neighborhoods that are wealthy and residentially stable. In poorer, less stable areas residents tend to move in and out often, know each other less well, have fewer resources for mutual support (less time, greater personal concerns such as money, safety), and have higher rates of crime that tend to increase fear of and isolation from neighbors. The authors note that collective efficacy is not necessarily geographically bounded. It can spillover, such that neighborhoods with high collective efficacy will tend to increase that of surrounding communities. Conversely, those with low collective efficacy will tend to reduce that of surrounding communities.

In sum, immigrants face disadvantages relative to the native-born, which may lead them to engage in crime for economic gain (Lee et al. 2001; Merton 1938) or violence out of frustration or retaliation (Messner and Rosenfeld 2000; Tonry 1997b; Agnew 1992). This is the conventional explanation for crime and violence within immigrant communities. It is routinely, though not exclusively, applied to immigrants because of the tendency in the past for those groups to locate themselves in transitional urban areas (cf. Gans 1962). The theory works well irrespective of immigrant status and has been applied to native-born whites and blacks in low-income areas (MacLeod 1987). It is important to note, however, that Shaw and McKay implicated the *process of immigration* as criminogenic, rather than immigrants themselves. For nativists, however, that gap has shown fairly easy to bridge and explanations abound pointing to the cultures of migrant populations as deficient and the source of criminality (Mullen 2005; Huntington 2004; MacDonald 2004a, 2004b).

Community Resource Perspective

Drawing largely from the literature on segmented assimilation theory, and in particular its focus on ethnic enclaves, scholars have begun to question whether the traditional notion of immigration as disorganizing applies as readily today as it may have in the past. An emerging line of thought holds that increasing immigration to an area, rather than fostering disruption, may in fact strengthen community cohesion, thereby possibly acting as a suppressant to local rates of crime, at least in certain communities. This view has received growing attention in recent years, though, testifying to its emergent nature, that attention has come under a variety of names. It has been referred to as an *immigrant concentration* view (Desmond and Kubrin 2009), the *ethnic community model* (Logan, Alba, and Zhang 2002), the *enclave hypothesis* (Portes and Jensen 1992), and a *residential instability* model of ethnic enclaves (Shihadeh and Barranco 2010a). Following Feldmeyer (2009), this line of thinking is here referred to as the *community resource perspective*, since this term most fully encapsulates both the structural focus and the multifaceted linkages between immigrant communities and crime.

Scholarly research in a variety of fields has begun to offer support for the notion that increasing concentration of immigrants in an area is associated with a range of positive outcomes, including economic stimulation (Parrado and Kandel 2008; Portes and Rumbaut 2006; Reid, et al. 2005; Kotkin 2000; Portes and Zhou 1993), mortality rates (LeClere, Rogers, and Peters 1997), and reduced crime and violence (Shihadeh and Barranco 2010a; Desmond and Kubrin 2009; Feldmeyer 2009; Morenoff and Astor 2006; Lee, Martinez, and Rosenfeld 2001). These findings have led to the development of the concept of the Latino Paradox, which refers to the tendency of heavily Latino communities to have lower rates of crime and disorder, despite high levels of traditionally disorganizing factors, such as poverty, reduced education, and an abundance of low-skill workers (Burchfield and Silver 2013; Shihadeh and Barranco 2013; Stowell, et al. 2009; Sampson and Bean 2006). While the full range of mechanisms at work remain somewhat unclear, evidence points to a number of key factors, including the preservation of cultural norms, networks of information and social control, and employment opportunities.

Established immigrant communities can help to foster cultural norms based on shared heritage and traditions that bond members together. Successive waves of immigrants refresh and reconnect community members to that shared heritage, again reinforcing traditional norms and strengthening cohesion among community members (Feldmeyer 2009; Martinez 2002; Martinez, Stowell, and Cancino 2008). Immigrant concentration has also been shown to strengthen norms underlying conventional institutions such as marriage, family, and work. Recent immigrants tend to have lower rates of divorce, greater tendency to live in extended family units, and greater attachment to the labor force, despite lower lifetime earnings, relative to their native-born counterparts. Research has shown that unacculturated Mexican immigrants have lower incidence of psychiatric disorders across the life course than their more acculturated Mexican-American counterparts (Portes and Rumbaut 2006; Escobar 1998). Finally, as others have noted, the benefits of cohesion are particularly helpful in reducing pressures on immigrant youth. Sutherland (1947) first pointed out the criminogenic "side effects" of the acculturation process for immigrant youth when exposed to the mainstream American culture. Portes and Rumbaut (2006) elaborate on this point in their discussion of "downward assimilation," whereby the pressures some youth face in their adopted schools and neighborhoods lead them to engage in drug use, participate in gangs, and drop out of school. According to those others, the cultural preservation offered by tight-knit immigrant communities can reinforce norms devaluing such behaviors, thereby buffering against peer group pressures.

Furthermore, concentrated immigration can foster tight-knit social networks that operate as sources of information, providing newcomers with information they can use to adjust to their new surroundings, such as local customs, language, and sources of aid. These networks also operate as sources of opportunity, connecting recent arrivals to sources of employment and income, thereby mediating the potential effects of poverty and unemployment. Such networks can also operate as sources of child care, enabling parents to maintain employment and ensuring children are supervised by community members, a key component of collective efficacy, which can help mediate the link between structural disadvantage and crime (Burchfield and Silver 2013). Portes and Stepick (1993) note the beneficial effects of immigration in stabilizing and revitalizing the local economy in Miami, as well as contributing to greater informal social control within the area.

Concentrated immigration also provides an important source of employment, particularly for those whose skills may be undervalued by the host culture. Desmond and Kubrin (2009: 586) note that "the enclave in particular allows immigrants to find employment that yields better returns to their human capital than would be found in the secondary labor market outside of the area." Additionally, Portes and Rumbaut (2006) note that enclaves offer important opportunities for financing entrepreneurial businesses, which then generating further employment opportunities for local residents in a spin-off effect. These sources of employment may be key not only in warding off the criminogenic consequences of poverty, but also in strengthening social control. Card (1990) finds that the infusion of Mariel Cubans, expected by both Fidel Castro and the American public to be a major source of economic and social disruption, was far less problematic than anticipated. Existing immigrant businesses essentially absorbed the newcomers, providing them and their families with important sources of income to establish themselves in their new communities. As these studies have shown, there is good reason to suspect that among some communities, immigrant concentration is likely to have suppressive effects on crime, whether by reinforcing norms against it, strengthening community ties and informal social control, or providing opportunities that make crime a less attractive alternative. In the last two decades, a number of criminological studies have offered empirical support to these claims.

Recent Research and Hypotheses on the Immigration-Crime Link

Over the last ten years, a number of social scientists have begun to test the tenets of social disorganization theory and the community resource perspective on the experiences of and outcomes for today's immigrants at varying levels of aggregation. While several studies have found limited support for social disorganization theory, in the form of null effects of immigration or positive effects for specific crime types, the majority of studies have tended to find suppressive effects of immigration on crime, controlling for a host of relevant factors.

At the individual level, Kposowa, Adams, and Tsunokai (2009) find no effect of citizenship status on the occurrence of being arrested for violent crime, but a significant negative effect on other types of crime. Specifically, those authors find that non-citizens are less likely to be arrested for property crimes, drug offenses, and weapons offenses than U.S. citizens.[9] Similarly, Desmond & Kubrin (2009) find that immigrant concentration has a negative and significant effect on self-reporting delinquent behavior, an outcome firmly in line with the community resource perspective's view of the role of family and community in exerting social control on youth. Sampson, Morenoff, and Raudenbush (2005) find lower rates of violence among Mexican Americans, compared to whites, a discrepancy they suggest is explained by the greater tendency for Mexican Americans to have married parents, live in a community with a high concentration of immigrants, and be an immigrant themselves. Their finding that rates of violence among first-generation Mexicans are lower than second-generation Mexican Americans, which are in turn lower than third-generation rates points to a process of downward assimilation, as outlined by segmented assimilation theory.

This effect of acculturation is highlighted by several more recent analyses. First, Peguero's (2011) study of school misbehavior indicates first-generation foreign-born youth are less likely to misbehave at school compared to their native-born counterparts, but through exposure to school social disorder, such as physical conflicts, crime, and alcohol use. Moreover, foreign-born youth are more likely to misbehave in schools with higher shares of native-born black and white youth. Similarly, Esbensen and Carson's (2012) study of youth gang-involvement suggests that foreign-born youth are less likely to be gang-involved at younger ages, but by their mid-teen years, these same youth constitute a disproportionate share of gang-affiliated young people. However, these authors note that even though foreign-born youth may be somewhat more likely to be involved in gangs, their rates of actual offending are significantly lower than those of native-born youth. Finally, Alvarez, Nobles, and Lersch (2013) analyze Latino arrest records in two southwestern cities, finding a consistent, significant, and positive effect of acculturation on criminal arrests. Taken together, these findings raise the question of whether immigrant youth learn to become more criminal from native-born youth. At the least, the results suggest that acculturating to American society does not always put the children of immigrants onto a trajectory toward middle-class success.

While individual-level analyses can address the question of whether immigrants are involved in crime to greater or lesser degrees than native-born Americans, aggregate level studies are required to address whether the *process* of immigration may be implicated as criminogenic. The last few years have seen an increase in these types of analyses. For example, an analysis of the effect of the percent foreign-born on the occurrence of homicide within census tracts reveals that increasing immigration has a depressive effect not only on foreign-born homicides, but also white and Latino homicides as well (Martinez, Stowell, and Lee 2010). Similarly, in a tract-level analysis of aggravated assault rates in Miami, Martinez, Rosenfeld, and Mares (2008) find that measures of social disorganization all exert significant effects, though not all in the expected direction. While population instability and economic deprivation are both positively correlated with assault rates, population heterogeneity actually has a negative indirect effect; that is, a heterogeneous population reduces the likelihood of drug market activity, thereby reducing rates of aggravated assault. The pattern is similar for robbery with the exception of a nonsignificant effect of deprivation. Consistent with social disorganization theory, instability and deprivation have positive significant direct effects on aggravated assault. Instability has a limited indirect effect on assault rates through drug activity. Inconsistent with social disorganization theory, heterogeneity has no direct effect on aggravated assault rates, but has a negative indirect effect on them by suppressing drug activity.

The findings on heterogeneity suggest, "either that the nature of immigration and ethnic relations has changed or that population heterogeneity—as distinct from racial disadvantage and isolation—is simply not the 'disorganizing' social condition that generations of theorists have assumed it is" (Martinez, Rosenfeld, and Mares 2008: 868). Stowell, et al. (2009) reach a similar conclusion in their metropolitan level analysis, arguing that it is not that today's immigrants are different from those who came before, but that the immigration-crime link is, as Hagan and Palloni (1999) argue, a myth. Results of a time series analysis for 1994–2004 and a cross-sectional analysis for 2000 for metropolitan areas with a population of at least 500,000 suggest, respectively, that immigration either was responsible for broad reductions in violent crime, especially robbery, or had no effect on most categories of crime.

In a tract-level analysis using multiple ethnic groups, Martinez, Lee, and Nielsen (2004) investigate whether drug violence in Miami and San Diego is influenced by a community's ethnic composition or the presence of enclaves. In Miami, Cubans were more likely to live in non-drug areas than drug areas (as measured by the number of drug homicides) while Haitians were more likely to live in drug, rather than non-drug areas. However, controlling for other factors, the percent of the population that is Cuban, Haitian, or Central American was found to have no significant effect on drug homicides. Predictors of drug homicide included economic deprivation (positive and significant) and the percent of the immigrant population that arrived in the 1960s (negative and significant). The results for San Diego were somewhat different. There, Mexican Latinos, African Americans, Southeast Asians, recent immigrants and those who arrived during the 1970s were all more likely to live in drug, rather than non-drug, areas. Unlike Miami, the percent of the population that was African American and the percent Southeast Asian were positively correlated with drug homicides. Also distinct, areas with more recent immigrants were more likely to be drug areas, a finding consistent with social disorganization theory. Areas with both Mexican Latinos *and* low-skill workers were less likely to be drug areas, suggesting a surprising buffering effect of low-skill immigration, an outcome more consistent with the community resource perspective. As with Miami, economic deprivation had a positive and significant effect on the occurrence of drug homicides in San Diego neighborhoods.

The results suggest the importance of ethnic enclaves like those found throughout Miami for reducing crime. In either city, those living in barrios or enclaves were less likely to live in drug areas. While San Diego "offers a wider range of economic opportunities than does Miami, it also offers a limited immigrant opportunity to move up the socioeconomic ladder. One potential result is that immigrants and ethnic minorities are concentrated in areas where exposure to drugs is more routine" (Martinez, Lee and Nielsen 2004: 149). In general, the authors' findings support community resource view, with Miami serving as the exemplar of immigrant revitalization and ethnic enclaves, and San Diego serving as an example of downward assimilation and the type of community whose ability to aid immigrants' incorporation is limited. In Miami, well-connected and well-established enclaves provide opportunities for advancement of successive groups of immigrants, which helps explain Card's (1990) finding that the influx of Mariel Cubans had no effect on the employment of the existing workforce. In San Diego, a lack of well-defined enclaves leaves successive immigrants to follow the path of earlier immigrants to low-skill, low-paying jobs in disadvantaged and marginalized communities.

At the city-level, recent research findings have as well tended to present a challenge to the social disorganization view. Ousey and Lee (2007) find that homicide rates declined in cities that experienced population growth and in cities that saw growth in relative size of their Latino population. These findings are inconsistent with social disorganization, broadly conceived, which would predict increasing rates of crime in areas marked by increasing immigration. Research findings by Ousey and Kubrin (2009) that growth in rates of immigration from 1980–2000 were associated with overall reductions in violent crime over the same period are also at odds with traditional expectations. The authors suggest that the effect may be a product of immigration's tendency to strengthen families, relative to the native-born. Immigration is negatively correlated with both the incidence of divorce and the presence of single-parent headed households, each of which is positively correlated with violence. Also within cities, Martinez (2000) finds no significant effect of immigration variables on total homicides, but positive effects on felony homicides, and negative effects on homicides in which the offender knew the victim.

In a place-level study of 459 cities with population greater than 50,000, Wadsworth's (2010) change-over-time analysis indicates a significant negative effect of foreign-born concentration on overall robbery rates, and a significant negative effect of recent foreign-born concentration on homicide rates. Both findings lend support to the community resource view, suggesting that immigrant incorporation may not be the socially disorganizing or criminogenic force once thought. Also at the place level, Feldmeyer (2009) finds support for both social disorganization theory and the community resource perspective. Consistent with the former, areas with greater Latino immigrant concentration tend to have higher rates of residential mobility, language heterogeneity, and racial and ethnic population heterogeneity, each of which is found to directly increase rates of violence. Consistent with the latter, however, immigration is found to directly reduce the occurrence of Latino robbery and works to reduce specific and general rates of violence indirectly by strengthening social institutions such as the family and social support systems. The overall effects of immigration, according to Feldmeyer are small but inverse; as immigrant concentration increases, rates of violence, especially robbery, decline.

At somewhat larger aggregations, research has tended to offer more support for social disorganization theory, though the distinction is far from finite, and may depend more on the type of analysis and question at hand. In a cross-sectional county-level study, for example, Lee and Slack (2008) find that, consistent with social disorganization theory, violent crime is higher in more disadvantaged areas and where there is greater population turnover. Also consistent with social disorganization, violent crime is lower in homogenous counties and in communities where people either tend to work from home or work outside of their county of residence. Lastly, the authors find that employment in low hour or seasonal work is associated with reduced rates of violence, suggesting that "even partial labor force participation can contribute to the regulation of group behavior and interactions" (Lee and Slack 2008: 765). Within metropolitan areas, cross-sectional analyses have found no significant effects of immigration on either total or violent crime (Butcher and Piehl 1998). In contrast, changeover-time analyses looking only at within-unit effects have found significant negative effects of the recent foreign-born population on homicide (Reid, et al. 2005), and significant negative effects of the total foreign-born population on overall violent crime, and robbery and aggravated assault in particular. These latter findings are more in line with expectations of the community resource view of immigration and crime.

Immigration, Crime, and the Challenge of New Settlement Patterns

The dynamic spread of immigrants to new locations poses a number of challenges to researchers, policy-makers, service providers, and even local residents. Because many of the new locations to which today's immigrants are moving have at best a limited history in dealing with and incorporating disparate groups, it is unclear what the overall effects will be. With respect to crime, then, there are factors that theoretically should predispose immigrants and their offspring to engage in crime and factors that should act as buffers, keeping crime rates low.

Recent research by Donato, et al. (2008) buoys these points. Those authors investigate the changing socioeconomic and demographic factors of the foreign-born, and in particular the Mexican-born, across metropolitan and non-metropolitan counties, as well as within what the authors term *offset* metropolitan and non-metropolitan counties—places where the arrival of the foreign-born has prevented population decline—from 1990 to 2000. Their findings suggest that not only are the settlement destinations for immigrants changing, but immigrants themselves are also changing on a host of key demographic and socioeconomic factors. From 1990 to 2000, as the overall native U.S. population aged, the overall foreign-born population grew younger. Moreover, the foreign-born in 2000 reported fewer years of formal education and fewer high school graduates than in 1990, despite the fact that in 2000 the foreign-born were *less likely* than in 1990 to live in poverty. They were also less likely to speak English well or to speak it in the home in 2000 than in 1990.

Comparing immigrants in non-metropolitan counties to those in metropolitan ones yields some interesting differences as well. In the former, both the foreign-born and Mexican-born experienced significant declines in poverty, while those in metropolitan counties experienced only tiny declines. This difference suggests the boom economy of the 1990s yielded weaker returns for those in major urban areas, such that by 2000, compared to natives and their counterparts in non-metropolitan counties, the foreign-born and Mexican-born in metropolitan counties grew more disadvantaged in terms of income and education.

Also, both the foreign-born and Mexican-born in non-metropolitan counties were much less likely to become naturalized citizens in 2000 than in 1990; the foreign-born experienced a decline from 46.6 percent to 36.9 percent, while the Mexican-born declined from 28.7 percent to 23.6 percent (the declines were even greater for those in non-metropolitan *offset* counties). In contrast, rates of naturalization for those in metropolitan counties remained steady at approximately 40 percent of the foreign-born and 22 percent of the Mexican-born.

There were also important differences between those who moved into areas offsetting native population decline and those who didn't. Compared to all non-metropolitan counties, both the foreign-born and Mexican-born in non-metropolitan *offset* counties were more geographically mobile, being more likely to have arrived within the five years preceding the study and having fewer mean years of U.S. residence. They were also likely to have more children under age 18 and less likely to speak English well or speak it in the home. Taken together, these comparisons across national origin and U.S. residence indicate a trend whereby, beginning in the 1990s, as increasing numbers of immigrants entered the country, not only did many eschew traditional urban destinations in favor of new non-metropolitan areas, but those who did so tended to rate higher on a host of criminogenic factors.

Research is just beginning to address whether patterns of association between immigration and crime differ across areas depending on their history of immigrant reception. While only a few such analyses exist, their results are instructive. At the place level, Lichter, et al. (2010) find that Latinos experience greater segregation within new destinations than traditional areas and find greater difficulty in either structural or cultural assimilation. With regard to crime, at the county level, research by Shihadeh and colleagues suggests that while in traditional receiving areas, Latino communities provide a buffer between economic deprivation and violence, the same buffer is absent within new destinations (Shihadeh and Barranco 2013; Shihadeh and Winters 2010). These results suggest that the re-organizing effects of contemporary immigration highlighted by the community resource perspective may not be consistent features of the process within new destinations. Instead, there is greater reason to expect the process to be more traditionally disorganizing in new receiving areas, perhaps owing to the lack of established networks to aid immigrant incorporation. The analyses presented in Chapters 4 and 5 seek to provide insight into this issue by determining whether patterns of association between immigration and crime differ between traditional and emerging immigrant destinations. Should the analyses indicate differential effects of immigration on crime across types of receiving areas, the results might suggest the limits of the community resource perspective and the continued applicability of social disorganization theory.

Hypotheses on the Relationship between Immigration and Crime

Despite the recent growth in research on the immigration crime link, questions regarding the nature of the connection still exist. Several studies continue to find support for the traditional model of social disorganization, with some noting null effects of immigration on crime, others finding positive effects, and still others suggesting effects mediated by disadvantage. The majority of recent research, however, offers support for the community resource perspective: new waves of immigrants exert no effect on crime either directly or indirectly, and in many cases, may offer a suppressive effect, particularly in the case of violent crime. With these findings in mind, this research proceeds with a number of key hypotheses. Consistent with the community resource view and existing place-level research findings, I expect to find changes in the concentration of the total foreign-born are (1) negatively correlated with changes in rates of overall, violent, and property crime. Within the overall sample, I also expect to find (2) the patterns do not substantively differ whether the independent variable represents the concentration of total foreign-born or only those recently arrived.

In contrast, for the subset of new destinations, I expect to find stronger support for social disorganization theory. Given that new destinations very likely lack mechanisms by which to aid in the incorporation of newcomers, their arrival is likely to manifest as more of a traditionally disorganizing force. Moreover, given the current cultural context of opposition and research indicating greater marginalization of ethnic minorities within new destinations (Lichter, et al. 2010), it is likely that foreign-born in these areas may experience blocked economic and employment opportunities. Consequently, in these areas, I expect to find that (3) changes in the concentration of total immigrants are positively and significantly associated with changes in the rates of property and overall crime (with the former driving correlation to the latter), but (4) no effect on changes in the rate of violent crime. Finally, while I expect significant findings with regard to total immigrant concentration, I expect (5) the patterns to be heightened for changes in the concentration of the *recent* foreign-born, given as well research indicating their greater likelihood of being young, male, poorly-skilled and a visible minority (i.e. Latino as opposed to white European immigrants). These hypotheses are offered for the relationship between immigration and traditional crime. As the next section will show, there are good reasons to suspect the relationships will differ when the crime in question involves the victimization of newcomers.

Immigrant Victimization

Discussions of the immigration-crime link have almost universally accepted that, where it does exist, it's a one-way correlation: that immigration leads to higher crime rates *because* immigrants engage in more crime or displace vulnerable members of the local population. One of the peculiarities of this view is that engaging in crime doesn't make a lot of sense for immigrants, especially those who are without documentation. Given the overall unsympathetic stance at the state and federal levels and the increase in deportation as a solution to immigrant crime, the costs of crime would seem to far outweigh any benefits (Sayad 2004; Hagan et al. 2008).

What is at least theoretically more likely is that even documented immigrants, lacking a firm grasp of the language, knowledge of their rights, or methods of calling advocates or agents of social control to their aid, are prime targets for victimization (Hopkins 2010). Undocumented immigrants are especially vulnerable as any invocation of official agents is likely to jeopardize their continued stay. This line of reasoning parallels the routine activities approach, which suggests that the crime rate can go up without any increase in the number of offenders (Felson 1996; Osgood et al. 1996). Cohen and Felson's (1979) routine activities theory focuses on criminal incidents, rather than criminals, and suggests there are three minimal elements necessary for predatory offenses: (1) a likely offender, usually a young male; (2) a suitable target for crime, determined by the value, inertia, visibility, and access to the item; and (3) the absence of a capable guardian. Immigration may increase the pool of potential targets or victims, simply by increasing the overall population but more pointedly by bringing in a vulnerable population of people who may not know their legal rights, may not speak the native language, and who may be construed negatively by the native population. Additionally, the changing structure of local labor markets coupled with the cheap source of labor that immigrants often represent to employers can displace native workers, especially native-born minorities (Reid et al., 2005), who then may be cast into in the pool of likely offenders. Previous research indicates that employers often prefer immigrant workers over African Americans for sound business reasons—native-born workers command higher pay, better working conditions, and greater benefits—and more overtly racist ones as well—immigrants are perceived as hard-working while native-born Blacks are viewed as lazy and a liability in the workplace (Waldinger 1997, 1996; Beck 1996).[10]

According to the Leadership Conference on Civil Rights (2009), the annual number of hate crimes against Latinos increased 40 percent from 2003 to 2007. Though in a larger sense, immigrants are victimized by a variety of social actors at every point from the start of their journey through their settlement and employment in the U.S. As McDonald (1997: 4) notes,

> Guides and organized gangsters have robbed, raped and killed them; abandoned them in the desert; tossed them overboard at sea or out of speeding cars under hot pursuit; or forced them to work in sweatshops or prostitution rings to pay off the cost of the trip. Bandits prey upon them during their journeys. Xenophobes

and hatemongers terrorize them. Some employers cheat them of their earnings. The fact that illegal immigration is a crime makes the immigrants particularly vulnerable because they are unlikely to seek the protection of the law.

All the while, the exploitation of immigrants is a lucrative business. By 1993, the market for smuggling Chinese immigrants into New York was an estimated $3.5 billion. Individual migrants were typically charged $1500 up front, with the rest of the debt amount vague and paid off via something akin to indentured servitude (McDonald 1997). By 1995, "Central America had become a free-trade zone in which government officials sold the visas and passports necessary to leave China via plane for $25,000 to $50,000 apiece" (McDonald 1997: 5).

At a more local level, a recent review of immigrant reception in Suffolk County in Long Island, New York by the Southern Poverty Law Center (SPLC 2009) highlights the potential for conflict between newcomers and the local population. As an exemplar of the violence that can occur, the authors of that report point to the November 8, 2008 murder of Marcelo Lucero, an Ecuadorian immigrant, in Patchogue, NY. The murder was committed by a group of local youth who referred to themselves as "the Caucasian Crew" and claimed to have targeted Latinos as "part of a sport they termed 'beaner-hopping'" (SPLC 2009: 5). According to the report, rather than an isolated incident, the attack on Lucero was part of a larger pattern rooted in a "climate of fear" developed out of anti-immigrant rhetoric and policy of political leaders.

Latino immigrants are drawn to Suffolk County in search of work in its wealthy seaside communities. Unable to afford residence in those same places, they settle in the area's more affordable inland towns, "alongside middle- and working-class American families who are more likely to view the brown-skinned newcomers as competitors for jobs than hired help" (SPLC 2009: 10). In less than two decades, some towns in Suffolk County have transitioned from homogenous white communities to 15 percent Latino; many of the newcomers are from Mexico and Central America. The pace of the change has been met with resistance. Latino immigrants report being regularly harassed, taunted, and attacked, typically by young white males, though incidents involving black males and white females have been reported as well. Interviews with immigrants suggest they are increasingly unlikely to report these attacks, believing law enforcement either indifferent or hostile. According to the SPLC, their fears may not be unwarranted. While Latinos make up 14 percent of Suffolk County's total population, they routinely make up roughly 50 percent of those charged in court for motor vehicle violations on any given day, and a review of police blotters suggests the same pattern for individuals fined for motor vehicle infractions (SPLC 2009).

Vocal opposition has come in particular from political leaders. For example, upon taking office, Suffolk County Executive Steve Levy proposed filing a Memorandum of Agreement with Immigrations and Customs Enforcement, which would empower Suffolk County police officers to detain Latinos they suspected of being undocumented immigrants and hand them over to the ICE for deportation.[11]

Addressing day laborers, who congregate in public places waiting for work and thus constitute a very visible subset of the population, County Legislator Michael D'Andre of Smithtown, NY stated in August 2001, "We'll be up in arms; we'll be out with baseball bats" (quoted from SPLC 2009: 8). Of the same issue, County Legislator Elie Mystal stated in March 2007, " 'If I'm living in a neighborhood and people are gathering like that, I would load my gun and start shooting, period. Nobody will say it, but I'm going to say it'" (ibid.).

The opposition toward immigrants in Suffolk County coalesced in the form of the anti-immigrant activist group, Sachem Quality of Life (SQL), founded in 1998 and disbanded in 2004. Following the 2003 murder of two Mexican day laborers, Suffolk County legislator Paul Tonna held a rally for racial unity. In response, SQL held a rally outside Tonna's home, and "hurled racial slurs at his adopted children, four of whom are Mexican-American and one a Native American" (SPLC 2009: 13). Two weeks later, SQL held a "Day of Truth" rally, featuring speakers from several established hate groups. At the meeting, SQL members stated: "'Farmingville is a one-day job, that's Farmingville! If the INS wanted to do it, they'd come in the morning with buses, with document people, and remove them all, repatriate them. One-day job. Farmingville would be restored'" (ibid.).[12] A few days later, on July 5, 2003, five local teenagers set fire to the home of a Latino family with firecrackers. When asked by the local District Attorney to explain their motives, one of the teens stated, "Mexicans live there" (ibid.).

Recent Research on Immigrant Victimization

While the situation in Suffolk County should not be taken as the norm, neither should it be discounted as an isolated incident. Valenzuela (2006) investigates the degree to which day laborers—the thousands of men and women, many of whom are immigrants, who congregate daily on street corners in major cities across the country looking for a day's work—in Los Angeles are victims of violence. Because of the scarcity of consistent work, competition among laborers is fierce and relationships with bosses tense (wages are often bartered for onsite). Valenzuela finds that day laborers are victimized by a variety of sources, including other day laborers, police, employers, local residents, and local merchants, and are victimized in a number of ways, ranging from hold-ups, to hate crimes, to death (cf. Pritchard 2004). Consistent with other research findings, they are vulnerable to violence because of language barriers, their immigration status, a fear of reporting, a lack of knowledge of their rights, and the cash-only nature of their employment (see Hendricks et al. [2007] for how these same factors affect victimization and perception of bias in Arab-American communities). Similarly, in her study of Latino migrants in post-Katrina New Orleans, Fussell (2011) finds that day laborers are at increased risk of experiencing wage theft, relative to other types of workers, while Latino migrant laborers in particular are also at risk for robbery and physical assault. Drawing from laborers' physical appearance, language use, and job-seeking behavior, employers and street criminals are able to identify laborers as likely undocumented and so easy targets. The abuses committed against laborers may go unnoticed as they lack documents or a formal relationship with their employer, they work "under the table," and may be unfamiliar with their rights. Fussell terms this condition the *deportation threat dynamic*, "a highly exploitative interpersonal dynamic between targeted migrants and those who seek to take advantage of them" (Fussell 2011: 594), which is fueled by two key conditions: the high and steady demand for cheap migrant labor and the continued enforcement of harsh migration policies, largely in the form of deportations.

This dynamic highlights what researchers have alternately referred to as state-sponsored violence, legal violence, or symbolic violence (cf. Aliverti 2012; Menjívar and Abrego 2012; Hagan, Levi, and Dinovitzer 2008; Hagan and Palloni 1999; for a discussion of the use of symbolic politics in the 2008 Presidential election, see Marion and Oliver 2012), a condition whereby the state uses existing—and, where necessary, creates new—laws to apply harsh punishment and enforce exceedingly strict requirements on the conduct and presence of immigrants. The actions of the state then serve to signal to its citizens that immigrants are unwelcome and worthy of harsh penalties. In analyzing the role of criminal law, Aliverti (2012) finds that it serves as much as a symbolic instrument as a protective one. She notes that passing anti-immigrant legislation is relatively easy and allows the state to 'do something' about the 'immigration problem.' whether the policies are enforced or not, and whether the flow of immigrants is stemmed or not are relatively extraneous; what matters is that something has 'been done.' But as others have pointed out, this symbolic effect can have important consequences on those it identifies as problematic. According to Menjívar and Abrego,

> legal violence is rooted in the legal system that purports to protect the nation but, instead produces spaces and the possibility for material, emotional, and psychological injurious actions that target an entire group of people with a particular set of shared social characteristics (2012: 1413–14).

As Fussell notes, when the economic demands of a capitalist system interact with the legal violence of the state, the result is a sort of carte blanche for employers and criminals to victimize newcomers. One of the ironies of this dynamic is that violence against day laborers may actually engender violence *by them* as well, as they may perceive few other alternatives for recourse (Valenzuela 2006).

While day laborers tend to occupy the lower echelons of the class hierarchy, upward mobility does not necessarily reduce the likelihood of victimization. Miller (2007) finds that contrary to popular belief, increasing acculturation results in more complex victimization that is often more difficult to uncover. Even those who possess greater human and financial capital have been victims of housing scams, education scams, workplace abuse, and so on. What may change with increasing mobility and acculturation is the predominance of violence by the victimizers, rather than the overall victimization.

Research by Biafora and Warheit (2007) provides insight into the complexity of the issue of immigrant victimization. Comparing victimization histories not only across the Latino-White-Black continuum, but also within the Latino group, disaggregating by immigrant status, those authors find that immigrant status had no effect on the likelihood of being a victim of violence among young adults in Miami-Dade County, Florida. Consistent with previous research, African Americans were more likely than Latinos or native whites to experience *vicarious victimization* (i.e., witnessing violence happen to another person) and males were more likely to be victims of street violence than females, regardless of race/ethnicity or immigrant status. Somewhat inconsistent with the literature, the authors find no effect of immigrant status or race on *personal exposure* to violence, nor a significant difference between the lifetime victimization rates for foreign-born and native-born Latinos. The lack of a finding is attributed to "the unique social environment awaiting Hispanic immigrants arriving in Miami-Dade county" (Biafora and Warheit 2007: 45); that is, a welcoming reception from a well-established immigrant community with available political power. The emergence of ethnic strongholds like Miami leads the authors to suggest that "we might be witnessing a trend towards more stable residency among inner city immigrant areas due to a composite of economic, political and culturally enhanced opportunities" (Biafora and Warheit 2007: 51). An implication of this research is that the context of immigrant reception, and thus the potential for victimization, likely varies geographically.

So while scholars are beginning to address the victimization of immigrants (see Cuevas, Sabina, and Milloshi 2012; McDonald and Erez 2007; Valenzuela 2006; Reid et al. 2005; Levin and Rabrenovic 2004; Levin and McDevitt 2002), to date there have been few large-scale studies focused specifically on rates of victimization of immigrants.[13] Several research pieces have relied on victimization rates as proxy measures for *offending rates* (Martinez and Nielsen 2006; Nielsen and Martinez 2006; Lee, Martinez and Rosenfeld 2001), yet their overall focus has been on connecting that victimization to crime *committed by immigrants*. Further, these studies have tended to focus on a limited number of immigrant groups and locations, typically those cities that have traditionally been points of entry or destination. The problem with regard to studying victimization in such places is that they have long histories of interactions between natives and nonnatives, which may potentially make those interactions routinized, thereby reducing the likelihood of victimization (cf. Shihadeh and Barranco 2013).

Immigration and the Place of Victimization

As with traditional forms of crime, the geographic diversification of immigration raises questions as to the likelihood of immigrant victimization within new destinations. As political rhetoric has appeared to "prime" residents of such areas to view newcomers as threats, it is likely that many will be met with opposition and that such opposition may crystallize into anti-immigrant collective action (Olzak 1992). There is potential for many to be victims of unfair housing practices, and to have difficulty procuring legitimate employment. The children of immigrants are likely to face significant pressure in school, particularly to the degree that they stand out socially, culturally, or phenotypically. That pressure can manifest itself in a number of ways, most prominently in either outperforming native-born peers or rejecting the school system. Attacks on immigrants are another potential outcome. Previous research has shown that "at the local level, hate crimes directed at Asians and Latinos have been found to increase when these groups move into traditionally white neighborhoods" (Citrin et al. 1997: 877).

Shihadeh and Winters (2010) are among the first to investigate victimization across types of settlement destinations. Their research finds that Latinos are more likely to be victims of crime, homicide in particular, in new destinations than in traditional settlement areas. The implication of these findings is that minority group movement into primarily dominant group areas leaves the newcomers without the support of an established community that can "compensate for poverty, unemployment, and other factors known to elevate crime" (Shihadeh and Winters 2010: 645). More recent research supports these findings. According to Shihadeh and Barranco (2013), Latinos are at increased risk of being the victims of homicide in new destinations, but not in traditional receiving areas. Moreover, in new destinations, victimization in general increases with Latino immigration, an effect found only for recent foreign-born, those entering after 1990. Consistent with Social Disorganization theory, Latino socioeconomic deprivation is associated with increased victimization only in new destinations, not in traditional receiving areas. This finding suggests a "clear duality in the experience of U.S. Latinos" (Shihadeh and Barranco 2012: 96), whereby those newcomers who settle in traditional receiving areas benefit from a social organization that provides a buffer against victimization, while those who settle in new destinations, places lacking in protective social organization, are more likely to experience criminal victimization. It would appear that the link between immigration and crime long ago predicted by social disorganization theory, may again be at work in new destinations.

Consequently, at least in the case of Latinos, the newcomers are at heightened risk of violent victimization. While Latinos make up the lion's share of contemporary immigrants, Shihadeh and colleagues' research captures both native- and foreign-born Latinos, and it remains to be seen whether the pattern holds for immigrants specifically. There is good reason to believe that as immigration spreads to ever newer and previously homogenous areas of the country, conflict will ensue in some of those areas and sometimes become violent, particularly where the incoming group is perceived by the majority as posing a threat and where local leaders benefit from potential conflict (Levin and Rabrenovic 2004; Rabrenovic 2007). Adequately addressing the issue requires attention to *demographic change* as a predictor of biased crime, a focus largely absent in the existing literature. Consequently, inferences about the effect of population shifts on the occurrences of biased crime must be culled from cognate research on racial attitudes.

Cognitive/Attitudinal Research and Hypotheses on Anti-Immigrant Crime

Insight into the native-born response to increases in local immigration can be drawn from the body of work on group threat theory.[14] Traditionally, this research has been applied to categories of race generally, and the black-white dichotomy in particular, as a way of interpreting reactions to increasing settlement of African Americans in predominantly white areas (Blumer 1958; King and Wheelock 2007). Recently, researchers have begun extending this line of thinking to other subordinated groups, including Latinos and Asians (Green, Strolovich, and Wong 1998) and the foreign-born (Vallas, Zimmerman, and Davis 2009; Semyonov, Raijman, and Gorodzeisky 2006; Quillian 1995).

In its traditional form, group threat theory suggests that prejudice toward immigrants is a function of the perceived—rather than the actual—size of the population of newcomers, relative to the dominant group and economic conditions (Wang 2012; Welch, et al. 2011). An analysis of attitudes toward immigrants across twelve European countries finds that indicators of threat—subordinate group size and economic conditions—explain most of the variation in levels of prejudice across the sample (Quillian 1995). A more recent extension of that research comes to virtually identical conclusions, stating that growth in the size of the immigrant population translates to "greater competition for rewards and resources and greater challenge to the actual interests and prerogatives of the dominant population" (Semyonov, Raijman, and Gorodzeisky 2006: 428). Research by Welch, et al. finds that "the rapidly growing U.S. Hispanic population represents a compelling crime threat, at least perceptually, which fosters consistent and strong support for punitive crime control" (2011: 832–33). Importantly, the authors also find that the effect is heightened in states where there is actually a smaller percentage of Latino immigrants, suggesting that native-born Americans' fear is strongest where the 'threat' is least, a finding that is consistent with the "clear duality of experience" identified by Shihadeh and Barranco (2013) between traditional receiving areas and new destinations.

Regarding economic conditions, research has tended to find opposition to out-groups is greatest in times of economic recession (Burns and Gimpel 2000), and greatest when the national, rather than individual, economic outlook is dim (Espenshade and Hempstead 1996). This pattern results from dominant group members' either blaming the subordinate group for the poor economic circumstances, or their perception of competition with the subordinate group for resources, such that "the greater the sense of threat to their prerogatives, the more likely are members of the dominant group to express prejudice against threatening outsiders" (Quillian 1995: 588). Accordingly, Wang (2012) finds that the level of unemployment in an area strongly predicts native-born Americans' perceptions of the undocumented as a criminal threat, more so than the actual size of the population, supporting the notion that the native-born "are not simply concerned about the actual size of the immigrant population, but instead, they are concerned about economic competition for limited economic resources and opportunities, especially job opportunities" (Wang 2012: 764).

While group threat theory offers expectations for and explanations of the link between increasing immigration and oppositional attitudes among the members of locally dominant groups, it does not specify the manner or mechanisms by which prejudice may manifest as biased crime. Subsequent variations of the theory have sought to address this aspect, though as Green, Strolovich, and Wong (1998) note, with conflicting hypotheses. For example, realistic group threat theory predicts that attacks on immigrants would be more common in places where their numbers are very large (Bobo 1988). The power-threat hypothesis suggests that immigrant victimization would be at its peak where size of the group is just large enough to present a challenge to the social, economic, political standing of whites (Tolnay, Beck, and Massey 1989), though it is unclear what that threshold would be and whether it is dependent on spatially or temporally variant factors. Alternatively, the power-differential hypothesis suggests that anti-minority crimes should be greatest when numbers of the minority group are small. In this situation, members of the dominant group "may be emboldened to attack by the perception that law enforcement officials and the majority of those living in the neighborhood are unsympathetic to the victim group. By the same token, where minorities are few in number, perpetrators have less to fear by way of reprisal" (Green, Strolovich, and Wong 1998: 375). Finally, research on the defended neighborhoods thesis indicates that anti-immigrant acts of intimidation will diminish once a critical mass establishes residence. Until that point, however, the influx of minorities "represents a catalyst for action among those who seek to preserve racial homogeneity" (ibid: 376). According to this perspective, increasing numbers of minority group members, including immigrants, function as a force of social disorganization, disrupting preexisting social networks which, among other effects, "foster whites' sentimental attachment to a racially homogenous image of the community" (ibid). The disruption of these networks, and presumably the larger socially disorganizing outcomes, provide the motivation for attacks against the newcomers by community members who feel most threatened and who are the most aggressive.

Despite the relatively limited research findings specific to immigrant reception to date, key hypotheses can be drawn from the existing literature. I expect that (1) across the sample as a whole, there will be no significant effect of changes in immigration—either total foreign-born or the recently arrived—on the occurrence of anti-immigrant hate crime, once controlling for relevant factors. This expectation is consistent with group threat theory's two key postulates, population size and economic conditions. First, in the majority of places sampled immigrants have had a consistent presence, such that changes in their numbers would be perceived as less threatening.[15] Second, the period under study—2000 to 2007—can be characterized generally as one of economic vitality, ending just prior to the onset of the global recession. However, within the new destination places—places to which immigrants have only arrived within the last 10 years—I expect that (2) changes in the shares of total foreign-born will be positively and significantly associated with changes in the occurrence of anti-immigrant hate crime. Further, (3) the effects within new destinations will be heightened for changes in the shares of the recently arrived foreign-born. Within new destinations, the arrival of even small numbers of foreign-born is likely to be noticed, and growth in their numbers may be viewed as more threatening.

Conclusions

Theories on the connection between immigration and crime are fundamentally rooted in the dominant views of the process of immigrant incorporation. Social disorganization theory, long held as the definitive model of immigration and crime, is rooted in the traditional assimilation view that immigration disrupts social cohesion and that once settled, immigrants experience social and economic marginalization and disadvantage that leads to criminal involvement. In contrast, the community resource perspective, rooted in the segmented assimilation perspective, suggests that immigrant status alone will not predict increased criminal activity. Rather, it is the complex interplay among a variety of factors—the range of human and social capital contemporary immigrants bring, their increased likelihood to settle away from impoverished urban enclaves, their specific historical experiences, and the context of reception received upon arrival—that will determine which *groups* of immigrants may be more likely to engage in crime. Moreover, this perspective, unlike social disorganization theory, can capture and explain recent findings of significant negative effects of immigration on crime.

Neither of these theories incorporates a focus on immigrant victimization; guidance for this how that phenomenon may play out can be found in the body of work known as group threat theory. While the existing group threat literature with respect to immigrants is still limited, it suggests that attacks on immigrants are a function of both increases in population size and economic conditions. As discussed, there are competing hypotheses about the nature of the linkages population size and victimization, specifically, the requisite size of the subordinate group to elicit violence from members of the dominant population. While several notable studies have investigated the causes and consequences of immigrant victimization, few studies have systematically addressed the effect of demographic change—in the form of increasing immigration—on the likelihood of victimization.

From the extant literature, this chapter has drawn a set of hypotheses to be tested in the chapters that follow. These include: (1) changes in the concentration of the total foreign-born are negatively correlated with changes in rates of overall, violent, and property crime; (2) within the overall sample, the patterns do not substantively differ whether the independent variable represents the concentration of total foreign-born or only those recently arrived; (3) in contrast, for the subset of new destinations, changes in the concentration of total immigrants are positively and significantly associated with changes in the rates of property and overall crime, but (4) no effect on changes in the rate of violent crime; (5) the patterns to be heightened for changes in the concentration of the *recent* foreign-born. With regard to the analysis of immigration and hate crime, and consistent with research on group threat theory, I offer three additional hypotheses: (6) across the sample as a whole, there will be no significant effect of changes in immigration—either total foreign-born or the recently arrived—on the occurrence of anti-immigrant hate crime; within the new destination sub-sample, (7) changes in the shares of total foreign-born will be positively and significantly associated with changes in the occurrence of anti-immigrant hate crime; and (8) the effects within new destinations will be heightened for changes in the shares of the recently arrived foreign-born. These hypotheses will be systematically tested in the analyses presented in Chapters 4 and 5. In preparation, the next chapter outlines the methodology employed in those analyses, including the sources of data, variables to be analyzed, and the analytical techniques employed.

Notes

1. Rubén G. Rumbaut, Roberto G. Gonzales, Golnaz Komaie, and Charlie V. Morgan (2006, July 1). Debunking the myth of immigrant criminality: Imprisonment among first- and second-generation young men. Migration Policy Institute. Retrieved from https://www.migrationpolicy.org/article/debunking-myth-immigrant-criminality-imprisonment-among-first-and-second-generation-young

2. ESOL is an emergent variation on what has previously been referred to in the U.S. as English as a Second Language (ESL), and what is referred to elsewhere as English as an additional language (EAL), and English as a foreign language (EFL). ESL is eschewed here in favor of ESOL because latter more clearly acknowledges the multilingualism of many who take these classes—that is, many already speak a second (or third, or even fourth) language, just not English.

3. For discussions of some of the broader problems with this view, see Kivisto and Rundblad (2000), Kivisto (2005) and Modood (2007).

4. The term "co-ethnic community" refers to a community inhabited largely by members from the same country of origin and so is fairly homogenous. As such, the term is akin to and often used interchangeably with "ethnic enclave".

5. Here the term *minority* is used in Wirth's original sense, rather than the constrained contemporary sense, which tends to denote only marginalized racial minority groups and in particular African Americans and Latinos. According to Wirth, a minority group is any "group of people who, because of their physical or cultural characteristics, are singled out from others in the society in which they live for differential and unequal treatment, and who therefore regard themselves as objects of collective discrimination" (1945: 347).

6. Interestingly, Shaw and McKay differentiated immigrants not only by country of origin, but also by specific *regions* of their home countries. Contemporary research has abandoned this approach (perhaps because statistical procedures require the aggregation of small groups to get large enough counts to run analyses) and is only now returning to it.

7. Byrne and Sampson (1986) later extended this work on the ecology of juvenile crime to adult crime.

8. Social disorganization theory is often categorized as a pure theory of social structure, though one can see that from its earliest conception, the focus on population heterogeneity and turnover point to the importance of social interaction, making it more a theory of social process than strictly social structure.

9. The only offense for which non-citizens are *more likely* to be arrested, according to the study by Kposowa, Adams, and Tsunokai (2009), is counterfeiting/forgery, an offense consistent with producing documentation of legal status.

10. Amazingly, Pager (2003) finds greater hiring discrimination against Blacks than against convicted felons.

11. The motion was ultimately quashed by police unions for fear that it would make victims and witnesses unlikely to comply with investigations.

12. At the time of the meeting, Immigration and Naturalization Services (INS) no longer existed. As of March 1, 2003 its administration duties had been transferred to Customs and Immigration Services (CIS) and its enforcement powers, to which the speaker quoted appears to refer, transferred to Immigration and Customs Enforcement (ICE), under the DHS restructuring.

13. A search of the *Sociological Abstracts* database for the terms "'immigra[]' and 'hate crime' " yielded not a single quantitative research item as of February 11, 2011.

14. Here, *group-threat theory* denotes the broad category of research including that theory in its original formulation (Blumer 1958; Blalock 1957; Quillian 1995) and its variants: realistic group conflict theory (Bobo 1988), the power-threat hypothesis (Tolnay, Beck, and Massey 1989), the power-differential hypothesis (Levine and Campbell 1972), and the defended neighborhoods thesis (Green, Strolovich, and Wong 1989).

15. This expectation is offered with the place-level unit of analysis in mind. At smaller aggregations, such as census tracts, even relatively small changes in immigrant population may be perceptible to neighborhood residents, and thus the expectation may more accurately be a positive correlation.

References

Agnew, Robert. 1992. "Foundation for a General Strain Theory of Crime and Delinquency." *Criminology* 30: 47–87.

Alba, Richard and Victor Nee. 1997. "Rethinking Assimilation Theory for a New Era of Immigration." *International Migration Review* 31: 826–74.

Alba, Richard D., John R. Logan, and Brian J. Stults. 2000. "How Segregated are Middle-Class African Americans?" *Social Problems* 47: 543–58.

Aliverti, Ana. 2012. "Making People Criminal: The Role of the Criminal Law in Immigration Enforcement." *Theoretical Criminology* 16: 417–434.

Alvarez-Rivera, Lorna L., Matt R. Nobles, and Kim M. Lersch. 2013. "Latino Immigrant Acculturation and Crime." *American Journal of Criminal Justice*. Forthcoming.

Beck, Roy. 1996. *The Case Against Immigration*. New York: Norton.

Biafora, Frank and George Warheit. 2007. "Self-Reported Violent Victimization Among Young Adults in Miami, Florida: Immigration, Race/Ethnic and Gender Contrasts." *International Review of Victimology* 14: 29–55.

Blalock, Hubert M. 1957. *Toward a Theory of Minority Group Relations*. New York: Wiley.

Bluestone, Barry. 1970. "The Tripartite Economy: Labor Markets and the Working Poor." *Poverty and Human Resources* 5: 15–35.

Blumer, Herbert. 1958. "Race Prejudice as a Sense of Group Position." *Pacific Sociological Review* 1: 3–7.

Bobo, Lawrence. 1988. "Group Conflict, Prejudice, and the Paradox of Contemporary Racial Attitudes." Pp. 85–114 in *Eliminating Racism*, edited by P.A. Katz and D.A. Taylor. New York: Plenum Press.

Burchfield, Keri B. and Eric Silver. 2013. "Collective Efficacy and Crime in Los Angeles Neighborhoods: Implications for the Latino Paradox." *Sociological Inquiry* 83(1): 165–176.

Burns, Peter and James G. Gimpel. 2000. "Economic Insecurity, Prejudicial Stereotypes, and Public Opinion on Immigration Policy." *Political Science Quarterly* 115: 201–225.

Bursik, Robert J., Jr., and Harold G. Grasmick. 1993. *Neighborhoods and Crime*. New York: Lexington.

Bursik, Robert J. 2006. "Rethinking the Chicago School of Criminology: A New Era of Immigration." Pp. 20–35 in *Immigration and Crime: Race, Ethnicity, and Violence*, edited by R. Martinez, Jr. and A. Valenzuela. New York: New York University Press.

Butcher, Kristin F. and Anne Morrison Piehl. 1998. "Cross-City Evidence on the Relationship between Immigration and Crime." *Journal of Policy Analysis and Management* 17: 457–493.

Byrne, James M. and Robert J. Sampson. 1986. *The Social Ecology of Crime*. New York: Springer-Verlag.

Card, David. 1990. "The Impact of the Mariel Boatlift on the Miami Labor Market." *Industrial and Labor Relations Review* 43: 245–257.

Carter, Prudence. 2005. *Keepin' It Real: School Success Beyond Black and White*. New York: Oxford University Press.

Citrin, Jack, Donald P. Green, Christopher Muste, and Cara Wong. 1997. "Public Opinion Toward Immigration Reform: The Role of Economic Motivations." *The Journal of Politics* 59: 858–881.

Cohen, Lawrence E., and Marcus Felson. 1979. "Social Change and Crime Rate Trends: A Routine Activities Approach." *American Sociological Review* 44: 588–608.

Crutchfield, Robert D. 1989. "Labor Stratification and Violent Crime." *Social Forces* 68: 489–512.

Crutchfield, Robert D., Ross L. Matsueda, and Kevin Drakulich. 2006. "Race, Labor Markets, and Neighborhood Violence." Pp. 199–220 in *The Many Colors of Crime: Inequalities of Race, Ethnicity and Crime in America*, edited by R.D. Peterson, L.J. Krivo, and J. Hagan. New York: New York University Press.

Cuevas, Carlos A., Chiara Sabina, and Riva Milloshi. 2012. "Interpersonal Victimization Among a National Sample of Latino Women." *Violence Against Women* 18: 377–403.

Desmond, Scott A., and Charis E. Kubrin. 2009. "The Power of Place: Immigrant Communities and Adolescent Violence." *The Sociological Quarterly* 50: 581–607.

Donato, Katherine M., Charles Tolbert, Alfred Nucci, and Yukio Kawano. 2008. "Changing Faces, Changing Places: The Emergence of New Nonmetropolitan Immigrant Gateways." Pp. 75–98 in *New Faces in New Places: The Changing Geography of American Immigration*, edited by D.S. Massey. New York: Russell Sage.

Esbensen, Finn-Aage and Dena C. Carson. 2012. "Who Are the Gangsters?: An Examination of the Age, Race/Ethnicity, Sex, and Immigration Status of Self-Reported Gang Members in a Seven-City Study of American Youth." *Journal of Contemporary Criminal Justice* 28: 465–481.

Escobar, J.L. 1998. "Immigration and Mental Health: Why are Immigrants Better Off?" *Archives of General Psychiatry* 55: 781–2.

Espenshade, Thomas J. and Katherine Hempstead. 1996. "Contemporary American Attitudes Toward U.S. Immigration." *International Migration Review* 30: 535–570.

Feldmeyer, Ben. 2009. "Immigration and violence: The offsetting effects of immigrant concentration on Latino violence." *Social Science Research* 38 (3): 717–731.

Felson, Marcus. 1996. "Routine Activity Approach." Pp. 20–22 in *Readings in Contemporary Criminological Theory*, edited by P. Cordella and L. Siegel. Boston: Northeastern University Press.

Fordham, Signithia. 1996. *Blacked out: Dilemmas of Race, Identity, and Success at Capital High*. Chicago: University of Chicago Press.

Fussell, Elizabeth. 2011. "The Deportation Threat Dynamic and Victimization of Latino Migrants: Wage Theft and Robbery." *Sociological Quarterly* 52: 593–615.

Gans, Herbert J. 1962. *The Urban Villagers*. New York: Free Press.

———. 1992. "Second-Generation Decline: Scenarios for the Economic and Ethnic Futures of the Post-1965 American Immigrants." *Ethnic and Racial Studies* 15: 173–92.

Gordon, Milton M. 1964. *Assimilation in American Life: The Role of Race, Religion, and National Origins*. New York: Oxford University Press.

Green, Donald P., Dara Z. Strolovich, and Janelle S. Wong. 1998. "Defended Neighborhoods, Integration, and Racially Motivated Crime." *American Journal of Sociology* 104: 372–403.

Hagan, John, Ron Levi, and Ronit Dinovitzer. 2008. "The Symbolic Violence of the Crime-Immigration Nexus: Migrant Mythologies in the Americas." *Criminology and Public Policy* 7 (1): 95–112.

Hagan, John and Alberto Palloni. 1999. "Sociological Criminology and the Mythology of Hispanic Immigration and Crime." *Social Problems* 46: 617–632.

Hargreaves, David H. 1967. *Social Relations in a Secondary School*. Routledge.

Hendricks, Nicole, Christopher W. Ortiz, Naomi Sugie, and Joel Miller. 2007. "Beyond the Numbers: Hate Crimes and Cultural Trauma Within Arab American Immigrant Communities." *International Review of Victimology* 14: 95–113.

Hopkins, Daniel J. 2010. "Politicized Places: Explaining Where and When Immigrants Provoke Local Opposition." *American Political Science Review* 104: 40–60.

Huntington, Samuel P. 2004. *Who Are We? The Challenges to America's National Identity*. New York: Simon and Schuster.

King, Ryan D. and Darren Wheelock. 2007. "Group Threat and Social Control: Race, Perceptions of Minorities and the Desire to Punish." *Social Forces* 85: 1255–1280.

Kivisto, Peter. 2005. *Incorporating Diversity: Rethinking Assimilation in a Multicultural Age*. Boulder, CO: Paradigm Publishers.

Kivisto, Peter and Georganne Rundblad (eds). 2000. *Multiculturalism in the United States: Current Issues, Contemporary Voices*. Thousand Oaks, CA: Pine Forge Press.

Kotkin, Joel. 2000. "Movers and Shakers." in *Urban Society*, 11th ed, edited by F. Siegel and J. Rosenberg. Guilford: McGraw Hill/Dushkin.

Kposowa, Augustine Joseph, Michelle A. Adams, and Glenn T. Tsunokai.2010. "Citizenship Status and Arrest Patterns in the United States: Evidence from the Arrestee Drug Abuse Monitoring Program." *Crime, Law, and Social Change* 53: 159–181.

Leadership Conference on Civil Rights. 2009. *Confronting the New Faces of Hate: Hate Crimes in America*. Washington, DC: Leadership Conference on Civil Rights Education Fund. (http://www.protectcivilrights.org/pdf/reports/hatecrimes/lccref_hate_crimes_report.pdf)

LeClere, Felicia B., Richard G. Rogers, and Kimberly D. Peters. 1997. "Ethnicity and Mortality in the United States: Individual and Community Correlates." *Social Forces* 76: 169–98.

Lee, Matthew R. and Tim Slack. 2008. "Labor Market Conditions and Violent Crime Across the Metro-Nonmetro Divide." *Social Science Research* 37: 753–768.

Lee, Matthew T., Ramiro Martinez, Jr., and Richard Rosenfeld. 2001. "Does Immigration Increase Homicide? Negative Evidence from Three Border Cities." *The Sociological Quarterly* 42: 559–580.

Levin, Jack and Gordana Rabrenovic. 2004. *Why We Hate*. Amherst, NY: Prometheus Books.

Levin, Jack and Jack McDevitt. 2002. *Hate Crimes Revisited: America's War on Those Who are Different*. Boulder, CO: Westview Press.

Levine, Robert A., and Donald T. Campbell. 1972. *Ethnocentrism*. New York: Wiley.

Lichter, Daniel T., Domenico Parisi, Michael C. Taquino, and Steven Michael Grice. 2010. "Residential Segregation in New Hispanic Destinations: Cities, Suburbs, and Rural Communities Compared." *Social Science Research* 39: 215–230.

Logan, John R., Richard D. Alba, and Wenquan Zhang. 2002. "Immigrant Enclaves and Ethnic Communities in New York and Los Angeles." *American Sociological Review* 67: 299–322.

MacDonald, Heather. 2004a. "The Illegal Alien Crime Wave." *City Journal* 14 (1) (http://www.city-journal.org/html/14_1_the_illegal_alien.html).

———. 2004b. "The Immigrant Gang Plague." *City Journal* 14 (3): 30–43 (http://www.city-journal.org/html/14_3_immigrant_gang.html).

MacLeod, Jay. 1987. *Ain't No Makin' It: Aspirations and Attainment in a Low Income Neighborhood*. Boulder, CO: Westview Press.

Marion, Nancy and Willard Oliver. 2012. "Crime Control in the 2008 Presidential Election: Symbolic Politics or Tangible Policies?" *American Journal of Criminal Justice* 37: 111–125.

Martinez, Ramiro Jr. 2000. "Immigration and Urban Violence: The Link Between Immigrant Latinos and Types of Homicide." *Social Science Quarterly* 81: 363–374.

———. 2002. *Latino Homicide: Immigration, Violence, and Community*. New York: Routledge.

———. 2006. "Coming to America: The Impact of the New Immigration on Crime." Pp. 1–19 in *Immigration and Crime: Race, Ethnicity, and Violence*, edited by R. Martinez Jr. and A. Valenzuela. New York: New York University Press.

Martinez, Ramiro Jr., Matthew T. Lee, and Amie L. Nielsen. 2004. "Segmented Assimilation, Local Context and Determinants of Drug Violence in Miami and San Diego: Does Ethnicity and Immigration Matter?" *International Migration Review* 38: 131–157.

Martinez, Ramiro Jr., and Amie L. Nielsen. 2006. "Extending Ethnicity and Violence Research in a Multiethnic City: Haitian, African American, and Latino Nonlethal Violence." Pp. 108–121 in *The Many Colors of Crime: Inequalities of Race, Ethnicity and Crime in America*, edited by R.D. Peterson, L.J. Krivo, and J. Hagan. New York: New York University Press.

Martinez, Ramiro Jr., Richard Rosenfeld, and Dennis Mares. 2008. "Social Disorganization, Drug Market Activity, and Neighborhood Violent Crime." *Urban Affairs Review* 43: 846–847.

Martinez, Ramiro Jr., Jacob I. Stowell, and Jeffrey M. Cancino. 2008. "A Tale of Two Border Cities: Community Context, Ethnicity, and Homicide." *Social Science Quarterly* 89: 1–16.

Martinez, Ramiro Jr., Jacob I. Stowell, and Matthew T. Lee. 2010. "Immigration and Crime in an Era of Transformation: A Longitudinal Analysis of Homicides in San Diego Neighborhoods, 1980–2000." *Criminology* 48: 797–829.

Massey, Douglas S. and Nancy A. Denton. 1985. "Spatial Assimilation as a Socioeconomic Outcome." *American Sociological Review* 50: 94–106.

McDonald, William F. 1997. "Crime and Illegal Immigration: Emerging Local, State, and Federal Partnerships." *National Institute of Justice Journal* 232: 2–10.

McDonald, William F. and Edna Erez. 2007. "Immigrants as Victims: A Framework." *International Review of Victimology* 14: 1–10.

Menjívar, Cecilia and Leisy J. Abrego. 2012. "Legal Violence: Immigration Law and the Lives of Central American Immigrants." *American Journal of Sociology* 117: 1380–1421.

Merton, Robert K. 1938. "Social Structure and Anomie." *American Sociological Review* 3: 672–682.

Messner, Steven F. and Richard Rosenfeld. 2001. *Crime and the American Dream,* 3rd edition. Belmont, CA: Wadsworth.

Miller, Linda. 2007. "The Exploitation of Acculturating Immigrant Populations." *International Review of Victimology* 14: 11–28.

Modood, Tariq. 2007. *Multiculturalism.* Malden, MA: Polity Press.

Morenoff, Jeffrey D. and Avraham Astor. 2006. "Immigrant Assimilation and Crime: Generational Differences in Youth Violence in Chicago." Pp. 36 63 in *Immigration and Crime: Race, Ethnicity, and Violence*, edited by R. Martinez, Jr. and A. Valenzuela. New York: New York University Press.

Mullen, Kevin J. 2005. *Dangerous Strangers: Minority Newcomers and Criminal Violence in the Urban West, 1850–2000.* New York: Palgrave MacMillan.

Nielsen, Amie L. and Ramiro Martinez, Jr. 2006. "Multiple Disadvantages and Crime among Black Immigrants: Exploring Haitian Violence in Miami's Communities." Pp. 212–233 in *Immigration and Crime: Race, Ethnicity, and Violence*, edited by R. Martinez Jr. and A. Valenzuela. New York: New York University Press.

Olzak, Susan. 1992. *The Dynamics of Ethnic Competition and Conflict.* Stanford, CA: Stanford University Press.

Osgood, D. Wayne, Janet K. Wilson, Patrick M. O'Malley, Jerald G. Bachman, and Lloyd D. Johnston. 1996. "Routine Activities and Individual Deviant Behavior." *American Sociological Review* 61: 635–655.

Ousey, Graham and Matthew R. Lee. 2007. "Homicide Trends and Illicit Drug Markets: Exploring Differences Across Time." *Justice Quarterly* 24: 48–79.

Ousey, Graham C. and Charis E. Kubrin. 2009. "Exploring the Connection between Immigration and Violent Crime Rates in U.S. Cities, 1980–2000." *Social Problems* 56: 447–473.

Pager, Devah. 2003. "The Mark of a Criminal Record." *American Journal of Sociology* 108: 937–75.

Park, Robert E. 1928. "Human Migration and the Marginal Man." *American Journal of Sociology* 33: 881–893.

Park, Robert E., and Ernest W. Burgess. 1924. *Introduction to the Science of Sociology*. Chicago: University of Chicago Press.

Park, Robert E., and Herbert A. Miller. 1921. *Old World Traits Transplanted*. New York: Harper and Brothers.

Parrado, Emilio A. and William Kandel. 2008. "New Hispanic Migrant Destinations: A Tale of Two Industries." Pp. 99–123 in *New Faces in New Places: The Changing Geography of American Immigration*, edited by D.S. Massey. New York: Russell Sage.

Peguero, Anthony A. 2011. "Immigration, Schools, and Violence: Assimilation and Student Misbehavior." *Sociological Spectrum* 31: 695–717.

Piore, Michael. 1970. "The Dual Labor Market: Theory and Implications." Pp. 55–59 in *The State and the Poor*, edited by S.H. Beer and R.E. Barringer. Cambridge, MA: Winthrop.

Portes, Alejandro and Leif Jensen. 1992. "Disproving the Enclave Hypothesis." *American Sociological Review* 57: 418–420.

Portes, Alejandro and Min Zhou. 1993. "The New Second Generation: Segmented Assimilation and Its Variants." *Annals of the American Academy of Political and Social Science* 530: 74–96.

Portes, Alejandro and Ruben Rumbaut. 2006. *Immigrant America: A Portrait*. Los Angeles: University of California Press.

Portes, Alejandro and Alex Stepick. 1993. *City on the Edge: The Transformation of Miami*. Berkeley, CA: University of California Press.

Pritchard, Justin. 2004. "Mexican-Born Workers More Likely to Die on Job: Risky Work, Compliant Attitude and Language Barrier Contribute to the Trend, AP Study Shows." *Associated Press*, March 14.

Quillian, Lincoln. 1995. "Prejudice as a Response to Perceived Group Threat: Population Composition and Anti-Immigrant and Racial Prejudice in Europe." *American Sociological Review* 60: 586–611.

Rabrenovic, Gordana. 2007. "When Hate Comes to Town: Community Response to Violence Against Immigrants." *American Behavioral Scientist* 51: 349–360.

Reid, Lesley Williams, Harald Weiss, Robert M. Adelman, and Charles Jaret. 2005. "The Immigration-Crime Relationship: Evidence Across US Metropolitan Areas." *Social Science Research* 34: 757–780.

Sampson, Robert J., Jeffrey D. Morenoff, and Fenton Earls. 1999. "Beyond Social Capital: Spatial Dynamics of Collective Efficacy for Children." *American Sociological Review* 64: 633–660.

Sampson, Robert J., Jeffrey Morenoff, and Steven Raudenbush. 2005. "Social Anatomy of Racial and Ethnic Disparities in Violence." *Public Health Matters* 95: 224–232.

Sampson, Robert J. and Lydia Bean. 2006. "Cultural Mechanisms and Killing Fields: A Revised Theory of Community-Level Inequality." Pp. 8–36 in *The Many Colors of Crime: Inequalities of Race, Ethnicity and Crime in America*, edited by R.D. Peterson, L.J. Krivo, and J. Hagan. New York: New York University Press.

Sayad, Abdelmalek. 2004. *The Suffering of the Immigrant.* Malden, MA: Polity Press.

Semyonov, Moshe, Rebeca Raijman, and Anastasia Gorodzeisky. 2006. "The Rise of Anti-foreigner Sentiment in European Societies, 1988–2000." *American Sociological Review* 71: 426–499.

Shaw, Clifford R. and Henry D. McKay. 1942. *Juvenile Delinquency in Urban Areas.* Chicago: University of Chicago Press.

Shihadeh, Edward S. and Raymond E. Barranco. 2010a. "Leveraging the Power of the Ethnic Enclave: Residential Instability and Violence in Latino Communities." *Sociological Spectrum* 30: 249–269.

———. 2013. "The Imperative of Place: Homicide and the New Latino Migration." *Sociological Quarterly* 54: 81–104.

Shihadeh, Edward S., and Lisa Winters. 2010. "Church, Place, and Crime: Latinos and Homicides in New Destinations." *Sociological Inquiry* 80: 628–649.

South, Scott J. and Steven F. Messner. 1986. "Structural Determinants of Intergroup Association: Interracial Marriage and Crime." *American Journal of Sociology* 91: 1409–30.

South, Scott J., Kyle Crowder, and Erick Chavez. 2005. "Migration and Spatial Assimilation among U.S. Latinos: Classical versus Segmented Trajectories." *Demography* 42: 497–521.

Southern Poverty Law Center. 2009. *Climate of Fear: Latino Immigrants in Suffolk County, NY*. Montgomery, AL: Southern Poverty Law Center. (http://www.splcenter.org/images/dynamic/main/splc_suffolk_report_lores.pdf).

Stowell, Jacob I., Steven F. Messner, Kelly F. McGeever, and Lawrence E. Raffalovich. 2009. "Immigration and the Recent Violent Crime Drop in the United States: A Pooled, Cross-Sectional Time-Series Analysis of Metropolitan Areas." *Criminology* 47: 889–928.

Sutherland, Edwin H. 1947. *Principles of Criminology, 4th ed.* Philadelphia: J.B. Lippincott Company.

Thomas, William I. and Florian Znaniecki. 1918. *The Polish Peasant in Europe and America.* Urbana: University of Illinois Press.

Tolnay, Stewart E., E. M. Beck, and James L. Massey. 1989. "The Power Threat Hypothesis and Black Lynching: 'Wither' the Evidence?" *Social Forces* 67 (3): 634–641.

Tonry, Michael, ed. 1997. *Ethnicity, Crime, and Immigration: Comparative and Cross-National Perspectives.* Chicago: University of Chicago Press.

Valenzuela, Abel Jr. 2006. "New Immigrants and Day Labor: The Potential for Violence." Pp. 189–211 in *Immigration and Crime: Race, Ethnicity, and Violence*, edited by R. Martinez, Jr. and A. Valenzuela. New York: NYU Press.

Vallas, Steven P., Emily Zimmerman, Shannon N. Davis. 2009. "Enemies of the State? Testing Three Models of Anti-Immigrant Settlement." *Research in Social Stratification and Mobility* 27: 201–217.

Velez, Maria B. 2006. "Toward an Understanding of the Lower Rates of Homicide in Latino versus Black Neighborhoods: A Look at Chicago." Pp. 91–107 in *The Many Colors of Crime: Inequalities of Race, Ethnicity and Crime in America*, edited by R.D. Peterson, L.J. Krivo, and J. Hagan. New York: New York University Press.

Vigil, James Diego. 2002. *A Rainbow of Gangs: Street Cultures in the Mega City.* Austin, TX: University of Texas Press.

Wadsworth, Tim. 2010. "Is Immigration Responsible for the Crime Drop? An Assessment of the Influence of Immigration on Changes in Violent Crime Between 1990 and 2000." *Social Science Quarterly* 91: 531–553.

Waldinger, Roger. 1996. *Still the Promised City? African-Americans and New Immigrants in Post-Industrial New York*. Cambridge, MA: Harvard University Press.

———. 1997. "Black/Immigrant Competition Re-Assessed: New Evidence from Los Angeles." *Sociological Perspectives* 40: 365–86.

Wang, Xia. 2012. "Undocumented Immigrants as Perceived Criminal Threat: A Test of the Minority Threat Perspective." *Criminology* 50: 743–776.

Warner, W. Lloyd, and Leo Srole. 1945. *The Social Systems of American Ethnic Groups.* New Haven, CT: Yale University Press.

Welch, Kelly, Allison Ann Payne, Ted Chiricos, and Marc Gertz. 2011. "The Typification of Hispanics as Criminals and Support for Punitive Crime Control Policies." *Social Science Research* 40: 822–840.

Whyte, William Foote. 1943. *Street Corner Society: The Social Structure of an Italian Slum.* Chicago: University of Chicago Press.

Wilson, William Julius. 1987. *The Truly Disadvantaged: The Inner City, The Underclass, and Public Policy.* Chicago: University of Chicago Press.

Wirth, Louis. 1945. "The Problem of Minority Groups." in *The Science of Man in the World Crisis*, edited by R. Linton. New York: Columbia University Press.

Zhou, Min. 1997. "Segmented Assimilation: Issues, Controversies, and Recent Research on the New Second Generation." *International Migration Review* 31: 975–1008.

DISCUSSION QUESTIONS

1. Identify and explain the traditional theories of assimilation that have historically guided our understanding of how immigrants become successful in society. How have those theories been challenged in more recent years?

2. What is social disorganization theory? What is collective efficacy? How do these theories relate to immigration and crime?

3. What does more recent research say about the link between immigration and crime? Please explain with examples.

4. In what ways are immigrants particularly susceptible to criminal victimization? What is routine activities theory? How might that theory explain why members of immigrant communities are particularly vulnerable to becoming crime victims?

5. What is group threat theory? Summarize some of the studies highlighted in the reading that relate to this theory. Based on your understanding of the theory, to what degree does it adequately explain crimes against immigrants committed by native-born offenders? Why?

CHAPTER EIGHT

Immigration and Terrorism

Introduction

On September 11, 2001, four commercial airliners were hijacked by Al Qaeda terrorists for the purpose of turning those aircraft into weapons. In all four planes, the pilots were killed or otherwise incapacitated. Three of the planes were flown into planned targets: both World Trade Center towers in New York City and the Pentagon outside of Washington, DC. The fourth plane is believed to have been destined for the White House or the U.S. Capitol building; however, passengers, having heard from loved ones via their cell phones about the fates of the other hijacked aircraft, attempted to overpower the terrorists who were by then in command of the cockpit. The outcome was that the airliner crashed in rural Pennsylvania as a result of the struggle for control of the plane.

These hijackings were carried out by 19 Arab men. Fifteen were from Saudi Arabia, two were from the United Arab Emirates, and one each were from Egypt and Lebanon. All 19 men had entered the United States legally. Most of them came on tourist visas; one entered on a student visa.

In the wake of the 9/11 attacks, which killed nearly 3,000 people, the United States entered a frenzied state of alertness and proactivity. Civilian aviation across the entire country was grounded for two days. America's skies over major cities were patrolled by NATO fighter jets. New laws were quickly passed that nationalized aviation security personnel at airports (the Aviation Transportation Security Act of 2001), expanded government powers to investigate terrorism (the USA PATRIOT Act), and created a new federal cabinet-level department to coordinate homeland security efforts, including those relating to border security and immigration (the Homeland Security Act of 2002).

Federal and local law enforcement also stepped up their counterterrorism investigative efforts, believing that another 9/11-scale attack could be imminent. Part of this effort included a large-scale, nationwide roundup and detention of hundreds of Arabs in the country illegally. These were individuals, and in many cases whole families, who were not thought to be tied to any terror organization, but who were indeed in the United States illegally—usually as a result of expired visas.

In the first piece presented in this chapter, Samantha Hauptman analyzes the "moral panic" that ensued in the United States following the 9/11 attacks. She argues that this panic, which focused on immigrant communities, was manifested in the actions of government officials and agencies, law enforcement, the media, and the public at large. Hauptman offers this autopsy of the post–9/11 panic as an object lesson for caution against broad generalizations and policy changes toward immigrants, who make easy but inaccurate and unproductive targets when anyone associated with their community engages in acts of terrorism or other serious offenses.

In the second piece for this chapter, authored by Fathali Moghaddam and James Breckenridge, the paradigms of assimilation (touched upon in previous chapters), multiculturalism, and omniculturalism are explored as societal frameworks for understanding one another, developing an appreciation for those outside of our groups, and for finding commonalities where they exist. Indeed, our relationships with one another inside and outside of our own ethnic, religious, and cultural communities have significant bearing on intelligence gathering and other forms of cooperation the government might gain from various subsets of society. In particular, omniculturalism is offered as the preferred paradigm of Americans, perhaps unbeknownst to them, given the dogma-like emphasis from different quarters on both immigrant assimilation and multiculturalism for society. The authors proceed to explore omniculturalism further and suggest it has merit for garnering the kind of intercommunity cooperation necessary for a successful fight against homegrown and imported terrorism.

READING 8

Terror of Immigration and War on Immigrants

By Samantha Hauptman

When investigating the moral panic conception, the most important tasks are to establish: "What characterizes the moral panic? [and] How do we know when a moral panic takes hold on a given society?" (Goode and Ben-Yehuda, 1994: 33). It is these questions that must necessarily be addressed through specific indicators, by means of appropriate measures that determine the sudden and unpredictable nature of a moral panic environment. Based on the moral panic model and theoretical concepts of social control and deviance, the three analyses utilized in this study examined each indicator individually, then used a combined approach to seek out the succinct symptoms, illuminating post-9/11 moral panic conditions where immigrants in general have been criminalized by the media, public, and federal government and particular immigrant groups were clearly defined as *folk devils*. It is evident from the results of this study that after September 11th 2001, each moral panic indicator was manifested at varying degrees and several have continued to linger in U.S. society.

Concern

Since 9/11 and the inception of the PATRIOT Act, the issue of immigration in the U.S. has been constructed as a social problem where immigrants are routinely associated with a variety of social dangers including crime, terrorism, and national security in the media. Although the media are not the sole actors in constructing social problems, the media do "play a pivotal and strong role in defining and legitimizing the problem as well as promoting official interventions, policies, and programs" (Altheide 2002:146). Therefore, the media are an effective form of informal social control that is imperative to the proliferation of a moral panic and instrumental in distinguishing the subject of concern during a panic.

Samantha Hauptman, "Terror of Immigration and War on Immigrants," *The Criminalization of Immigration: The Post 9/11 Moral Panic*, 1st ed., pp. 125-142, 157-166. Copyright © 2013 by LFB Scholarly Publishing. Reprinted with permission.

After the 9/11 terrorist attacks, the media's campaign against immigrants was evident as it began almost immediately with focused reporting on immigrants as related to a variety of criminal activities, thus aiding the increase in public fear and anxiety against them. As Welch (2006) asserts the overall effect of this type of reporting results in:

> Framing the issue in that manner reflects and reinforces not only public fear of terrorism, but also an undifferentiated social anxiety over national security, economic woes, crime, racial/ethnic minorities, immigrants, and foreigners. Those tensions compound the need to assign blame even if it means falsely accusing innocent persons for terrorism along with a host of other social problems. (p. 35)

This analysis discovered that there was in fact a comprehensive increase in the post-9/11 levels of reporting making the association between immigrants and criminality. These increases were discernible as a heightened anxiety over immigration that was prevalent in the media throughout the country; illuminating the concern indicator as a measurable and verifiable condition required to discern panicked condition (Welch 2002; Cohen 1972; Goode and Be-Yehuda 1994). The results showed increases in both the number of relevant articles and negative articles published, and even revealed an increase in the reporting of an individual's ethnicity or country of origin when reporting criminal activities; even in cases where the articles that had an entirely different focus and an individual's ethnic origin was immaterial.

Media Concern

By naming particular groups or adding foreign descents or ethnicities to U.S. citizens involved in crime or articles with an unrelated focus, the media effectively increased the coverage of immigrants as related to criminality within its publications; thus perhaps criminalizing immigrants and also those of foreign descent. One common tactic in reporting after 9/11 was the addition of a subject's ethnicity or descent in articles recounting criminal activities, even as the article's focus was not immigration or if the subject associated with crime was not necessarily foreign born but in many cases was in fact a U.S. citizen. Although the reference to a foreign descent did not enhance or further clarify the subject's motivation for engaging in criminal activity, the mere mention potentially criminalizes the immigrant group when it is included for no immediately obvious or apparent reason.

This method of informal social control suggests identifies foreign born groups are *folk devils* and further may provide the public with a target of hostility or "scapegoat". In an informal social control role, the media uses "scapegoating [which] by its very nature targets 'the other', a person or group that is perceived as being not only different from 'us' but potentially threatening to 'our' society. Especially when the 'the other' is different in terms of race, ethnicity, and religion" (Welch 2006: 71). Therefore, even in cases where criminal activities may have been perpetrated by U.S. citizens, the addition of an ethnic or foreign descent label further defined the subject as an "other" or outsider, needlessly suggesting a potential threat or need for increased suspicion against the immigrant groups referenced.

In the media analysis, there were many examples of articles where adding or implicating a foreign born descent seemed gratuitous. For instance, one article reporting a theft from a research lab in California described that the accused as "a naturalized citizen of Chinese descent" but did not elaborate on why the detail was relevant to the arrest or explore the issue further, it simply implied that as the accused is foreign born, he does not really belong to U.S. society and was in effect, although a citizen, clearly identified as an being an 'other'.

In another article, there was a report of an investigation into an identity theft crime where "an American born woman and an Israeli man" were accused; the article later clarifies the female suspect's ethnicity further by indicating that the American was of Russian descent, again a seemingly irrelevant but pejorative detail. In articles where immigration was not the primary issue and need not have been included in the reports, the criminal association of immigrants was still included, for example:

> Trailed early Thursday by news cameras, state game wardens arrested Mark Golmyan, 54, owner of the Gastronom Russian Deli on Geary Street, along with four other San Francisco residents accused of buying the caviar for up to $140 a pound and then selling it to Bay Area residents, mostly of Russian descent. ("Sturgeon Poaching Leads to Caviar Sting", The *Associated Press State & Local Wire,* May 5, 2005)

The article therefore, implicates the immigrant group as being involved in criminal activity even though the report was simply relaying an incident of sturgeon poaching and subsequent arrest of a deli owner.

Another example of the kinds of reporting that included ethnicity or named and immigrant group where there was no further enhancement to the story, except to implicate the criminal association to a particular immigrant group, was:

> A doctor arrested and charged with illegally providing prescription drugs to addicts has been freed on $2,500 bail. Prosecutors argued that Dr. Sarfraz A. Mirza, who is of Pakistani descent, is a flight risk and that his bail should be consistent with those charged with serious drug offenses. Brevard County Judge George Turner disagreed. We argued for higher bond because these are serious offenses," Assistant State Attorney Wayne Holmes told The Orlando Sentinel for its Thursday editions. "In our view, it's no different than cocaine or other illegal substances harming our community. ("Brevard County Doctor Freed After Prescription Drug Arrest", *The Associated Press State & Local Wire,* July 30, 2003)

In this article, no further details were presented therefore the casual reader's assumption is that given the foreign descent of the accused, there is an inherent suspicion that the subject may be considered a flight risk although the article did not indicate if the subject was a U.S. citizen or native born, instead the assumption of criminality rests entirely with the fact that the subject is of foreign descent.

Concern was also evident among the public as the heightened level of anxiety was directed at specific immigrant groups, determined by an increase in the number of reported hate crimes. Although these articles were not accusing the immigrants of committing criminal acts, the association between immigrants and criminality and the frequency of hate crime occurrences both suggest an overall heightened anxiety against particular immigrant populations in society. In fact, the sharp increase in the number of hate crimes occurring against Asian groups and especially Middle Eastern groups, further illustrates the notion of labeling or "othering", where specific immigrant groups were targeted for attacks as a means to protect the public from the perceived threat of outsiders (Welch 2006). These tactics were especially common after 9/11 and often directed toward Muslim/Arab Americans where a variety of forms of harassment or assault, acts of vandalism, and instances of boycotting were frequently reported (Mukherjee 2003). It is evident from this study that after September 11 and throughout the U.S., "the dynamic of 'othering' abounds ... [the attacks] serve to sharpen an otherwise vague notion of 'them' ... they have quickly emerged as the 'usual suspects' eligible for suspicion, blame, and persecution" (Welch 2006: 73).

Public Concern

In a moral panic environment, hate crime proliferates as concern over a particular group is amplified by the media, as a form of informal social control (Welch 2006; Cohen 1985). The media messages are subsequently responded to by the public and then manifest as the public labels or identifies particular groups as threatening and valid targets of hostility (Becker 1963). With the well documented wave of hate crimes that occurred after September 11th, the media reports provided persistent examples of the presence of the concern indicator among the public against particular immigrant groups.

As the concern indicator was proliferated in media reporting, concern among the general public was further evidenced in the post-9/11 public opinion poll results. Poll participants continually indicated immigration as an important domestic problem and the poll trends suggested that it was becoming more of a problem than the other typically related issues of national security and terrorism. With the assistance from the media in making increased associations of immigrants engaging in criminal activities, changes in the perception of immigrants among the public were noted and as expected in a moral panic environment, infers a higher level of suspicion toward particular groups in society and the groups' impact on society (Rothe and Muzzatti 2004; Slone and Shoshani 2010).

Although the number of respondents in support of a decrease in immigration peaked immediately following 9/11 and had never reached the height of pre-9/11 levels, since 9/11 there has been an overall increase in support for maintaining present levels and a corresponding decline the respondents indicating support of an increase in immigration which greatly fluctuated near the end of the period of study. The last poll considered in this study fluctuated in its sentiment toward immigration as a "good or bad thing". Although the evidence was not as strong as in the other poll results, the poll taken in 2005 displayed a sudden and abrupt drop in respondents' "good thing" reactions, typifying the episodic, heightened anxiety of the concern indicator.

This analysis focused on three polls however, other public opinion research conducted since September 11th (*See* Cainkar 2004, Kettl 2004, McLean 2004, Parenti 2002, Welch 2002, and Welch 2006) supports the assertion that public sentiment with regard to immigration had been generally negative and especially accusatory towards Arab and Middle Eastern groups since the attacks. In this study, there was evidence of a successful campaign by the media and followed by the public, which clearly defined several immigrant groups as *folk devils* thus criminalizing these immigrants and making them the object of concern in the post-9/11 panicked society. Finally, as perhaps the most influential source in shaping public opinions and attitudes about crime and crime victims (Chermak 2004), the news media's informal controls are enhanced by the government, the primary formal social control group, through policy support and by providing legitimacy to the panic against immigrants, resulting in the preservation of political, economic, and social goals (Paletz and Entman 1981).

Governmental Concern

The concern indicator was evident by the federal government's heightened anxiety which denoted by the comparative reduction in the number of regionally issued LPRs between 2002 and 2003 and the decline in issuances in four of the five LPR categories during the same period. As observed in the 1996 federal legislation changes affecting immigration and LPR issuances, changes resulting from the PATRIOT Act did not fully materialize immediately but were certainly palpable by the 2002–2003 period. Also targeting immigrants as potential threats to security, lower levels of government including state and local agencies displayed heightened anxiety and provided support to federal efforts by furthering the goals of formal social control at a the regional or community levels.

Although the federal government's response to 9/11 was a general "crusade against terror" (Welch 2006: 64), on a more localized level, government agencies responded to the 9/11 attacks by questioning foreign born residents as a means of reducing potential threats and heightening public safety, again implying threats from specific foreign residents in the community. In Maine, for example, "local and federal agencies have interviewed dozens, if not hundreds, of foreign-born Maine residents. Most of those from northern Africa, the Middle East and South Asia" (*The Associated Press State & Local Wire* 2001). Even two years after 9/11, continued increased vigils targeting immigrants were common but cast more of a general and ambiguous suspicion and against groups as was the case where "agents in Oklahoma have been keeping an eye on suspicious individuals doing suspicious things, including those of Middle Eastern descent who may be conducting unusual financial transactions" (*The Associated*

Press State & Local Wire 2003). It is these types of generalized concerns and continual ambiguous vigils that typify the concern indicator in a moral panic environment.

With all the common moral panic participants or claims makers involved, it is apparent that concern indicator unfolded immediately after the attacks in 2001 and continued to linger throughout the post-9/11 five-year time span. With an immediate increase in articles relating immigrants to criminality, concern was initiated by the media in September 2001 and continued vacillating, but elevated, until the end of the period of study. The media reaction coincided with the implementation of the PATRIOT Act in 2001 however; it was not until the 2002 and 2003 period when new federal legislation exhibited its full effect, and among other changes, a consequential and terse decline in LPRs issuances found in this study. Finally, the public's anxiety in general began immediately after 9/11 with the reported frequency of hate crimes, continued with an overall "bad" public opinion of immigration, and has lingered with a steady increase in the public's sentiment that immigration is an ongoing, principal problem in the U.S.

Hostility

With the concern indicator revealed, it follows that the media, public, and federal government's heightened anxiety must next be directed at a target of apprehension, represented by a specific "folk devil" in moral panic terms. The essence of the hostility indicator then may be measured as an increase in both formal and informal controls are directed at a particular group, as was elucidated by the concern indicator. From the results of this investigation there was a definite labeling of immigrant groups that materialized in both general and specific manifestations and as increased levels of formal and informal controls.

Targeted Informal Controls

Given the increases in hate crimes directed at immigrant groups and in the reporting of immigrants associated with criminality, "The fact that the terrorists of 9/11 were not US citizens ... seemed to justify a certain 'state of general suspicion' (of being a terrorist) against all foreigners, but particularly against those who shared a common Arab origin with those terrorists" (Saux 2007: 58). This is the fundamental nature of hostility in a moral panic environment as heightened informal social controls imposed upon immigrants were indeed evident along with an immediate and obvious increase in the post-9/11 period that named Asian groups, especially Middle Eastern ethnicities and descendants, as targets of hostility. Several polls that were conducted during the period of study also indicated an increased focus on terrorism and national security as the primary cause of the attacks, blaming immigration controls as the main area of concern (Adelman 2004) and more specifically targeting the Middle Eastern/Arab population as the primary target of concern (Cainkar 2004).

Therefore, although media attention to the generic "foreign born/descent" reference remained high throughout the period of study, in post-9/11 articles the greatest increases in references were clearly made in the Middle Eastern immigrant groups, making them the most well defined and apparent *folk devils* in media reporting. The Middle Eastern group was also the most frequently targeted victim of the publics' heightened anxiety, in the form of hate crimes, exceeding the second most victimized group by 168.3%. Another conspicuous development in the post-9/11 reporting within the immigrant references was discovered. In addition to the top referenced general "Middle Eastern" category, more particularized groups were also recognized, including broader geographical mentions and added Middle Eastern ethnicities referenced; thus expanding the overall number of immigrants in the population that the media associated with criminality and "attracting greater scrutiny to otherwise undifferentiated 'Middle Easterners'" (Welch 2006: 73).

Targeted Formal Controls

As the primary agency, responsible for implementing formal social controls, the federal government's responses to terrorist threats or similar devastating events in U.S. history have been well documented. Similar to the crisis controls implemented during the suspension of habeas corpus after the civil war, the Palmer Raids of WWI, and the Japanese Internment of WWII (Chang 2002; Gerstle 2004; Zinn 2002), the PATRIOT Act legislation responded to 9/11 with similar sweeping legislation, clearly targeting immigrants as a primary source of trepidation in society. The extent of the new federal powers are unprecedented and also somewhat ambiguous, in that the new laws permitted nearly all of the current 20 million U.S. immigrants to be subjected to military tribunals, increased surveillance, expedited deportation, and indefinite detention (Zinn 2002).

Further, PATRIOT Act legislation targets immigrants especially in its ability to question and detain noncitizens without even a criminal conviction for an extended period of time if attorney general "certifies" that there are "reasonable grounds to believe" that they are somehow connected to terrorist activities and release would likely threaten national security (Chang 2002, Kuzma 2004). Therefore, not only did the PATRIOT Act allow the imposition of a variety of general restrictions and controls on immigrants but also it specifically targeted Middle Eastern groups by rounding up and detaining more than 1,200 immigrants within two months of 9/11, deeming them as suspicious, for questioning and indefinite detention (Welch 2002). Already subjected to informal controls, it is evident that with the implementation of these types of sweeping formal social controls, "Immigrants and asylum-seekers are perfect candidates to be considered 'folk devils' in the context of counter-terrorism policy" (Saux 2007: 63).

Increased governmental formal controls were most evident in this study's results as overall declines in LPR issuances over the period of study were evident in all regions. Although these declines affected virtually all immigrant groups, the decreases were particularly noted in the North American and Asian regions and in the latter region, were very pronounced in the Employment Based category, historically the highest LPR beneficiaries. It is the immigrants seeking LPR status only for employment purposes that do not usually have familial ties or necessarily any additional connections to the U.S. and therefore; the candidates may be seen as the LPR group that garners the most suspicion in the application process, in view of all the LPR categories. Given the many applicant classifications, also noted was also a more general, overall decline in LPR issuances that was evident across all categories.

Similar to the federal government's response to drug users in the "war on drugs" and given the wholesale radical declines in LPR issuances between 2002 and 2003, the new PATRIOT Act regulations have effectively erased all defining lines that identified particular groups of immigrants as potentially threatening, instead criminalizing all immigrant groups seeking LPR approvals in the post-9/11 period. This all inclusive response was however anticipated as:

> [B]eing that law precepts have necessarily a general nature and given that a distinction between foreigners (Arabs and not-Arabs) would certainly not be in accordance with the rule of law and would not respect the principle of equality, all foreigners were put at a disadvantage, irrespective of their origin. (Saux 2007: 58)

Essentially, as the federal effort was aimed at national security, reducing terrorism, and protection against *folk devils* targeted formal control have breached their boundaries in this pursuit when it comes to identifying particular immigrant groups as targets of suspicion; it has started "pushing the pendulum from care to control" (Lyon 2003: 11).

Consensus

The consensus indicator is characterized by widespread agreement that a particular group is considered suspect and potentially threatening to society. Consequently, during a moral panic, some resistance or opposition to the purported menace must occur. As discovered in the document analyses, increases in post-9/11 negative articles and media references to foreign born groups associated with criminal activity were evident in all regions of the country, elucidating an extensive concurrence among media publications in reporting immigrants, potentially as likely and frequent sources of peril.

Similar to the concern and hostility indicator outcomes, the increase in poll respondents' anxiety over immigration and in the number of hate crimes reported in all regions gives the indication that the public's response to immigrants was observable throughout the country as a response to the corresponding perceived threat from the foreign born population.

Public Consensus

Thompson (1998) asserts that publicly perceived social problems do not suddenly materialize in the moral panic environment. Essentially, societal conditions beset with anxiety must first exist and be equipped with a receptive or risk-conscious public which is open to the media and government's agitation of particular social problems (Thompson 1998: 29). As is the case since 9/11, issues of immigration, national security, and terrorism have been habitually linked (Aldeman 2004) and have provided a social context for responding to perceived societal threats, garnering much of the media's attention and necessitating formal solutions, in the form of government action (Cainkar 2004; Zucconi 2004). It is under these conditions that opinion polls revealed a moral panic against immigrants across the country, given government's response to the "war on terror", by the implementation of the PATRIOT Act, and the post-9/11 social environment that existed, fueled by the media, the public was highly susceptible to hostility against immigrants.

Although not as explicit as public opinion toward terrorism and national security, the fact that immigration was indicated as one of the most important problems for almost every poll in the post-9/11 period of study, and so infrequently in the pre-9/11 data, indicates a clear and increased public perception of the potential threat that immigrants pose. This indication was also observable in the changes to respondents support for a "decrease" or maintenance of "present levels" of immigration when compared to those in support of an "increase" in levels. This illustration does not suggest that all of society was engulfed in the panic as the element of consensus in a moral panic does not require that the whole society is in fact consumed (Cohen 1985; Goode and Ben Yehuda 1994). Instead, it must be established that at least a fairly widespread segment of the population (Goode and Ben-Yehuda 1994) is engaged in some amount of public disquiet which agrees that "where social control has disappeared, it must be put back in place" (Baerveldt et al. 1998: 36).

Federal Consensus

In observing the historical practice of responding to terrorism, federal crime and social controls are frequently prone to the expansion of criminal laws and criminalization of targeted and ostensibly threatening populations (Saux 2007). In fact, over the last few centuries, U.S. immigration policy has been based on directing restrictions towards groups that threaten national security, and at different times, "permitting exclusion, deportation, detention, or heightened scrutiny" (Engle 2004: 64) to targeted groups, when applicable.

The federal response to 9/11 was therefore predictable as "political actors in ... America have repeatedly chosen to respond to widespread public concern about crime and security by formulating policies that punish and exclude" (Garland 2001: 202), an especially important task in response to immigration policy where federal institutions are responsible for both the protection of the country from terrorists and foreign threats and balancing the "positive benefits which immigration has and continues to provide" to U.S. society (Lebowitz and Podheiser 2002). The PATRIOT Act implementations with regard to immigration therefore have addressed the issues of terrorism however; it appears that the residual effect has also punished particular categories of immigrants that have historically enjoyed favorable and long-established admission.

With regard to LPR approvals, this examination found that all regions have not continued to experience decreases that were indicated in the 2002–2003 period. However both Europe and North America, traditionally large LPR recipients, have not yet been restored to their pre-9/11 levels. By LPR category, these data indicate that while the "Immediate Relatives of U.S. Citizens" category, where immigrants already have some close family ties to the U.S., has experienced substantial increases. Conversely, the Employment Based approvals, the LPRs with the most rigorous background checks and scrutiny of qualifications, using a complex labor certification process and employability, skill, and advanced education requirements (Ting 2003) are in fact on the decline. Again, although new PATRIOT Act policies are targeted at reducing terrorism and security threats, the LPR declines clearly indicate a shift in time-honored confidence that scrutinized LPR immigrants have come to depend on, casting a new suspicion on LPR groups that have historically earned much confidence from the U.S. immigration system, both by region and application category.

Disproportionality

Although the disproportionality indicator may be observed and measured using a variety of methods (Goode and Ben-Yehuda 1994), previous moral panic studies suggest that disproportionality is often the most elusive and difficult to determine (Baerveldt et al., 1998; Waddington 1986). Goode and Ben-Yehuda (1994) assert that the measure must be empirical in nature and some indication that public concerns exceed the relative level of genuine hazards or tangible threats posed. Therefore, as was selected for this study, examining the developing concern over the problem through a historical comparison would yield the most dependable measure (Baerveldt et al. 1998) of disproportional moral panic conditions.

From the results of the regional document analyses, indicating an increase in overall reporting relating immigrants with criminality, perceived threats that immigrants posed did not correspond with specific events occurring in U.S. society, such as additional major terrorist attacks, which customarily increase anxiety over immigration or would imply comparative dangers from immigrants that are directed specifically towards U.S. society. Rather, it was found that "social anxieties instigated either at decision/opinion-making levels or in localized settings by the general public can be and [were] spread by national and local media" (Pijpers 2006: 94).

Disproportionality was also evident from both the public and federal governments' perspective. After 9/11, poll respondents have consistently indicated immigration as one of the "most important problems" in varying degrees which equates to an overall comparative rise and strong indication that the issue is an undoubtedly more significant concern to the public on a continual basis, especially when compared to the pre-9/11 poll responses. The public's general preoccupation, continued anxiety, and enduring concern over immigration is seemingly unwarranted given that federal regulations have not changed significantly since the PATRIOT Act was implemented and since there are have not been any major terrorist attacks against the country, nor have there been any other major civil disturbances directly involving immigrants since 9/11 that would draw suspicion or garner additional scrutiny towards immigrant groups.

As noted from the consensus indicator, the federal response to the threat of immigrants was again conspicuous in the overall sharp decline in LPRs granted between 2002 and 2003 and some of the developing category trends since 9/11. Indicative of the overall changes to antiterrorist legislation and governmental strategies that have developed since 9/11, disproportionality was indicated as the target of new PATRIOT Act policies addressed immigration as a whole, rather than just targeting particular groups associated in the media or by the public as potential threats. Similarly, the volatility indicator was prevalent in all regions and across all included categories in varying degrees.

Volatility

With all of the other moral panic conditions present, the volatility indicator aids in determining the length and measuring magnitude of the episode. Volatility is characterized as an oscillating disquiet over a particular issue that is observable among the media, public, and government, appearing in short and sudden episodes, then just as abruptly, dissipating for periods of time (Goode and Ben-Yehuda; Thompson 1998; Critcher 2003). Although the initial panic subsides, the volatility indicator is typified as the issues do not dissipate entirely but instead recur and may abruptly rise as sporadic episodes of panic occur. Essentially, as the distinct episodes of a panic may be brief and sporadic in nature, the fundamental issue that is the source of the panic remains as a more permanent and continuous focus (Critcher 2003; Baerveldt et al. 1998).

Intermittent Episodes

As this study considered the issue of immigration a 10-year span, using 9/11 as the midpoint, overall trends indicated that the episodic nature of moral panics was indicated several times over the post-9/11 period among the media, public, and federal government. Firstly, volatility was evident since 2001 in the media as sudden and sweeping negative reports of immigrants and articles relating immigrants to criminality began immediately after 9/11, which dissipated quickly, and then continued to erratically rise and fall over time. Secondly, as noted in the concern indicator, given the opinion polls that identified immigration as an important among a range of other social problems, both intermittently and continuously, meets the criterion for volatility. Finally, with the sharp changes in LPR issuances between 2002 and 2003, then equally as dramatic rises that followed, typifies the characteristic of volatility as displayed in the federal government's response to immigration in a moral panic environment.

Enduring Issues

Pijpers (2006) asserts that the episodic nature of a panic environment may be attributed to the introduction of new social problems that pose additional or greater threats, thus quelling the original panic, but allowing the broader issues to remain in focus. As non-citizens and foreign visitors are often associated with a host of other recurring social issues, such as legal versus illegal immigration, crime, national security, and terrorism, it is anticipated that over time the larger issue of immigration among the public, media, and government will therefore logically endure. Interestingly, previous moral panic research has entirely excluded elaborating on the presence of this indicator (Burns and Crawford 1999) given that the nature of the fluctuations depicted by the volatility indicator are very similar to the characteristics found in the concern and disproportionality indicators however, it is the enduring, episodic panic against immigration that differs, making its inclusion in this study not only warranted but also indispensable.

With the media and public opinion over immigration showing sharp fluctuations in the post-9/11 era, support levels for immigration shifted suddenly and unpredictably, possibly in response to a variety of domestic occurrences involving immigrants or perhaps other social problems occurring abroad. At the same time the federal governments' abrupt increases and subsequent declines in the number of LPR issuances in a range of areas indicated an elevated level of anxiety which manifested as volatility against immigrants since 9/11. These episodes fluctuated unpredictably; similar to the action observed both the concern and disproportionality indicators.

The next and last chapter will conclude this investigation with a discussion of the outcome of the application of the moral panic conception to immigration in the post-9/11 U.S. society, prospects, and implications for future studies.

References

Adelman, Howard. 2004. "Governance, Immigration Policy, and Security: Canada and the United States Post 9/11". Pp. 109–130 in *The Maze of Fear: Security and Migration after 9/11*, edited by John Tirman. New York, NY: The New Press.

Altheide, David L. 2002. *Creating Fear: News and the Construction of Crisis*. New York: Aldine de Gruyter.

Baerveldt, Chris, Hans Bunkers, Micha De Winter, and Jan Kooistra. 1998. "Assessing a Moral Panic Relating to Crime and Drugs Policy in the Netherlands: Towards a Testable Theory". *Crime, Law & Social Change* 29: 31–47.

Becker, Howard S. 1963. *Outsiders: Studies in the Sociology of Deviance*. New York, NY: The Free Press of Glencoe.

Burns, Robert and Charles Crawford. 1999. "School Shootings, the Media, and Public Fear: Ingredients for a Moral Panic". *Crime, Law & Social Change* 32: 147–168.

Cainkar, Louise. 2004. "The Impact of the September 11th Attacks on Arab and Muslim Community in the United States". Pp. 215–239 in *The Maze of Fear: Security and Migration after 9/11*, edited by John Tirman. New York: The New Press.

Chang, Nancy. 2002. *Silencing Political Dissent*. New York: Seven Stories Press.

Chermak, Steven. 2004. "Crime in the News Media: A Redefined Understanding of How Crimes Become News". Pp. 95–130 in *Media, Process, and the Social Construction of Crime*, edited by Gregg Barak. New York: Garland Publishing, Inc.

Cohen, Stanley. 1972. *Folk Devils and Moral Panics: The Creation of the Mods and Rockers*. London: MacGibbons & Kee.

———. 1985. *Visions of Social Control: Crime, Punishment and Classification*. Cambridge, MA: Polity Press.

Critcher, Chas. 2003. *Moral Panics and the Media*. Philadelphia, PA: Open University Press.

Engel, Karen. 2004. "Constructing Good Aliens and Good Citizens: Legitimizing the War on Terror(ism)". *Colorado Law Review* 75: 59–114.

Garland, David. 2001. *The Culture of Control: Crime and Social Order in Contemporary Society*. Chicago, IL: University of Chicago Press.

Gerstle, Gary. 2004. "The Immigrant as a Threat to American Security: A Historical Perspective". Pp. 87–108 in *The Maze of Fear: Security and Migration after 9/11*, edited by John Tirman. New York: The New Press.

Goode, Erich and Nachman Ben-Yehuda. 1994. *Moral Panics: The Social Construction of Deviance*. Cambridge, MA: Blackwell.

Kettl, Donald F. 2004. *System Under Stress: Homeland Security and American Politics*. Washington, DC: CQ Press.

Kuzma, Lynn M. 2004. "Security versus Liberty: 9/11 and the American Public". Pp. 160–190 in *The Politics of Terror: The U.S. Response to 9/11*, edited by William Crotty. Boston, MA: Northeastern University Press.

Lebowitz, Lawrence M. and Ira L. Podheiser. 2002. "A Summary of the Changes in Immigration Policies and Practices After the Terrorist Attacks of September 11, 2001: The USA PATRIOT Act and Other Measures". *University of Pittsburgh Law Review* 63: 873–888.

Lyon, David. 2003. *Surveillance after September 11*. Cambridge, UK: Polity Press.

McLean, Scott L. 2004. "The War on Terrorism and the New Patriotism". Pp. 64–94 in *The Politics of Terror: The U.S. Response to 9/11*, edited by William Crotty. Boston, MA: Northeastern University Press.

Mukherjee, Roopali. 2003. Between Enemies and Traitors: Black Press Coverage of September 11 and the Predicaments of National "Others". Pp. 29–46 in *Media Representations of September 11th*, edited by Steven Chermak, Frankie Y. Bailey, and Michelle Brown. Westport, CT: Praeger Publishers.

Paletz, David L. and Robert M. Entman. 1981. *Media Power Politics*. New York: The Free Press.

Parenti, Michael. 2002. *The Terrorism Trap: September 11 and Beyond*. San Francisco, CA: City Lights Books.

Pijpers, Roos. 2006. "Help! The Poles are Coming: Narrating a Contemporary Moral Panic". *Geografiska Annaler* 88 B(1): 91–103.

Rothe, Dawn and Stephen L. Muzzatti. 2004. "Enemies Everywhere: Terrorism, Moral Panic, and US Civil Society". *Critical Criminology* 12: 327–350.

Saux, Maria Soledad. 2007. "Immigration and Terrorism: A Constructed Connection". *European Journal of Crime and Policy Research* 13:57–72.

Slone, Michelle and Anat Shoshani. 2010. "Prevention Rather than Cure? Primary or Secondary Intervention for Dealing with Media Exposure to Terrorism". *Journal of Counseling & Development* 88(4):440–448.

The Associated Press State & Local Wire. 2001. "Foreign-born Mainers Differ on Inquiries". December 9, Sunday, BC cycle.

———. 2003. "FBI Agent Says Terrorism Still a Threat in Oklahoma". March 30, Sunday, BC cycle.

Thompson, Kenneth. 1998. *Moral Panics.* New York: Routledge.

Ting, Jan. 2003. "Immigration Law Reform After 9/11: What Has Been and What Still Needs to Be Done". *Temple International and Comparative Law Journal* 17: 503–521.

Waddington, P.A.J. 1986. "Mugging as a Moral Panic: A Question of Proportion". *The British Journal of Sociology* 37(2): 245–259.

Welch, Michael. 2002. *Detained: Immigration Laws and the Expanding I.N.S. Jail Complex.* Philadelphia, PA: Temple University Press.

———. 2006a. "Seeking a safer society: America's anxiety in the war on terror". *Security Journal*, 19, 93–109.

———. 2006b. *Scapegoats of September 11th.* Piscataway, NJ: Rutgers University Press.

Zinn, Howard. 2002. *Terrorism and War.* New York: Seven Stories Press.

Zucconi, Mario. 2004. "Migration and Security as an Issue in U.S.-European Relations". Pp. 142–154 in *The Maze of Fear: Security and Migration after 9/11*, edited by John Tirman. New York: The New Press.

READING 9

Homeland Security and Support for Multiculturalism, Assimilation, and Omniculturalism Policies among Americans

By Fathali Moghaddam and James Breckenridge

This article presents data suggesting that Americans' views of policies toward immigrants are pertinent to matters of homeland security. "Homeland" is a concept shaped partly by how people psychologically differentiate "citizen" from "immigrant." The differentiation of these categories is critical to individuals' political and social identity. Homeland security scholars are unlikely to be aware, however, of this country's substantial majority preference for an alternative to the traditional, yet deeply divided, incompatible policies of assimilation and accommodation. Moreover, the publics' appraisal of the threat of terrorism, the priority they assign to homeland security institutions, their trust and confidence in homeland security organizations, and their support for counter-terrorism measures are linked to their immigration policy preference even after accounting for their race/ethnicity and socioeconomic status. Homeland security professionals would do well to consider the potential implications of these preferences.

Practitioners and researchers in the domain of security have been engaged for several decades in an important debate concerning the relative merits of a "realist" versus a "human security" approach.[1] The realist approach focuses primarily on military security, and represents the dominant school in the domain of security studies. The human security approach is newer and involves an emphasis on health security, food security, shelter security, and other "humanitarian" concerns that are argued to be a priority for ordinary people in their everyday lives. Although the debate between the realist and human security camps has been constructive, there is a danger that both approaches are being left behind by new challenges created by accelerating globalization. Among the most important

Fathali M. Moghaddam and James N. Breckenridge, "Homeland Security and Support for Multiculturalism, Assimilation, and Omniculturalism Policies Among Americans," *Homeland Security Affairs*, vol. 6, no. 3, pp. 1-14. Copyright © 2010 by Naval Postgraduate School, Center for Homeland Defense and Security. Reprinted with permission. Provided by ProQuest LLC. All rights reserved.

of these challenges is rapid and large-scale movement of people around the world bringing about "sudden" intergroup contact.[2]

Humans have always been migrating, starting from Africa to reach all the major landmasses by about 10,000 years ago.[3] But until fairly recently, migrations were relatively slow. The human groups in interaction had more time to adapt to one another. In the modern era, using jet planes and rapid trains, large numbers of people can move long distances in a relatively short time. The availability of rapid transportation systems has been coupled with the globalization of the economy, so that a demand for cheaper labor in one part of the world can be met with a speedy supply of cheaper labor from other parts of the world. Consequently, in the last few decades there has been a rapid increase of South Asians in the United Kingdom, North Africans in France, and Turks in Germany, with the result that there are now about twenty million Muslims in the European Union.

Rising intergroup contact in recent decades has created new tensions in the European Union, and these tensions have been further intensified by a series of terrorist attacks. The most well-publicized of these attacks are the March 11, 2004, bomb explosions on trains in Madrid which resulted in close to 200 deaths and over 1,000 serious injuries, and the July 7, 2005, bomb explosions on the London public transportation system, which also resulted in multiple fatalities and serious injuries. An outcome of terrorist attacks has been a re-examination of policies for managing diversity; Europeans have been forced to ask, are we integrating minorities the best way? For example, Andrew Jakubowicz assessed reactions to the London terrorist bombings in this way: "The updraft from the bombings carried a message about the critical importance of working out what 'multiculturalism' could continue to mean."[4] This question was brought into sharp focus when the Dutch filmmaker Theo Van Gogh was brutally murdered in Amsterdam by an Islamic fanatic on November 2, 2004. Van Gogh's "crime" was that he had, in collaboration with the Dutch Muslim feminist Ayaan Hirsi Ali, made a short film, *Submission*, critical of the treatment of women in Islamic societies. Van Gogh's murder put the spotlight on the Muslim fanatics in Europe, and forced Europeans to critically re-think their policies for managing diversity. Similarly, the threat of home-grown terrorism in the United States, highlighted by the case of about twenty young Somali-Americans apparently recruited by violent Islamic fanatics, has fueled a debate about the best policies for managing diversity in the United States, as well as the threat of terrorism, trust in government, and related security issues.

Two main policies have been used to manage cultural and linguistic diversity: *assimilation*, the washing away of intergroup differences, and *multiculturalism*, the highlighting, strengthening, and celebration of intergroup differences.[5] Both these policies are founded on psychological assumptions, some of which are questionable.[6] An assumption underlying assimilation policy, for example, is that intergroup differences can be washed away through contact, to eliminate any important basis for group-based divisions. But social identity research using the minimal group paradigm demonstrates that group members can use even trivial criteria as a basis for intergroup differentiation and ingroup favoritism.[7] By implication, no matter how similar the members of a society become through assimilation, it will be possible to manufacture dissimilarity, even on seemingly trivial criteria. Some of the key psychological assumptions underlying multiculturalism are also questionable, including the *multiculturalism hypothesis*, the idea that confidence in one's own ethnic heritage will lead one to be open and accepting toward the outgroup members. Empirical evidence does not provide solid support for this hypothesis,[8] nor do historical examples, such as the Nazis, who arguably showed high confidence in their ingroup heritage, but were not open and accepting toward outgroups (although there is support for some interpretations of multiculturalism, particularly among minorities).[9]

There is continued debate between supporters of multiculturalism and assimilation,[10] and some efforts to compare the two policies using empirical evidence.[11] However, given that the psychological assumptions underlying both policies are in important ways flawed, we should also explore alternative policies that are already an implicit part of psychological discussions of intergroup relations.[12] Muzafer Sherif's concept of superordinate goals,[13] and Gaertner and Dovidio's Common Group Identity Model both suggest a third alternative policy, whereby groups emphasize commonalities such as identities and goals.[14] This third alternative is reflected in the policy of omniculturalism, which proposes a two-stage process in the socialization of individuals: during stage one, the focus is on human commonalities; during stage two, intergroup differences and distinctiveness are introduced.[15] The objective of omniculturalism is to establish a solid basis of commonality between people within the framework of a primary identity, before adding an emphasis on how people also belong to groups that in some respects differ from one another.

The present study examines three research questions. The first concerns the extent to which Americans would support omniculturalism, as compared with multiculturalism and assimilation. The second concerns the support of majority and minority group members for the different policies. Some previous research has demonstrated that African Americans and other minorities show stronger support for multiculturalism, whereas white Americans show stronger support for assimilation policy.[16] A third set of research questions—the central focus of this article—concern possible differences in the attitudes of supporters of assimilation, multiculturalism, and omniculturalism, toward homeland security threats, how America should react to such threats, and the extent to which individuals trust authorities to do the right thing.

In summary, terrorist attacks in Western democracies, such as the United States, the United Kingdom, and Spain, have resulted in a re-assessment of multiculturalism and other policies for managing diversity.[17] Because assimilation has been endorsed to a greater degree by majority groups (primarily of western European descent), and because terrorist attacks are perceived as arising from minority (primarily Middle Eastern) communities, we expected support for assimilation to be associated with greater concern about future terrorist attacks, as well as stronger American reactions to terrorist attacks. Growing concerns about the possibility of "home grown" terrorism may increase the salience of these issues for American security practitioners and researchers, especially in light of current population projections, which suggest that by 2050 whites will represent a minority and one out of five Americans will be an immigrant.[18]

Methods

Participants in this research were a nationally representative probability sample of 4,000 adults age eighteen and older selected randomly from an internet-enabled panel maintained by Knowledge Networks (KN) in November 2008. KN panel members are recruited through a random digit telephone dialing system based on a sample frame covering the entire United States. In contrast to "opt-in" Web surveys, which recruit participants of unknown characteristics via "blind" Internet solicitations, KN panel members are selected on the basis of known, non-zero probabilities. Individuals are not permitted to volunteer or self-select for participation in the KN panel. In addition, individuals who lack either computers or Internet access are provided equipment or access without charge. KN panel-based surveys have demonstrated acceptable concordance with a variety of "benchmark" large-scale surveys.[19]

In the present study, the response rate to invitations to participate was 71 percent. To reduce the effects of potential non-response and non-coverage bias, post-stratification sample weights,[20] incorporating the probability of participant selection based on age, gender, race, and ethnicity benchmarks from the most recent available Census Bureau *Current Population Survey* and supplements were employed in all statistical analyses using algorithms modified for complex survey designs in the statistical software packages STATA.[21]

Measures

Cultural policy preferences. Participants were grouped into one of three perspectives on cultural differences policies according to participants' response to the following question:

"Which statement below best fits your view about immigration to the United States: When people come to America,

1. People should set aside their cultural differences and "melt into" the American mainstream;

2. People should maintain and celebrate their distinct group culture

3. People should first recognize and give priority to what they have in common with all other Americans, and then at a second stage celebrate their distinct group culture."

We label responses 1 thru 3 Assimilation, Multiculturalism, and Omniculturalism, respectively. Participants could also choose not to declare any preference.

Political ideology. Participants identified their favored political ideology as "extremely liberal," "liberal," "somewhat liberal," "moderate or middle of the road," "slightly conservative," "conservative," or "extremely conservative." In the following analyses, participants were grouped into three categories: *liberal* (extremely liberal or liberal), *conservative* (extremely conservative or conservative), or *other* (all other responses).

Terrorism risk perceptions. Participants rated the probability over the next five years of terrorist attacks using an anchored scale from zero ("totally unlikely to occur") to 100 ("absolutely certain to occur") and assessed the probability of acts of terror within the country (*risk to nation*—"How likely do you feel a terrorist attack is somewhere within the United States?"), as well as attacks directly involving the participant (*risk to self*—"How likely do you feel that you personally will directly experience an act of terrorism?"). An additional dichotomous indicator variable was included representing participants who reported that they were "very concerned" or "extremely concerned" about terrorism ("How concerned or worried are you about a terrorist attack happening in the area of the country where you live sometime during the next 12 months?").

Emotional response to the threat of terrorism. Following the instructions, "Please help us to understand how you feel when you think about threats of terrorism using the following scale," participants completed the *Positive and Negative Affect Schedule—Expanded Form*,[22] which requires participants to rate sixty emotional adjectives on a five-point scale from one ("slightly or not true of your feelings") to five ("extremely true of your feelings"). Composite subscales assessing the degree of fear and anger were employed in the present study. These subscales have demonstrated good psychometric properties in other samples and have been significantly correlated with public perceptions about terrorism and support for various counterterrorism policies.[23]

Confidence in government, preparedness, counterterrorism measures, and security priorities. Participants were also asked whether they "agreed," "strongly agreed," "disagreed," or "strongly disagreed" with a series of statements related to terrorism and terrorism policies. To simplify the presentation of results, responses were collapsed into categories indicating either agreement or disagreement. Statements assessed *confidence* in certain government organizations (i.e., the federal and state governments, the Immigration and Customs Enforcement agency, the Border Patrol, in response to the statement "This organization will do a good job carrying out its role in fighting terrorism"), community terrorism *preparedness* ("I believe my community is sufficiently prepared for a terrorist attack if it happened here"), and the *importance of revenge* ("It is important for United States to take revenge on the people and countries responsible for terrorist acts against this country"). In addition, participants were asked whether they agreed that in order to "protect against terrorism" the government should adopt certain *measures*, including "Engage in racial or ethnic profiling," "Restrict the rights of non-citizens and foreign visitors," or "Require all Americans to have a national identification card." Finally, participants were asked to rank terrorism-versus disaster-related activities as the top "homeland security priority for the United States."

Results

More than three out of five American adults preferred omniculturalism.[24] Among those who preferred another policy, more favored assimilation over multiculturalism (Table 9.1). Gender, age, race and ethnicity, education, income, political ideology, and urban residential status distributions within policy preference groups are listed in Table 9.2.

Table 9.1 Distribution of Endorsements

Cultural View	Percent	95% C.I.
Assimilation "People should set aside their cultural differences and 'melt into' the American mainstream."	19.67%	(18.19–21.24)
Multiculturalism "People should maintain and celebrate their distinct group culture."	13.81	(12.43–15.30)
Omniculturalism "People should first recognize and give priority to what they have in common with all other Americans, and then at a second stage celebrate their distinct group culture."	62.71	(60.77–64.61)
Elected not to respond	3.81	(3.04–4.77)

Though most members of each sociodemographic category preferred omniculturalism, distinct sociodemographic profiles differentiated proponents of assimilation or multiculturalism. Significantly greater proportions of women, adults under age forty-five, members of non-white races or ethnicities, urban residents, or political liberals, characterized multicultralists. Conversely, white non-Hispanics, older adults over age fifty-nine, individuals with annual household incomes from $10,000 to $20,000, and political conservatives were more prevalent among assimilationists. Assimilationists were also more apt to have partial or full high school educations, but were less likely to have pursued or completed college educations.

Average predicted probabilities of a terrorist attack on the nation or against the self, as well as average levels of fear and anger experienced in response to terrorism within each group are shown in Figure 9.1. Responses for the omnicultural group closely tracked the average national response. Assimilationists reported the most elevated appraisals of the probability of attacks against the nation or self, as well as the greatest degree of anger in response to terrorism. Omniculturalists, however, reported significantly less fear than either assimilationists or multiculturalists, but averaged significantly higher appraisals than multiculturalists of the likelihood of a terrorist attack on the nation.

Table 9.2 Distribution of Sociodemographic Variables by Policy Preference

Variable	Cultural Policy Preference — Assimilation (19.7%)	Multiculturalism (13.8%)	Omniculturalism (62.7%)	Total Sample (100%)
Gender				
Female	47.5%	*60.8%*[a]	49.5%	51.3%
Age				
18–29	15.4	*32.0*[a]	21.4	21.7
30–44	24.3	*31.4*[a]	26.7	26.9
45–59	30.1	25.5	28.3	28.3
60+	30.2	*11.1*[a]	23.6	23.2
Race/Ethnicity				
White, Non-Hispanic (NH)	77.7	*56.9*[a]	75.9	73.5
Black (NH)	8.6	*12.9*[a]	8.8	9.4
Other (NH)	3.6	*8.6*[a]	4.1	4.6
Hispanic	9.2	*20.6*[a]	10.1	11.4
Multiple Race/Ethnicities	1.0	1.0	1.1	1.1
Education				
< High School	*16.6*[b]	14.1	9.9	11.9
High School	*38.6*[b]	25.6	29.6	30.9
Some College	*24.1*[b]	31.4	29.4	28.6
B.A. or higher	*20.7*[b]	28.9	31.1	28.7
Income				
< $10,000 ($10k)	6.3	5.3	4.9	5.3
$10k–$19k	*12.9*[b]	6.3	8.7	9.2
$20k–$39k$	25.9	25.1	22.5	23.6
$40k–$59k	20.1	23.6	20.0	20.6
$60k–$99k	23.4	25.8	26.8	26.0
$100k–$174k	9.0	11.6	14.0	12.6
$175k+	2.4	2.4	3.0	2.8
Urban-Rural Classification				
Urban	81.3	*86.9*[a]	82.3	82.8
Political Ideology				
Conservative	*26.1*[b]	13.6	22.5	21.9
Liberal	11.6	*24.8*[a]	16.0	16.2

[a] Differs significantly from Assimilation and Omnicultural groups $p < .005$ (two-tailed)
[b] Differs significantly from Multicultural and Omnicultural groups $p < .003$ (two-tailed)

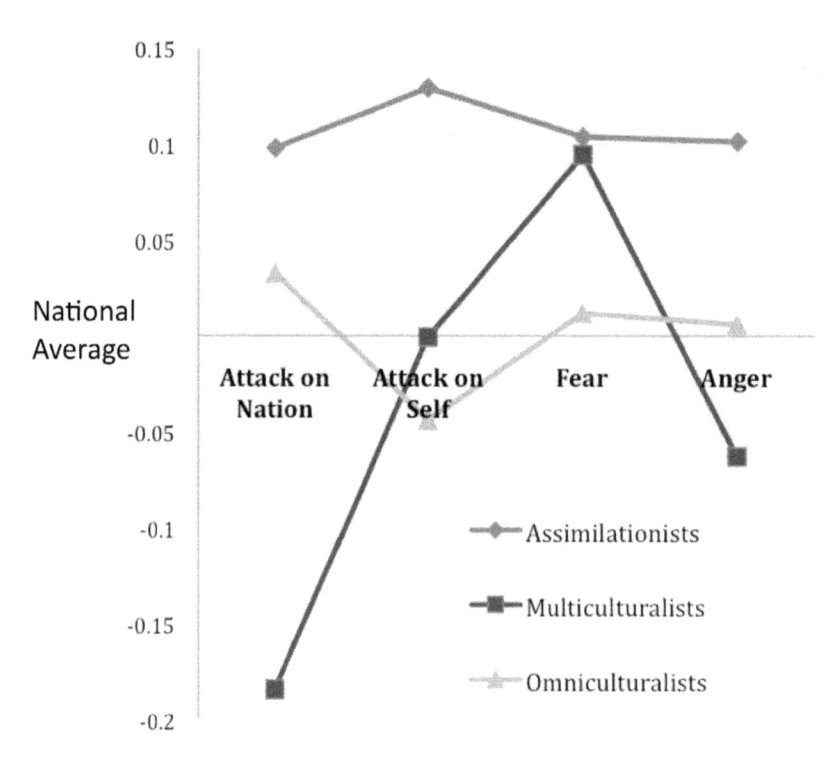

Figure 9.1 Average Perceived Threat and Emotional Response by Cultural Policy Preference

(Vertical axis indicates deviation from national averages as a percentage of one standard deviation. Differences are significant at $p < .01$)

Participants' priorities and support for particular responses to the threat of terrorism reflected these divergent views of threat and emotional response (Table 9.3). Intense worries about terrorism were least common among multiculturalists and most prevalent among assimilationists. Significantly more assimilationists—in contrast to significantly fewer multiculturalists—viewed terrorism as the top homeland security priority, and also asserted the importance of seeking revenge against terrorist actions. Moreover, support for modifying civil liberties to prevent terrorism—racial profiling, restricting the rights of non-citizens, and requiring a national identity card—was most prevalent among assimilationists and once again, least prevalent among multiculturalists. While more assimilationists had confidence in the federal government's capacity to counter terrorism, more multiculturalists had confidence in the Immigration and Customs Enforcement. Omniculturalists were more likely to view disaster preparedness as the top homeland security priority and to judge their communities as better prepared for crises.

With respect to security priorities and responses, omniculturalism was situated between the extremes of the alternative cultural policy preferences. Moreover, when multivariate procedures were employed to adjust statistically for sociodemographic differences among cultural preference groups,

Table 9.3 Terrorism Concerns, Priorities, Confidence & Support for Aggressive Measures by Cultural Policy Preference

Variable	Assimilation	Multiculturalism	Omniculturalism
"Very" or "extremely" worried about terrorism	**26.7%**[b]	**12.8%**[a]	22.6%
Top priority for Homeland Security:			
Terrorism	**77.7**[b]	**64.4**[a]	68.5
Disasters	11.6	12.7	**18.8**[c]
Confidence in:			
Federal Government	**71.1**[b]	65.9	65.9
Immigration & Customs Control	53.3	**61.2**[a]	53.2
Border Patrol	66.4	65.6	**59.9**[c]
State Government	66.1	65.6	66.8
Views community as unprepared for terrorist attack	60.5	61.2	**66.7**[c]
Believes it is important for U.S. to seek revenge	**75.1**[b]	**54.1**[a]	64.7
In order to prevent terrorism, supports:			
Racial profiling	**46.9**[b]	**21.8**[a]	35.2
Restrict rights of non-citizens and foreign visitors	**78.2**[b]	**54.7**[a]	70.5
Require national ID card	**68.6**[b]	**49.6**[a]	56.4

[a] Differs significantly from Assimilation and Omnicultural groups $p < .001$ (two-tailed)
[b] Differs significantly from Multicultural and Omnicultural groups $p < .001$ (two-tailed)
[c] Differs significantly from Multicultural and Assimilation groups $p < .001$ (two-tailed)

the differences among omniculturalists, multiculturalists, and assimilationists in perceived threat, emotional response, security priority, confidence in government, perceived community preparedness, and support for aggressive responses to terrorism were sustained.

Discussion

The objective of this study was to explore attitudinal support among Americans for the traditional policies of assimilation and multiculturalism, as well as the new policy of omniculturalism. A second research question focused on the support of majority and minority groups for the different policies. Third, we explored the relationship between support for different policies for managing cultural diversity and security issues, specifically related to the threat of terrorist attacks, how America should react to attacks, feelings about the possibility of terrorist attacks, and trust in authorities to do the right thing in response to terrorist attacks.

With respect to support for different cultural diversity policies, omniculturalism represented a clear majority preference across all sociodemographic groups, although there were some sub-group differences: whites, men, and older adults were more prevalent among assimilationists; non-whites, women, and younger adults were more prevalent among multiculturalists. Consequently, any future exploration of the omnicultural perspective must also attend to the generational and diversity differences that underlie dissenting perspectives among a significant portion of the population. That such differences predicted the roughly 4 percent of participants who declined to state a cultural preferences, as well as the 29 percent of those who declined to participate in this survey further,[25] underscores the need for careful scrutiny of the pattern of minority preferences identified in the present study.

Preferences for cultural policies were correlated significantly with terrorism threat perceptions and emotional responses, as well as attitudes towards homeland security priorities, confidence in certain governmental organizations' capacities to carry out their counterterrorism missions, and willingness to modify civil liberties to prevent terrorism. Although assimilationists did not differ from multiculturalists in reported fear, assimilationists expressed the highest levels of anger, an affective response associated strongly with support for aggressive counterterrorism policies in other studies.[26] Indeed, support for aggressive measures was most common among assimilationists, a group which also judged the likelihood of future attacks as more probable than those who endorsed alternative cultural policies, and least prevalent among multiculturalists, a group which appraised national threats of terrorism as less likely than other groups. In several respects, the attitudes towards homeland security among omniculturalists represented a middle ground between the divergent views of assimilationists and multiculturalists.

Omniculturalism arises in part out of well-researched ideas in the social psychology of intergroup relations. Both the earlier field research of Sherif and the more recent experimental research of Gaertner and Dovidio have demonstrated that the re-categorization of the members of different groups as a single group can reduce the original intergroup biases.[27] The applied benefits of superordinate goals have been demonstrated in culturally and ethnically diverse classrooms.[28] The Common Ingroup Identity Model has taken the further step of carefully exploring potential antecedents, consequences, and mediating processes of re-categorization that results in a superordinate category.[29] However, missing from this picture has been empirical evidence to suggest that a "third alternative" along these lines would be supported among the general population.

This study presented participants a third alternative, omniculturalism, with two steps: First, recognizing what is common to all Americans, second, celebrating distinct group cultures. Endorsement of this alternative policy represents positive feedback for research exploring the path of re-categorization, but it also highlights a need for additional research on developmental questions. In particular, at what age should the education of children emphasize what is common to everyone, and at what age should the focus be on distinct group cultures? Input from developmental science should guide schools and other socialization agents on this question. In future research, more attention also needs to be given to the difference in support shown by majority and minority group members for the three policies for managing diversity. An important limitation to the present study is that perspectives on cultural policy were measured by a single item. Future studies should include multiple measures, as well as, perhaps, comparisons among each pair of alternatives. Our statistical analyses utilized post-stratification weights to adjust for sampling biases. Nevertheless, the sociodemographic factors we found associated with a preference for assimilation or multiculturalism in this study also tended to characterize individuals in the KN panel who declined to participant. Thus, the magnitude of support for omniculturalism—albeit, considerable (i.e., 60 percent)—could well have been attenuated if all invited participants had been recruited successfully for the survey.

We believe that the alternative policy of omniculturalism also has potential to both gain support from diverse populations internationally and serve as an effective policy at the international level. This is because omniculturalism presents opportunities for groups to both find common ground in shared human characteristics and establish their own special (and perhaps unique) characteristics at a secondary level. A challenge in future research is to further explore these possibilities internationally.

Support for different policies for managing diversity was systematically associated with different patterns of attitudes toward security issues. Support for assimilation was associated with greater concern and anger about the possibility of a terrorist attack, as well as support for stronger reactions in the case of an attack. This included greater willingness to seek revenge, to carry out racial and ethnic profiling, and to restrict the civil liberties of foreigners in case of a terrorist attack. In contrast, supporters of multiculturalism policy downplayed the possibility of a terrorist attack and were least likely to seek revenge and agree to racial and ethnic profiling, as well as to impose restrictions on the civil liberties of foreigners as a protection against terrorism. We believe this pattern of results is explained in part by the fact that support for multiculturalism was most prevalent among minority groups, whereas support for assimilation was most prevalent among majority groups. At the same time, terrorist attacks have been seen as emanating from Islamic communities (within and outside Western societies), and the target of such attacks have often been major urban centers in the West, such as New York, London, and Madrid. Thus, majority groups support assimilation of minorities into mainstream society, and perceive terrorism (emanating from minority communities) as a greater threat and something to be angry about and avenged.

The pattern of distrust toward authorities shown by supporters of assimilation and multiculturalism was also different. Whereas supporters of assimilation expressed greater confidence in the counterterrorism capacity of the federal government, supporters of multiculturalism expressed greater trust and confidence in the present capabilities of Immigration and Customs Enforcement. These differences might be attributed to controversy regarding illegal immigration. Multiculturalists' confidence in the status quo perhaps reflects a reluctance to support strengthening immigration controls; conversely, assimilationists' lack of confidence might reflect greater willingness to strengthen immigration controls.

The finding that support for different policies for managing cultural diversity was systematically related to attitudinal differences toward security issues reflects back in important ways on the traditional debate between the two main sides in debates about security, suggesting an interactive link between factors identified by realists and human security advocates. On the one hand, the large-scale movement of people and sudden contact between human groups can result in "host" majority groups feeling threatened, desiring the minority to assimilate, and wanting revenge for terrorist attacks.[30] Furthermore, in this context the majority seems to have less confidence in federal and immigration authorities to do the right thing. These trends are no doubt to some extent associated with the majority groups perceiving the influx of "aggressive" minorities as increased competition for scarce resources. However, more than material resources are involved: minority groups support multiculturalism and seem to want to maintain their distinct identities. They are less fearful about terrorist attacks and do not support America "avenging" such attacks. Clearly, both material factors, identified by realists, and "soft" factors such as identity, identified by advocates of human security, are involved in these intergroup processes.

Since the 1990s there has been increased focus on the approximately 12–15 million illegal immigrants believed to be in the United States. For many, illegal immigrants represent a "threat" that requires an immediate solution. However, even if the "problem" of illegal immigration is solved, the far greater challenge of managing an increasingly diverse population of United States citizens looms ahead of us. In the long term, even if all 12–15 million illegal immigrants either become legal or leave the country (an unlikely event), effective policies are still urgently required for managing inter-group relations among the enormously diverse population of over 300 million Americans, which today includes 37 million legal first-generation immigrants. Such policies must receive greater attention from authorities, researchers, and others concerned with homeland security. The findings of this study highlight the value of exploring alternative policies for managing diversity, as well as critically re-thinking links between both alternative and traditional policies and homeland security.

Fathali M. Moghaddam is professor, Department of Psychology, and director of the Conflict Resolution Program, Department of Government, Georgetown University. His most recent book is The New Global Insecurity (2010); more details about his research and publications can be found at his website: www.fathalimoghaddam.com.

James N. Breckenridge, PhD, is professor of psychology and co-director of the PGSP–Stanford Consortium at the Palo Alto University. He is also associate director of the Center for Interdisciplinary Policy, Education and Research on Terrorism (CIPERT) and a senior fellow at the Center for Homeland Security and Defense (CHDS).

Correspondence regarding this paper should be directed to the first author.

This research was supported in part by funding from the Department of Homeland Security through the Center for Homeland Defense and Security at the Naval Postgraduate School, Monterey, CA.

Notes

1. A. Collins, ed., *Contemporary Security Studies* (Oxford University Press, 2007); M.I. Midlarsky, *Handbook of War Studies* (Boston: Unwin Hyman, 1989); R. Paris, "Human Security: Paradigm Shift or Hot Air?" *International Security* 26 (2001):87–102; M. Weissberg, "Conceptualizing Human Security," *Swords and Ploughshares: A Journal of International Affairs* XIII (2003): 3–11.

2. F.M. Moghaddam, *Multiculturalism and Intergroup Relations: Psychological Implications for Democracy in Global Context* (Washington, DC: American Psychological Association Press, 2008).

3. S. Wells, *The Journey of Man: A Genetic Odyssey* (Princeton, NJ: Princeton University Press, 2002).

4. A. Jakubowicz, "Anglo-multiculturalism: Contradictions in the Politics of Cultural Diversity at risk," *International Journal of Media and Cultural Politics* 2 (2006): 255.

5. W.E. Lambert and D.M. Taylor, *Coping with Cultural and Racial Identity in Urban America* (New York: Praeger, 1990).

6. Moghaddam, *Multiculturalism and Intergroup Relations.*

7. H. Tajfel, C. Flament, M.G. Billig, and R.F. Bundy, "Social Categorization and Intergroup Relations," *European Journal of Social Psychology* 1 (1971): 149–177.

8. Lambert and Taylor, *Coping with Cultural and Racial Identity.*

9. M. Verkuyten, "Ethnic Group Identification and Group Evaluation among Minority and Majority Groups: Testing the Multiculturalism Hypothesis," *Journal of Personality and Social Psychology* 88 (2005): 121–138.

10. B.J. Fowers and B.J. Davidov, "The Virtue of Multiculturalism: Personal Transformation, Character, and Openness to the Other," *American Psychologist* 61 (2006): 581–594.

11. J.A. Richeson and R.J. Nussbaum, "The Impact of Multiculturalism versus Color-blindness on Racial Bias," *Journal of Experimental Social Psychology* 40 (2004):417–423; C. Wolsko, B. Park, C.M. Judd, and B. Wittenbrink, "Framing Interethnic Ideology: Effects of Multicultural and Color-blind Perspectives on Judgments of Groups and Individuals," *Journal of Personality and Social Psychology* 78 (2000): 635–654.

12. B. Park and C. M. Judd "Rethinking the Link between Categorization and Prejudice within the Social Cognition Perspective, *Personality and Social Psychology Review* 9 (2005): 108–130.

13. M. Sherif, *Groups in Harmony and Tension: An Integration of Studies on Intergroup Relations* (New York: Octagon Books, 1973).

14. S.L. Gaertner and J.F. Dovidio, *Reducing Intergroup Bias: The Common Ingroup Identity Model* (Philadelphia, PA: Psychology Press, 2000).

15. F.M. Moghaddam, "Omniculturalism: Policy solutions to Fundamentalism in the Era of Fractured Globalization," *Culture & Psychology* 15 (2009): 337–347.

16. J.D. Vorauer, A. Gagnon, and S.J. Sasaki, "Salient Intergroup Ideology and Intergroup Interaction," *Psychological Science* 20, No. 1, (2009): 444–446; Wolsko et al., "Framing Interethnic Ideology."

17. Jakubowicz, "Anglo-multiculturalism."

18. J.S. Passel and D.V. Cohn, *Pew Social and Demographic Trends: U.S. Populations Projections: 2005–2050*, http://pewsocialtrends.org/pubs/703/population-projection-united-states.

19. L.C. Baker, M.K. Bundorf, S. Singer, and T.H. Wagner, *Validity of the Survey of Health and the Internet and Knowledge Network's Panel and Sampling* (Palo Alto, CA: Stanford University, 2003), http://www.knowledgenetworks.com/ganp/reviewer-info.html; J.M. Dennis and R. Li, "More Honest Answers to Web Surveys? A study of Data Collection Mode Effects," *Journal of Online Research* (October 2007):1–15; T. Heeren, E.M. Edwards, J.M. Dennis, S. Rodkin, and R.W. Hinson, "A Comparison of Results from an Alcohol Survey of a Prerecruited Internet Panel and the National Epidemiologic Survey on Alcohol and Related Conditions," *Alcoholism: Clinical and Experimental Research* 32 (2008): 222–229.

20. In contrast to "opt in" Internet-based surveys, in which only the reported demographics of participants who choose to volunteer for the survey are available, complete population demographics for the KN Panel are known prior to survey recruitment. Consequently, a unique advantage of sampling from a pre-recruited web-enabled panel is that the sociodemographic characteristics of panel members who declined the invitation to participate can be unambiguously described. In this study, people who declined to participate were more likely to be female, under age thirty, black or Hispanic, and have a high school or less education. Statistical analyses that fail to account for response rate differences among such subgroups of participants can bias estimates of effects and yield imprecise and misleading standard errors and confidence intervals. Sampling weights are typically employed to reduce bias of this kind. Details regarding the Knowledge Networks panel design and post-stratification sample weighting are available on-line at http://www.knowledgenetworks.com/ganp/docs. Briefly, an iterative process is used to create weights that are inversely proportional to the probability of selecting each subject, i.e., the proportion of people in the population belonging to each "cell" or cross-classification by age, gender, race/ethnicity, education, income, and geographic region groups. Participants in over-represented cells are weighted less; participants in under-represented cells are weighted more. Iteration is continued until the distribution of weighted data converges on the most recently available U.S. Census distributions for each cell. Sampling weights are employed in subsequent statistical analyses to adjust for response rate and coverage biases and to strengthen the representativeness of results.

21. Bureau of Labor Statistics and U.S. Census Bureau, *Current Population Survey,* (Washington, DC: U.S. Census Bureau, 2008), http://www.census.gov/cps/; StataCorp, *Stata Statistical Software: Release 10* (College Station, TX: StataCorporation, 2007).

22. D. Watson and L.A. Clark, *The PANAS-X. Manual for the Positive and Negative Affect Schedule—Expanded Form* (Iowa City, IA: University of Iowa, 1994).

23. J.N. Breckenridge and P.G. Zimbardo, "The Political Psychology of Terrorism Five Years after September 11," paper presented at the International Society of Political Psychology (2007); Breckenridge and Zimbardo, "The Psychology of Political Violence: Implications for Constructive Public Policy?" paper presented at the American Psychological Association (2007).

24. Some participants (3.8 percent) declined to state a cultural policy preference. A logistic regression of response status (no stated preference versus any stated preference) on the sociodemographic variables listed in Table 9.2 was statistically significant ($F(17, 4000) = 2.57$, $p < .001$), indicating that non-response could not be construed as randomly missing data. Participants who had received some college education were twice as likely as those with less than a high school education to endorse one of the three cultural policy perspectives (AOR (adjusted odds ratio) = .484, $p < .01$). Participants with annual incomes between $60,000 and $174,000 were from three to five times more likely to respond than participants in the lowest income category (AOR = .319, $p < .001$ and AOR = .179, $p < .001$, for incomes $60,000–99,000 and $100,000–174,000, respectively). The remaining analyses in this paper are confined to participants who chose one of the three perspectives on cultural differences, but include all demographic indicators as covariates throughout. A multinomial logistic regression of declared cultural policy alternatives (assimilation, multiculturalism, omniculturalism) on all predictors (gender, age, race and ethnicity, education, income, political ideology, and urban/rural status) was also statistically significant ($F(40,3840) = 4.62$, $p < .0001$).

25. See previous note.

26. See note 23, Breckenridge and Zimbardo.

27. Sherif, *Groups in Harmony and Tension*; S.L. Gaertner and J.F. Dovidio, "Understanding and Addressing Contemporary Racism: From Aversive Racism to the Common Ingroup Identity Model," *Journal of Social Issues* 61 (2005): 615–639.

28. E. Aronson, C. Stephan, J. Sikes, N. Blaney, and M. Snapp, *The Jigsaw Classroom* (Beverly Hills, CA.: Sage, 1978).

29. Gaertner and Dovidio, "Understanding and Addressing Contemporary Racism."

30. F. M. Moghaddam, "Catastrophic Evolution, Culture, and Diversity Management," *Culture & Psychology* 12 (2006):7415–434.

DISCUSSION QUESTIONS

1. According to the piece written by Samantha Hauptman, in what way did the media contribute to a moral panic with regard to immigration after the 9/11 terror attacks?

2. What evidence is there from the public at large that a moral panic regarding immigrants had taken hold in the United States after the 9/11 attacks?

3. What informal and formal controls were placed on immigrants in the post–9/11 era that were consistent with the existence of a moral panic?

4. Post–9/11, describe how consensus, hostility, and volatility, by both the government and the public, contributed to the conditions of moral panic directed toward immigrants, according to Hauptman.

5. What is omniculturalism? How is it different from multiculturalism and from assimilation?

6. What are the findings of the Moghaddam and Breckenridge study? What are the implications of omniculturalism for the discussion of immigration generally? Do you agree with the authors that omniculturalism has merit? Explain.

7. In what way would American society, were it to explicitly identify with the omnicultural perspective, be more (or less) capable of countering and preventing terrorism? How would homeland security public policy be affected?

CHAPTER NINE

Immigration and Elections

Introduction

In the 2016 presidential election, Donald Trump beat Hillary Clinton pretty handily in the electoral college (304–227), which of course secured him the presidency. But he lost the popular vote to Clinton by roughly three million votes. Much of Clinton's popular vote victory can be credited to California, which alone gave Clinton more than four million votes over what Trump received.

In January 2017, Trump began to claim he would have won the popular vote but for the fact that millions of noncitizens voted in the election, which itself would constitute the federal crime of voter fraud. Critics decried the president's claims as completely baseless. Some pundits went so far as to declare that there has been no documented case of voter fraud in the United States for years—a claim that itself is patently absurd. Some supporters of President Trump argued that studies had been done that buttress Trump's assertions. One such study is presented in this chapter. The study, by political scientists Jesse Richman, Gulshan Chattha, and David Earnest, found there had been votes cast by noncitizens in the federal elections of 2008 and 2010. Of course, any such votes would have been cast illegally, as noncitizens are not allowed to vote for federal office candidates.

Proponents of the president's theory of noncitizen voter fraud embraced this study and extrapolated from it to conclude that as many as three million to five million immigrants (legal and illegal) voted in the election. They further concluded from polling data that the majority of these votes went for Clinton. Others who disagreed with the president were quick to point to other political science studies that challenged the Richman et al. findings on methodological grounds. For his part, Richman, who is a tenured political scientist at Old Dominion University, has been reluctantly engaged in the war of claims and counterclaims. He has published several responses to the users and detractors of his and his colleagues' study. He has simultaneously defended the study's methodology and findings that there are indeed noncitizens voting in our elections, while also disabusing anyone of the notion that the numbers of noncitizen voters are as large as the president has touted. Richman would say that the number is certainly more than zero and almost certainly not in the millions. In any case, the study by Richman and his colleagues has become Exhibit A in the debate over policing our elections from unauthorized voters through voter ID laws and other measures.

Of course, immigrants' connection to American elections is not exclusively, or even primarily, a matter of their voting practices. More substantially, immigration is a theme that frequently drives election campaign rhetoric. The propensity of immigration to be an election issue is the subject of the article written by Damien Arthur and Joshua Woods. Interestingly, the authors observe that presidents, from Clinton through Obama, have tended to frame the discussion of immigrants in a negative light more often than in a positive one. Negative framing involves connecting immigrants and immigration to negative themes, such as crime, terrorism, economic woes, etc. The use of negative frames has occurred across all three presidencies (i.e., Bill Clinton, George W. Bush, and Barak Obama) to a greater or lesser degree, despite each president's ostensibly sympathetic posture toward the plight of immigrants in the United States. The tendency toward negative framing, where immigration is concerned, is particularly observed when societal conditions are such to foster it.

# READING 10

Do Non-citizens Vote in U.S. Elections?
By Jesse T. Richman, Gulshan A. Chattha, and David C. Earnest

Introduction

This analysis provides some of the first available nationwide estimates of the portion of non-citizen immigrants who vote in U.S. elections. These estimates speak to an ongoing debate concerning non-citizen voting rights within the United States (DeSipio 2011; Earnest, 2008; FAIR, 2004; Fund and von Spakovsky, 2012; Hayduk, 2006; Immigration Policy Center, 2012; Munro, 2008; Song, 2009; Von Spakovsky, 2012) and they also speak to broader global questions concerning the normative political place of non-citizens in democratic politics.

Most state and local governments in the United States bar non-citizens from participating in elections (the exception: a few localities in Maryland), but the question of whether non-citizen immigrants can, and should, participate receives varied answers globally (Earnest, 2008) with many countries offering at least some opportunity for some resident non-citizens to participate in local elections, and some countries offering full participation in national elections.

The United States also has a long history of noncitizen voting at the local, state and national levels. Aylsworth (1931) notes that "during the nineteenth century, the laws and constitutions of at least twenty-two states and territories granted aliens the right to vote." From the founding of the Republic to the early 20th century, various territories and states enfranchised noncitizen residents for several reasons. During westward expansion, several territories offered the franchise to entice European migrants to settle so that territories would meet the population criterion for admission to the Union. Similarly, during Reconstruction several southern states offered the franchise to migrants who would replace slave labor. Later, some states enfranchised so-called "declarant aliens" (resident aliens who declared their intent to naturalize) to educate them about the interests and issues of their communities. Yet the practice of enfranchising noncitizens served less salutary goals as well. By enfranchising only propertied white European men, the practice of noncitizen voting

Jesse T. Richman, Gulshan A. Chattha, and David C. Earnest, "Do Non-citizens Vote in U.S. Elections?," *Electoral Studies*, pp. 149-157. Copyright © 2014 by Elsevier Science and Technology - Journals. Reprinted with permission.

reinforced extant prohibitions on voting by women, African Americans, Asian Americans, the poor and others. By the 1920s, however, following the large migrations of the early 20th century, all states had revoked the voting rights of noncitizens (Earnest, 2008, 25–26). Non-citizens voted legally in every presidential election through 1924. By 1928 the last state constitution that protected non-citizen voting (Arkansas') had been amended.

The decision to (dis)enfranchise non-citizens falls within the states' authority to define qualifications for voting. The nineteenth-century practices in various states produced a case-law legacy that most legal scholars conclude permits states to enfranchise noncitizens if legislators so choose. Similarly, on several occasions the Supreme Court has upheld the constitutionality of noncitizen voting because states have the authority to set voter qualifications (Earnest, 2008, 25–26). The question of noncitizen voting is, in the end, a political rather than a legal one.

Within the context of the current nearly universal ban on non-citizen voting in the United States, this study examines the voting behavior of non-citizens. To what extent do non-citizens ignore legal barriers and seize ballot access in U.S. elections? We find that non-citizen participation in U.S. elections is low, but non-zero, with an unusual set of covariates with participation, and the potential to change important election outcomes.

Data

The data used for this paper is from the 2008 and 2010 Cooperative Congressional Election Studies, based on the files released by Stephen Ansolabehere (2010, 2011). The 2008 and 2010 Cooperative Congressional Election Studies (CCES) were conducted by YouGov/Polimetrix of Palo Alto, CA as an internet-based survey using a sample selected to mirror the demographic characteristics of the U.S. population. In both years survey data was collected in two waves: pre-election in October, and then post-election in November. The questionnaire asked more than 100 questions regarding electoral participation, issue preferences, and candidate choices.

Four design characteristics make this survey uniquely valuable for our purposes. 1. It has an enormous sample size, which makes feasible sub-population analyses (n = 32,800 in 2008 and n = 55,400 in 2010). 2. It included a question about citizenship status. 3. Many non-citizens were asked if they voted, unlike other large surveys which filter out non-citizens before asking about voting. 4. Participation and registration were verified for at least some residents in nearly every state for the 2008 survey (Virginia state law barred voting verification).

Inclusion of a validated voting measure is particularly valuable in this context because of important and contradictory social and legal incentives for reporting non-citizen electoral participation. Although variation in the social desirability of voting may skew estimates (Ansolabehere and Hersh, 2012) as for other populations, legal concerns may lead some non-citizens to deny that they are registered and/or have voted when in fact they have done both. Validation of registration and voting was performed by the CCES research team in collaboration with the firm Catalyst. Of 339 non-citizens identified in the 2008 survey, Catalyst matched 140 to a commercial (e.g. credit card) and/or voter database. The vote validation procedures are described in detail by Ansolabehere and Hersh (2012). The verification effort means that for a bit more than 40 percent of the 2008 sample, we are able to verify whether non-citizens voted when they said they did, or didn't vote when they said they didn't. For the remaining non-citizens, we have only the respondent's word to go on concerning electoral participation, although we do attempt to make inferences about their true participation rate based upon the verified portion of the sample.

About one percent of the respondents in each survey identified themselves as non-citizen immigrants (339 in 2008, 489 in 2010)[1].In both years the sample likely includes individuals drawn from more than one category of non-citizen (ranging from permanent resident aliens to those on short-term student visas). In the context of the 2010 CCES, it is possible to identify the exact citizenship status of some respondents because many provided an open-ended response about their citizenship status when asked why they did not vote. For instance, "I'm a permanent resident," "I have a green card," "waiting on US Citizenship to come through!" and most commonly simply, "not a citizen." No individual specifically identified themselves as an illegal or undocumented resident, although one did indicate that he or she hadn't voted because the individual "didn't have green card [sic] yet." It is possible that some respondents were without any documentation whatsoever (popularly called "illegal aliens"), though this cannot be confirmed or rejected with the information available as no respondent specifically self-identified themselves as illegal or undocumented (but many did not specifically identify themselves as having permanent resident status).

A critical question for this project is whether respondents' self-identification as non-citizens was accurate. If most or all of the "non-citizens" who indicated that they voted were in fact citizens who accidentally misstated their citizenship status, then the data would have nothing to contribute concerning the frequency of non-citizen voting. Appendix 1 includes demographic, attitudinal, and geographical analyses designed to assess whether those who stated that they were non-citizens were in fact non-citizens. It builds a strong construct or concurrent validity case for the validity of the measure. We demonstrate that self-reported non-citizens who voted had similar racial, geographic, and attitudinal characteristics with non-citizens who did not vote, and that as a whole the non-citizens in our sample had racial, attitudinal, and geographic characteristics consistent with their reported non-citizen status. Given this evidence, we think that the vast majority of those who said they were non-citizens were in fact non-citizens.

For 2008, the median length of residence at the current address for non-citizens was 1–2 years, with 16.9 percent residing at the current address for less than seven months, and 25.7 percent residing at the current address for 5 or more years. This is considerably more mobile than the overall sample, which has a median length of residence of over 5 years (57.1 percent). In 2010 the median time spent at the current address by non-citizens was 3 years, and respondents were also asked how many years they had lived in their current city with a median response of 5 years. A few respondents have been in the U.S. for a long time. One 2010 respondent explained "I am English although I've lived here for 26 years and am balking at becoming a citizen for multiple reasons although I know I really need to do this for my family's financial future. So I am active in politics and know more than most Americans."

It is impossible to tell for certain whether the non-citizens who responded to the survey were representative of the broader population of non-citizens, but some clues can be gained by examining education levels. Census bureau estimates (Census, 2012) suggest that the sample contains slightly more college-educated respondents (30.6 percent) than the overall foreign born population (26.8 percent), and many fewer respondents with less than a high-school education (8.3 percent versus 33.3 percent). The paucity of uneducated non-citizens in the sample would in most circumstances be expected to bias sample voting participation upward. However, given our results concerning the association between participation and education (discussed below) it may well be that the paucity of uneducated non-citizens in the CCES sample biases the turnout estimates down rather than up. We confront this issue primarily by weighting the data.

Throughout the analysis (with the exception of the appendix) we report results produced from weighted data. Weight construction began with CCES case weights, but then adjusted these by race to match the racial demographic of the non-citizen population. Our concern with using regular CPS case-weights was that weights were constructed based upon overall demographic characteristics without attention to the demographic character of the non-citizen population. For instance, the Census Bureau estimates (Census Bureau, 2013) that 6.7 percent of non-citizens are Black[2]. The unweighted 2008 CPS dataset slightly over-counts non-citizen respondents who identified their race as "Black" at 9.1 percent. The weighted 2008 CPS by contrast dramatically over-counts non-citizen respondents who self-identified their race as "Black" at 14.1 percent. We constructed a new weight variable that adjusted the CCES case weight to (1) preserve the actual number of respondents in the sample in the face of a tendency for non-citizens to be in demographic groups receiving higher weights, and (2) match Census Bureau (CPS, 2011) estimates of the racial characteristics of the non-citizen population. Results for weighted data were qualitatively similar to (but somewhat lower than) results with un-weighted data for the key voting variables. Weighting produces a non-citizen sample that appears to be a better match with Census estimates of the population. For instance, 32.5 percent of the weighted sample had no high school degree.

Participatory Stages

Participation in U.S. elections requires that would-be voters complete a series of steps including: registering to vote, traveling to a polling place or requesting an absentee ballot and presenting any required identification, and casting a ballot. At each stage, legal barriers to non-citizen voting may lead to lower participation. Only if all stages are surmounted will the non-citizen cast a ballot in a

U.S. election. At any stage, concern about the potentially high legal costs of non-citizen voting, or enforcement of official requirements for ballot access may prevent non-citizen voting.

Registration

Non-citizen voter registration is a violation of election law in almost all U.S. jurisdictions, the lone exceptions are for residents of a few localities in Maryland. Most non-citizens did not cross the initial threshold of voter registration, but some did. In 2008, 67 non-citizens (19.8%) either claimed they were registered, had their registration status verified, or both. Among the 337 immigrant non-citizens who responded to the CCES, 50 (14.8%) indicated in the survey that they were registered. An additional 17 non-citizens had their voter registration status verified through record matches even though they claimed not to be registered. Perhaps the legal risks of non-citizen registration led some of these individuals to claim not to be registered. In 2010 76 (15.6%) of non-citizens indicated that they were registered to vote in either the pre-election or post-election survey waves.

In 2008, the proportion of non-citizens who were in fact registered to vote was somewhere between 19.8% (all who reported or had verified registration, or both) and 3.3% (11 non-citizen respondents were almost certainly registered to vote because they both stated that they were registered and had their registration status verified). Even the low-end estimate suggests a fairly substantial population of registered-to-vote non-citizens nationwide. Out of roughly 19.4 million adult non-citizens in the United States, this would represent a population of roughly 620,000 registered non-citizens[3]. By way of comparison, there are roughly 725,000 individuals in the average Congressional district.

The "adjusted estimate" row presents our best guess at the true percentage of non-citizens registered. It uses the 94 (weighted) non-citizens from 2008 for whom Catalyst obtained a match to commercial and/or voter databases to estimate the portion of non-citizens who either claim to be registered when they are not (35%) or claim not to be registered when they are (18%). We then use these numbers to extrapolate for the entire sample of non-citizens in 2008 and 2010. Because most non-citizens who said they were registered were in fact registered, and quite a few who said they were not were actually registered, the adjusted estimate is the highest of the three estimates, indicating that roughly one quarter of non-citizens were likely registered to vote (Table 10.1).

Table 10.1 Estimated Voter Registration by Non-citizens.

	2008	2010
Self reported and/or verified	67 (19.8%)	76 (15.6%)
Self reported and verified	11 (3.3%)	N.A.
Adjusted estimate	84 (25.1%)	124 (25.3%)

Voter Identification

Post-registration, another barrier to voting by non-citizens might come in the form of the credential checking that occurs before individuals are permitted to vote on Election Day. In 2008 14 respondents indicated that they did not vote because "I did not have the correct form of identification," and in 2010 29 indicated that they did not vote because of the absence of necessary identification.

Nonetheless, identification requirements blocked ballot access for only a small portion of non-citizens. Of the 27 non-citizens who indicated that they were "asked to show picture identification, such as a driver's license, at the polling place or election office," in the 2008 survey, 18 claimed to have subsequently voted, and one more indicated that they were "allowed to vote using a provisional ballot." Only 7 (25.9%) indicated that they were not allowed to vote after showing identification. These results are summarized in Fig. 10.1. Although the proportion of non-citizens prevented from voting by ID requirements is statistically distinguishable from the portion of citizens[4] (Chi-Square = 161, $p < .001$), the overall message is that identification requirements do not prevent the majority of non-citizen voting. The fact that most non-citizen immigrants who showed identification were subsequently permitted to vote suggests that efforts to use photo-identification to prevent non-citizen voting are unlikely to be particularly effective. This most likely reflects the impact of state laws that permit non-citizens to obtain state identification cards (e.g. driver's licenses).

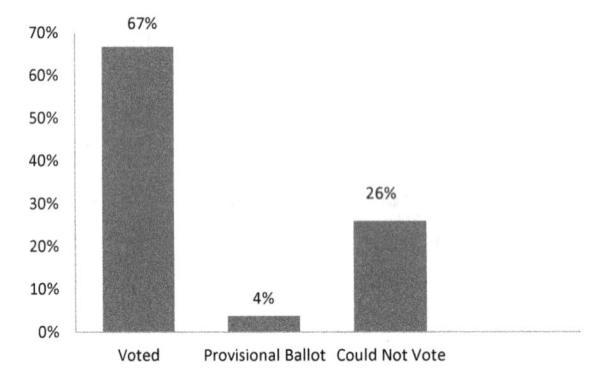

Figure 10.1 Outcome of Polling-Place Photo-Identification Request among Non-citizens.

Voting

There is evidence that some non-citizen immigrants voted in both 2008 and 2010. In 2008, thirty eight (11.3%) reported that they voted, had their vote verified, or both. As with registration, claims of voting and validated voting did not intersect very often, in part because the voting question was not asked for all non-citizens who had verified voting, and voter file matches were not available for all non-citizens who claimed that they voted. Twenty seven indicated that "I definitely voted in the November General Election" and 16 had validated general election votes. Only five (1.5%) both claimed that they definitely voted and had a validated vote. In 2010 thirteen non-citizens (3.5% of respondents to the post-election survey) indicated that they voted. All 2008 and 2010 reported votes by non-citizens were in violation of state election law as no votes were cast by non-citizen respondents from the Maryland localities which allow non-citizen voting (Table 10.2).

Table 10.2 Estimated Voter Turnout by Non-citizens.

	2008	2010
Self reported and/or verified	38 (11.3%)	13 (3.5%)
Self reported and verified	5 (1.5%)	N.A.
Adjusted estimate	21 (6.4%)	8 (2.2%)

How many non-citizen votes were likely cast in 2008? Taking the most conservative estimate—those who both said they voted and cast a verified vote—yields a confidence interval based on sampling error between 0.2% and 2.8% for the portion of non-citizens participating in elections. Taking the least conservative measure—at least one indicator showed that the respondent voted—yields an estimate that between 7.9% and 14.7% percent of non-citizens voted in 2008. Since the adult non-citizen population of the United States was roughly 19.4 million (CPS, 2011), the number of non-citizen voters (including both uncertainty based on normally distributed sampling error, and the various combinations of verified and reported voting) could range from just over 38,000 at the very minimum to nearly 2.8 million at the maximum.

The "adjusted estimate" represents our best guess at the portion of non-citizens who voted. As with voter registration, we extrapolate from the behavior of validated voters in 2008 to estimate the portion of non-citizens who said they voted but didn't, and the portion who said they didn't vote but did. 71 non-citizens answered a survey question indicating whether they voted, and also had their vote validated. Among these, 56 indicated that they did not vote (but two of these cast a validated vote), while 13 indicated they voted, of whom five cast a validated vote[5]. The adjusted estimate of 6.4 percent for 2008 is quite substantial, and would be associated with 1.2 million non-citizen votes cast in 2008 if the weighted CCES sample is fully representative of the non-citizen population. To produce an adjusted figure for 2010 we cut by three quarters the estimated number of non-citizens who voted but claimed they did not (somewhat larger than the drop in the number who self-reported voting). This produces an overall estimate that 2.2 percent voted in 2010.

There has been significant debate in the literature concerning the ideological or political leanings of non-citizen voters. In Belgium for instance, Jacobs (2001) found indications that non-citizens often voted for right wing parties, while others (Bird et al., 2010; Howard, 2009; Janoski, 2010; Joppke, 2003; Rath, 1990) find evidence that left-leaning parties and noncitizens tend to align together. In the 2008 and 2010 U.S. elections, non-citizen voters favored Democratic candidates. Non-citizens who reported voting were asked their candidate preferences, and these preferences skewed toward Democrats. In 2008 66.7 percent reported voting for the Democratic House candidate, while only 20.8 percent reported voting for the Republican candidate. 81.8 percent reported voting for Barack Obama compared to 17.5 percent for John McCain. The difference of proportions is statistically significant using both Chi-Square and z tests ($p < .005$) and substantively large for both the House and Presidential vote cases. Similarly in 2010, 53.8 percent of non-citizens reported voting for the Democratic House candidate while 30.7 percent indicated that they voted for the Republican. These results are summarized in Fig. 10.2.

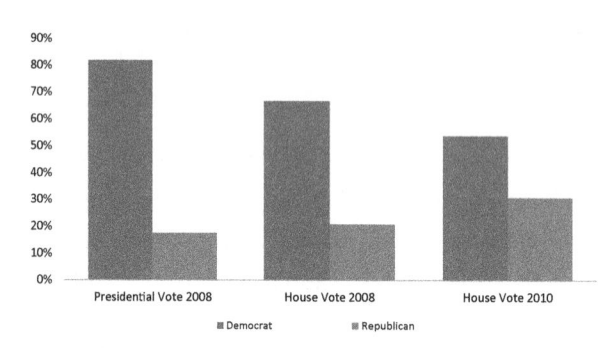

Figure 10.2 Partisan Vote Choice by Non-citizens in 2008 and 2010 U.S. Elections.

These results allow us to estimate the impact of non-citizen voting on election outcomes. We find that there is reason to believe non-citizen voting changed one state's Electoral College votes in 2008, delivering North Carolina to Obama, and that non-citizen votes have also led to Democratic victories in congressional races including a critical 2008 Senate race that delivered for Democrats a 60-vote filibuster-proof majority in the Senate. It is possible to evaluate whether non-citizen votes have changed election outcomes by pairing data on the number of adult non-citizens per state with election margins and our estimates of the frequency with which non-citizens supported Republican and Democratic candidates. For instance each additional non-citizen vote adds an expected 0.643 votes to Obama's vote margin based on the portion of non-citizens who supported Obama and McCain. By multiplying this decimal by the victory margin for Obama (Federal Election Commission, 2009) and then dividing by the number of adult non-citizens in the state (Census Bureau, 2013), we can determine the level of non-citizen voter turnout required for non-citizen votes to have given Obama a state-level victory, and assess whether such a turnout is plausible in light of our turnout estimates.

There were five states in 2008 where less than 100 percent turnout among non-citizens could have accounted for Obama's victory margin. These states, and the required turnout among non-citizens, are shown in Table 10.3. Virginia (85 percent turnout required) and Nevada (68 percent) are clearly not cases in which non-citizen votes could have changed the outcome. Our estimates of non-citizen turnout are much lower. Similarly, the turnout required for non-citizens to have made the difference in Florida and Indiana (22 percent and 27 percent respectively) is larger than the upper bound of our turnout estimate. By contrast, North Carolina is a plausible case. If more than 5.1 percent of non-citizens residing in North Carolina turned out to vote in 2008, then the vote margin they gave Obama would have been sufficient to provide Obama with the entirety of his victory margin in the state. Since our best estimate is that 6.4 percent of non-citizens actually voted, it is likely though by no means certain that John McCain would have won North Carolina were it not for the votes for Obama cast by non-citizens.

Table 10.3 Non-citizen Turnout Required to Account for 2008 Obama Win of State.

State	Obama Victory Margin (FEC, 2009)	Number of Adult Non-citizens (Census Bureau, 2013)	Non-citizen Turnout Required to Account for Obama Victory Margin
North Carolina	14,177	432,700	5.1%
Florida	236,450	1,684,705	21.8%
Indiana	28,391	165,210	26.7%
Nevada	120,909	275,565	68.2%
Virginia	234,527	427,535	85.3%

A similar analysis reveals that there was one House race and one Senate race during the 2008 and 2010 election cycles which were close enough for votes by non-citizens to potentially account for the entirety of the Democratic victor's margin. As before this analysis merges Census estimates of the number of adult non-citizens by House district and State with FEC tabulations of final election results. In 2008 there were 22 House races and two Senate races in which the Democratic candidate's winning margin was small enough that less than 100 percent turnout among non-citizens could account for Democratic victory, and in 2010 there were 24 such House districts and three Senate races.[6] In the two instances shown in Table 10.4 the required turnout is small enough that it is quite likely non-citizen participation led to victory by the Democratic candidate e the necessary non-citizen turnout is within the range of our turnout estimates. As with the presidential-election results above, this analysis suggest that non-citizen turnout is large enough to have had a modest, but real, influence on election outcomes in the US.

The most important race identified in Table 10.4 is undoubtedly the Minnesota 2008 Senate contest. This race, ultimately decided by 312 votes for Democrat Al Franken, was of critical national importance. It gave Democrats the filibuster-proof super-majority needed to pass major legislative initiatives during President Obama's first year in office. The Patient Protection and Affordable Care Act, for instance, would have had a much more difficult path to passage were it not for Franken's pivotal vote. The MN 2008 Senate race is also the race where the smallest portion of non-citizen votes would have tipped the balance—participation by more than 0.65% of non-citizens in MN is sufficient to account for the entirety of Franken's margin. Our best guess is that nearly ten times as many voted.

Table 10.4 Non-citizen Turnout Required to Account for Democratic Congressional Victories.

State, District, and Year	Democratic Candidate Victory Margin (FEC)	Number of Adult Non-citizens (Census Bureau, 2013, 2014)	Non-citizen Turnout Required to Account for Victory Margin
MN Senate (2008)	312	180,020	0.65%
VA 5 (2008)	727	19,845	6.94%

Is Non-citizen Voting Intentional or Accidental?

The fact that non-citizen voting is illegal in most parts of the United States means that those who voted were potentially violating the law. The decision to participate in spite of de-jure barriers may at times be an intentional act of protest against the failure to enfranchise non-citizen residents. On the other hand, some may have violated election laws accidentally because they were unaware of legal barriers to electoral participation.

Education rates may provide some clues concerning the balance between ignorance and activism. If activism drives non-citizen voting, then participation rates should be higher among better educated individuals who are more likely to be attentive to normative arguments in favor of enfranchising non-citizen residents. If ignorance of legal barriers drives voting, then participation rates should be higher among those who are more poorly educated.

Unlike other populations, including naturalized citizens, (Bass and Casper, 2001; Mayer, 2011) education is not associated with higher participation among non-citizens. In 2008, non-citizens with less than a college degree were significantly more likely to cast a validated vote (Somers'd -0.17, $p < .001$), and no non-citizens with a college degree or higher cast a validated vote. Non-citizens with more education were also not significantly more likely to self-report voting in 2008 or 2010. This hints at a possible link between non-citizen voting and lack of awareness about legal barriers.

Conclusions

Our exploration of non-citizen voting in the 2008 presidential election found that most non-citizens did not register or vote in 2008, but some did. The proportion of non-citizens who voted was less than fifteen percent, but significantly greater than zero. Similarly in 2010 we found that more than three percent of non-citizens reported voting.

These results speak to both sides of the debate concerning non-citizen enfranchisement. They support the claims made by some anti-immigration organizations that non-citizens participate in U.S. elections. In addition, the analysis suggests that non-citizens' votes have changed significant election outcomes including the assignment of North Carolina's 2008 electoral votes, and the pivotal Minnesota Senate victory of Democrat Al Franken in 2008.

However, our results also support the arguments made by voting and immigrant rights organizations that the portion of non-citizen immigrants who participate in U.S. elections is quite small. Indeed, given the extraordinary efforts made by the Obama and McCain campaigns to mobilize voters in 2008, the relatively small portion of non-citizens who voted in 2008 likely exceeded the portion of non-citizens voting in other recent U.S. elections.

Our results also suggest that photo-identification requirements are unlikely to be effective at preventing electoral participation by non-citizen immigrants: In 2008, more than two thirds of non-citizen immigrants who indicated that they were asked to show photo-identification reported that they went on to cast a vote. A potential response to the inefficacy of photo-id at preventing non-citizen voting is found in laws recently passed by Kansas and Arizona that require voter registrants to prove citizenship. By highlighting and emphasizing the citizenship requirement (and by requiring documentation non-citizens should be unable to provide) it seems likely that such laws would prevent more non-citizens from voting. That said, enforcement would be critical for efficacy (and much would depend here upon local election officials), particularly since federal voter registration forms do not require proof of citizenship. In addition, already registered non-citizens might well be able to continue voting. In any case such measures would come with significant costs for some citizens for whom the necessary documentation could be challenging to provide.

Ultimately, the results of our analysis provide a basis for informed reflection concerning the role of non-citizens in U.S. elections. They demonstrate that in spite of de-jure barriers to participation, a small portion of non-citizen immigrants do participate in U.S. elections, and that this participation is at times substantial enough to change important election outcomes including Electoral College votes and Senate races. For those who wish to further restrict participation by non-citizens, however, our results also provide important cautions. Simple resort to voter photo-identification rules is unlikely to be particularly effective.

Appendix 1: Validating Citizen Status Self Reports

One potential concern about the results presented in this paper is that they might reflect survey response errors. Specifically, if some citizens intentionally or inadvertently indicated that they were non-citizens, this could produce the pattern we find—a small number of apparent non-citizens engaging in the political process. While we find it implausible that citizens would intentionally claim to be non-citizen immigrants, it is possible that some citizens could have inadvertently selected this response. This appendix evaluates that possibility.

Given confidentiality and legal issues, it is not ethically possible to directly verify whether individuals who voted were/are non-citizens. Instead, we examine the construct or concurrent validity by showing that self-reported non-citizens had demographic and attitudinal characteristics one would expect them to have if they were in fact non-citizen immigrants, and that the non-citizens who voted had similar attitudes and characteristics to the non-citizens who didn't vote on questions where one might expect those who were in fact non-citizen immigrants to be distinct from the broader population.

A.1. Demographic Characteristics

Given immigration patterns in recent decades, non-citizens should be more likely to be non-white than the general population surveyed. Table A.1 summarizes the racial characteristics of individuals with various immigration statuses among 2008 survey respondents. Non-citizen immigrants had the lowest percentage of whites, and the highest percentages of Hispanics and Asians. None identified as Native Americans. All analyses in the appendix use unweighted data because the goal is to evaluate the characteristics of the sample.

Table A.1 Race and Citizenship Status.

		Immigrant Citizen	Immigrant Non-citizen	First Generation	Second Generation	Third Generation	Total
Race	White	647	150	1622	6442	18,002	26,863
		47.0%	44.2%	62.3%	89.1%	85.3%	82.3%
	Black	134	31	91	68	1668	1992
		9.7%	9.1%	3.5%	0.9%	7.9%	6.1%
	Hispanic	353	91	581	405	550	1980
		25.6%	26.8%	22.3%	5.6%	2.6%	6.1%
	Asian	167	55	156	36	30	444
		12.1%	16.2%	6.0%	0.5%	0.1%	1.4%
	Native American	5	0	8	38	260	311
		0.4%	0.0%	0.3%	0.5%	1.2%	1.0%
	Mixed	20	5	68	94	270	457
		1.5%	1.5%	2.6%	1.3%	1.3%	1.4%
	Other	40	5	66	147	320	578
		2.9%	1.5%	2.5%	2.0%	1.5%	1.8%
	Middle Eastern	11	2	13	2	3	31
		0.8%	0.6%	0.5%	0.0%	0.0%	0.1%
Total		1377	339	2605	7232	21,103	32,656
		100.0%	100.0%	100.0%	100.0%	100.0%	100.0%

If the self-declared non-citizens who voted were actually non-citizens, their racial distribution should be similar to that of non-citizens who did not vote.[7] In Table A.2, we divide non-citizens into two groups: those who voted (said they voted, had a verified vote, or both) and those who did not, and compare their racial characteristics. Non-citizen immigrants who voted are not statistically distinguishable from non-citizen immigrants who voted, and several of the non-significant differences in demographic characteristics skew in the direction of demographics less like those of citizens. For instance, there are fewer Whites among the voters than the nonvoters, and more Hispanics and Blacks. Results from 2010 are omitted in the interest of saving space, but they reveal the same patterns, with non-citizens who voted reporting slightly (but not significantly) more racial diversity, and fewer whites than even among non-citizens who did not vote.

Table A.2 Racial Characteristics of Non-citizen Voters and Non-voters, 2008.

		Did not Vote	Voted	Total
Race	White	129	21	150
		44.3%	43.8%	44.2%
	Black	24	7	31
		8.2%	14.6%	9.1%
	Hispanic	77	14	91
		26.5%	29.2%	26.8%
	Asian	50	5	55
		17.2%	10.4%	16.2%
	Mixed	5	0	5
		1.7%	0.0%	1.5%
	Other	4	1	5
		1.4%	2.1%	1.5%
	Middle Eastern	2	0	2
		0.7%	0.0%	0.6%
Total		291	48	339
		100.0%	100.0%	100.0%

A.2. Immigration Attitudes

The 2010 CCES included a battery of questions on immigration attitudes. These questions provide a good opportunity to use attitudinal variables to check the validity of the citizenship measure. Non-citizen immigrants might be expected to have distinctive positions on immigration issues, given the potential for immigration policy choices to directly affect themselves or their families. The specific immigration questions asked respondents to select as many options as they wished from among a list of items:

What do you think the U.S. government should do about immigration. Select all that apply.

- Fine Businesses
- Grant legal status to all illegal immigrants who have held jobs and paid taxes for at least 3 years and have not been convicted of felony crimes.
- Increase the number of guest workers allowed to come legally to the US.
- Increase the number of border patrols on the U.S.-Mexican border.
- Allow police to question anyone they think may be in the country illegally.
- None of these.

For all of these items, the choices selected by non-citizen immigrants were statistically different from those made by other respondents. The number of respondents and the percent supporting each policy is summarized in Table A.3 below.

Table A.3 Immigration Attitudes of Citizens and Non-citizens (2010 CCES).

	Citizens	Non Citizens	Total Responses
Fine businesses	1786	6	2438**
	73.7%	35.3%	
Grant legal status	21,162	310	55,234**
	38.7%	63.4%	
Increase border patrol	34,057	201	55,234**
	62.2%	41.1%	
Increase guest workers	659	8	2438*
	27.2%	47.1%	
Allow police to question	26,531	96	55,234**
	48.5%	19.6%	

Chi-Square test: ** difference significant at $p < .001$ level. * Difference significant at $p < .10$ level.

Across all five issues, the difference between citizen and non-citizen responses is statistically significant and substantively large. Those who identified themselves as non-citizens have views that are distinctly different from those who identified themselves as citizens.

To further investigate whether those self-declared non-citizens who voted might have mis-stated their citizenship status, Table A.4 compares the immigration attitudes of non-citizens who said they voted with the immigration attitudes of non-citizens who said they did not vote. Only three questions are included because none of the non-citizens in the subsamples asked the other two questions identified themselves as voters.

Table A.4 Immigration Attitudes of Non-citizens by Voting Status (2010 CCES).

	Didn't Vote	Voted	Total Responses
Grant legal status	285	25	489
	62.6%	73.5%	
Increase border patrol	186	15	489
	40.9%	44.1%	
Allow police to question	87	9	489
	19.1%	26.5%	

Note: All voting status is based on self-reported vote as no votes were verified for 2010 CCES. ☐ Chi-square difference significant at $p < .10$ level.

As expected, there are no significant differences in attitudes toward immigration among respondents who identified as non-citizens, irrespective of whether or not they voted. This is what we would expect if respondents' self-identification is valid. On one of three questions (grant legal status) non-citizens who voted were slightly (not significantly) more likely to take the pro-immigrant position.

A.3. State Non-citizen Population

If respondents who indicate they are non-citizens are in fact non-citizens, then they should be more likely to reside in states with larger non-citizen populations. To test this idea, we computed the percentage of adult non-citizens per state using Census Bureau (2013) data (2007–2011 American Community Survey 5 year estimates). We then used this percentage to predict whether respondents would indicate they were non-citizens across states on the 2008 CCES. The percentage of non-citizens was a very statistically significant predictor of self-identified non-citizen status in a binary logit analysis ($B = 11.34$, S.E. = 1.05, $p < .0005$), and remained statistically significant with a very similar effect size when analysis was restricted to only individuals who had self-identified or verified votes ($B = 11.25$, S.E. = 2.77, $p < .0005$). Similar results were obtained for 2010, with the analysis of all respondents producing the following coefficient and significance levels ($B = 8.86$, S.E. = 0.88, $p < .0005$) and the analysis of voters producing the following results ($B = 6.4$, S.E. = 3.3, $p < .053$). In 2010 it is once more not possible to reject the null hypothesis that the coefficients are the same.

A.4. Conclusion

The results presented in this appendix support the conclusion that those who identified themselves as non-citizens had the demographic characteristics one would expect non-citizens to have, and non-citizens who voted were not appreciably different from non-citizens who did not vote in terms of their political attitudes towards immigration, their geographic distribution, and their racial demographics. Therefore, it is unlikely that a substantial number of citizen respondents (inadvertently) indicated that they were non-citizens.

Notes

1. Since the total legal permanent resident population in 2008 of 12.6 million (Rytina, 2012) was approximately four percent of the overall U.S. population, and the total non-citizen adult population in 2011 was 19.4 million (CPS, 2011), the non-citizen population was under-sampled. Nonetheless, the sample that was collected provides the first nation-wide sample from which analysts can draw inferences concerning electoral participation by non-citizens in United States elections.
2. Here we combine the categories Black or African American, Black or African American and White, or Black or African American and Native American—6.6 percent were Black or African American alone.
3. The Census Bureau (CPS, 2011) estimates that there were 19.4 million non-citizens age 18 or over living in the United States in 2011.
4. 0.6 percent of all survey respondents were prevented from voting after showing identification.
5. This should produce a very conservative measure of the portion who actually voted, as most of the drop off is among individuals for whom registration status could not be verified (and this could be a result of errors in matching—a match to consumer data could occur even though a match to voter data has been missed). Among non-citizens with verified registration status, 75 percent of those who reported voting had a verified vote, while 30 percent who reported not voting cast a validated vote.
6. Each analysis assumes that non-citizens voted for D and R candidates at the relevant national percentages from that election year and for that office. E.g. 68 percent voted for House Democrats in 2010.
7. One important caveat is in order. To the extent that non-citizen voting is dependent upon an ability to 'pass for' a citizen at the polling place, respondents who looked less like immigrants to election officials might have an easier time voting.

References

Aylsworth, L.E., 1931. The passing of alien suffrage. Am. Polit. Sci. Rev. XXV (1), 114–116.
Ansolabehere, S., 2011. Cooperative Congressional Election Study, 2008: Common Content [Computer File] Release 4: July 15, 2011. Harvard University [Producer], Cambridge, MA. http://cces.gov.harvard.edu.
Ansolabehere, S., 2010. CCES Common Content, 2010. http://hdl.handle. net/1902.1/17705. V3 [Version].

Ansolabehere, S., Hersh, E., 2012. Validation: What Big Data Reveal About Survey Misreporting and the Real Electorate. Paper Prepared for Presentation at the Society for Political Methodology Annual Meeting. Downloaded on May 29, 2013 from. http://polmeth.wustl.edu/media/Paper/hershpolmeth2012.pdf.

Bass, L.E., Casper, L.M., 2001. Impacting the political landscape: who registers and votes among naturalized Americans? Polit. Behav. 23 (2), 103–130.

Bird, K., Saalfeld, T., Wust, A.M. (Eds.), 2010. The Political Representation of Immigrants and Minorities: Voters, Parties and Parliaments in Liberal Democracies. Taylor & Francis, Hoboken, NJ.

CPS, 2011. Current Population Survey—March 2011 Detailed Tables: Table 10.1. Population by Sex, Age, Nativity, and U.S. Citizenship Status: 2011. Downloaded on December 11, 2013 from. http://www.census.gov/population/foreign/data/cps2011.html.

Census Bureau, 2012. Educational Attainment in the United States: 2009. Downloaded June 29, 2014 from. http://www.census.gov/prod/2012pubs/p20-566.pdf.

Census Bureau, 2013. Voting Age Population by Citizenship and Race (CVAP) Data File. Downloaded December 11, 2013 from: http://www.census.gov/rdo/data/voting_age_population_by_citizenship_and_race_cvap.html.

Census Bureau, 2014. Table B05003: Sex by Age by Nativity and Citizenship Status—Universe: Total Population, 2007–2011 American Community Survey 5-Year Estimates Downloaded June 27, 2014 from. http://factfinder2.census.gov/faces/nav/jsf/pages/download_center.xhtml.

DeSipio, L., 2011. Immigrant incorporation in an era of weak civic institutions: immigrant civic and political participation in the United States. Am. Behav. Sci. 55 (9), 1189.

Earnest, D.C., 2008. Old Nations, New Voters: Nationalism, Trans-nationalism, and Democracy in the Era of Globalization. SUNY Press, Albany NY.

FAIR (Federation for American Immigration Reform), 2004. Illegal Aliens in Elections and the Electoral College (2004). Downloaded on May 29, 2013 from: http://www.fairus.org/issue/illegal-aliens-in-elections-and-the-electoral-college.

Federal Election Commission, 2009. 2008 Official Presidential Election Results. Downloaded December 21, 2013 from. http://www.fec.gov/pubrec/fe2008/2008presgeresults.pdf.

Fund, J., von Spakovsky, H., 2012. Who's Counting?: How Fraudsters and Bureaucrats Put Your Vote at Risk. Encounter Books, New York, NY.

Hayduk, R., 2006. Democracy for All: Restoring Immigrant Voting Rights in the United States. Routledge, New York, NY.

Howard, M.M., 2009. The Politics of Citizenship in Europe. Cambridge, New York.

Immigration Policy Center, 2012. Chicken Little in the Voting Booth: the Non-existent Problem of Non-citizen Voter Fraud. Downloaded on May 3, 2013 from: http://www.immigrationpolicy.org/sites/default/files/docs/chicken_little_in_the_voting_071312.pdf.

Jacobs, D., 2001. Immigrants in a multicultural sphere: the case of Brussels. In: Rogers, A., Tille, J. (Eds.), Multicultural Policies and Modes of Citizenship in European Cities. Ashgate, Aldershot, UK.

Janoski, T., 2010. The Ironies of Citizenship: Naturalization and Integration in Industrialized Countries. Cambridge, New York.

Joppke, C., 2003. Citizenship between de- and re-ethnicization. Eur. J. Sociol. 44 (3), 429–458.

Mayer, A.K., 2011. Does education increase political participation? J. Polit. 73 (3), 633–645.

Munro, D., 2008. Integration through participation: non-citizen resident voting rights in an era of globalization. Int. Migr. Integr. 9, 43–80. http://dx.doi.org/10.1007/s12134-008-0047-y.

Rath, J., 1990. Voting rights. In: Layton-Henry, Z. (Ed.), The Political Rights of Migrant Workers in Western Europe. Sage Publications, London.

Rytina, N., 2012. Estimates of the Legal Permanent Resident Population in 2011. Population Estimates, DHS Office of Immigration Statistics. http://www.dhs.gov/xlibrary/assets/statistics/publications/ois_lpr_pe_2011.pdf. Downloaded May 28, 2013.

Song, S., 2009. Democracy and noncitizen voting rights. Citizsh. Stud. 13 (6), 607–620.

Von Spakovsky, H., 2012. The Problem of Non-citizen Voting. The Foundry: Conservative Policy News Blog from the Heritage Foundation. Downloaded May 3, 2013 from. http://blog.heritage.org/2012/07/20/the-problem-of-non-citizen-voting/.

READING 11

The Contextual Presidency
The Negative Shift in Presidential Immigration Rhetoric

By Damien Arthur and Joshua Woods

Party platforms from 1993 through 2008 show a positive approach to immigration policy. Presidential rhetoric, however, does not match the tone of the platforms. There are negative frames (illegality, criminality, terrorism, and economic threats) in nearly 50% of immigration speeches. We argue that social context motivates presidents to talk about immigration negatively. This analysis provides insight into rhetoric as responsive to context rather than a mechanism of power. We coded each speech on immigration from Presidents Bill Clinton, George W. Bush, and Barack Obama, and found statistically significant results that show that immigration rhetoric is more negative when certain social conditions are present.

Neustadt's (1991) claim that presidential power is the *power to persuade* highlights the expectation for what presidents are supposed to do with their rhetoric. The rhetoric is supposed to bring about a desired result. Therefore, the literature on presidential rhetoric often focuses upon what presidents attempt to accomplish with the use of their rhetoric (Smith 1983). Kernell (2007) maintains that presidents "go public" with their requests with the hope that it will translate into policies. The most celebrated studies research the presidents' ability to shape the agenda with what is discussed in the *State of the Union Addresses* (Cohen 1995; Edwards and Wood 1999), how presidents can influence Congress (Barrett 2005; Canes-Wrone 2004), how they can control what the media decides to report (Cohen 2008; Eshbaugh-Soha and Peake 2008), and how they are able to shape the bureaucracy (Whitford and Yates 2009), as well as their ability to influence

Damien Arthur and Joshua Woods, "The Contextual Presidency: The Negative Shift in Presidential Immigration Rhetoric," *Presidential Studies Quarterly*, vol. 43, no. 3, pp. 468-489. Copyright © 2013 by Center for the Study of the Presidency. Reprinted with permission. Provided by ProQuest LLC. All rights reserved.

how the public approves of their performance (Druckman and Holmes 2004; Edwards, 2003), how they can change attitudes and perspectives on public policies (Eshbaugh-Soha and Peake 2006), and how they can manipulate public opinion (Brace and Hinckley 1992; Edwards 2003; Welch 2000).

Presidential behavior is often situated within a social structure and incentivized by historical context. Beasley's (2006) edited volume on presidential immigration provides an interesting, qualitative look at how presidents have historically addressed immigration and used their rhetoric to frame the public's perception of immigrants. The contained essays point out, through selected case studies, how presidents have discussed specific immigrant groups as a positive, beneficial addition to American life while at the same time, in many contexts, repeatedly acting xenophobically and framing immigrants and the immigration process as detrimental.

The scope of this analysis is not to determine if presidents are effective with using their rhetoric to influence immigration policy, however. We simply looked at presidential party platforms to see how each president discussed their policy positions on immigration. These presidential preferences provided a baseline for the tone and content one could expect presidents to have in their immigration rhetoric. We used this understanding of each president's policy preferences for immigration to ascertain what other conditions or variables may influence the president to say something substantively different from that which was articulated in the party platform. As researchers, we need to step back and consider the impetus for negativity and themes in presidential rhetoric. We argue that the content of presidential rhetoric on salient issues such as immigration can often be determined by the context in which it is given rather than an autonomous entrepreneurial policy exposition advocated by the president (Cook 2002; Doherty 2007; Miroff 2003).

We argue that the negativity in immigration rhetoric, a highly salient and controversial policy, is more likely the result of the context in which presidents find themselves speaking (see Figure 11.1). Aside from Rottinghaus' (2006) study on public opinion, Peterson and Djupe's (2005) study on negative primary campaigns, and Wood's (2007) study of presidential rhetoric and the tone of the economy, as well as Hart's (1987) analysis of rhetorical leadership, a literature on the rhetoric of modern and conspicuous policies as shaped by context has not been fully developed, especially given the rise in the salience of immigration by the public and the media. Zarefsky's (2004) assessment of presidential rhetoric says that it is theoretically possible that presidents pay attention to the context of their speeches but does not provide substantial empirical analysis that addresses the issue. As scholarship develops, more emphasis needs to be placed on studying the antecedent conditions of presidential speeches. We argue that ascertaining what conditions can motivate presidents to discuss immigration so negatively needs further inquiry, particularly since the president-controlled party platforms are so positive. Further, providing analyses that correlates specific conditions with negative presidential immigration rhetoric will add to the literature that treats rhetoric as fastidiousness and furthers presidential studies. Therefore, this study provides a noteworthy look into the inducements of presidential immigration

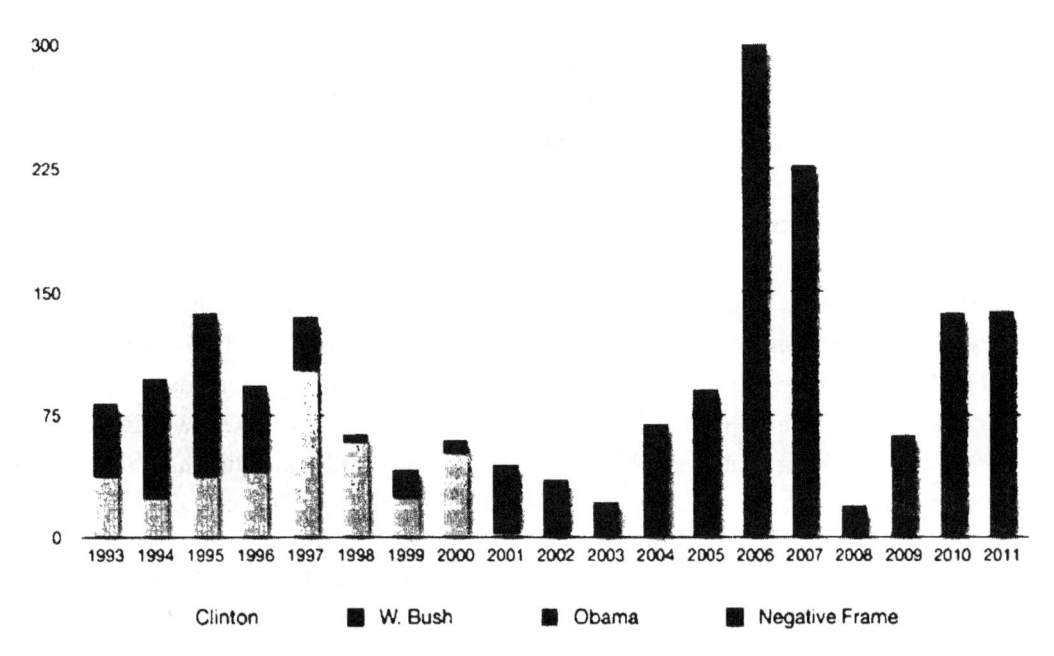

Figure 11.1 Presidential Speeches on Immigration Differentiated by Year and the Presence of a Negative Frame.

rhetoric, rather than the more common instances wherein it is seen as a mechanism of power or a tool through which presidents accomplish their goals (Canes-Wrone 2004; Woods 2007).

We, however, want to ascertain how specific circumstances are able to predict the negativity in the immigration frames in presidential rhetoric. Such an assessment will offer insight into the motivations and conditions that surround presidential rhetoric on such a consequential topic like immigration. This study, using multimethod analyses, offers findings that demonstrate correlation between the presence of specific conditions and the presence of negative immigration frames in presidential rhetoric. We begin the article by explaining the theoretical framework and hypotheses justifications. Next, we discuss the statistical model wherein we used the *American Presidency Project* to determine the presidential speeches by keyword from January 20, 1993, through November 7, 2011, and the strong predictors of negativity that accompany the rhetoric. We provide a discussion of the significance of our findings and future analysis of the context of presidential rhetoric.

Theoretical Framework

As Rottinghaus (2006) stated, presidents tailor their policy statements on salient issues to match the majority public opinion polls. Maintaining this "rhetorical congruency" with public opinion enables the president to strategically connect to the public (Canes-Wrone and Shotts 2004). The president is familiar with the national circumstances that engender the tone of the discussion of immigration by elite policy makers and the public. The public's negativity toward immigration saw a 20% increase directly after 9/11, from 38% to 58% (Woods and Arthur forthcoming). The public's concern over "illegal immigration" also saw an increase (28 to 45) of nearly 20% after 9/11 (Segovia and Defever 2010). The economy before 9/11 is considered to be one of the largest expansions in history. The economy, after the attacks on 9/11, seriously slowed down and nearly collapsed into a depression in 2008.

Presidents tailor their message to specific groups in geographical areas in order to influence the coverage of themselves in local newspapers, which can help their ability to lead the public on issues of pertinence to that group (Cohen 2010). Before 9/11, the president's approval rating ranged from 36% to 71%. In the years following 9/11, the president's approval rating ranged from 89% to 25% (Woolley and Peters 2013). Moreover, the majority party in congressional government changed during the administrations of Bill Clinton, George W. Bush, and Barack Obama. Therefore, we maintain that it is pertinent to ascertain if the context in which the president discusses immigration has the potential to predict the presence of negative rhetoric on a consequential topic of public policy such as immigration.

The Period before or after 9/11 as a Predictor of Negative Framing

The attacks on 9/11 and the fear of terrorism hardened public attitudes toward immigrants and encouraged negative stories about those who could be classified as non-American in the news media (Woods and Arthur forthcoming). The most recent economic crisis only added to the public's sense of insecurity and further encouraged the negative reactions that transpired. There is research that argues that 9/11 had a substantial impact upon how the public perceives, and the media portrays, those considered outsiders (DeParle 2011; Golash-Boza 2009; Segovia and Defever 2010; Woods and Arthur forthcoming). The fear and threat of terrorism causes the public and the government to restrict outsiders' access to public life. Pyszczynski, Greenberg, and Solomon (2003) maintain that threats to the status quo cause a rejection of outsiders. Threats can enable groups to use negative stereotypes to frame the image of those they consider outsiders, causing a transformation of the immigrant narrative (Adorno et al. 1950). When the threat of terrorism is coupled with the immigrant threat narrative, the conversation about immigration policy is different after 9/11, particularly in the news, media, and the public (Andreas 2002; Elliot 2011; Shenon 2003). However, little research has investigated whether the shift in negativity that occurred in the media and the public can be found in the rhetoric of government actors, particularly in the speeches that presidents give on immigration.

> H_1: It is significantly more likely that presidential rhetoric after 9/11 will have a negative immigration frame.

Economic Indicators as a Predictor of Negative Framing

Cohen (1995) claims that the public attention to a weak economy can draw negative attention to the president. Economic indicators provide a direct correlation to reelection and presidential approval

(Wood 2007). When the economy does not do well, the public typically holds the president accountable for this, whether through approval ratings, midterm elections, and/or his reelection. As Edwards and Wayne (1985) maintain, the presidents' responsibilities toward the economy have increased, but their abilities to meet those expectations have decreased. According to Gallup's "Most Important Problem" list, the economy or an economic issue, such as unemployment, tops the list nearly every year since 1936 (Dolan, Frendreis, and Tatalovich 2008). The Gallup Poll of presidential approval ratings can be correlated to economic performance. In other words, when the economy is doing well, Americans say that the president is doing his job well. The inverse is also true; when the economy is doing poorly, Americans say that the president is doing his job poorly.

Nonetheless, when economic indicators are not where the presidents think they need to be, they often attempt to refocus the public's attention from the economy and direct it toward something that can rally constituency support (Baum 2002; Wood 2009). Doing what is politically viable is the best economic strategy (Edwards and Wayne 1985). Given the public's sentiment toward immigration, the presidents know that immigration "saber-rattling" can create the "rally" effect they need to boost approval ratings, their reelection, or policy proposal successes (Wood 2009).

Therefore, we maintain that when the economic indicators (unemployment, inflation rate, gross domestic product [GDP]) are at levels that are not conducive to the presidents' plans, they discuss immigration negatively in order to refocus the public's attention. In other words, presidents are going to be more negative about immigration when unemployment is high, which enables them to blame immigration policies and immigrants for the rise in unemployment. The same is true when the inflation rate increases. Moreover, as the GDP decreases, presidents will resort to the aforementioned. We have chosen these economic indicators because they are those that best represent the health of the overall economy (Dolan, Frendreis, and Tatalovich 2008).

> H_2: The strength of the economy when the speech was given will make a significant difference in the frequency of negative immigration frames used in presidential rhetoric.

Geographical Location of Speech as a Predictor of Negative Framing

Cohen (2010) maintains that "going public" is not effective, and presidents have recognized this in recent years, particularly the going national element of his argument. He argues that there has been a steady change in the presidential leadership strategies due to the changing circumstances in which they find themselves governing. These circumstances have caused alterations in presidential behavior. Cohen avers that there are two main transitions in presidential governance. The first transition consists of what he calls "institutional pluralism (1940s to 1970s) to individual pluralism (1970s-mid-1980s)" (2010, 3). This transition is the movement from presidential appeals to the leaders (committee chairs) in

Congress to appeals to the public. The president knew that those members of Congress could mobilize their members to accomplish what the president wanted (Cohen 2010). The problem, however, was that the institutional power of those committee members diminished tremendously so the president was forced to "go public" with his proposals (Cohen 2010).

The second transition goes from "individual pluralism to the current era of polarized parties and fragmented media (mid-1980s-present)" (Cohen 2010, 3). Cohen (2010) maintains that during the 1980s, the president began losing his influence with the mass media. They were less likely to provide him with the airtime necessary to promote his programs and policies to the public. Such actions seriously limited his ability to "go public" in the same capacity. Moreover, during this time, there has been an increase in divided government and party polarization. The two major parties are becoming more partisan and less likely to work together on policy compromise.

The increasingly constraining circumstances imposed upon presidents, according to Cohen, have forced them to change their "going public" strategy to "going narrow" in local venues (2010, 4). In other words, he argues that presidents think they can influence the coverage of themselves in local newspapers, which can help their ability to lead the public. Essentially, Cohen maintains that the data show that presidents have simply adjusted their behavior to meet the demands/expectations of their office by appealing to their "party base, interest groups, and opinion in localities" (2010, 4). Therefore, we maintain that presidents will go to the regions, states, and localities that face questions and issues dealing with immigration as well as those areas that they believe will be the most receptive to their messages about immigration, particularly during elections (Hart 1987). In other words, presidents are going to be more negative about immigration in states that border Mexico.

> H_3: The geographical location/state will make a significant difference in the frequency of negative immigration frames used in presidential rhetoric.

Control Variables for Analysis of Negative Presidential Frames

The three hypothesis presented above are the primary justifications for the analysis; however, we also consider how the negativity differs among the control variables: whether or not there was an election transpiring, whether or not the audience to which the president is speaking has a vested interest in immigrants or immigration, the major political parties, the type of speech given, how the discussion of the different type of immigrant groups contribute to the negativity, how the make-up of government contributes, how the presidents' approval ratings play a role, whether there is a recession, and how the presidents' calls for congressional action affect negativity and the type of negative frames present.

Brace and Hinckley (1992) state that presidents "go public" because of the declining party mechanisms. The president cannot form coalitions with Congress any longer. Ragsdale (1987) found that the differentiation of speeches could determine effectiveness. The 2004 and 2008 Republican party platforms discuss how immigration policy is connected to Mexican border security, weapons of mass destruction, and illegal migrants, as well as drug contraband and terrorism (Woolley and Peters, 2013). Canes-Wrone (2006) argues that the presence or absence of divided government or unified government can significantly influence presidential success in legislative outcomes. Canes-Wrone and de Marchi (2002) argue that presidents seek to make their approval ratings higher because it will provide them with the opportunity to secure more policy success. Calling on Congress to take action is an attempt to give the presidents more legislative power and to help them accomplish goals (Kernell 2007). Canes-Wrone and de Marchi's (2002) research justifies including all of these variables in the analysis.

Given the importance of these variables in prior research, we investigate their influence on the negative framing of immigration in presidential rhetoric with the following research questions:

Research Question 1: Does the type of audience, those with or without a vested interest in immigration or immigrants, the president is addressing make a significant difference in the frequency of negative immigration frames used in their rhetoric?

Research Question 2: Does it make a significant difference in the frequency of negative immigration frames used in the presidential rhetoric when there is an election transpiring, midterm or presidential?

Research Question 3: Does the type of speech given by the president make a significant difference in the frequency of negative immigration frames used in their rhetoric?

Research Question 4: Does the social identification of those involved in the immigration system mentioned in the speech make a significant difference in the frequency of negative immigration frames used in presidential rhetoric?

Research Question 5: Does the make-up of who is in control of the government make a significant difference in the frequency of negative immigration frames used in presidential rhetoric?

Research Question 6: Does the presidents' approval rating make a significant difference in the frequency of negative immigration frames used in presidential rhetoric?

Research Question 7: When the presidents propose legislation to address immigration, does it make a significant difference in the frequency of negative immigration frames used in presidential rhetoric?

Research Question 8: Does it make a significant difference in the frequency of negative immigration frames used in presidential rhetoric when the presidents mention reforming the immigration process?

Empirical Design/Model

This analysis was conducted to determine whether the conditions surrounding Presidents Clinton, Bush, and Obama, at the time of their speeches on immigration, are capable of predicting how they discuss immigration and the narratives framed in their rhetoric. We have selected these administrations because their speeches and the data they provide will give us an accurate narrative of the negative conversations of U.S. immigration policy before and after 9/11.

Independent Variables

Each presidential mention of immigration was coded with 13 variables, including

- whether the speech was made before 9/11 or after (1 = after; 0 = before)
- the audience the president is addressing (1 = groups with a vested interest in immigration or immigrants; 0 = groups with no apparently vested interest in immigration or immigrants)
- whether or not there was an election transpiring when the speech was given (1 = election year; 0 = no election year and 1 = midterm election; 0 = no midterm election)
- divided government (1 = president and Congress are a *different* party; 0 = president and Congress are the *same* party)
- Chamber control (House—1 = Democrat; 2 = Republican) & (Senate[1]—1 = Democrat; 2 = Republican)
- the approval rating of the president the day before the speech (expressed as a percentage = 0 % to 100%)
- type of speech given (1 = news conference; 2 = town hall meeting; 3 = other (written, proclamations, radio addresses); 4 = major speech (televised); 5 = interview; 6 = remarks, whether the president proposed legislation dealing with immigration (1 = yes; 0 = no)
- whether there was a recession happening (1 = yes; 0 = no), the unemployment rate (continuous variable expressed in percentage)
- the inflation rate (continuous variable expressed in percentage)
- the GDP (continuous variable expressed in billions of chained dollars)
- the social identifiers (1= Mexico, Central America, Caribbean, South America [also Latino or Hispanic]; 2 = Europe; 3 = Asia; 4 = Africa; 5 = Arab/Middle East; 6 = Oceania; 7 = Canada; 8 = none mentioned)
- the geographical area wherein the speech was given (1 = Northeast; 2 = South; 3 = Midwest; 4 = West; 5 = DC; 6 = outside of the United States)[2]
- whether or not the president mentioned reforming the immigration process (1 = immigration reform; 0 = reform not mentioned)
- whether the speech was given in a border state (1 = yes; 0 = no).

Each continuous variable in the analysis was recoded into a dummy variable so as not to bias the results.

Dependent Variable

We used the *American Presidency Project* to determine the presidential speeches by keyword from January 20, 1993, through November 7, 2011. The *American Presidency Project* is a digital search technology that allowed us to search the *Public Papers of the President.* This enabled us to create a document of the compiled rhetoric of when and how the presidents negatively address immigration. As other scholars have done, we did not use content analysis software to compile and categorize the language, but instead we used human coding accompanied by a detailed and systematic codebook so that this study could be replicated in the future (Barrett 2004, 2005; Cameron 2000; Woods and Arthur forthcoming).

Many of the speeches mention "immigration" multiple times. Therefore, the word "immigration" was our coding trigger and the *day* is the unit of analysis. In many instances, there are different social identifiers or negative frames in the same thought that includes the word "immigration" in the speech. For instance, a speech might mention "immigration" and "Mexico" and "securing the borders" from "terrorists" and "drug cartels" as well as discuss the "Canadian border" and the issue of "illegality." In such an instance, the coding was consistently treated in the same fashion: we took the closest coding trigger for each mention of "immigration" in the speech. We broke each mention of "immigration" into as many separate recording units that the speech included, one for each "immigration" word mentioned. In total, 1850 recording units were found in the 769 speeches from January 20, 1993 through November 7, 2011.

For each mention of "immigration," we coded the presence of a negative frame. To accomplish this, we created the dependent variable: presence of negative frame (0 or 1). The outcome variable is dichotomous, wherein "1" represents at least one negative immigration frame was present. The "0" will represent no negative immigration frame in the mention of immigration. The negative frames are defined as illegality, criminality, terrorism, or economic threats (Woods and Arthur forthcoming). The first negative frame is the legal status of immigrants. Discussing immigration and immigrants within the framework of legality produces an "us" verses "them" mentality that constructs an image of immigrants that are "illegally" in the United States, one that questions their legitimacy. The second framework is that of criminality. Associating immigrants as those who have committed crimes, such as drugs, violence, or theft, differentiate this from the aforementioned. This narrative constructs a reality that portrays immigrants as something to be feared or threatening to the equilibrium of society. The third framework has to do with terrorism and how it relates to immigration policy and immigrants. Such a framework creates a rhetorically constructed reality wherein immigrants are seen as terrorists or threats to national security. The fourth framework has to do with the notion that immigrants pose a threat to the economic stability of the United States.

This rhetorically constructed framework is one where immigrants are seen as taking jobs and economic security from U.S. citizens.

Reliability of Coding

Testing the reliability of the data was a significant concern for the researchers. We employed standard intercoder agreement tests on all the variables using roughly 30% of the total units. The percentage of agreement on the 11 variables ranged from 86% to 100%. We used *Scott's Pi,* which corrects for chance agreement. It ranged from .78 to .95 on the variables. According to Riffe, Lacy, and Fico (2005), this measure is a better method to determine reliability. We used alpha levels of .80 or higher as the measure of significant reliability (Krippendorff 1978).

Testing the reliability of negative frames involved two well-trained coders who spent many hours perfecting this method. One might state that such well-trained coders would, in fact, tailor their interpretations to ensure reliability. Therefore, providing statistical validation of intercoder reliability does not prove that others would come to the same conclusions, as did the trained coders. In order to control for this, we carried out an additional reliability assessment using 12 coders who received only minimal training on how to code the content according to the codebook and protocol. These tests showed that a very high level of intersubjectivity exists on each of the issues in the codebook. The average percentage of agreement among the 12 coders was roughly 92% on mentions of illegality, 98% on criminal acts, 98% on references to terrorism, and 94% on mentions of immigrants as economic threats.

Measurement

This analysis will determine the difference in the frequency of negative frames in the presidents' "immigration" rhetoric before 9/11 and the negative "immigration" rhetoric after 9/11. Analyzing the data in this way will allow us to determine the shift in negativity that transpired. The dependent variable is the type of negative frame in presidential rhetoric addressing immigration. In order to determine how the independent and control variables predict the frequency of negative frames per recording unit, we dichotomized a variable so that each mention of immigration either had or did not have a negative frame for that unit. The variable enabled us to create various pertinent measures of percentages and bivariate relationships with the other independent variables.

The logistic regression model predicts the frequency with which negative frames were used. Moreover, by using the logistic regression analyses, we model and graph the predicted probabilities that the independent variables can have on the frequency of negative immigration frames in presidential rhetoric. We want to determine if the predictors (before 9/11 or after, the unemployment rate, the inflation rate, the GDP, and the geographical area wherein the speech was given) can predict the frequency with which negative frames were used. Such an analysis enabled us to obtain the probability that the control variables (elections, audience, presidential party, divided government, the approval rating of the president, type of speech given, whether the president proposed legislation, whether there was a recession, and the social identifiers) will change the frequency with which negative frames were used in presidential rhetoric.

Findings/Results

To try and find the predicted probability of the specific indicators on the presence of negative frames in the immigration rhetoric of Presidents Clinton, Bush, and Obama, a Logistic Regression Analysis was performed. The Logistic Regression Analysis uses a *Maximum Likelihood Estimator,* an iterative method that measures the effect of the predictor variables on the tone of immigration rhetoric. Tables 11.1 and 11.2 present the coefficients, odds ratios, and *p*-values as well as the standard errors and the measures of fit. The model, overall, is in line with the hypotheses; the predictor variables in this analysis significantly affect whether the president uses negative immigration frames in his rhetoric. Moreover, the log likelihood chi-squared values prove that the model will allow for a rejection of the null; it is highly significant that the model we have created works better than one with no predictors.

TABLE 11.1 Summary of Logistic Regression Analysis (logit) for Variables Predicting Negativity in Presidential Immigration Rhetoric

Dependent Variable: Pr (Success = 1) N = 1850				
Log Likelihood—1149.6984			χ^2 = 239.91 (p < .0000)	
	Coefficients	Odds Ratios	*p* Values	Standard Errors
Period	2.736	15.43	.000	.4079
Border State	.7200	2.054	.001	.2266
Mexico	.4325	1.541	.003	.1463
Africa	1.659	5.252	.003	.5652
Middle East	−.1183	.8885	.935	1.459
Europe	−1.063	.3455	.049	.5409
Recession	.3535	1.424	.175	.2604
Inflation Rate	.1819	1.203	.016	.0770
Unemployment	.0514	1.053	.276	.0472
Gross Domestic Product	−.0009	.9991	.000	.0001

TABLE 11.2 Summary of Logistic Regression Analysis (logit) for Variables Predicting Negativity in Presidential Immigration Rhetoric

Dependent Variable: Pr (Success = 1)
N = 1850

Log Likelihood—1149.6984			χ^2 = 239.97 (p < .0000)	
	Coefficients	Odds Ratios	p Values	Standard Errors
Proposed legislation	.4393	1.552	.000	.1255
Approval Ratings	−.0191	.9808	.011	.0077
Major Speech	1.156	3.176	.001	.3357
Divided Government	−.1881	.8283	.331	.1919
Audience	−.2774	.7577	.030	.1276
Election Year	−.0214	.9788	.902	.1742
Midterm Election	.1472	1.159	.461	.1997
Democrat House	.0012	1.001	.997	.3007
Democrat Sen.	−.3318	.7177	.278	.3059
Republican House	−.0012	.9989	.997	.3007
Republican Senate	.3317	1.393	.278	.3059
Reform	.0236	1.024	.861	.1383

A one unit change in the presence of a negative frame (0 = no negative frame to a 1 = a negative frame), in our analysis of 1,850 units, shows that it does make a significant difference in the frequency of negative immigration frames when considering our predictor variables. The log odds of a negative frame occurring after 9/11 (versus before 9/11) increases by 2.736. Confirming Hypothesis 1, it is significantly more likely that presidential rhetoric after 9/11 will have a negative immigration frame. In fact, when the presidents discuss immigration after 9/11, the presence of a negative frame increased by a factor of 15.43. This was highly significant, both statistically and in terms of the magnitude of the odds ratio (see Figure 11.2).

During the Clinton administration, the percentage of the rhetoric with negative frames actually increased until his first midterm election. For 1993 through 1996, President Clinton's overall "immigration" rhetoric was negative over 50% of the time, topping 70% in 1994 and 1995. He was not as negative for the rest of this administration, however, with the exception of 41% negativity in 1999. For instance, in 1998 only about 8% of his rhetoric was negative. Moreover, in 1995 and 1996, over 45% of his "immigration" mentions discussed the illegality frame. After the midterms, his use of negative frames dropped significantly. There were similar numbers in 1997 (25%) and 2000 (14%). There was a slight increase, however, in 1999; about 40% of his rhetoric was negative. President Clinton rarely mentions the other negative frames, with two exceptions. In 1995, 17% of his "immigration"

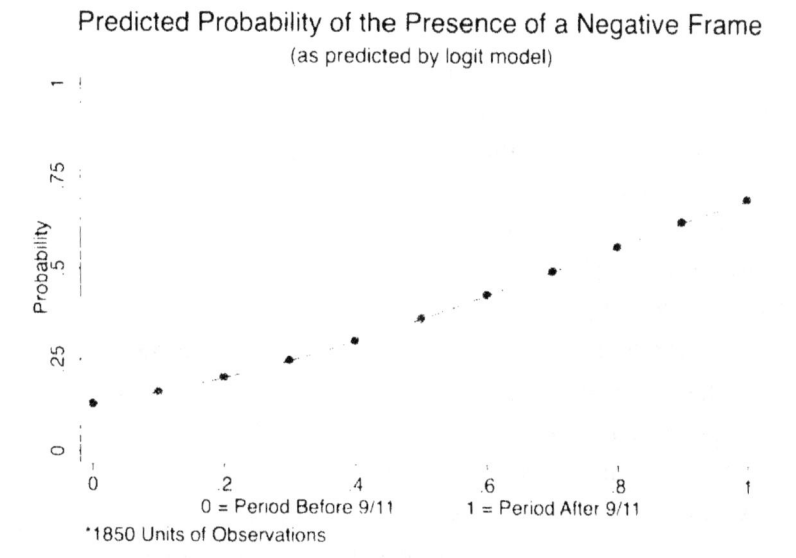

Predicted Probability of the Presence of a Negative Frame
(as predicted by logit model)

0 = Period Before 9/11   1 = Period After 9/11
1850 Units of Observations

Figure 11.2 Presence of a Negative Frame in Presidential Rhetoric as a Result of the Period in which the Speech was Given.

rhetoric mentioned the criminality frame, which was 28% of all criminality frames for each president. Moreover, in 1994, 34% of his "immigration" rhetoric mentioned the economic threat frame, which was nearly 45% of the total economic threat frames for all presidents.

President Clinton had to address the issue that was transpiring in Haiti when he assumed office, which created a significant amount of Haitian refugees in 1994. One may assume that this would account for some of this negativity. In order to correct our model to account for this suggestion, we removed all observations wherein President Clinton was addressing Haitians. We had already, as our model shows, accounted for the social identification of the immigrant community discussed by the president in each speech. This accounted for 23 observations of presidential rhetoric. According to our model, 10 of the 23 observations were negative, which is about 44% of presidential mentions are negative when addressing Haitians. We ran the same regressions for each model, one that included rhetoric that addressed Haitians and another model that did not include rhetoric that addressed Haitians. There were no statistical differences in the substantive effects of the regressions.

In 1995, this number was about 10% of his "immigration" rhetoric, which was nearly 18% of all economic threat frames. We speculate that the budget battle of 1996 and the opposition Congress that President Clinton faced, after the midterm elections, engendered the perfect opportunity for presidential rhetoric to be responsive to context rather than create entrepreneurial meaning. Most importantly, however, we argue that the backlash President Clinton is facing from the signing of the North American Free Trade Agreement (NAFTA) increases the likelihood that he mentions NAFTA and immigration together. On multiple occasions, President Clinton, in his rhetoric, is responding to the criticisms of NAFTA and argues that it will significantly decrease the amount of "illegal" immigrants who come to America. In fact, he claims that NAFTA will or has created the type of economic growth in Mexico that will lead to the slowing of "illegal" immigration, which, in turn, will keep "legal" immigration running smoothly. These conditions motivated him to deviate from the tone of his party platform. Given the decreasing percentage of negative frames and the lack of mentions of NAFTA in his rhetoric after 1996, one has to consider this rationale.

During the second Bush administration, the trend of negative immigration rhetoric changes, significantly. The negativity in his rhetoric is consistently over 30%, until 2008 where it was 21%. His negativity peaked in 2004 (52%), 2005 (69%), and 2006 (52%). The year 2006 accounts for about 20% of the total negative rhetoric for all of the presidents. For instance, about 39% of Bush's "immigration" rhetoric used the negative frame terrorism in his first year in office. The percentage dropped slightly in 2002 (29%), 2003 (29%), and 2004 (23%), before rising again in 2005 (34%), right before the midterm elections. There was a steady decline in the terrorism frame in 2006 (25%), 2007 (13%), and 2008 (10%). In 2006, however, President Bush used the terrorism frame 74 times, which is about 39% of the total terrorism frames for all of the presidents in this study. The next closest negative frame President Bush used regularly was the illegality frame, in 2004 (20%), 2005 (26%), and 2006 (26%). In 2006, he used this frame the most, 77 times, which is almost 17% of the total illegality mentions for all of the presidents.

Directly after 9/11, the president's approval rating and image as a leader was unparalleled. His approval topped 85% at one point. The president did not need to remind the public of 9/11 directly after the event to garner any support for his policies, particularly the largest reorganization of American bureaucracy since the Department of Defense. Again, his approval rating was still high in 2003 (70% at some points), the Republican Party took the House and Senate, which gave them unified government, and he initiated the invasion of Iraq; the conditions were not conducive to negative rhetoric. However, the conditions in which President Bush found himself governing began to change in 2004 and 2005, and after his second election. The context had changed; his approval ratings were dropping (36%), people were growing weary of the wars, and the midterm elections were nearing. This context is where we start to see the increase in President Bush's negativity. For instance, we do not see the negative frames of terrorism and illegality reaching their peak until 2006. We observe President Bush increase his usage of the negative frames the closer he gets to the 2006 midterm elections, wherein the Republicans are expecting to lose many House and Senate seats. As President Bush's conditions changed, the perfect context was created for presidential rhetoric to respond to externalities rather than set or create new agendas. The deviations from the tone of his first party platform are a result of the aforementioned context, which gave rise to the negative 2004 party platform.

The negativity in President Obama's rhetoric was higher than expected, given the language his administration used in the party platform. This is the first platform to move away from language that addresses immigrants as "illegal" and begins referring to them as "undocumented." His total "immigration" rhetoric was negative, however, over 25% for 2009 (30%), 2010 (40%), and 2011 (26%). The negative frames used by President Obama change significantly from that of the Bush administration. This change transpires, primarily, in the use of terrorism frames. President Obama only uses the terrorism frame once from 2009 through 2011. Moreover, he uses about 18% of the total economic threat frames. One might speculate that his use of the economic threat frame is a response to the economic crisis he encountered upon entering the presidency. President Obama's use of the illegality frame, in 2009 (24%), 2010 (37%), and 2011 (18%), is similar to the other presidents in that it decreases the longer they are in office, with the exception of the midterm elections. This is surprising given his party platform and his massive push for the Dream Act legislation that changes U.S. policy toward so many immigrants.

Hypothesis 2 is mostly supported by the data. The strength of the economy makes it more likely that there is a significant difference in the frequency of negative immigration frames. The indicators consist of the inflation rate, the unemployment rate, and the GDP (Dolan, Frendreis, and Tatalovich 2008; Wood 2007). When the inflation rate increases by .1849, the presence of a negative frame increases by a factor of 1.203. This is exactly what we would expect it to do. When the purchasing power of the public is mitigated, they want action from the president (Beck 1982). When the unemployment rate decreases by .052, the president becomes more negative. This is not, on the surface, what one would expect the president to do. In other words, one would expect the president to become more negative as the unemployment rate *increased*. High unemployment is detrimental to presidential reelections. We speculate that low unemployment might keep the president from "rattling the immigration saber" and securing his policy goals (Wood 2009). Nonetheless, the presence of a negative frame in his rhetoric increases by factor of 1.053 when this economic indicator decreases. The result was not statistically significant, however.

When the GDP decreases, the president is more negative in his discussion of immigration; in fact, the presence of a negative frame in his immigration rhetoric increases by a factor of .999. Again, this is exactly what one would expect (see Figure 11.3). If the GDP decreases too much, the United States slips into a recession, which is consequential for an incumbent president (Dolan, Frendreis, and Tatalovich 2008). The indicators that determine the health of the economy provide the context to which the president responds. These indicators of the economy's health are essential to the presidents' goals (Baum 2002). The president needs someone or something to blame for the economy's decline. If the indicators are doing poorly, the president has to refocus the public's attention from that which may lead them to not vote for the president or the incumbent's party. Given the public's sentiment toward immigration, the presidents know that immigration "saber-rattling" can create the "rally" effect they need to boost approval ratings, their reelection, or policy proposal successes (Wood 2009).

Hypothesis 3 is also supported by the data and the analysis. It is more likely that the geographical location/state will make a significant difference in the frequency of negative immigration frames used in presidential rhetoric. In other words, for every one-unit change in whether the speech occurred in

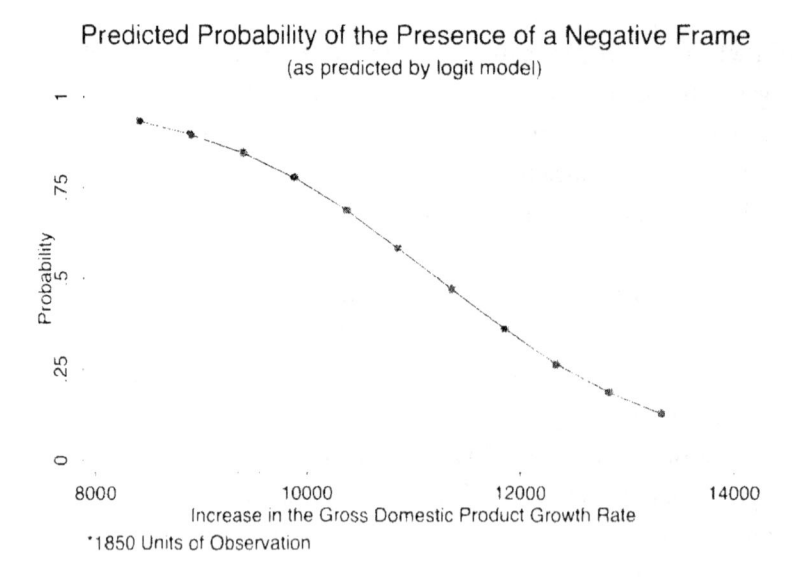

Predicted Probability of the Presence of a Negative Frame
(as predicted by logit model)

Figure 11.3 The Presence of a Negative Frame in Presidential Rhetoric as a Result of the Gross Domestic Product Growth Rate when the Speech was Given.

a state that borders Mexico, the odds of it being negative toward immigrants increase by a factor of 1.541. However, the majority of the negative frames (507) presidents used occurred while they were in Washington, DC. Slightly over half of the negative frames (156) used outside of DC occurred while they were in a state that bordered Mexico.

Moreover, of the 95 negative frames that were given while the president was in the south, 80 of those mentions took place in Texas, which borders Mexico. Presidents are more negative while they are in DC, but they are in DC more often than they are anywhere else. Moreover, given the rhetoric about "border security" that transpired after 9/11, we find it profoundly interesting that Canada is mentioned only once, December 31, 2001. It did have a negative terrorism frame attached to the mention, however. This led us to question why the Bush administration focused so much of its terrorism/ immigration/border security rhetoric on only one of the borders in the United States, namely, Mexico.

In regard to the research questions, there is statistical significance for many of the variables in the model. In the first question, we were concerned with the audience that the president addressed. We identified those groups/audiences that are closely tied to immigrants and immigration, those groups that have a direct and substantial interest in making sure that immigrants are treated positively and that the immigration process works well for those that are trying to migrate to the United States. We identified these groups by their mission statements. Not conducting the analysis in this way would mean that every group the president addresses has a vested interest so there would be no variation, and the "audience" would not matter, particularly given that presidents have a great deal of say in the audiences they address. We determined that when the president addresses these groups, he is less negative about immigration. In fact, when presidents address these groups, the negativity in their speeches decreases by a factor .7577, which is, again, evidence that the context in which the president speaks has an impact on the tone of their speeches about salient policy topics. We thought it interesting to note that presidents speak to these groups far more often when there is not an election year. This enables them to speak about immigration more authoritatively and negatively during the election when they are appealing to their bases and not performing the ceremonial obligations of the office of the presidency.

The second research question helped us ascertain whether or not the increase of negative rhetoric in an election year made a substantive difference. This addition provided a unique element to the analysis, particularly the substantive differences between the amount of negative frames in the presidents' rhetoric in the midterm elections and the general presidential elections. Of the 817 total negative frames in the presidents' rhetoric, 402 of them occurred during an election. Presidents are significantly more negative during the midterm elections (301 negative frames) than they are during the general presidential elections (101 negative frames). Our analysis, however, suggests that there is no statistically significant difference between the negativity in an election year or nonelection year. We speculate that presidents are simply trying to appeal to their party (ideological) bases during the midterms and are vying for the more moderate voters during the general presidential elections; again, this is another instance wherein presidents respond to their context.

The third research question addresses the type of speech the president gives when discussing immigration and how it matters for the amount of negativity present in the rhetoric. By far, the president mentions immigration more in his various remarks (989 total and 404 negative frames), interviews (146 total and 76 negative frames), and news conferences (173 total and 80 negative frames) as well as their written rhetoric (452 total and 204 negative frames), which is essential for establishing and maintaining an engendered environment of policy perspectives. However, the public is more likely to pay attention to their major speeches (49 total and 35 negative frames), the ones televised for extended periods of time. Therefore, we controlled for this in our analysis and found that the presence of a negative frame in presidential rhetoric in a major speech increases by a factor of 3.176 (see Figure 11.4).

The fourth question addresses the social identification of the immigrant mentioned in the speech. Our analysis found that it does make a significant difference in the frequency of negative immigration frames used in presidential rhetoric. We were concerned with what type of social identifications presidents would discuss negatively when considering immigration, particularly after 9/11. One might simply assume it would be Arabs/Middle Easterners, especially given the fact that the United States was involved in two large-scale wars after immigrants of Arab/Middle Eastern social identification used the immigration system to enter America and then commit terrorist attacks. Nonetheless, presidents only mentioned Arabs/Middle Easterners two different times and only one of those mentions

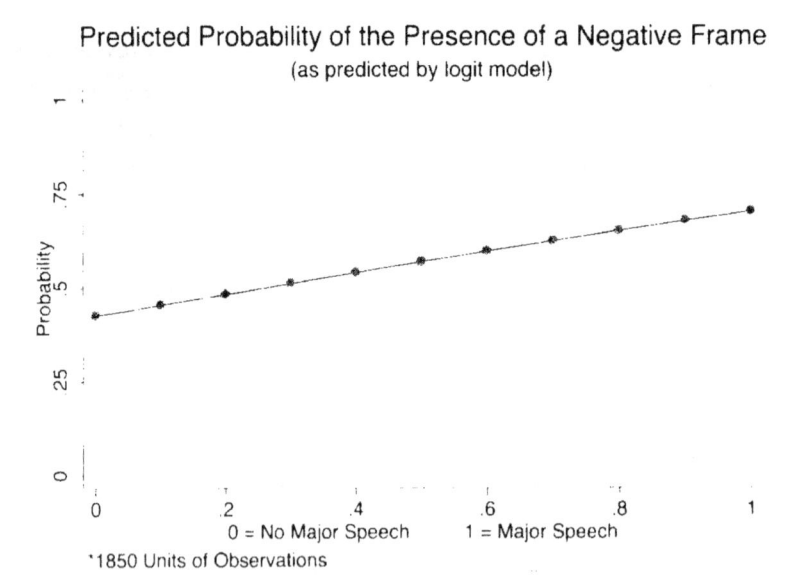

Predicted Probability of the Presence of a Negative Frame
(as predicted by logit model)

*1850 Units of Observations

Figure 11.4 The Presence of a Negative Frame in Presidential Rhetoric as a Result of the President Giving a Major Speech.

had a negative frame (terrorism) attached to it. In fact, however, presidents were mostly concerned with Mexico, Central America, and the Caribbean, as well as South America (also Latino or Hispanic). Presidents mention this social group 358 times, of which 176 mentions had a negative frame attached to it. In other words, when presidents mention Mexico, Central America, or Caribbean, as well as South America (also Latino or Hispanic), the presence of a negative frame attached to this social identification increased by a factor of 1.541. Interestingly, when presidents are discussing European immigrants, they are significantly less likely to use a negative frame in their rhetoric. In fact, the presence of a negative frame in their rhetoric decreases by a factor of .3445. Further, when presidents are discussing African immigrants, they are significantly more likely to use a negative frame in their rhetoric. In fact, the presence of a negative frame in their rhetoric increases by a factor of 5.252.

The fifth research question addresses the dynamics of congressional government and its relation to presidential rhetoric. Our research indicates that the party that is in control of Congress as well as whether there is divided government, particularly between congressional control and presidential control, does not have a significant effect on the frequency of negative immigration frames. There were more negative frames in presidential rhetoric during Republican control of the Senate (479) than in Democratic control of the Senate (338). Moreover, there were more negative frames in presidential rhetoric during Republican control of the House (549) than in Democratic control of the Senate (268). Nonetheless, presidents are more likely co use negative immigration frames when there is no divided government.

The sixth research question with which we were concerned addressed the presidents' approval ratings. Our analysis indicates that it does make a significant difference in the frequency of negative

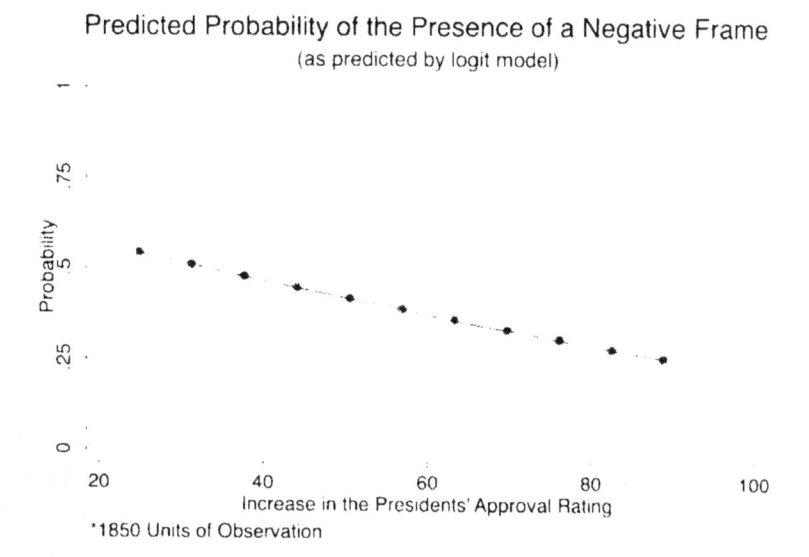

Predicted Probability of the Presence of a Negative Frame
(as predicted by logit model)

Figure 11.5 The Presence of a Negative Frame in Presidential Rhetoric as a Result of the Presidents' Approval Ratings.

immigration frames used in presidential rhetoric. In fact, when the presidents' approval-ratings decrease by 1 percentage point, presidents use more negative frames in their rhetoric. The reality is that the presence of a negative immigration frame in their rhetoric increases by a factor of .988 when approval-ratings decrease (see Figure 11.5).

The seventh research question we discussed addressed whether the presidents' proposed immigration legislation made a significant difference in the frequency of negative immigration frames used in presidential rhetoric. Our analysis indicates that when presidents propose legislation that addresses immigration, they use more negative frames in their rhetoric. In fact, the presence of a negative frame in their rhetoric increased by a factor of 1.552 when immigration legislation was proposed. We speculate that presidents are using the most dramatic and negative frames they can to try and convince Congress to pass legislation.

The eighth research question addressed whether the presidents' calls for immigration reforms made a significant difference in the frequency of negative immigration frames used in presidential rhetoric. Our analysis indicates that President Clinton did not specifically call for immigration reform during his time in office. There is essentially no mention of immigration policy reform until 2004 (18 mentions) and 2005 (29 mentions). There was a significant increase in mentions of immigration policy reform in 2006 (147 mentions) and 2007 (131 mentions), with a dramatic drop in 2008 (4 mentions). Again, there was a steady increase in the mentions of reform under the Obama administration in 2009 (44 mentions), 2010 (98 mentions), and 2011 (89 mentions).

However, when presidents mention reforming the immigration process, there was no statistical validity to the presence of more negative frames in their rhetoric. Nevertheless, presidents increased their rhetoric about immigration reform when others did the same. Interestingly, according to our analysis, presidents mention reforming the immigration process more often when they are speaking to audiences that do not have a vested interest in immigration policy or immigrants. There are 169 mentions of reform to groups that do have a vested interest and 289 mentions of reform to groups that have no vested interest, according to our measurement.

Conclusions

Little research has investigated whether the negative shift in the discussion of immigration that occurred in the media and public opinion can be found in the rhetoric of government actors, particularly in the speeches that presidents give on immigration (Woods and Arthur forthcoming). Therefore, the rationale for this study was to determine how certain conditions can motivate presidents to talk about immigration and provide a basis for future studies on the context of presidential rhetoric, particularly how specific contexts can alter or frame the conversation on salient policy discussions. We were able to gather this information and provide the analysis for over 750 speeches (1,850 units of analysis) from Presidents Clinton, Bush, and Obama. We examined several years of presidential rhetoric from before and after 9/11 and during the post-9/11 economic crisis in order to determine whether the presidents' discussion of immigration can be influenced by the context in which they find themselves speaking. It is clear that presidential rhetoric possessed more negative frames about the issue of immigration when certain conditions were present.

As shown earlier, there is a vast literature on presidential rhetoric as an independent variable. Speeches are conceptualized as attempts to set the agenda or accomplish some action or goal. Yet, the literature has not fully developed wherein scholars ascertain whether presidential rhetoric on immigration issues is responsive to a particular context. Our research suggests that presidents change the negativity of their rhetoric on immigration policy issues depending on when the speeches are given, where they are when they give the speech, and in response to externalities that they are mostly unable to control. In other words, presidents pay attention to the context in which they find themselves. They maintain a "rhetorical congruency" with public opinion, which enables them to strategically connect to the public (Canes-Wrone and Shotts 2004). In fact, they are responding to that very context, to other governmental actors, and to the public as well as the media and other special interests.

Presidents are not always setting the agenda or creating new meaning for and in the political process. As Miroff (2003) argues, they are to be seen in the framework of leadership rather than entrepreneurship. Skowronek (1997) says that this is true because the presidents are constrained by the institutional framework created by their predecessor and that their efforts at entrepreneurship are a part of a larger drama that is always evolving. Presidents are always struggling to gain control over the arrangements that are imposed upon them. Light asserts that presidents do not have time for new policy perspectives or an innovative agenda. The political process is too fragmented and competitive to accommodate another entrepreneur. His "derivative presidency" shows that president must use "old" policy ideas rather than create them anew (1999, 285). This forces presidents to try to accomplish their ideal goals, laid out in the party platform, by responding to the context in which they find themselves. Therefore, we argue that context sets the agenda rather than the presidents' entrepreneurial rhetoric.

Despite the fact that presidents define their party's approach to immigration with positivity, circumstances exist during their administrations that motivate/compel them to discuss immigration negatively. These findings necessitate further inquiry into the context surrounding presidential speeches on immigration and presidential speeches in general, particularly how they match the tone of their party platforms. We maintain that the implications from this analysis engender two questions that need further research.

Now that we know that the presence of certain conditions or control variables can predict the probability with which presidents will use a negative frame in their rhetoric to discuss immigration, we need to ascertain if the same context (conditions and control variables) can predict the type of negative frame (illegality, criminality, terrorism, economic threat) the president uses, not just the frequency of negative frames.

Future research should also consider what other salient policies for which this analysis would work. Considering that we only looked at one complex policy over three presidential administrations, the research agenda is widely open to consider how other salient policies were impacted by context and how it mattered for multiple other administrations in the *Rhetorical Presidency* (Tulis 1987). We look forward to ascertaining how context has influenced presidential rhetoric over time and in various other salient policies.

Notes

1. If the congressional chamber is tied, it is assumed that the vice president will vote along with his party to break the tie. Thus, whichever party the vice president is, that party is in the majority.

2. Each continuous variable in the analysis was recoded into a dummy variable so as not to bias the results.

References

Adorno, Theodor W., Else Frenkel-Brunswik, Daniel Levinson, and Nevitt Sandford. 1950. *The Authoritarian Personality, Studies in Prejudice Series*. Vol. 1. New York: Harper and Row.

Andreas, Peter. 2002. "The Re-Bordering of America after 11 September." *Brown Journal of World Affairs* 3 (2): 195–202.

Barrett, Andrew W. 2004. "Gone Public: The Impact of Going Public on Presidential Legislative Success." *American Politics Research,* 32 (3): 338–70.

Barrett, Andrew W. 2005. "Going Public as a Legislative Weapon: Measuring Presidential Appeals Regarding Specific Legislation." *Presidential Studies Quarterly* 35 (March): 1–10.

Baum, Matthew A. 2002. "The Constituent Foundations of the Rally-Round-the-Flag Phenomenon." *International Studies Quarterly* 46 (December): 263–98.

Beasley, Vanessa B. 2006. *Who Belongs in America? Presidents, Rhetoric, and Immigration.* College Station: Texas A&M University Press.

Beck, Nathaniel. 1982. "Presidential Influence on the Federal Reserve in the 1970s." *American Journal of Political Science,* 26 (3), 415–45.

Brace, Paul, and Barbara Hinckley. 1992. *Follow the Leader: Opinion Polls and the Modern Presidents.* New York: Basic Books.

Cameron, Charles. 2000. *Veto Bargaining: Presidents and the Politics of Negative Power.* New York: Cambridge University Press.

Canes-Wrone, Brandice. 2004. "The Public Presidency, Personal Approval Ratings, and Policy Making," *Presidential Studies Quarterly,* 34 (3): 477–90.

———. 2006. *Who Leads Whom? Presidents, Policy, and the Public.* Chicago: University of Chicago Press.

Canes-Wrone, Brandice, and Kenneth Shotts. 2004. "The Conditional Nature of PresidentialResponsiveness to Public Opinion." *American Journal of Political Science* 48 (4): 690–706.

Canes-Wrone, Brandice, and Scott de Marchi. 2002. "Presidential Approval and Legislative Success." *Journal of Politics* 64 (2): 491–509.

Cohen, Jeffrey. 1995. "Presidential Rhetoric and the Public Agenda." *American Journal of Political Science* 39 (February): 87–107.

———. 2008. *The Presidency in the Era of 24-Hour News.* Princeton, NJ: Princeton University Press.

———. 2010. *Going Local: Presidential Leadership in the Post-Broadcast Age.* New York: Cambridge University Press.

Cook, Corey. 2002. "The Contemporary Presidency": The Permanence of the "Permanent Campaign": George W. Bush's Public Presidency. *Presidential Studies Quarterly* 32 (4): 753–64.

DeParle, Jason. 2011. "The Anti-Immigration Crusader." *New York Times,* April 17.

Doherty, Brendan. 2007. "Elections: The Politics of the Permanent Campaign: Presidential Travel and the Electoral College, 1977–2004." *Presidential Studies Quarterly* 37 (4): 749–73.

Dolan, Chris, John Frendreis, and Raymond Tatalovich. 2008. *The Presidency and Economic Policy.* New York: Rowman and Littlefield.

Druckman, James, and Justin Holmes. 2004. "Does Presidential Rhetoric matter? Priming and Presidential Approval." *Presidential Studies Quarterly* 34 (December): 755–77.

Edwards III, George C. 2003. *On Deaf Ears: The Limits of the Bully Pulpit.* New Haven, CT: Yale University Press.

Edwards, George, and Stephen Wayne. 1985. *Presidential Leadership: Politics and Policy Making.* New York: St. Martin's Press.

Edwards III, George, and Dan Wood. 1999. "Who Influences Whom? The President, Congress, and the Media." *American Political Science Review* 93 (2): 327–44.

Elliot, Justin. 2011. Debunking the Latest Sharia Scare. *Salon,* April 2.

Eshbaugh-Soha, Matthew, and Jeffrey Peake. 2006. "The Contemporary Presidency: 'Going Local' to Reform Social Security." *Presidential Studies Quarterly* 36 (December): 689–704.

———. 2008. "The Presidency and Local Media: Local Newspaper Coverage of President George W. Bush." *Presidential Studies Quarterly* 38 (4): 609–31.

Golash-Boza, Tanya. 2009. "The Immigration Industrial Complex: Why We Enforce Immigration Policies Destined to Fail." *Sociology Compass* 3 (2): 295–309.

Hart, Roderick. 1987. *The Sound of Leadership: Presidential Communication in the Modern Age.* Chicago: University of Chicago Press.

Kernell, Samuel. 2007. *Going Public: New Strategies of Presidential Leadership.* 4th ed. Washington, DC: Congressional Quarterly Press.

Krippendorff, Klaus. 1978. "Reliability of Binary Attribute Data." *Biometrics* 34 (1): 142–44.

Light, Paul. 1999. *The President's Agenda: Domestic Policy Choice from Kennedy to Clinton.* Baltimore: Johns Hopkins University Press.

Miroff, Bruce. 2003. "Entrepreneurship and Leadership." *Studies in American Political Development* 17 (Fall): 204–11.

Neustadt, Richard. 1991. *Presidential Power and the Modern Presidents: The Politics of Leadership from Roosevelt to Reagan.* New York: The Free Press.

Peterson, David, and Paul Djupe. 2005. "When Primary Campaigns Go Negative: The Determinants of Campaign Negativity." *Political Research Quarterly* 58 (1): 45–54.

Pyszczynski, Thomas, Jeff Greenberg, and Sheldon Solomon. 2003. *In the Wake of 9/11: The Psychology of Terror.* Washington, DC: American Psychological Association.

Ragsdale, Lynn. 1987. "Presidential Speechmaking and the Public Audience: Individual Presidents and Group Attitudes." *Journal of Politics* 49 (August): 704–36.

Riffe, Dan, Stephen Lacy, and Frederick Fico. 2005. *Analyzing Media Messages: Using QuantitativeContent Analysis in Research.* Hillsdale, NJ: Erlbaum.

Rottinghaus, Brandon. 2006. "Rethinking Presidential Responsiveness: The Public Presidency and Rhetorical Congruency, 1953–2001." *Journal of Politics* 68 (3): 720–32.

Segovia, Francine, and Renatta Defever. 2010. "The Polls—Trends: American Public Opinion on Immigrants and Immigration Policy." *Public Opinion Quarterly* 74 (2): 375–94.

Shenon, Philip. 2003. "New Asylum Policy Comes Under Fire." *New York Times,* March 19.

Skowronek, Stephen. 1997. *The Politics Presidents Make: Leadership from John Adams to Bill Clinton.* Cambridge, MA: Belknap Press of Harvard University Press.

Smith, Craig. A. 1983. "The Audience of the 'Rhetorical Presidency': An Analysis of President-Constituent Interactions." *Presidential Studies Quarterly* 8 (Fall): 613–22.

Tulis, Jeffrey. 1987. *The Rhetorical Presidency.* Princeton, NJ: Princeton University Press.

Welch, Reed. 2000. "Is Anybody Watching? The Audience for Televised Presidential Addresses." *Congress and the Presidency* 27 (March): 41–58.

Whitford, Andrew, and Jeff Yates. 2009. *Presidential Rhetoric and the Public Agenda: Constructing the War on Drugs.* Baltimore: Johns Hopkins University Press.

Woolley, John, and Gerhard Peters. 2013. *The American Presidency Project.* http://www.presidency.ucsb.edu/ (accessed April 19, 2013).

Wood, B. Dan. 2007. *The Politics of Economic Leadership: The Causes and Consequences of Presidential Rhetoric.* Princeton, NJ: Princeton University Press.

———. 2009. "Presidential Saber Rattling and the Economy." *American Journal of Political Science* 53 (July): 695–709.

Woods, Joshua, and Arthur, C. D. Forthcoming. "The Authoritarian Turn: The Changing Public Discourse on Immigration after 9/11."

Zarefsky, David. 2004. "Presidential Rhetoric and the Power of Definition." *Presidential Studies Quarterly* 34 (September): 607–19.

DISCUSSION QUESTIONS

1. What are the consequences of votes cast by noncitizens in national elections? Are there negative consequences even if the number of such votes are not enough to change an election outcome?

2. What measures do you believe should be put in place to ensure that only those individuals eligible to vote in an election actually cast votes? Is there a concern that measures considered too cumbersome could suppress legitimate voter turnout?

3. What were the findings of the Richman et al. study? What data was used as the basis for this study? Do you believe the study's findings are important? Why or why not?

4. On what basis could President Trump use the Richman et al. study to arrive at millions of noncitizen voters in the 2016 election? In other words, explain how one would use the findings regarding the 2008 and 2010 elections to extrapolate that result. On what basis would the authors most likely push back against the idea that millions of noncitizens voted in 2016 or in any election?

5. In what ways do the following conditions serve as predictors of negative framing: the periods before and after 9/11? Economic indicators? Geographic location of speech?

6. In what years do you find the most frequent negative framing of immigration-related issues? Why do you believe that is the case?

7. Summarize what you believe are the most important findings of the Arthur and Woods study? What makes the finding important? What are its implications?

CPSIA information can be obtained
at www.ICGtesting.com
Printed in the USA
LVHW100033250720
661461LV00005B/33